HEIR
NOT
APPARENT

HEIR NOT APPARENT

SUZANNE FINSTAD

TexasMonthlyPress

Dustjacket photograph courtesy of United Press International.

Texas Monthly Press, Inc.
P.O. Box 1569
Austin, Texas 78767

A B C D E F G

Library of Congress Cataloging in Publication Data

Finstad, Suzanne, 1955–
 Heir not apparent.

 1. Hughes, Howard, 1905–1976—Estate. 2. Executors and administrators—Texas. I. Title.
KFT1347.F56   1984   346.76405'6   83-15619
ISBN 0-932012-57-4   347.640656

*For
my parents*

Contents

Preface

Howard Robard Hughes, Jr., came into this world quietly, on Christmas Eve in 1905, and departed it sadly, tragically on April 5, 1976, the victim of his own delusions. In the seventy-one years between, a legend grew around him. So powerful was his personal mystique, so vast his empire, that the name Howard Hughes came to symbolize Money and Power and all that went with them.

With his death came the usual speculation about the distribution of his multimillion-dollar estate. This idle speculation took on a more urgent tone as it became increasingly apparent that one of the world's wealthiest men had died, unbelievably, without leaving a valid will. The Hughes domain was, in a sense, up for grabs, and there was no shortage of bidders.

In the ensuing mad scramble for heirs, a mystery story unfolded. Hughes' genealogy, like the man himself, is bizarre and enigmatic, full of twists and turns and unanswered questions. In the end, the seeming survivors of the family tug-of-war over the Hughes inheritance seemed to be a stately maternal aunt, three paternal cousins-once-removed (two of whom Hughes never met and probably didn't know existed), and a pair of common-law "cousins" who didn't even pretend to be blood relations. An exhaustive investigation of Hughes' family background, however, raises some uncomfortable suspicions concerning the chosen few, and perhaps some uncertainty about those who were left out.

The chaos surrounding Howard Hughes' death was dramatic in the extreme, given the man's eccentricities and the enormous size of his estate, but it also raises larger questions about the way our legal system operates when a person dies intestate.

This book is the fruit of more than six year's labor. When in 1976 I first became involved in the estate proceedings of Howard Hughes, Jr., I was twenty and a recent college graduate. Hughes had recently died, and by chance my clerkship with a Houston law firm coincided with the litigatioin of his tangled estate. A partner at the firm, O. Theodore Dinkins, Jr., had been appointed the "attorney ad litem," a watchdog of sorts over estate matters in Texas. Dinkins was also assigned the formidable task of confirming *or finding* the heirs-at-law of billionaire Howard R. Hughes, Jr., a legendary eccentric and recluse with no known relatives, and, allegedly, no valid will. It was an assignment that, not surprisingly, became fraught with controversy and intrigue. As Dinkins' law clerk and later associate, the heirship investigation largely fell on my shoulders, and it was this extraordinary experience that formed the springboard for *Heir Not Apparent*. As my sleuthing into the Hughes family intensified, I grew more suspicious about the family tree that was ultimately approved by the court. These suspicions still haunt me today.

The research that forms the basis of this book is prodigious indeed. Over the course of six to seven years, I have interviewed nearly two hundred individuals (Hughes family members, those who would like to be, or others with various connections to Hughes or his interests), analyzed thousands of pages of documents, court transcripts or records (including over 6,000 pages of deposition testimony alone), scoured books, obscure reference works, newspaper clippings, diaries, magazines, county histories, church records, cemetery records (and gravestones), passport applications, vital statistics, census reports, correspondence, memoirs, and all other forms of literature imaginable. I have also from time to time screened films, studied photographs, and analyzed handwriting. Fundamental to the development of the text was my participation in, preparation, for, or observation of the two major trials in the Hughes estate proceedings in Texas: the 1977–78 trial to establish Hughes' legal residence and the 1981 trial to determine his heirs-at-law.

In writing this book I have strived to be objective at all costs. Faced with many different versions of the "truth," I have attempted to analyze the facts available, offer hypotheses wherever possible, or simply report when this was not feasible. Because the majority of the subjects of my research are dead, certain important questions must remain answered. This was at once the fascination and frustration of my task, and hence this book. Any mistakes or misimpressions are therefore mine alone.

Acknowledgments

It is a particularly overwhelming task to acknowledge other's help in a work of such magnitude. Special gratitude is due my editors, Barbara Rodriguez, Chester Rosson, and Barbara Burnham who cheerfully and skilfully guided me through an undertaking that seemed to grow more enormous with each passing week, and to the rest of the Texas Monthly Press staff, who have been friendly and supportive at every turn. A note of thanks is in order to my former colleagues at Butler & Binion, especially Ted Dinkins, who provided me with the experience of a lifetime; and to the individuals I have interviewed, whose cooperation exceeded all expectations. Finally, to those friends and family members who provided encouragement and support when it was needed most, I offer my heartfelt thanks.

Houston
January 1984

Introduction

When Howard Hughes, Jr., was sixteen, his mother died unexpectedly from an overdose of anesthesia preceding minor surgery. She was by all accounts a beautiful and sensitive woman, devoted to her only child; Howard, Jr., then known as "Sonny," was a shy and socially awkward boy, just as strongly attached to his mother. Two and a half years later Sonny's father, "Big Howard", dropped dead at the age of fifty-four in the middle of a business meeting at his office in Houston, Texas, leaving behind a very large estate, his position as President of the Hughes Tool Company, and an orphaned son. Significantly, he also left a will.

At the time of Howard, Sr.'s, death in January 1924, the Hughes estate was valued at $871,518 according to the Inventory filed among his probate proceedings in Harris County, Texas. More important than the dollar value of his estate, however—though that was sizable—was his sole interest in the Hughes Tool Company, which he had founded and would pass on through his untimely death. With the advent of an oil age, Howard Hughes, Sr.'s, enterprise, which manufactured the revolutionary cone drilling bit, was just beginning to realize the enormous profits that were to be its due. The beneficiaries of this windfall, as set forth in a will Howard Hughes, Sr., executed on April 23, 1913 (and amended by a codicil dated November 25, 1919), were his late wife, Allene Gano Hughes, his parents, a brother, and Sonny.

Allene Hughes was to receive half of her husband's estate, both by his design and by virtue of Texas community property law, a vestige of the state's Spanish heritage. The remaining half was to be divided among Sonny, Felix and Jean Hughes (Howard Hughes, Sr.'s, parents), and Felix Hughes, his youngest brother. Sonny would receive half of this half, or a fourth of his father's estate, while the other fourth would be split equally among the other three. Since Mrs. Hughes had died, the bequests to the others doubled, leaving Sonny 50 percent and his grandparents and Uncle Felix one-sixth share of the Hughes Tool Company.

The rest has become part of the Hughes folklore, the events that signified the end of "Sonny" and the beginning of the Howard Hughes legend. At the time of his father's death, Sonny, barely eighteen, was living with his maternal aunt, Annette Gano Lummis, and attending the Rice Institute (now Rice University) in Houston. He was a peculiar boy, quiet and hard-of-hearing, who seemed to be interested only in airplanes, and his saxophone, and Hollywood. As Felix and Jean Hughes—possibly encouraged by Howard, Sr.'s, other brother, Rupert

1

Hughes, who was conspicuously omitted from Howard, Sr.'s will—pushed to establish a guardianship for their orphaned grandson, he took steps to determine his own fate. Howard, Jr., persuaded Judge Walter Monteith of Houston, an old family friend, to grant his petition to be declared an adult for legal purposes, though he was only eighteen.

Young Hughes quickly bought out his uncle Felix and his grandparents' interests in the Hughes Tool Company and assumed total control; like his father before him, Howard, Jr. was now sole owner of the goose that laid the golden eggs. His next acquisition was a bride, Ella Rice, a Houston thoroughbred two years his senior, and he approached that goal with the same single-mindedness of purpose. "Came to me and asked me to go and convince Aunt Mattie, who was a Rice, to let Ella marry him," described his aunt, Annette Lummis, "and I was against it, but I went and asked her. I said, 'I can't send him with all that money to California with all those vampire movie picture people,' and Aunt Mattie said she agreed with me. And Ella and Howard were married in her sister's garden."

So it came to pass that Howard Hughes, Jr., took control of the Hughes Tool Company, married his Sunday School sweetheart, and established himself in the Hollywood movie colony by the age of nineteen, despite efforts to appoint a guardian for him, and amid rumored counterplots engineered by his uncle Rupert to muscle in on the Hughes Tool Company.

It is no small irony that the architect of such an elaborate scheme should die without making any provision for the family fortune he fought so hard to obtain.

PART ONE
Hughes Who

1

Send In The Clowns

By the summer of 1981, Howard Hughes, Jr., had been dead for five years, his body laid to rest in the family plot in Houston next to his beloved parents. In a courtroom in downtown Houston not ten minutes away from the cemetery, a probate judge and a jury of six had just carved up and served the estate his father had created and he had expanded to a set of distant relations, most of whose names Hughes would not have recognized, had he been alive.

Ironically, the catalyst for this extraordinary legal drama was Hughes himself. By either not executing a valid will, or keeping its whereabouts too secret—or possibly due to foul play, although no real proof of this has surfaced—Howard Hughes opened a Pandora's box of designing or deluded would-be heirs to an enormous unsettled fortune.

5

In a well-meaning but ultimately futile attempt to impose order on certain chaos, the judge, the Honorable Pat Gregory, had divided the heirship determination of Howard Hughes into three separate minitrials:

Phase One was to determine whether Hughes had left any wives, children, parents, brothers, or sisters. (If he had, the ball game would be over, since anyone in those relationships would be Hughes' closest living kin and thus sole heir to the Hughes millions. If not, Phases Two and Three would come into play.)

Phase Two was to ascertain his relations on his mother's side of the family.

The third, last, and only phase tried before a jury was to determine Hughes' relatives on the paternal side. (Phases Two and Three were necessary because, under Texas law, a person who dies without a will and with no immediate family survivors has his estate split evenly between the maternal and paternal closest living relatives.)

The first phase, certainly the most spectacular of the three, began and ended on a sultry Monday in mid-July. The courtroom and adjacent lobby were filled with a gaggle of curiosity seekers, a small army of media people, and wall-to-wall lawyers. With almost more cameras than people, the event had the aura of a movie premiere. Flashbulbs and camera lights were glaring everywhere, as if awaiting the grand entrance of the stars who never came. There was no Jean Harlow, no Jane Russell, nor even a Jean Peters—none of the glamorous stars or starlets who had graced Hughes' arm over the years. Only a rather pathetic pair of ladies was on hand, each of whom claimed to have been married to Hughes in years past, and each with a bizarre tale to support her belief.

Alyce Hovsepian Hughes, a snappy-looking strawberry blonde well into her fifties, dressed in black and wearing a straw bowler, sat in the front row of the courtroom and kept a close eye on the proceedings as Wayne Fisher, a lawyer representing some Hughes cousins, described her claim to the judge. She contended she had met Hughes at a hospital in Philadelphia in March 1946. According to Ms. Hughes, he arranged an unusual "screen test" for her, promising to make her either a star or Miss Atlantic City. Part of the test had led to her shoplifting jewelry from Black's Department Store in Philadelphia at Hughes' request. He had also taken her blood sample; and on June 6, 1946, the two of them had taken part in what Alyce thought was a rehearsal for a civil marriage ceremony. He had later told her it was real, and had asked her to take the name Jean Peters. They had never lived together, although Hughes had visited her at her family home in Atlantic City several times that year, usually bringing oranges, and never identifying himself to Alyce's mother. She had seen him only once more, in the fall of 1946, while she was a patient at the Trenton State Psychiatric Hospital. During the visit,

Hughes had raped her, she alleged, in the presence of a man known variously as Sam the Actor or Sam the Jew.

Judge Gregory denied Ms. Hughes' claim.

Fisher next outlined the case of Alma Hughes, who maintained she had met Hughes in Shreveport, Louisiana, in the summer of 1931, when he was operating a dollar-a-ride airplane concession. She had run into him again at the local Peacock Jewelry Store, where she was selecting an engagement ring to marry another man. Hughes had proposed to her on the spot, but she had refused him. "I didn't want to marry someone who'd be flying all the time," she explained. They later had met each other regularly at a medical club in Alexandria, Louisiana, and in August 1951 Alma had borne his child, Margie, out of wedlock. Hughes denied paternity because Margie had blue eyes. In 1968 Alma moved to Dallas at Hughes' request, where they had met in secrecy at the Neiman-Marcus department store. He used the name Conroe and was undergoing hair transplant surgery. They had finally married in 1973 after she had agreed to be artificially inseminated by Hughes. (This was the only way he could be certain the child was his.) Hughes had arranged the implant while Alma underwent hemorrhoid surgery, and she had borne his child at age sixty-four.

Since Alma Hughes was "unable to get counsel," she presented her own case before the judge, apologizing in advance, "I'm not very good at making public speeches." Ms. Hughes, a tiny gray-haired woman clad in a green polyester pantsuit, became very emotional during her speech. She explained that during her pregnancy, Hughes kept several mistresses, because "he was rough in bed with a woman." He also had midgets working for him, and lost a foot in a plane crash. His autopsy, which does not reveal a missing foot, was falsified. "Money is one thing. Honor is another," wept Ms. Hughes to Judge Gregory. "One day all those who falsified these things will have to pay for it. God is a just God." Although Judge Gregory was sympathetic to her emotional breakdown, he quickly disposed of Alma Hughes' case. "May I ask what recourse I have?" she queried, and walked out to plan her appeal.

No one turned up claiming to be a brother or sister of Howard Hughes, but a woman called Claire Benedict Hudenberg tried to prove she was his daughter. Ms. Hudenberg, an ordained minister in a cult church, professed to have been born with supernatural powers. She was both clairvoyant (seeing future events) and clairaudiant (hearing things from the other world "where we'll all go"). She was employed as a "counselor" in a restaurant owned by Paul Anka, and had regressed back seventeen lives through hypnosis, she claimed. (In sixteen of them she was a king.) That she was Hughes' natural daughter was based on the following evidence:

7

In 1969 she was working in the Bahamas and living next door to Howard Hughes.

In 1974 she tried to buy a house in Bel Air and found it once belonged to Hughes. Later she saw a picture of Hughes in the newspaper and was "stunned" by their physical resemblance.

A man called Claude Haag told her in 1979, in Las Vegas, that she looked like Howard Hughes.

A man at the Desert Inn Hotel told her she walked just like Howard Hughes.

While Hudenberg was counseling in Las Vegas, a daughter of a former Hughes pilot mentioned the resemblance to her.

She believed Harold Robbins' book, *The Carpetbaggers,* to be an accurate portrayal of Howard Hughes' life. In the novel, one of the tycoon-hero's children is the daughter of a Chicago newspaperwoman. Ms. Hudenberg's adoptive mother was a newspaperwoman.

She had been harassed by twenty-five men "with great big necks," who had followed her around Las Vegas to get her picture. This must have been because she was Howard Hughes' daughter.

She had found arsenic in her pool and black cyanide on the roof of her house. She attributed these acts to "either the Mormons or Summa people."

Like the claims of the two alleged wives of Hughes before her, Judge Gregory dismissed Hudenberg's claim. As opposing counsel Fisher put it, "there was not a piece of supporting evidence other than wild speculation." He further characterized the trio of claims as "bizarre and unbelievable," the product of "minds controlled by delusion, fantasy, and paranoia."

To complete the day in court and prove under the law that Howard Hughes, Jr., died without leaving any parents, wives, children, brothers, or sisters, the lawyers involved introduced a small number of official documents. Chief among them were the death certificates of his parents, Howard, Sr., and Allene Gano Hughes; the marriage and divorce records of Howard, Jr., to and from Ella Rice and the real Jean Peters; and Howard, Jr.'s, birth and death certificates.

The will that started it all—Howard, Sr.'s—was then introduced into evidence. This was done to show that Howard, Sr., provided for no children except Howard, Jr., and no wives except the late Allene. In short, no surprises. The will was followed into the record by the other document that altered the course of young Sonny's life: the petition that removed his disabilities as a minor. The lawyers representing distant cousins wanted to illustrate that when the petition was executed Sonny was an orphan, and that he acknowledged no brothers or sisters, thereby clearing the path for their more remotely related clients to inherit a chunk of the estate.

And then it was over. In one morning, attorneys for cousins on both sides of Hughes' family had eliminated the possibility that his estate would go to a brother, sister, wife, or child. They were now ready to go on to Phases Two and Three of the trial, putting them one step closer to their final objective.

But was it really that simple? One cannot help but wonder how it came to this, how Hughes himself would have felt about where his money was going, and whether this scene from *One Flew Over the Cuckoo's Nest* was an accurate reflection of the individuals who fell within this first category of heirs.

To answer these questions, one must go back in time, first to the death of Howard Hughes, Jr., and the events that followed, to understand why his estate was put on the auction block. And finally, to the lives and loves of Howard Robard Hughes, Junior and Senior. If either of these men had had a child—kept from public view for whatever reason—the estate would have its heir apparent, and the journey into Hughes' genealogy would go no further. Or if, on the other hand, Howard, Jr., had died a married man, his wife would indeed be a merry widow, for the great Hughes fortune would all belong to her.

It is an interesting phenomenon when the private pasts of two rich, notorious womanizers are put on public display, more interesting still when their romantic adventures can lead to millions of dollars, and irresistible when one of them is perhaps the most legendary recluse of modern times.

2

Where There's a Will . . .

Many surprises concerning Howard Hughes, Jr., had crept into public view after his death. Foremost of these was the death itself. Although nearly everyone had paused now and then to speculate about the goings-on of the billionaire whose pursuit of solitude had assumed near-mythical proportions, few were prepared for what his corpse so chillingly proved—that the world's richest man spent the last years of his life in no better physical condition than the average inner-city derelict. His frame had shrunk at least an inch, to 6'2'', and he weighed 92.4 pounds—less than a teenage anorexic. On top of that, his shriveled body was covered with huge bed sores and his forearms were dotted with puncture wounds, like an old junkie left to waste away.

Just as talk about Hughes' death and rumors about his condition reached a fever pitch, the public gasped at the biggest surprise of all. HOWARD HUGHES DIES WITHOUT A WILL was the shocking headline that dominated the papers of Houston and the nation during the spring of 1976.

How could this be? As everyone knew, Howard Hughes had a nearly insane hatred for taxes, had driven away his top executives because he wanted complete autonomy, and had jealously refused even to grant them stock options in his companies. Instead, he had rewarded them with lavish salaries, which were all but consumed by income taxes.

Noah Dietrich, Hughes' first and best chief executive, likes to tell the story of how his long and successful business relationship with Hughes came to an abrupt end when he gave Hughes his ultimatum: accept his profit-sharing plan or Dietrich would quit. "You're holding a gun to my head, Noah," was all Hughes would say, even though he knew that the plan would allow Dietrich to keep more of the money intended to compensate him for his considerable services. But Hughes would have none of it. According to Hughes lore, his father once had a partner and lived to regret it; from this knowledge, young Howard resolved to retain exclusive ownership of his companies. Whether this tale is apocryphal or not is unimportant; Hughes kept total control of his enterprises. It seemed especially strange that a man with this attitude would die without a will, leaving his wealth in the hands of lawyers and Uncle Sam to dispose of.

The Heirs Apparent

Meanwhile, the press and populace were having a field day with the absurdity of it all. Who would have dreamed that one of the world's largest private fortunes would go unclaimed? This brought to mind the inevitable question: where would the Hughes empire go, without direction from the man responsible for it? Most people have some hazy notion that without a will, their money would go to their relatives, whoever they might be. But little was known about Howard Hughes at the time he died, and even less about his family. However, less than two months after his demise, on May 31, 1976, the respected *Philadelphia Inquirer* published a chart called "The Heirs of Howard Robard Hughes," setting forth the names of the individuals then thought to be related to the industrialist—individuals made millionaires overnight if Hughes had truly neglected to make a will. For this group, obscurity would become a thing of the past.

The *Inquirer* chart was the first of what would be many backward glances into Howard Hughes' genealogy. Like everything else about

12

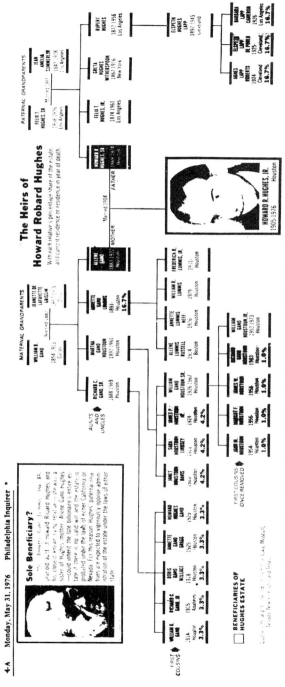

Sole Beneficiary?

The Heirs of
Howard Robard Hughes

With each relative's percentage share of the estate and current residence or residence in year of death.

BENEFICIARIES OF HUGHES ESTATE

FIRST COUSINS

FIRST COUSINS ONCE REMOVED

AUNTS AND UNCLES

PATERNAL GRANDPARENTS

MATERNAL GRANDPARENTS

FATHER

MOTHER

If no valid Howard Hughes will is found, and the estate is probated under Texas laws, the father's and mother's sides of the family divide the estate equally. Three granddaughters of Rupert Hughes would divide among themselves 50 percent of the estate. For every $100 million distributed they would receive $16.7 million each.

Note: The chart as provided above was reproduced from the clearest copy available for use in this book. The author apologizes for its quality.

Reprinted by permission of the Philadelphia Inquirer, *May 31, 1976.*

13

him, it was atypical. Normally, when one thinks of "heirs," the word calls to mind a family tree, with children and grandchildren, nieces and nephews, sisters and brothers, all extending from the deceased person like leafy branches. In the *Inquirer*'s chart, it was just the reverse. Howard Hughes appeared, in this topsy-turvy money tree, at the bottom, like the trunk, and the branches led back to generations past—to individuals to whom, under usual circumstances, Hughes himself would have been heir. But this preliminary report of Hughes' family only pointed backward.

According to the statistical information readily available to the *Inquirer* reporters, Hughes died without a wife, without any children, and without brother or sister. This left only his parents in the family circle, but they were both dead. It was this extraordinary development—the apparent lack of any close family to collect this unexpected inheritance—that led to a full-scale investigation of Hughes' ancestors, an investigation that provided more questions than answers, with much more at stake than family pride or family history. The motivation for this search into the past was money—lots and lots of it. This was genealogy played for high stakes, a game in which skeletons in the family closet could mean unanticipated windfalls, and family secrets might yield family fortunes. There was no shortage of either of these in Howard Hughes' ancestry, a fact that is hardly remarkable. Actually, it is rather predictable: when one traces the bloodline of a champion, he often finds another champion; when he traces the bloodline of an eccentric, he should not be too surprised to find an eccentric or two lurking about. This was certainly the case with Howard Hughes.

The Heir-Finder

About the time the *Inquirer* article came out, with its provocative diagram of Hughes' heirs, Judge Gregory, into whose lap fell the Hughes estate administration in Texas, offered his own significant contribution to the celebrated heir-hunt. On August 10, 1976, he appointed a lanky Houstonian to serve as his "attorney ad litem" in the estate of Howard R. Hughes, Jr. His choice was O. Theodore Dinkins, Jr., a canny lawyer from a prestigious local law firm with a near-encyclopedic knowledge of the Texas Probate Code. Dinkins' mind for probate matters was as quick as his East Texas drawl was languid. This background would serve him well in his new position, for his role was awkward, ill-defined, and unusual. "I'm in a unique position," Dinkins said of his function. "I'm not on anybody's side, and I'm technically against everybody." To make matters more uncomfortable, Dinkins' fees were paid out of Hughes' estate, since he was actually providing it a service. This no doubt made him extremely popular back at his law firm, but put a strain on relations with those who claimed a part of the estate. To them, Dinkins could only be an expensive thorn in the side.

Just what was the attorney ad litem's role? "I have been appointed by the Probate Court Number Two," explained Dinkins shortly after receiving the honor, "to represent the interests of any unknown heirs of Howard Robard Hughes, Jr., and any heirs suffering from legal disability. I have an obligation to protect their interests, and I intend to see that obligation is carried out." What did this noble statement mean, in practical terms? It meant that Ted Dinkins' task was to locate any and all rightful heirs of Howard Hughes—people who, if they existed, were either not aware of their relationship to the dead magnate, or chose, for whatever reason, not to pursue it. This cast him in a role not unlike the lead in the old television series, *The Millionaire,* in which a gentleman stranger selected a person at random each week to receive a million dollars, no strings attached. This fantasy would become a reality for someone, if Dinkins' search uncovered a name missing from the *Inquirer* chart. But his research could also burst the bubble of one or all of the lucky heirs named on the chart, if he found an "unknown heir" more closely related than they, or if he came up with something to discredit any one of them.

On April 4, 1977, one day short of the first anniversary of Howard Hughes' death, Dinkins hired a professional genealogist, Mrs. Mary Smith Fay, to assist him in preparing a list of the late billionaire's heirs-at-law—a case that had to be a genealogist's dream come true. A longtime member of the Texas Society of the Daughters of the American Revolution, Mrs. Fay was a lady who relished poking around in the past, whose eyes lit up at the sight of a pension application by a Civil War veteran, or the opportunity to review an old census record. In appearance and by temperament, Mrs. Fay was a replica of Miss Marple, Agatha Christie's matronly sleuth. She accomplished her research through a combination of persistence, unfailing politeness, and a twinkling, inquiring nature.

Together, she and Dinkins made a most unlikely team. Their assignment was to conduct an independent investigation into the heirs of Howard Hughes, representing no one in particular, with no objectives other than truth and fairness. Based on their findings, Dinkins would recommend to Judge Gregory who should inherit the Hughes estate. It was a most memorable case full of surprises, occasionally more enigmatic then Hughes himself. And it was an investigation in which most of the findings never made it to court.

15

The Truth About Hughes' Will

In the meantime, Judge Neil Lake, Gregory's California counterpart, was having a difficult time accepting the notion that Howard Hughes had died without a valid will. As the official in charge of the Hughes estate in California, he could do something about it. On January 25, 1977, eight months after the presumed "heirs of Howard Robard Hughes" were charted in the *Inquirer,* and ten months after the billionaire's death, Judge Lake ordered the special administrator of the Hughes estate in California to search for a will and prepare a report of the findings for his approval. It was to describe everything that had been done to locate a valid Hughes will—every person contacted, every place searched, and every document found. The man in charge of the search had a name that was becoming increasingly familiar in Hughes circles. In fact, it could be found on the *Inquirer* chart. The name, and the man, was Richard C. Gano, Jr., a first cousin of Hughes on his mother's side.

Two months later, on March 15, 1977, Gano filed his report. He could find no valid will executed by his late cousin.

The California public administrator later challenged Gano's appointment, on three grounds: that there was no notice given; that the choice of Gano was an abuse of discretion; and that Gano was allegedly not doing a good job. The challenge continued in the courts for approximately a year, but the public administrator eventually lost the case.

Whether a will exists, and if so, where it is, remains a mystery. One thing is clear, however, after reading the report Gano put together: as everyone suspected, the subject of his will was never far from Hughes' mind. In fact, he referred to it regularly and revised or tinkered with it with the relentless attention of an over-conscientious probate lawyer. Based on interviews with 397 people and a search that extended from Las Vegas to the Bahamas, Gano found numerous indications that Howard Hughes had made a will, or wills. Here is a summary of his findings:

The 1925 will

Howard Robard Hughes, Jr., first made out a will in May 1925, at the tender age of nineteen, when he was still known as Sonny. It was a part of the series of moves designed to propel him to adulthood after his father's death, and he approached it with the same sense of straight-ahead responsibility. He assigned the task of its creation to Frank Andrews, founding partner of the old-line Houston law firm of Andrews, Streetman, and a close friend and trusted legal adviser to his late father. The will that young Hughes and Andrews devised was carefully drafted and, for the most part, extremely conventional. Interestingly, there are provisions in it for three of Sonny's maternal relatives: his uncle Chilton Gano (the father of Richard C. Gano, Jr., the man responsible for the will search in California) and aunts Martha Gano Houstoun and Annette Gano Lummis, the brother and sisters of his late mother, Allene Gano Hughes. His father's relatives, however, were cut off completely.

The other bequests were thoughtful, if predictable, ones for a young man of Hughes' age and station. He remembered his "colored household servants"; a childhood friend, Dudley Sharp (a son of the man who was once Howard, Sr.'s, partner; in what was then known as the Sharp-Hughes Tool Co.); and his wife-to-be, Ella Rice. (They married a few days after the will was executed.)

Sonny also pledged to continue the operations of the Hughes Tool Company, in a touching tribute to his father. "This institution was founded by my father and promoted through his genius and ability, to the success which it now enjoys," he began, "and it is my purpose and intention . . . to continue its development and progress . . . thus building to my father a permanent monument marking his initiative, judgment, and foresight in the founding and upbuilding of a great business."

It was his final request, however, the only provision even slightly out of the ordinary in an otherwise routine will, that would become exceedingly significant in the chaotic power struggle over his estate.

Though only nineteen years old, Howard, Jr., had witnessed the early and sudden deaths of both his mother and father. Raised as an only child, Sonny was spoiled and coddled, particularly by his mother, who would go to any lengths to avoid exposing her son to germs. (She once withdrew him abruptly from Dan Beard's Outdoor School, a summer boys' camp in the Pocono Mountains operated by one of the founders of the Boy Scouts of America, because of a polio scare in the East.)

Perhaps influenced by his parents' preoccupation with his health and by the unexpected loss of their lives, Sonny wished, by the last clauses of his will, to use his money to establish a research center "devoted to the discovery of ways, means, antitoxins, and specifics for the prevention and curing of the most serious diseases with which this country may from time to time be afflicted." It was to be a corporation, known as the Howard R. Hughes Medical Research Laboratories, operated by the executors of his estate, who included Frank Andrews and Sonny's uncle, Frederick R. Lummis, Annette Gano Lummis' husband. All things considered, it was a remarkably serious and philanthropic gesture for one still in his teens, and it was a goal that would stay with Hughes to the very end.

17

Unfortunately, Richard Gano, Jr., found no signed or conformed copy of this will, though it is clear that it was executed with the necessary formalities. But because the original is missing, the unsigned copy has no legal significance.

Surprisingly, this early document is the most tangible evidence of a Hughes will produced during the search.

1929–30 and 1938 wills

Apparently Hughes wrote a new will approximately five years later, in the 1929–30 period. By this time, his marriage to socialite Ella Rice had crumbled, and he wanted to revise his earlier will to keep pace with the changes in his life. He evidently intended to leave the bulk of his fortune to medical research, cutting out his family altogether. Though he was still only twenty-five years old, his estrangement from his relatives, at least in a financial sense, was already complete.

Eight years later, in 1938, Hughes once again turned his attention to updating his will. In this case, it was a matter of life or death. Ever the daredevil pilot, he was about to embark on a dangerous test flight, and his lawyers and he thought it would be prudent to make out a new will before he set off. The grand design of the will remained essentially the same, however: his money would go to the proposed Medical Research Laboratories.

Gano could not find either of these instruments, though he did discover a codicil, handwritten by Hughes and dated June 10, 1939. True to form, in the codicil the imperial Hughes struck a former employee from his earlier will. Without the will to which it refers, though, the codicil is meaningless.

Early 1940s

In his later years, Hughes gave the impression that he had made a holographic (handwritten) will during this period. If this is true, it has remained elusive.

1947 Will

In 1944, Hughes hired Nadine Henley, a bright and ambitious young woman from Minneapolis, as his private secretary. She became his confidante as well and rose through the ranks of the organization, eventually advancing to the Board of Directors of Summa Corporation in 1972. Shortly after she began to work for Hughes, he engaged her in a meticulous revision of his will over a period of several years. It called for the creation of a medical research laboratory, to which he planned to leave his fortune. Hughes was actively involved in every aspect of the will's creation and was even known to draft memos over the most picayune matters, such as the placement of commas in the will.

Hughes was a great procrastinator, however, and Ms. Henley claims he never got around to signing and executing the document. Though the final version was typed in 1947, he didn't arrange a signing session until 1950, three years later. "Well, I'm not going to sign it today," he reportedly said at the time, and that was the end of it. Consequently, the document has remained, unsigned, in a safety deposit box or safe in California.

Ms. Henley never knew whether her boss, the world's foremost tycoon, ever made a valid will.

An important and highly consequential event occurred in Hughes' life after this. In 1953, he established a foundation known as the Howard Hughes Medical Institute (HHMI). Like the Howard Hughes Medical Research Laboratories he had proposed at age nineteen, HHMI was a nonprofit corporation devoted to medical and scientific research. The press release announcing its creation made this revealing statement: "For more than 25 years his will has provided for the creation of such an institution and the transference to it of the bulk of his estate, but five years ago he made the definite decision to create this foundation during his lifetime."

Hughes then transferred to HHMI all the assets of one of his most successful companies, now known as the Hughes Aircraft Company, still wholly owned by the Medical Institute.

1950–1966

By this time Howard Hughes was already in the early stages of the bizarre lifestyle now associated with him. His contact with the outside world was diminishing, and he would soon develop a system of round-the-clock aides to attend him like nursemaids. His communication with Nadine Henley was waning and would deteriorate completely by the 1960s, though she would remain an important force in his organization.

He was, in short, already a man unto himself, so his activities during this period are difficult to monitor. According to Gano's report, sources close to Hughes believe he made a holographic will around this time, leaving everything to medical research. Why he switched to a handwritten form, and who if anyone helped him prepare it, are not precisely known.

However, he did solicit the legal opinion of Gregson Bautzer, counsel for Hughes Productions and personal attorney to Hughes in the 1950s and 1960s. Bautzer was also a trusted friend and intimate. Hughes asked Bautzer to determine whether he could, "without witnesses and/or lawyers, make and execute a will that would be valid subsequent to his death.'' Bautzer was instructed to do the research alone, after which he would fly to Hughes' side to deliver the information personally. Bautzer informed Hughes that this procedure was perfectly legal under the laws of Texas, California, and Nevada, Hughes' successive domiciles. Hughes questioned Bautzer in great detail, always pressing him for a ''guarantee'' that such an instrument would be valid. Despite their three meetings and frequent discussions concerning the holographic will concept during the 1950s, Bautzer never saw a document signed by Hughes that appeared to dispose of his estate upon his death. Hughes did mention HHMI on these occasions and briefly stated to Bautzer his intention to leave the majority of his estate to the institute.

Actress Jean Peters was an important force in Hughes' life during the 1950s (they married in 1957), and she and Hughes occasionally discussed how he should dispose of his huge estate. She felt he should make frequent grants to various charities, spread his wealth around, and ''have some fun'' with his fortune. In contrast, Hughes thought it important to keep the corpus of his estate in one large sum, saving it for medical research to benefit HHMI, making it the most valuable and powerful organization of its kind. During his conversations with Jean, Hughes was frequently upset because he had not ''revised his will'' and because it was completely out of date. At some point, no doubt after one of his briefings with Bautzer, Hughes explained the holographic will concept to Peters, describing what made it legal. He told her he could do as good a job ''if not better, where it was concerned, than any lawyer setting down on a piece of paper what he wanted to say.''

The only tangible evidence to support the belief that Hughes made a handwritten will at this time is a memorandum apparently written by Hughes in 1971 or 1972 to one of his Mormon assistants. ''I don't know how many more summers I have left, Howard, but I don't expect to spend all of them holed up in a hotel room on a Barca-lounger,'' the Hughes memo begins. ''I have had in existence for some time, a holographic will. . . . however, I intend to replace this will with a witnessed conventionally drawn will, as the will, to which I refer above, was purely an interim document, written only for temporary protection.''

This is consistent with Peters' opinion, based on her husband's ''personal style,'' that Hughes would have had a typewritten, formally drafted, witnessed, and signed will as opposed to a holographic document, his occasionally disparaging comments about lawyers notwithstanding. Hughes never actually showed his wife a testamentary document, however, during their marriage or at any other time.

1966–1976

Hughes' world was now confined to the interiors of darkened hotel suites, where he screened movies endlessly, often repeating the same film over and over until he knew the dialogue by heart. He received few visitors, not even his wife, reducing his contact with human beings to his rotating staff of Mormon aides. Several of these men have said that Hughes made comments about "his will" during this period of seclusion, that it was holographic, and that the greater part of his estate went to HHMI.

This was the extent of Gano's report. Now that his unsuccessful effort to locate a valid will for his cousin was duly recorded, the door to inheritance by Hughes' relatives, including Gano himself, was wide open. Or so they thought.

A Lost Will ?

A group of Hughes' former top associates thought otherwise, and they had a novel legal theory behind them. These individuals, including Hughes' former secretary, Nadine Henley, were convinced that Howard Hughes had made a valid will that left his estate to the Howard Hughes Medical Institute. Somehow they had to get around the fact that they had never seen it and did not know where it was. It was here that the law stepped in to help them, at least initially.

"Wills are carelessly lost and misplaced and a reasonable opportunity should be given to establish such a will. Likewise wills are sometimes suppressed or destroyed for an ulterior purpose. The defeat of that purpose ought not to be made too difficult or impossible." This language from a court opinion expresses the general philosophy of most states concerning attempts to prove a lost or destroyed will, and it was precisely the ammunition that the supporters of Howard Hughes Medical Institute needed. They marched into court with the theory of a lost will tucked under their arms, anxious to defeat the hopes of what they called the "remote relatives" of Howard Hughes, who were already poised to inherit his estate by intestacy.

Though the cause that these former associates of Hughes supported was charitable, there was speculation in the media and Hughes' inner circle that the motives of some of them were at least open to question. Despite Nadine Henley's lack of proximity to Hughes in the last fifteen or twenty years of his life, she formed part of a power base within Summa Corporation that included William Gay, a former Hughes driver groomed by Henley, and Chester Davis, the fiery, intimidating general counsel of Summa. By the December after Hughes' death, Henley was

21

named corporate secretary of HHMI, and Gay and Davis were serving on the Executive Committee. Obviously, a will naming HHMI the chief beneficiary of the Hughes estate was in their best interests as well.

The medical institute lost the first round in the legal battle staged in Judge Gregory's courtroom over the so-called lost will. The difficulty, in their case, was the Texas requirement that they produce one credible witness to the will and its contents. Since no one connected with the medical institute had actually seen an executed will, producing a witness to the document was a problem. The identity of this individual was as unknown as the heirs whom Ted Dinkins was hired to find.

Because of this, Judge Gregory ruled against the group. HHMI immediately filed an appeal in the Court of Civil Appeals in Houston, ultimately moving to the Texas Supreme Court, where it was again defeated. If the institute had been successful on appeal, everything that had occurred since its day in court—all the results of the three-part heirship determination trial—would have been forgotten, and the money would have passed to the foundation. Instead, the estate will go to distant relatives and the United States government, the two beneficiaries it is most clear Howard Hughes would not have chosen.

In another development, Melvin Dummar, a former gas station attendant from Willard, Utah, claimed he picked up an old bum in the desert outside Tonopah, Nevada, on a cold winter night in 1968. He gave the old geezer a ride into Las Vegas and some loose change for the telephone. In return, the man thanked Dummar and told him he was Howard Hughes.

On April 27, 1976, an envelope with a holographic will written on yellow legal paper and signed "Howard R. Hughes" arrived under slightly mysterious circumstances at the Mormon headquarters in Salt Lake City. The beneficiaries named in the document were the "Hughes Medical Institute of Miami"; the University of Texas; the University of Nevada; the University of California; the Mormon Church; "orphan cildren" (sic); the Boy Scouts; Jean Peters; Ella Rice; William R. "Lommis" (Annette Gano Lummis' son); "personal aids" (sic); "key men" in Hughes' companies; a school scholarship fund; and, not least, Melvin Dummar. Noah Dietrich, whom Hughes had not seen or spoken to since they parted company over the stock dispute in the 1950s, was named executor.

A jury in Las Vegas declared the will invalid, after a trial that had to be the most sensational show ever to play Vegas. A Houston jury declared the will a forgery after only about two hours of testimony.

Did Howard Hughes leave a will? From everything known about his business actions, there is certainly a question mark hanging over his estate. He clearly executed at least one will, back in 1925, and he was closely involved in the creation of several others, up through the early 1950s. In all of them, he wished to leave most of his fortune to medical research, in the form of a research laboratory to bear his name. But he established such a foundation during his lifetime, the Howard Hughes Medical Institute, which he funded through the Hughes Aircraft Company; perhaps he felt that was enough. After HHMI was created, Hughes became a recluse, and we have only the belief of his former wife Jean Peters (whom he divorced in 1971 and who did not even see her husband during the last four years of their marriage) and the word of his Mormon aides, who believe he made a handwritten will leaving everything to the medical institute, plus a smattering of comments and memos Hughes himself made at various times.

If Hughes did make a valid will, why can't anyone find it? Surely Hughes was shrewd enough to choose a trustworthy location and custodian for the safekeeping of his will—unless, that is, it was suppressed or destroyed for some ulterior purpose. The only logical motivation for that would be if the holder of the will were dissatisfied with Hughes' choice of beneficiaries and had a chance to benefit directly or indirectly by some other result. This raises a spectre of doubt about nearly everyone close to Hughes, and places his family, friends, and business associates under suspicion. The possibilities for intrigue are always present in the disposition of an estate, and with an accumulation of wealth the size of Hughes', they are multiplied a hundredfold.

It is possible that Hughes never executed any of the documents drafted after his 1925 will. First, there is the matter of his procrastination. Putting things off was a way of life with Hughes. Moreover, as possessive as he was about his fortune, perhaps he just couldn't go through with the process of signing away his estate, even knowing it would not take effect until his death. Maybe Hughes thought that by pressuring him to sign his will, his lawyers and colleagues were "holding a gun to his head." Certainly, with all the willmaking activity surrounding him for years, it seems strange that no signed and executed copy should turn up. For a man who inspired such curiosity during his lifetime, this last act of omission would guarantee him the same aura of mystery after his death.

So the drama of who will inherit the Howard Hughes estate is a complex one, where the motives are mixed and the stakes are high; where the world's richest man appears to have died without a valid will, despite his intense dislike for taxes and a clear intention to cut his family out of any inheritance; to know whether he actually left a valid will they have never seen; and where those closest to Hughes, those in the best position to know whether he actually left a valid will, say they have never seen one. Instead, they lend their support to a medical institute which they serve as officers, claiming the estate under a "lost will," whose chief beneficiary is the medical institute.

Against such a background, it is difficult if not impossible to sort out the truth, and the one person who knows, Howard Robard Hughes, Jr., isn't talking.

3

Will the Real Mrs. Howard Hughes Please Stand Up?

Just as Howard Hughes' cousins began to consider themselves his heirs, a former Hollywood starlet known as Terry Moore made a surprise appearance. She informed the astonished group, their befuddled lawyers, and anyone else who would listen, that she was actually the secret Mrs. Howard Hughes, and she had come out of the closet to claim his estate. To their further consternation, there was something more than fantasy to support her story.

Howard and Ella

Howard Hughes, Jr., as they already knew, had a peculiar history where women were concerned, particularly his wives. This pattern was established early with Ella Rice, his first wife—and his first girl friend. They met as very young children at the Christ Church Cathedral School in Houston where they were both students, and Sonny evidently knew what he wanted even then. "She was the queen," recalled his aunt Annette Lummis, "and apparently he was in love with her from then on." As would become his trademark in later years, Hughes let nothing stand in the way of himself and his goal.

His first such obstacle came in the form of his father's aspirations for him. Big Howard desperately wanted Sonny to attend college. "My son, Howard, Jr., is booked for Harvard, '26," he wrote his former classmates in the Class of 1897 Harvard Alumni Report. This was not to be, however. Allene Hughes died in 1922, and her grief-stricken husband took his son and moved to California, away from the Hughes family home on Yoakum Boulevard and all its bittersweet memories. "He wouldn't come out to the house," his sister-in-law Mrs. Lummis remembered. "He just had a phobia . . . after his wife died." So he persuaded Mrs. Lummis, then Annette Gano, and one of Allene's favorite first cousins, Katherine (Kitty) Callaway, to accompany him to California for one year to raise Sonny. He was still determined that his son would have a college education at all costs, despite the setback, and he somehow arranged for Howard, Jr., to attend Cal Tech, though Sonny was only sixteen at the time. The school claims to have no record of his attendance. "The reason is they were bribed to let him [in]; he wasn't old enough to go then," Mrs. Lummis said, laughingly. "They just claimed he never went there, but I was there one year at the Vista del Arroya and he went every day to Cal Tech."

When the year was up, Sonny returned to Houston with his aunt but without his father, moved back into the Yoakum house, and attended the Rice Institute for two semesters. Then his father died, and Big Howard's plans for Sonny's higher education died with him. "I desire and request that my son be given as good an education as possible," Hughes, Sr., wrote in his will, his last attempt to influence Howard, Jr.'s, behavior. It was to no avail. Sonny had other ideas. He planned to drop out of Rice Institute and marry a Rice instead: Ella, the object of his childhood fantasies. "I told him my opinion," Mrs. Lummis volunteered, "which is he ought to finish Rice and have a degree before he got too independent. He paid no attention to me."

Ella Rice, Sonny's bride, was a great dark beauty from a distinguished family considered "old money" by Houston standards. That she married Howard Hughes at all is somewhat remarkable, considering the circumstances. She was two years older than Sonny, and a belle of Houston society; he was a shy nineteen-year-old orphan, and socially backward. There was no courtship, and the two probably never even dated as such. James O. Winston, Jr., Ella's only husband after Hughes, acknowledged that the couple knew each other just as children in the same Sunday School. The marriage was in effect arranged by their mutual families, in part to please the headstrong Sonny, but more likely to provide a stabilizing influence for him in his encounters with the "vampire movie picture people" in Hollywood. For her part, poor Ella could not have been less prepared for the life she would lead as Mrs. Howard Hughes.

The marriage began conventionally enough. Howard and Ella moved into the Hughes family home on Yoakum with all their wedding presents, the very picture of traditional newlywed respectability in Houston's polite society. "Not awfully long," recalled Mrs. Lummis. "Howard decided he wanted to go out and make movie pictures." Hughes' year in California with his aunt and cousin Kitty Callaway had awakened an interest in him for something other than higher education. To fill the hours when his father was away, Sonny did what everyone else in California was doing at the time: he went to the movies, and he took his aunt and cousin with him. "The story I've heard through the years and through the family," repeated Mrs. Callaway's son-in-law, "is . . . he would go to movie after movie and he'd sit through the movies and say, 'This stinks,' and get up and walk out after just looking at it for about half an hour. . . . And this, I suppose, spawned at a very early age his interest in the movies, because he really thought that most of what they turned out was trash." Whatever the motivation, Hughes closed up the Yoakum house once more, uprooted his bewildered bride, and settled in at the Ambassador Hotel in Los Angeles to make movies.

"I think it was a heckuva life, if you ask me," related Mrs. Lummis, who is also Ella Rice's best friend, in addition to being her cousin by marriage. "He was making *Hell's Angels*, and he wasn't home at all. He would come home for two hours in the daytime and get a sandwich and he would go out and fly." Now that Hughes had acquired his prize, he didn't seem to know what to do with her. His all-consuming interest was making motion pictures, yet he wouldn't allow his wife to participate in any way. "In the first place, Howard did not want Ella to meet any of the movie people he had. He thought she shouldn't associate with them," Mrs. Lummis added. "I don't think he thought they were her equal. I think he tried to keep Ella where she belonged, in the Pasadena social group, and he was mixed up with all the movie people. It was a very difficult situation."

27

Hughes revealed other eccentricities, as well. "He was overly protective of her," said a source close to Ella. "He wouldn't even let her go out of the hotel without a—I wouldn't say a guard, but at least without a chaperone." To serve this purpose, Hughes hired an Englishwoman to be Ella's *duenna*. "But she finally just told him," the source continued, "said, 'Now, I'm not gonna live this secluded life. I'm gonna get out and make friends.' And she joined the Junior League out there."

In spite of Ella's efforts, the marriage simply collapsed after four years. Just as she had been at the beginning of the relationship, Annette Lummis was called in at the end. "I was in Honolulu," she recollected, "and I got a wire from Libby (Libby was Mrs. W. S. Farish, whose husband was president of the Standard Oil Company, and in whose garden Ella had been married). And Libby wired me to meet her in Los Angeles, that Ella and Sonny were having trouble—that is Ella. And I stayed at their house with Libby, and they were having trouble, the reason being that Howard was producing *Hell's Angels* and was never home. . . . They just weren't getting along, understandably. . . . Ella wanted to go home and get a divorce."

In December 1929, Ella Rice Hughes was granted a divorce in Houston, ending what would seem to have been a mismatch from the start, and what was surely a very difficult marriage for the displaced and neglected Ella. "He was a very peculiar man," admitted an intimate of Ella's, "even then." "He was very odd, from all reports; that is, from her reports." Ella Rice Hughes went on to marry James O. Winston, Jr., founder of Rowles, Winston Investments, whom she had met thirteen years earlier on a blind date, before her ill-fated marriage to Hughes. Reflecting back on his wife's troubled first marriage, Winston seemed to attribute much of the problem to Howard, Jr.'s, "genius," and expressed gratitude to Hughes for letting her go. For the devoted Winston, who had fallen in love with Ella at first sight those thirteen years ago, it was the happy ending to a storybook romance.

As for Howard Hughes, Jr., he assumed, at twenty-four, one of the most enviable positions in the world: he was rich, handsome, unmarried—and living in Hollywood, California.

Leading Ladies

Howard, Jr.'s, earlier visits to California as a teenager had introduced him not only to the movies, but also to the actresses who made them, and he was as fascinated by one as by the other. His early acquaintances with the women of Hollywood could hardly be called successful, however. In fact, the young Howard Hughes, Jr., was so ill at ease around women that his father often had to use his influence to get dates for his son.

"He was the rich son of a rich father," is how one California comrade remembered Howard, Jr., during this period. Big Howard's brother Rupert Hughes was then a well-known screenwriter and director living in California. Through him, the popular Texas millionaire widower and his shy son met and mingled with movie stars. Rupert would invite his brother to visit him on his movie sets, and included him in the Sunday luncheons that he hosted at his Hollywood mansion, a gathering place for screen luminaries. More often than not, Howard, Jr., would tag along.

Eleanor Boardman, then an ingenue making her debut in a Rupert Hughes film called *Souls for Sale,* accompanied Howard, Jr., to one of these luncheons, and admits that the date was "arranged" by Howard Hughes, Sr. Apparently this practice was not unusual. In contrast to his outgoing father, Howard, Jr., was more scientific-minded, serious, and slightly intense. Long periods of silence were not uncommon for him. This characteristic may have been acceptable to the old guard society back in Houston, but it did not make him a popular escort in Hollywood. Even his Uncle Rupert privately described Howard, Jr., as "very strange," according to Miss Boardman.

However unattractive Howard, Jr.'s, social shortcomings made him appear to the young actresses, his father's fortune in drill bits must have more than compensated, because the starlets seldom refused to accompany the taciturn young man on his father's arranged dates.

When Howard Hughes, Jr., returned to Hollywood after his divorce from Ella Rice, he carried with him the experiences of his early years in California. Those first awkward and prearranged encounters with leading ladies aroused in him a strong attraction for actresses and demonstrated to Hughes the enormous and seductive power of his wealth. It was a combination that would gradually lead him to a notorious and slightly demented obsession with starlets, and into one— and possibly two—strange and ultimately doomed marriages to screen personalities.

Leading Man

The new bachelor Hughes hit Hollywood, the second time around, like a Texas cyclone. He began to make movies with a frenzy, already displaying a tendency toward compulsive behavior. Hughes did everything in excess, nothing in moderation. And since movies were his passion, he dedicated himself to their creation twenty-four hours a day, often becoming so engrossed in his work that he would forget to change clothes or go home for several days at a time.

By leaving the tool company in the hands of its competent Houston executives and settling instead in the libertine new community of Los Angeles, Howard, Jr., found a way to escape his "genius" father's tall shadow. Hollywood in the 1920s and 1930s was the brave new world, and Howard Hughes, Jr., had the keys to the kingdom. He no longer needed his father to arrange dates for him. Now the starlets came to Hughes.

And why not? He had everything a struggling actress could want in a man: he could make her a star. This ability, more than any dubious Hughes mystique, was his drawing card with the women of Hollywood. Clearly, it was not a dramatic personality change that transformed the Texas wallflower into a Hollywood Don Juan. Indeed, the adult Hughes displayed many of the faults that made him such a loser with the opposite sex as a teenager. He was, to the end, almost painfully shy; he made little effort to please, and certainly no attempt at small talk— hardly the traditional components of a man-about-town.

Betty Westbrook, a distant cousin who was thrown together with Hughes during their teen years, remembers how they would "sit and glare at each other . . . because he was bored to death, and I know I was." Apparently this awkwardness persisted to adulthood with the majority of Howard's dates. Whatever charm Hughes possessed was buried deep as the oil his drill bits tapped. The real change in Hughes was in his attitude. Now he knew that none of that mattered. He had power, and he knew that power was the ultimate aphrodisiac. So he did little to polish the rough edges of his social behavior; he simply sat back and let his money do the talking.

As an indication of how little Hughes had changed in his ability—or inclination—to court women, he hired a flamboyant public relations man, Johnny Meyers, to set up his dates for him. Meyers' public relations title was little more than a front for his true service to Hughes: to procure girls. If an actress or chorine survived Hughes' careful scrutiny, Meyers would approach her with the news that she had been chosen by Hughes to be his companion for the evening. Under the Hughes system of courtship, it was not so much an invitation as a command performance. To be summoned by Hughes was a status symbol in the starlet community, so most of the objects of his attention accepted breathlessly. Thus, oddly enough, though he was internationally recognized as a playboy, the truth is that Hughes' dates were largely still arranged. Where once his father served as the go-between, now it was Johnny Meyers.

30

If Hughes remained in temperament much the same toward women, his lifestyle certainly changed dramatically. This is perhaps best demonstrated from the perspective of actress Eleanor Boardman. When she first met Hughes in the early 1920s, she and her set either snubbed him or agreed to an occasional mercy date to appease his father. At their next encounter, over a decade later, Howard was attempting to rent Boardman's house as a pied-à-terre for his string of girlfriends.

The years in Hughes' life from 1930 (after his divorce from Ella Rice) to 1949 can best be described as one big party. This is the period that earned him his reputation as a ladykiller. With the help of Meyers or through his own peculiar panache, Hughes embarked on two decades of debauchery, leading to reports of his involvement with what would seem to be half the women in Hollywood. In this period, Hughes courted or pursued such diverse personalities as Bette Davis, Cyd Charisse, Ava Gardner, Billie Dove, Jean Simmons, Elizabeth Taylor, and more.

Interestingly, two women with whom Howard Hughes apparently was not romantically involved are the actresses most often associated with him: Jean Harlow and Jane Russell. He discovered both and made each a star, Harlow as the femme fatale in the ambitious aviation-adventure film *Hell's Angels*, and Russell and her famous cleavage in *The Outlaw*. Probably the mogul in Hughes taught him not to mix business with pleasure, because Harlow and Russell remained his platonic friends before, during, and after filming; Russell continues to hold Hughes in high esteem.

In addition to his other endeavors, Hughes was a regular at the madcap parties at San Simeon given by William Randolph Hearst, whose guests included the most glittering of the Hollywood beautiful people. Yet in pictures taken at these gala affairs, Hughes typically appears sullen and withdrawn, although surrounded by glamorous and fawning women.

Despite the determination of his many female companions, Hughes somehow managed to elude matrimony during this period—not that the subject was not discussed. Several of the actresses whom Hughes dated during his romantic heyday claim to have received proposals from him, including but certainly not limited to Ginger Rogers, Debra Paget, and Elizabeth Taylor. The women who fall within this category describe Hughes as an ardent suitor, and several have suggested that Hughes offered enormous sums as an inducement to matrimony. Ginger Rogers has said that Hughes proposed to her on a hillside in Hollywood, where he vowed to buy the entire mountaintop for their dream house. How much of such reports is true and how much the product of romantic embellishment will never be known. It is clear, however, that none of these proposals, however impassioned, resulted in marriage.

Certainly Howard Hughes would not be the first man to make promises in the dark he would later deny, regret, or at least qualify, and that may be the explanation for this rash of proposals. Hughes' track record bears this out. A random survey of his girl friends suggests that such pillow talk was Hughes' modus operandi. He used the same line and the same technique on many different women, apparently saving his originality for his business encounters. Evidently, a "proposal" from Hughes was worth about as much as a Confederate dollar.

It is unlikely that marriage was seriously on Howard Hughes' mind at this time in his life. He had just been through a painful divorce, and he seemed to enjoy playing the man-about-town. Colleen Moore, a successful actress of the 1920s and 1930s, first met Hughes in 1922 while she was starring in a Rupert Hughes picture called *The Wallflower*. The two became friends, and when, in the early thirties, Howard began dating Billie Dove, a stunning actress and a close friend of Moore's, Colleen asked him, "Why don't you two get married?" According to Moore, Hughes replied, "I will never marry again, ever, ever, ever."

If Hughes had been inclined to marry during this period, the most likely woman would have been Katharine Hepburn. They were both independent, private, stubborn, inflexible, domineering, intelligent, accomplished, and emphatically antimarriage. In Hepburn, Hughes more than met his match.

As told by Ben Lyon, a social friend of Hughes', and the lead in his film *Hell's Angels*, Howard's primary interests in the thirties were movies and aviation. Glenn Odekirk, an employee and close friend of Hughes' for many years, remembered much the same thing, adding that Howard loved girls even more.

Another Hollywood crony of Howard's, Pat deCicco, added golf to the list of Hughes' chief interests during this period. Ginger Rogers, who dated Hughes off and on between 1933 and 1940, remembers how they often played golf or went riding in planes during their times together.

This arrangement fit the athletic and adventurous Kate Hepburn like a designer glove. Always eager for a challenge, she was keen competition for Hughes in golf and even learned to pilot a plane under his tutelage. The only interest Hughes shared with the typical Hollywood nymphet was his money. With Hepburn, he had at last found a woman whom he could meet on his own terms, an equal, not an object.

Both feverishly busy with their careers, they met briefly in out-of-the-way places during the 1930s and 1940s. Hughes would occasionally visit Hepburn at her home in Connecticut, and they often dodged the press from hotel to hotel. Joanna Madsen, first Hepburn's and later

Hughes' maid, recalled how she first came to meet Hughes in 1936. Madsen was on location with Hepburn during the filming of one of her movies, when Hughes landed his private plane on a beanfield next to the set to visit with Kate. This sort of rendezvous was typical of their relationship. The next year, Hepburn moved into Hughes' house on Muirfield Road in Hollywood, and Madsen stayed on with Hughes after Kate left, working as his maid until 1944, when the house was sold.

When Hepburn was scheduled to appear in Houston in a road show of her hit, *The Philadelphia Story*, in 1941, Hughes wrote his aunt Annette Lummis in advance, asking her to invite Hepburn to the house one afternoon. "She was the first woman I ever saw in trousers," recalled Mrs. Lummis. "She came out in the most beautiful yellow trousers that ever was. . . . Oh, we had a great time." Hughes' tender letter to his aunt is a measure of his respect and affection for Miss Hepburn:

Dear Annette,

Kate Hepburn arrives in town Jan. 10. She is an exceptionally good friend of mine, and one of the nicest people in the world—next to you, of course.

Will you please invite her out to see the house one afternoon? Please don't invite anyone else, as she is shy and it gets her upset to meet strangers. She is very tired at the end of a long road tour.

She would love to see the house and you and the children—noone [sic]else—not even Martha or Fred. [Martha Houstoun, another Hughes maternal aunt; and Dr. Frederick Lummis, Annette Lummis' husband.]

If she asks to see the plant, please drive her out but not in the gate. I have specific reasons for this, and you can find some excuse—'Fletcher, or Noah, the only ones you know, are out of town, etc.' You had better tell Noah about that so he won't do it himself—by any chance.

Please see that she gets back to the hotel by four-thirty for her nap before the show. This is most important, as she won't take care of herself and is headed for complete exhaustion and a break-down. Tell her I said I was writing to you on the specific condition that she promise to get her nap and go to bed immediately after the show both nights, and that if you did anything to interfere with it I would be terribly disappointed. And I mean this.

33

Well, Annette, I'm afraid I am imposing a great deal.
Please forgive me—and I do thank you ever ever so much.

My love to you,

Son.

I want to tell you also how much I appreciate your
phoning.

Howard and Jean

It was several years later, over the Fourth of July holiday, 1946, that
Howard Hughes met actress (Elizabeth) Jean Peters. He was forty years
old, she was nineteen, when they were introduced at the home of a
mutual friend, Bill Cagney, in Newport Beach. Two days later, Hughes
was nearly killed when a plane he was test flying crashed into the second floor of a house in Beverly Hills. Thus their courtship began at the
Good Samaritan Hospital in Los Angeles, where Peters visited Hughes
from time to time during his two-week hospitalization. She continued
to call upon the convalescing Hughes at his home in Beverly Hills,
where they would frequently have dinner and view movies together.
That October, Peters traveled to Mexico for the filming of *Captain from
Castille* with Tyrone Power. Hughes flew down twice to be with her on
location.

Thereafter, between 1947 and 1950, Hughes continued to see
Peters, but with less intensity. She was being groomed for stardom, and
Hughes was busy pursuing his other business and romantic interests,
dividing his time between hotels or rented houses in Palm Beach, Los
Angeles, Las Vegas, and Palm Springs. The Hughes-Peters relationship
continued into the early fifties, but clearly with less fervor. Hughes,
unbeknownst to Miss Peters, was going through something of a transition period in his life in the early 1950s, gradually phasing out of his
playboy-entrepreneur stage and into a more reclusive life.

Of course, he was still active, both in a business and a social sense,
during these years, maintaining an office at Goldwyn Studios, meeting
his appointments at the Beverly Hills Hotel, and playing the field with
Hollywood's newest faces. (In fact, it was during this stage that Hughes
would dispatch ''drivers'' to chauffeur his collection of starlets, with
specific instructions to avoid any bumps in the road that might un-
necessarily jostle their bosoms. He also preferred devout Mormons for
his corps of drivers, thinking they might be less inclined to socialize
with their passengers.) And Hughes continued to see old friends like

Cary Grant and celebrity lawyer Gregson Bautzer, along with the usual movie crowd. However, a pattern was developing in his behavior: his dress and eating habits seldom changed. He was typically attired in beige gabardine trousers, a white shirt, and an occasional jacket, and he consistently dined on steak, vegetables, and ice cream once a day.

Finally, on May 29, 1954, seven years after she met Hughes, Jean Peters grew tired of waiting and married someone else, Stuart W. Cramer III. Her marriage to Cramer seemed to heighten Hughes' interest in her, and she saw him fairly frequently from 1954 to 1957, though still married to Cramer at the time. By this point, Hughes had acquired several of the employees who would later become known as his "aides," although their duties as such had not yet developed, and they performed instead a miscellany of services for Hughes Productions, euphemistically described as "public relations," but which in practice meant such tasks as chauffeuring and message delivery. One of these individuals, Roy Crawford, observed that by about 1955, Hughes' outside contact with business associates had decreased "drastically," and he came to depend more and more on the network of "special services" assistants he was devising. As before, he maintained floating residences in Palm Beach, Miami, and either the Beverly Hills Hotel or a rented mansion in the Bel Air section of Los Angeles.

The strain of Hughes' attention no doubt contributed to the Cramers' eventual divorce, and on January 12, 1957, Hughes, the reluctant bridegroom, chartered a TWA Constellation and flew himself and Jean Peters to the dusty desert town of Tonopah, Nevada, where they were married in a secret wedding ceremony on the second floor of a small motel. Although they used the assumed names of Marian Evans and G. A. Johnson, Hughes leaked the scoop to gossip columnist Louella Parsons, thereby dashing the hopes of his legion of groupies back in Hollywood.

The marriage of Jean Peters and Howard Hughes was destined to be unusual, as Hughes' eccentric behavior pattern worsened. After a brief stay in the house that Jean had occupied before the wedding, she and Hughes moved into one of the private bungalows on the grounds of the Beverly Hills Hotel, an arrangement that Mrs. Hughes hoped would be temporary. After several weeks, she departed for Palm Springs to set up a house for the two of them. Hughes later joined her there, staying for only three days. Then the lure of hotel life beckoned once again, and he set off for Nassau in the Bahamas, leaving his wife behind in the home she had selected for their new life together. Jean Hughes joined her husband shortly afterwards, and they spent six weeks on holiday together. On their return, it was back to the Beverly Hills Hotel, Hughes' old haunt, this time for good. It was here that Howard Hughes' life took its turn from the merely eccentric to the increasingly bizarre.

Hughes' setup at the Beverly Hills Hotel was unique, to say the least. He maintained from five to eight bungalows, as well as various rooms and suites in the hotel proper, all rented on a day-to-day basis. Hughes occupied Bungalow number 4, his wife lived in Bungalow number 19, and Bungalow number 3 housed John Holmes and Roy Crawford, two of Hughes' "special services" employees, now "on call" to Hughes, who often never called at all. The other luxury bungalows were used to store video equipment, house employees, or serve some similarly prosaic purpose. Hughes' preference for the hotel style of life, once understandable in one who had traveled widely and had no family, had now assumed monstrous proportions.

His appearance was described as "appalling" by Jack Egger, a "PR/bodyguard" for Hughes from 1957 to 1960. Hughes, always lanky, carried only 140 pounds on his 6'4" frame, and wore a "bushy" five-to seven-inch beard and longish brown-gray hair. His fingernails and toenails were also long, often a half-inch to one inch beyond his fingers and toes. Although he kept a chef and two waiters on twenty-four-hour call either at home or at the hotel, Hughes was a "cyclical" eater, preferring one food for an extended period of time. He was also partial to Hershey bars and cakes. Perhaps because he had no occasion to dress, reducing his world to the room around him and receiving few, if any, guests, Hughes usually remained in the nude or in pajamas, only occasionally putting on a pair of trousers.

Hughes' system of communication was equally extraordinary. He employed a three-man team (of which Egger was one) to work an eight-hour shift, seven days a week in Bungalow number 1—basically to answer the telephone or to run an occasional errand for Mr. or Mrs. Hughes. Like some character in a John le Carré novel of international espionage, this employee was designated "the Third Man" by Hughes. No one called Hughes directly. All calls were screened through the Third Man, who was instructed to answer the telephone using four layers of tissue as "insulation." Just as in any good spy thriller, Hughes also had a girl friend during his Beverly Hills Hotel period. This was aspiring actress Yvonne Schubert, known in the Hughes code as "the Party." To Egger's knowledge, Hughes and the Party, for all their extended phone conversations, enjoyed only one evening together during the four years the entourage occupied the bungalows.

Understandably, Crawford and the other employees in special services began to notice a "strain" in Howard and Jean's relations. Though Peters knew she had married a man whom others considered strange, she could not have imagined the kind of lifestyle Hughes would establish for their marriage. There is a slight difference of opinion among the bungalow staff, but all agree that Howard and Jean saw each other very seldom during their four-year residence at the Beverly Hills Hotel. Egger can recall only one meeting. The occasion was Thanksgiving, and Mrs. Hughes (whose code name was "the Major"), was escorted by an entourage of staff assistants from her bungalow to Howard's, where she spent an hour, presumably to have dinner. Despite their lack of physical contact, the two kept in touch by telephone, and Hughes took great pains to instruct Jean's chef to classify as "restricted" from her diet certain foods such as onions, garlic, and pork.

During his luxurious exile at the hotel, Hughes spent his time screening films, as he had done most of his life, chatting on the phone for hours, sleeping, and reading. The Third Man was responsible for delivering sundries to "the Boss" (as Hughes was known among the staff), and Egger notes that Hughes' reading list included the *Los Angeles Times* and *Herald-Examiner*, an occasional *Wall Street Journal*, all the business and general news publications, and "every girly magazine."

Hughes apparently left the hotel grounds for an extended period, secreting himself at Nosseck Studios in Hollywood, where he screened movies nonstop. His assistants delivered his food and an occasional clean shirt to him at the studios, but they were under strict instructions from Hughes to keep his whereabouts concealed from Mrs. Hughes, whom he phoned regularly. (He reportedly finally told her he was in the hospital, to "get her off his back.") Sometime after his return to the bungalow, two 35mm movie projectors and a screen were installed so he could create his own projection room, and two of the drivers became projectionists.

Hughes' love for movies was exceeded only by his distrust for television. He believed that television emitted radiation that made one sterile and caused constipation. He never watched it himself, and if his staff insisted, they were to view it from a distance and without touching it. His fear of radioactivity was so extreme that he once banished an employee from the vicinity of the hotel because he was observed shaking hands with Walter Winchell, who had been to Las Vegas during the original atomic bomb tests. Hughes considered Winchell to be radioactive, and thought that the handshake transferred this condition to the staff member. The same paranoia prompted Hughes' directive to his employees to avoid crowded spots such as amusement parks and cinemas, which of course they ignored. It was this phobia that led to Hughes' much-publicized Kleenex insulation system.

In late 1960 Hughes surprised his elated wife with a house, albeit rented, in Rancho Santa Fe, California, an exclusive community north of San Diego. He flew her over it and talked about the house for a month before they actually moved in. Nothing could have pleased Peters more. It was her continuing dream to establish the two of them in a house; she hoped this would stabilize both Howard and their marriage. The move to Rancho Santa Fe did signal a return to normalcy in some respects, beginning with the drive out of Los Angeles on Christmas Eve, Howard's fifty-fifth birthday. For the first time in years, Hughes sat behind the wheel of a car, driving himself and his wife away from the Beverly Hills Hotel bungalows to their new home. Hughes would never drive an automobile again.

Rancho Santa Fe was not much different from the restricted environment that Hughes had created at the Beverly Hills Hotel. He received no visitors, and spent his time wandering about the house or making and receiving his continual phone calls, mostly business-related. His hearing was deteriorating, and an amplifier had been added to the telephone, his lifeline to the rest of the world. His diet had improved slightly, as had his personal hygiene, and a barber came in to trim his beard from time to time. Hughes' wardrobe remained unchanged, however; he still wore pajamas morning, noon, and night, possibly because he never left the house for even five minutes. Jean Hughes tried to interest him in golf, his former passion, but Hughes remained indoors throughout their residence at Rancho Santa Fe. More ominous was the continuation of his system of rotating attendants. Both Roy Crawford and John Holmes, another special services employee, accompanied the Hugheses to Rancho Santa Fe, and one or the other was "on call" at all times, commuting to and from the nearby Rancho Santa Fe Inn, four days off and four days on. And for the first time, Hughes began stationing guards outside the house, a practice he would continue thereafter.

The Hugheses' occupation of the Rancho Santa Fe house was short-lived. Within eleven months, they were again packing their bags for another move. Peters attributes this decision to the collapse of the plumbing system at the house. Hughes "would not tolerate" working under the conditions necessary to bring it to full repair. Instead, they relocated to another rented mansion, at 1001 Bel Air Road, high in the hills of Los Angeles, where they resided for four years, their last time together under the same roof.

Immediately upon their arrival at the Bel Air house, Hughes requested that one of his assistants be available to him twenty-four hours a day. Initially, the aide stayed in Hughes' room, but in a matter of months an office was set up and Hughes would ring a bell to summon the man on duty. This was a turning point both in Hughes' life and in his marriage. Jean Peters notes that it was here that his aides took on increasing importance to Hughes, and their marriage, fragile at its best, crumbled under the strain.

Within the same house, Hughes and Peters had separate suites and for the most part led separate lives. Jean Hughes struggled to establish a normal lifestyle under abnormal conditions. She went shopping with friends, attended the ballet on occasion, entertained guests (in her division of the house), and used her considerable spare time to make recordings for the blind. She generally saw Hughes briefly once a day, and did her best to encourage him to escort her to social functions, but he resisted, and in fact never left the house for any reason. George Francom, yet another aide, claims that Hughes never even left his room, except once, "improperly clothed," when he embarrassed the maids and returned immediately to his sanctuary.

The quality of Hughes' life had declined to an alarming degree. Roy Crawford, placed in charge of Hughes' staff of round-the-clock attendants, was one of the few even to see Hughes at this stage of his life, and the picture he paints of his employer is indeed pathetic. Hughes had completely given up dressing; his bathing habits were irregular, and he stayed bedridden most of the time. He ate only one meal a day, usually at 3 A.M. The telephone, his life support system, was his constant companion. His only exercise was the short walk between his bed, the bathroom, and a favorite lounge chair. Hughes was apparently very sentimental about the chair, which was sent to him at his request by Kitty Callaway, the cousin who accompanied him to California with Annette Lummis. Carl Callaway, Kitty's husband, recalls how it came about. "There was a certain piece of furniture—I don't know what you call it, is there a certain type of couch you call a La-Z-Boy?—that was an old family piece of furniture. And Howard was very much interested in his family, evidently, at the time, and someway this piece of furniture came into focus. And Mrs. Callaway fixed it up and crated it up and sent it to Mrs.—to Jean Peters—for Howard." The Callaways certainly had no clue that it would play such an important role in Hughes' life.

Hughes, a man of unique talents, even genius, became a witness to his broken dreams. He knew that he had lost control over his life, and he deeply regretted what he had become. In 1956, the year before he married Jean Peters and began his course toward self-destruction, he telephoned his old and dear friend, Dudley Sharp, with whom he had not spoken in many years. Sharp was the son of Howard, Sr.'s, partner in the early days of the Hughes Tool Company, and had served as best man in Howard, Jr.'s , wedding. Sharp still lived in Houston and traveled in the world Hughes had abandoned. "I've messed up my life very badly," Hughes confessed to Sharp. The two did not communicate afterward, and Hughes seemed to have broken the silence in order to convey that message to the friend from his childhood.

One other major event occurred in Hughes' life in 1957 (in addition to his marriage to Peters), which helped trigger the drastic changes manifest in his behavior. This was the year he fired Noah Dietrich, his longtime chief executive, with Hughes since he was a teenager.

Hughes felt trapped by the role he had created of the wealthy man of solitude, according to Jean Peters, and often seemed confused about life in general. At one point, Peters remembers Hughes saying that the only person who made any sense was Cary Grant, one of his closest friends from their years together at RKO Studios. Although her marriage to Howard was by now little more than a sham, they were still emotionally attached, and Hughes continued to share with her his feelings, his hopes, and his sorrows. "He used to call me a shotgun talker, and he was a rifle talker. That is, he would hone in. I kinda talked around things. He was very precise." During these conversations, Hughes told his wife he felt it was immoral that one person should have so much money. The shy, withdrawn young man who first traveled to California with his father reemerged in these private moments with his wife, and Hughes admitted that he would have much preferred being an aeronautical engineer working in a shop some place. The man who had carved out an international reputation for himself as a high-powered financier did not enjoy business dealings. "Unfortunately," he told Peters, "I am very good at (them)."

The more sensitive of his aides, such as Jack Egger, not only liked and respected him, but sensed his loneliness and empathized with him. Hughes' basic outlook on life, as described by Peters, was negative. If he had a goal during this period of decline, it was to get his life back in order, get back into aviation, into designing and inventing new forms of aircraft. It was a great disappointment to him, Peters reveals, that though aviation had been so important in his lifetime, all of his records were eventually broken. Accordingly, she feels, he transferred all his hopes and goals to the formation of the medical institute that would bear his name. This was something he could feel proud of and look forward to, his last statement, his lasting monument. His feelings about the Howard Hughes Medical Institute, as Miss Peters' recollections suggest, were highly personal. He did not want the institute to become another "successful Disneyland in which hot dog stands were seen rimming . . . the park." He saw HHMI instead as a "utopian kind of model city where not only would research be going on but where lifestyles and problems of pollution and air pollution, water pollution, everything would be so perfectly designed . . . it would be a model for the rest of the world."

40

Sadly, Hughes was progressively less able to pursue this idealistic dream, as his private world took on its nightmarish characteristics. Midway into 1966, Hughes sold his substantial stock holdings in Trans World Airways, ending fifteen troubled years of dominance over the airline. The $546,549,171 check he had received as a result of the stock transaction would have been gobbled up by California's stiff state income tax, and Hughes was far too possessive about his wealth to allow that to happen. On the advice of his tax attorney, Milton H. West of the Andrews, Kurth law firm in Houston, Hughes began casting about for a new residence. As a ruse, he chose Boston, and in late 1966 vacated the Bel Air house, never to return to the state where he had spent so many years. He discussed his destination beforehand with his aides, but apparently not with his wife. Jean Hughes heard her husband leaving, but chose to stay in her room as he departed. Hughes turned up at the Ritz-Carlton Hotel in Boston, staying two weeks, just long enough to plot the direction of his new life. As had been the pattern in their marriage, beginning with Hughes' disappearance from the Palm Springs house shortly after their honeymoon, Jean Hughes, the constant wife, hopped on a plane to join her vagabond husband.

"My hat is off to Jean Peters. She really stuck with him," marveled Annette Lummis, when asked about her nephew's second marriage. "I don't know anything about it. I don't know her at all, but from what the papers said about his life . . ." Even Mrs. Lummis shuddered to contemplate the odd, reclusive style of living that "Sonny" had adopted in his later years. Miss Peters has testified that she and Hughes were not separated emotionally when he left for Boston, only due to "business circumstances"; this slender hope nourished her faith in their marriage. While in Boston, she discussed possible residences with Hughes, and the two studied maps together. Hughes was keen on settling in Las Vegas, a move Peters strongly opposed. They also considered several states on the East Coast, and Peters left the Ritz-Carlton for 1001 Bel Air Road certain that her husband would consult her before he made a final decision. Events proved her wrong, and although she would remain married to Hughes another four years, she never saw him again.

Jean Peters Hughes learned about her husband's decision in the newspapers, along with everyone else. Rejecting Montreal, Atlanta, and Nassau, Hughes ignored his wife's wishes and established himself and his traveling family of aides in the Desert Inn, which he swiftly purchased to avoid eviction. "Las Vegas was kind of an afterthought," reflected George Francom, another Hughes driver/aide who was privy to the Boss's decision-making process. "Everything that happened there was by chance." For Hughes, it was his final journey into madness.

41

He eventually phoned his wife to tell her what she had already discovered, and for the first time in their marriage, she did not rush to join him. Jean Hughes despised Las Vegas and remained instead at the house in Bel Air, from which she sustained a telephone marriage with Hughes throughout his period of residence at the Desert Inn. They spoke by phone daily, and as always, Hughes was full of talk about their future. His plan was to one day have a ranch "with everything on it to make them both happy"—a private landing strip, a good projection room, and so on. He even sent Peters a scrapbook. Still susceptible to Hughes' considerable powers of persuasion, she consented to come to the ranch, if Hughes would leave the hotel permanently. He told her, as he had so many times in the past, that he planned to abandon the hotel style of living and spend the rest of his life on their dream ranch.

But by the time Hughes left the Desert Inn in 1970, their talk had turned to divorce. His isolation at the hotel had extended to four years, and Peters' patience had simply given out. As she later explained it, Hughes' tendency to procrastinate, in combination with his growing dependence upon his aides, finally drove her to seek an end to the marriage. (By this time, it was certainly not jealousy over suspected infidelity. The truth is, Hughes never even saw a woman face to face during the four years he spent at the Desert Inn.) After fourteen extraordinary years of marriage, Peters finally divorced Hughes in February 1971.

Father Knows Best

The squadron of lawyers preparing for the determination of Hughes' wives and children in Phase One of the heirship trial of Howard Hughes saw him revealed as a man who was unsuccessful in personal relationships and indifferent to the needs of his wives, characteristics that led to two failed marriages, each of which ended childless. About this there was no dispute. It was clear that Hughes was duly divorced from both Ella Rice and Jean Peters, leaving them with no claim to his estate, either personally or through any offspring. More surprising was the absence of any serious claim to inheritance by an individual coming forward as an illegitimate child of Howard Hughes. Hughes' philandering had certainly created the opportunity, and his death supplied the motive.

There have always been rumors about Hughes' sexual prowess, and his history with women is the stuff of legends. Still, there seems never to have been a paternity claim brought against Hughes that was taken seriously. Greg Bautzer, who served as Hughes' personal attorney on a retainer basis from 1947 until his death, would have been the person in the best position to know about any lawsuits of this kind, and he maintains Hughes never had any children. Dr. Norman Crane, personal physician to Hughes intermittently from 1938 on, has testified there were no paternity claims during the period he treated Hughes. Hughes once told Colleen Moore he didn't like children, and apparently he succeeded in remaining childless. "I said to him once," she recalled, "I said, 'Your father is a genius and you're pretty good yourself. I think you should be married and have a child to leave these wonderful genes to.' " According to Moore, he replied, "I will never marry again, I told you that, and I don't like children."

And yet, there was always the possibility that Hughes' confidantes were mistaken, creating an atmosphere of continuing expectation in Ted Dinkins' office back in Houston. "It was very unpredictable," recalls Darlene Cameron, Dinkins' secretary throughout the heir search. "It was exciting from the standpoint of all the research that was going on, and you kept thinking, well, maybe something's gonna turn up." In the five years between Hughes' death and the legal determination of his heirs, Dinkins received numerous letters from "sons" or "daughters" of Howard Hughes, each seeking official recognition of his or her paternity. And as the court-appointed attorney representing unknown heirs, it was Dinkins' duty to investigate each claim to his satisfaction.

It was not an unusual occurrence to pick up the telephone in Dinkins' office during this period and have "Howard Hughes III" on the other end of the line. "The one that really sticks in my mind is the Queen of Russia," chuckles Cameron. The "Queen of Russia" was an elderly woman from Great Britain who was convinced she was the daughter of Howard Hughes and aviatrix Amelia Earhart. She wrote to Dinkins regularly, always sketching her royal seal of office on the outside of each envelope, signifying her position as queen of Russia and all "eight" continents. "Poor Missus Little," Dinkins would often drawl as he read her latest epistle, "I feel sorry for her." Then he would compose, as he did with his countless other correspondents, a sympathetic but discouraging response.

Occasionally these individuals appeared at his law offices, much to the amusement of Dinkins' partners and associates, not to mention the flustered receptionists, who were accustomed to the routine parade of blue- and gray-suited corporate clients characteristic of a large and conservative law firm. Typical of this sort of individual was the black man who waited patiently for an audience with Dinkins, identifying himself to the receptionist as Howard Hughes III. The fact that Hughes entertained an extreme prejudice against blacks did not disturb his fantasy in the slightest.

For all the flurry of correspondence that Dinkins received, no claim of any substance materialized. Most of the so-called children of Howard

Hughes who knocked on his door suffered from psychological problems, and after Hughes' death, the billionaire had become the focus of their paranoid delusions.

There was some speculation among the Hughes aides that their boss might have fathered a teenaged boy who occupied one of the Hughes suites at the Beverly Hills Hotel during Hughes' residence there with Jean Peters. The lad resided with a couple in their mid-fifties called Adolph and Elsa Fuchs, and he was identified as their son. The Fuchs' room was paid for by Hughes Productions, although they were not on the payroll; their food was on the "restricted" list, delivered by the Third Man; and they were assigned a maid named Viola. According to Jack Egger, their presence was something of a mystery among the staff, particularly since the thirteen-year-old "son" did not attend school, and bore a "startling" resemblance to Hughes, especially around the eyes. Alas, to the aides' disappointment, Jean Peters later testified that Elsa Fuchs was nothing more remarkable than a cleaning woman, and nothing further has been heard of or from the Fuchses.

The crackpot stories and letters that surfaced concerning Hughes' paternity—tales that ranged from venereal disease to sterility to impotence to miscegenation—stimulated a great deal of idle gossip and much titillation among the attorneys preparing their clients' heirship claims, but fostered little real apprehension. After several years of studying Hughes' life and habits, all were convinced that he had died a divorced man and childless. It was then, right on cue, that Terry Moore joined the cast of characters in the drama to establish Hughes' heirs, ready to collect the estate she considered rightfully hers as the widow of Howard Hughes.

Howard and Terry?

When Terry Moore's name first appeared on pleadings in the Hughes estate proceedings, most of the lawyers concerned dismissed her as just another fantasizing female, in a category with Alyce Hovsepian Hughes and Alma Hughes. However, it soon developed that Moore's claim differed from the others in several respects that caused attorneys for the distant relatives to take her more seriously. First, Terry Moore was not just another anonymous crank, but a legitimate actress, one of the many glamorous movie starlets of the 1950s. She had even been nominated for an Academy Award (for her role in *Come Back, Little Sheba*). Second, and most important, it soon became clear that she, unlike the other previously unheard of "wives," had actually had a relationship of some sort with Howard Hughes.

The story that unfolded in the legal effort to determine the nature of her relationship with Howard Hughes could easily have been the script for one of the famous "screwball" comedies produced at Hughes' RKO Studios in the 1940s and made popular on the screen by two of his best friends, Cary Grant and Katharine Hepburn. In this real-life comedy, the leading lady, Miss Moore, was a daffy but lovable actress, impossibly naive, playing opposite Hughes at his madcap best. The plot involved a wedding on the high seas, performed by the ship's captain, but kept secret to protect the heroine's career as an innocent ingenue. The couple never divorced, though each went on to marry again, resulting in hysterical complications when the millionaire hero died without a will and his secret wife showed up to claim his estate.

Here, at last, was a story just zany enough to be true. Whether or not the alleged marriage was legal made millions of dollars worth of difference.

To explore the specifics of Miss Moore's claim, her deposition was taken, in numerous installments, by opposing counsel anxious to dispose of her case—or at least determine its legal merit. Although there were generally seven to ten attorneys present during these question-and-answer sessions, they came to provide the setting for a running battle of wills and personalities between Moore's attorney, Arthur Leeds, a quick-witted, fast-talking Los Angeles entertainment lawyer, and Paul Freese, the deliberate and excruciatingly polite attorney representing several grandchildren of the late Rupert Hughes.

The mise-en-scène was often a long oak conference table in a private conference room in the Houston offices of Andrews , Kurth, Campbell, and Jones. Gathered about were the distinguished attorneys, most of them from old-line, socially prestigious law firms, representing interests as diverse as the state of Texas, the unknown heirs, the administrators of Hughes' estate, and of course the distant cousins, all vitally interested in the outcome of the heirship determination. At the center of this group sat Terry Moore. Though she was now in her mid-fifties, her era in Hollywood a thing of the past, the old star system still lived in Miss Moore. Trained at a time when actors and actresses were under contract to a major studio and fussed over and pampered from dusk to dawn, she still operated by these rules. Every session found her in full makeup, her strawberry blonde page-boy coif groomed to perfection, every inch the glamour queen.

For most, deposition testimony is a solemn and nervous undertaking; the witness is placed under oath, and a court reporter is present to record the questions and answers. Not so for Moore. Her deposition had the atmosphere of a Mary Kay Cosmetics party. Not in the least daunted by the imposing circle of legal talent that surrounded her, firing questions, she prattled on, happily drawing doodles, relaying inside

45

Hollywood scoop during breaks in her interrogation. Without missing a beat, she would occasionally pull out a full-sized makeup mirror, set it up on the conference table, and touch up her face. This was deposition, Hollywood style, *Gidget Goes to Court*. As further proof of her longtime romance with and romantic marriage to Hughes, Moore clutched a copy of her unpublished manuscript, then entitled, *Howard Be Thy Name*. (It has since been changed to *Beauty and the Billionaire*.) It is a tribute to the self-restraint of the lawyers present that any pretense of decorum was maintained.

As developed through Terry's testimony, the Hughes-Moore relationship began in the late 1940s, during the period when Hughes was, in his fashion, courting Jean Peters. They met in the usual way, for Howard. Terry had been in show business since she was a child and was struggling for her "big break" into the movies. Like most starlet hopefuls, she went out a lot, to see and be seen, anxious to be "discovered," often with her boyfriend of the moment. "Wherever we would go," she recalls, "we would run into Johnny Machio, who was a man very much like Walter Kane. They both supplied introductions to Mr. Hughes, which I did not know about. . . . We always refused having a drink with him," she went on. "This one particular day we were at the tennis matches, Mr. Machio came along. Jerome [then her beau] felt that we . . . refused him so many times, let's not hurt his feelings. Let's go."

There followed the historic meeting.

"We went to the Beverly Wilshire Hotel. We were sitting in the center of what is now the El Padrino. Mr. Machio called over and said, 'Oh, there is Howard.' He was sitting alone against the wall. He said, 'Are you alone?' He nodded. He said, 'Come join us.' So he came over and said, 'This is Howard Hughes.' He came over and he introduced him to Jerry and me."

Jerry thereafter receded into the background, as Hughes moved in for his latest conquest. Just as he did with his other "girls," Howard pursued Moore relentlessly. At the beginning of their romance, Terry was still in her late teens, living at home with her parents, and Hughes was in his mid-forties. Furthermore, Moore was a devout Mormon who prided herself on "holding onto her virtue" with her young swains, despite the almost constant temptation. On one of her early dates with Howard, the couple drove up to Mulholland Drive, a famous lover's lane in the Hollywood hills. It was there, Moore contends, that she first "married" Howard Hughes. The ceremony was extremely private, just Hughes and Miss Moore, and it took place alongside their parked car on Mulholland, where Hughes recited a few words of his own composition. He then asked his date to do the same, after which he pronounced them man and

46

wife. Hughes, according to Moore, was not a religious man in the traditional sense, and in his eyes this exchange united them in marriage. "I felt very much married after that," reflects Miss Moore, "very much so. I mean, to me that is when I gave myself to Howard in spirit—whatever you want to call it." She was not convinced to Hughes' complete satisfaction, however. "I didn't think I should go to bed with him [afterward]," she admitted. (According to Moore, Elizabeth Taylor later told her that Hughes once tried the same approach on her, but Taylor apparently saw through it. It would be interesting to discover how many others "exchanged vows" with Hughes on Mulholland Drive.)

Not long thereafter, in November 1949, Hughes invited Moore aboard his private yacht, and it was there that their "legal" ceremony took place, she claimed. "It was a last-minute thing," Moore volunteered. Hughes apparently phoned her the same morning with an invitation for a short cruise and casually mentioned the idea of a shipboard wedding. Without obtaining a license and asking no further questions, Moore met Hughes later that day, bringing along her mother (as she often did) and Lillian Barclay, who was her best friend and "like another mother" to Terry. "It never occurred to Mother and me to question Howard," she explained. "We didn't question Howard." As his guest, Hughes brought either Lloyd Wright, a friend and one of his stable of attorneys, or Noah Dietrich, who was still in his good graces at the time. Miss Moore was not sure which. "I always thought it was Noah Dietrich, and so did my mother," she declared. "Noah said it was him, and then he changed and said he wasn't there, that he thought it was Lloyd. . . . I don't know. I used to get Mr. Dietrich and Mr. Wright mixed up all the time. . . . It was a—he was white-haired, I remember that."

From Los Angeles, the group, whatever its composition, flew to San Diego, where the Hughes yacht was docked. From San Diego, they boarded the yacht and "headed south"—to Mexico, Miss Moore supposed, "because I asked somebody where we were going and they said Mexico." Several hours later—Miss Moore did not know exactly how long or where—the "ceremony" took place in the main salon, performed by a Captain Flynn, now deceased. "I think it was Psalms or something like that," mused Moore. "He read some very pretty things. It was very beautiful, I know, because I was surprised at how beautiful it was." After this occurred, Terry recalled, "It seems to me Captain Flynn asked if he [Howard] had a ring, and he said, 'No,' and somebody loaned me a ring that we used, and I gave it back. I don't remember who it was. . . . I just used the ring for the ceremony; that was all."

A short time after this event, the party returned to San Diego, within

47

seven or eight hours after they had set sail. There the guests disembarked, leaving Hughes and Terry alone on the yacht overnight. Assured she was now officially Mrs. Hughes, Terry consummated her marriage to Howard while the boat remained docked in the San Diego harbor. Moore had no qualms about the legality of the ceremony, even though there was no marriage license and she had never observed the captain's logs recording the event, because she remembered "seeing movies where people were married on shipboard. . . . I knew a sea captain with unlimited Master's papers could marry you at sea," she elaborated. "Who told me, I don't remember. But I knew that. I know it now. I knew it then, and I don't know how I knew it. I just knew it—from books, from motion pictures—and I knew it." The next morning, true to Hughes' style, the couple returned to Los Angeles to Bungalow 19 at the Beverly Hills Hotel.

During the months immediately following the episode on Hughes' yacht, the pair "moved around a lot," occasionally using pseudonyms, often going as Howard Hughes and Terry Moore, but never referred to as Mr. and Mrs. Hughes. "I told everyone I was not married because I promised Howard I wouldn't ever admit to the marriage at that time until we told," Moore explained. "It was a secret. It was a very secret marriage." According to Terry, the secrecy was for her protection. "I made animal pictures and I was the eternal virgin," she disclosed. "Howard was a roué and had a reputation for being a roué, and it would be very harmful to my reputation to be married to him or anybody." Somehow this was impressed upon the guests and conveyed to Howard, although Moore cannot recall when these discussions took place or what was said. "I don't know," she admitted. "I don't know when. I can't remember that far back."

Under any circumstances, the Hughes-Moore friendship, whatever its legal status, continued over the next year. The alleged marriage was certainly never made public, nor was it acknowledged privately by Hughes' friends or his aides. "He was years older," Moore offered by way of explanation. "I made little girl roles. I was the eternal virgin at that time. It was because of the roles I made." Moore did not even inform her father she was married, "because he was so much against it," said Terry. "You know, he just—my father did not care for Mr. Hughes and I just didn't bring the subject up." For his part, Hughes continued to see other women, and basically go about his business, much as he always had. Moore continued to pursue her career. "My career started at the age of eleven," she said proudly. "I had worked very hard, and I was just on the brink of making it big from '49 to '51." Things, in effect, had not changed much for the two of them since the purported marriage at sea.

About a year into their secret marriage, Moore surprised Hughes at a very awkward moment. "My father hired an ex-FBI agent named Leckie," she revealed, "and we caught Howard in Las Vegas with another woman. . . . I was with the detective. I caught him. I confronted him right in front of the woman." Rather than filing for divorce on grounds of adultery, the conventional reaction for a newlywed in her position, Moore decided to follow the maxim, "Don't get mad, get even." She reestablished contact with Glenn Davis, the famous Army halfback whom she had met some months earlier through her friend Elizabeth Taylor, to whom he was then engaged. "In the meantime," she recalled, "they had broken up. Time had elapsed; he had asked me out. I always said no to him and on this particular occasion I said yes." The two made a date to attend the Rose Bowl game on New Year's Day 1951, and their appearance together made quite a splash with the Hollywood gossip columnists. "With Glenn," Terry remembers, "it was suddenly the big star treatment where everybody was talking about it. Everywhere we went they grabbed pictures."

The popular couple continued to date, and within several weeks they announced their engagement, even though Moore insisted at the deposition she believed she was still married to Hughes. "I just kept going on and on and on until it happened," she tried to explain. "The studio publicity department started pushing this marriage. Everybody did. It flew into a crescendo like a snowball, and I was just too scared to stop it. It just kept, like a snowball, growing bigger and bigger, and I just went along with the people who pushed the hardest." When she told her alleged husband of her intention to marry Davis, "He just laughed and said I couldn't marry him." For once, Hughes was evidently wrong, because on February 7, 1951, a month after their first date, Davis and Moore were married in a Mormon church in Glendale, California, Terry's hometown. "I married him because no one was there to stop it," is Moore's explanation. "I thought Howard would stop it. . . . Neither one of us thought I would do it." On her marriage license, Moore stated under oath she had never been married previously. "My fear of telling the truth was far greater than saying I had been denying a marriage," she rationalized. She also told her new husband she was a virgin. "He didn't know I had been married to [Howard], because I couldn't tell him that. I didn't dare."

"You don't know what it is like . . . to be a star," Moore told attorneys representing some Hughes cousins, in defense of her actions. As one exasperated lawyer commented, weary after taking her deposition for the third or fourth time: "I don't understand this pressure, exactly. I really don't understand Hollywood." As usual, Miss Moore had a ready answer. "When you see or date anybody," she explained, "they all try to get you married. The moment you get married, they try to get you divorced. That is just Hollywood.''

Even though she had been exposed to publicity since she was a child, Moore blamed the ''giant publicity machine'' for propelling her into her dilemma. When asked by the same frustrated adversary how she could reconcile bigamy with her strict Mormon upbringing, Moore snapped: ''Excuse me. That is a very childish remark. That is what Howard used to say to me all the time—hold religion over my head. . . . I wasn't going along every day saying I wasn't married, and suddenly put down I had been married.'' In Moore's simple world view, this was sufficient explanation.

After Terry's marriage to Davis was a fait accompli, Hughes made no further effort to get his ''wife'' back, and in fact the two never spoke until at some point Terry telephoned Hughes—at the request of her new husband. ''I didn't want to call Howard,'' she says, ''and I couldn't imagine why Glenn would want me to, knowing that I was in love with him. They weren't acquainted at all. Glenn just stood there and made me make the phone call . . . made me call Howard and ask him if he could [get him a job with] Hughes Pipe and Supply Company, and so I did.'' Apparently Hughes bore no ill will toward Davis, because ''Howard arranged for us to meet the president, whoever that was.'' According to Terry, ''after he made me call Mr. Hughes, the marriage was over as far as I was concerned. . . . I figured he was using me, that he didn't love me.'' However, she said nothing to Davis. ''No, I just telephoned. I didn't tell him how I felt.'' As usual, fear was her primary motivation. ''I was afraid to tell my parents. I was afraid to tell Howard—afraid to tell anybody.''

Instead, she returned to Hollywood and moved back in with her parents. ''I didn't want to be with either of them at that time,'' she observed. Before long, it became necessary for her to see Hughes to discuss costume fittings for a movie she was making at Goldwyn Studios. ''After I saw Howard at Goldwyn,'' she remembered, ''I called up Glenn and then I saw him again. I knew I could never go back. I was just wildly in love with him [Howard], and I called Glenn and told him I wanted a divorce.'' Although only two years had elapsed since her ''secret marriage'' to Hughes, Terry claimed her situation had changed and the adverse publicity stemming from a relationship with Hughes no longer concerned her. ''I am trying to think—'' she paused; ''by this time I don't think I cared as much, because at that time Howard—always my career was the most important thing in the whole world to me. At this time Howard became the most important thing in the whole world to me.'' She goes on, ''My career was changing. I was beginning to go into sexy roles and different roles. For the first time I was coming out of animal pictures—for the first time.''

In yet another magnanimous gesture for a man who should have been outraged over his wife's peculiar ménage-à-trois, Hughes arranged for Terry to meet with attorney Lloyd Wright to discuss divorce proceedings against Davis. If Wright were the ''white-haired man'' who witnessed her shipboard marriage to Hughes, as a lawyer he should have felt some ethical nudgings to counsel her on the legal implications of bigamy during this conversation. No such discussion took place, however—merely the routine dialogue incidental to a conventional divorce. The only obstruction to the divorce was Davis' macho attitude. As Terry perceived the problem, ''Glenn thought he was married to me, and Howard knew he was married to me. I guess he wanted to talk things over with Howard, that was all.'' What exactly he wanted to discuss with Hughes is unclear, because Terry had never informed Davis of her alleged marriage to Hughes. Nevertheless, such a meeting apparently did take place, at Davis' instigation.

Eventually, the couple filed for divorce, still with no word about Moore's prior marriage to Hughes. As soon as she made her plans clear to Davis, it was back to Hughes again. ''I was still married to Howard,'' Terry insisted. ''I wasn't really—for the *public* we [Moore and Davis] were trying to get a divorce.''

Sometime between 1951 and 1952, Moore claimed that she gave birth to Howard's baby. The child was allegedly born prematurely in Germany, where Terry was then making a movie, and the little girl lived only twelve hours. It is Moore's position that Hughes sent his personal physician (Hughes himself stayed behind in the States), Dr. Verne Mason, to deliver the infant, and that much seems to be true. Although Dr. Mason is deceased, his son can recall Mason flying to Germany during this period to attend to Moore. Nevertheless, her memory of these events was remarkably hazy. She received no pre- or postnatal care, either in Germany or the United States; she never saw the child; and she played no part in the funeral arrangements. ''Dr. Mason took care of all that,'' she acknowledged, ''because I was too sick and too depressed to do anything.'' When, during her deposition, counsel Freese asked Miss Moore what she and Hughes named their daughter, she froze for a moment, and then replied, to the astonishment of the attorneys present: ''Let me tell you later. I just can't think of it right now. . . . I have gone blank.''

Later in her testimony, Moore suddenly blurted, ''Our daughter's name was Maria or Marie!'' Freese, by now accustomed to her erratic system of responding to questions, asked calmly, ''Which was it?'' Moore's reply is a study in confusion. ''It was,'' she began, ''well, we discussed several things. . . . We discussed Marie, and Anna Marie. I remember years later when we saw a boat called the *Marie Analie* that reminded us of it. I remember years later seeing a boat. I was trying to recall the name of the boat. If they put it on any records of anything it would be either Anna Marie or Marie." Freese listened patiently, then asked hopefully, "Does this boat have anything special to do with the case otherwise?" In her usual nonresponsive fashion, Moore replied: "We just discussed that we saw the name of a boat, and it reminded us—we mentioned it at the time." "To be clear," Freese persisted, "the boat had nothing to do with you and Mr. Hughes otherwise; is that correct?" "Right," Moore answered.

Terry Moore's divorce from Glenn Davis became official in April 1953. "I remember when my divorce was final from Glenn Davis," she thought back, "that I was making a movie in Florida called *Beneath the Twelve-Mile Reef*. When that became final, Howard and I gave a big yahoo over the telephone." When the yahoos subsided, Moore returned to Hughes, after a fashion. "During that time," she recalled, "if we had fights, I would get mad and go home to my parents. . . . I usually would stay with them if Howard were away or if I had a fight with him. We were fighting a lot by this time." The problem, cited Moore, was "other women." There weren't enough detectives in Las Vegas to keep track of Hughes' infidelities, as Terry had done earlier with the former FBI agent her father hired. According to Moore, Hughes was seeing both Mitzi Gaynor and Debra Paget in Las Vegas at the same time, and his romance with Jean Peters hobbled along concurrently with these affairs, not to mention the continuation of his "marriage" to Moore. Still, hope sprang eternal in Terry.

"Well," she reflected, "after my divorce from Glenn Davis became final, we were going to have a marriage and let the entire world know that we were married, and that was to be at Jack Frye's ranch. I was with Howard when he made arrangements with him to be married for a third time, the first time being on Mulholland, and the second time being on the boat, and the third time being at Jack Frye's ranch in Tucson, Arizona, or thereabouts." Alas, the Tucson wedding ceremony never materialized, nor did any other. Hughes' philandering continued, and Terry, never one to be left to wither on the vine, met Howard McGrath, soon to be husband number two (or three), well into 1955. As usual, it happened at the Beverly Hills Hotel. "I remember where I met him," she reminisced. "I met him at the Beverly Hills Hotel. He was lunching with John Wayne, and John Wayne introduced me to him." Still Hughes and Moore did not divorce; nonetheless, Terry married McGrath in 1956, never mentioning her liaison with Hughes. In the meantime,

Hughes himself had married, as Jean Peters became Mrs. Howard Hughes—publicly and privately—in 1957.

After her marriage to McGrath broke up in 1958, Moore met a wealthy businessman at a party given by Ann Miller. They dated for eight or nine months, then decided to marry. The businessman was Stuart Cramer III, the husband Jean Peters had divorced to marry Hughes a year earlier. This situation inspired a rather humorous colloquy between Moore and Freese during her deposition testimony:

Freese:	At the time he asked you to marry him, did you consider whether you were still married to Mr. Hughes?
Moore:	I was still married to him.
Freese:	The question was: did you have any discussion about him?
Moore:	No. I never told Stuart. He had already lost one wife to Howard Hughes. Are you aware of the fact that Howard Hughes had broken up Stuart Cramer's one and only marriage at that time?
Freese:	I don't know who broke up what in that period. That is a whole other set of interesting relationships, I gather.
Moore:	Howard Hughes was not a popular subject.

Moore's marriage to Cramer lasted twelve years, during which time she never brought up her relationship with Hughes. "We usually avoided the subject," she offered. "He asked me not to talk about him." Nor did Moore talk *to* him, as her direct communication with Hughes ceased in the 1950s. Moore went on to date countless other men after her divorce from Cramer in the early 1970s, but he was her last adventure in matrimony, at least as of this writing.

After riding on the dizzy merry-go-round of Moore's relationships, Freese, Dinkins, and their co-counsel were left to ponder her legal position vis-à-vis the Hughes estate. Unfortunately for Moore, she needed more than charm to win her case. In her favor was the almost unanimous opinion of those close to Hughes that she did indeed have a relationship of long standing with the millionaire. "I don't remember the exact years," said Glenn Odekirk, one of Howard's closest friends, "but I'll tell you one thing, that . . . after I quit flying with him and my brother-in-law flew with him, that she was with him quite a lot then. However, I spent a week with her and her mother in New York. In fact, it happened to be at the same time, and I was there and Howard had me even teach her to fly, preliminary part of teaching her to fly, so he went with her quite a while." However, when asked by Dinkins if Hughes ever told him he had actually married Moore, Odekirk responded, "Definitely not."

Greg Bautzer, Hughes' occasional rival, trusted friend, and legal counsel, has acknowledged his colleague's romance with Moore but never indicated that it was more than that. "He told me," declared Moore, "that Howard had told him that he loved me more than any woman in the world. He always tells me—he calls him Sam—and also says, 'Sam always asked about you right up to the end.' Also always stated, 'You were the only woman he ever loved, or the one he loved the most.' "

There is little argument that Hughes and Moore were involved, and it may well be that Moore believed they were indeed husband and wife. Circumstances point to the fact that there was some sort of "ceremony" aboard Hughes' yacht that day in November, and in Terry's mind it may have signified a bona fide wedding ceremony. But the critical question is whether they were legally married, both on Hughes' boat, and at the time of his death. Moore herself admitted, "Howard always talked more of the anniversary of when we met and when he married me on Mulholland. He did that. Those points were important to him. . . .Howard always thought that was the most meaningful." As adept as Hughes was at saying what he thought others wanted to hear in order to get what he wanted from them, the wedding ceremony by a sea captain, if it truly happened, may have been nothing more than a contrivance designed to get his reluctant amour into bed.

It is Terry Moore's contention that she and Howard Hughes were legally married by a Captain Flynn aboard Hughes' yacht in international waters in November 1949. Since they never divorced, she further asserts, her subsequent marriages to Davis, McGrath, and Cramer were bigamous and therefore illegal, as was Hughes' eventual marriage to Jean Peters—all of which makes her his lawful widow and sole beneficiary of his estate.

It certainly weakens Miss Moore's legal position that the only witness to her wedding still living is her mother, with the possible exception of Noah Dietrich, who may or may not be the mysterious "white-haired man"—and he denies it. Also damaging is the absence of the ship's logs. Moore insists that they were destroyed, either by Hughes after one of their many rows, or by his associates, to destroy evidence that might endanger the Hughes empire. The fatal flaw from a legal standpoint, however, came out at the trial to determine the merit of her claim. As a testament to the more serious nature of her assertions, Moore's arguments were heard at an earlier separate trial from the others who claimed inheritance as wives, brothers, sisters, or children.

Ultimately, however, hers fared no better. After hearing the arguments of counsel, Judge Pat Gregory ruled that Terry Moore was not entitled to share in the estate of Howard Hughes. Since she had married three other men subsequent to her alleged marriage to Hughes, he determined that she was legally "estopped" from now claiming to be Hughes' wife, and it was therefore unnecessary for him even to consider the substantive issues in her case.

Consequently, Gregory was spared the pages of romantic and melodramatic testimony that Freese and his colleagues had endured for months and months. Since her June 27, 1981, date in court with Judge Gregory, Moore has appealed all the way to the Texas Supreme Court and fought similar battles in California and Nevada, each claiming Hughes as a resident, but all to no avail. Mrs. Howard Hughes is one role the courts have not let her play.

Behind the scenes during her seven-year legal effort to establish her relationship to Hughes, Moore's attorney, Arthur Leeds, made repeated attempts to settle out of court with representatives of Hughes' estate, without success. As recently as February 1983, certain of the maternal heirs joked privately about Terry's claim. One Hughes cousin was heard to remark, "Terry Moore. Isn't she the one who says she and Hughes were married on a boat by Errol Flynn?" (Referring, obviously, to the mysterious Captain Flynn whom Moore insists performed the nuptials.)

Yet on May 24, 1983, just three months after this comment, Moore called a surprise press conference in Los Angeles. In her best Old Hollywood tradition, she announced triumphantly to the startled assembly of reporters that the Hughes heirs had at last recognized her as Howard Hughes' "widow" and agreed to give her an undisclosed sum of money. "It's more than $100,000 and less than $99 million," she tittered. Her attorney Leeds was less coy. "It's closer to the first figure," he later acknowledged laughingly. Though the exact amount of the settlement is to remain unpublicized as one of the terms of the agreement, Leeds described it as a "modest sum." (Recent leaks to the press by sources outside the Moore camp put the figure in the $390,000 range. Other estimates are as high as $14 million. Asked to comment, Leeds was evasive. "Anyway," he observed, "the way the agreement is worded it's very difficult to determine exactly how much Terry is getting. It's set up so that she gets her money tax-free.") Whatever the sum, Moore was radiant; the heirs were noticeably silent, and their attorneys unavailable for comment. Confidentially they groused about Terry's distorted portrayal of the settlement, and grumbled that she was paid off merely to enable attorneys for the family to "move the ball down the field."

As usual, none of this fazed Moore. For one afternoon she had, as her attorney put it, ''her moment in the sun.'' ''It has never been a question of the money for me,'' she remarked afterward. ''I . . . enter[ed] into this . . . to defend myself and my integrity.''

4

The Sins of the Father

Thus far, Phase One of the heirship determination trial of Howard R. Hughes, Jr., left little room for doubt or controversy. Faced with the available facts, few would dispute what was presented in court, that the millionaire industrialist died without leaving a widow or children to inherit his estate (Terry Moore notwithstanding). It was similarly clear that his parents predeceased him, and were therefore unable to inherit his wealth, leaving open only one question in this first stage of the litigation: whether Hughes had any brothers or sisters.

It was considered common knowledge during his lifetime that Hughes was the only child of Howard and Allene Gano Hughes, and not a soul stepped up to claim a birthright; therefore the possibility that Howard, Jr., had siblings seemed unlikely. Nevertheless, no evidence could be left unexplored in Dinkins' search for unknown heirs, in light of the billions of dollars at stake. With this thought in mind, his associates turned their attention to the man who created the Hughes legacy, Howard Robard Hughes, Sr. Was Sonny his only child, or did his past contain secrets heretofore suppressed?

Annette Gano Lummis was a logical person to begin with in a search for Sonny's potential brother or sister. She was Allene Gano's treasured younger sister, Howard, Jr.'s, maternal aunt. And she was one of the few still living at the time of Hughes' death who had known the family well. Public records confirm that Howard Hughes, Sr., married debutante Allene Gano on May 24, 1904, in Dallas, Texas. "And it was on Masten Street in our home," the former Annette Gano recalls. About a year and a half later, Howard, Jr., was born. One possibility that Dinkins had to consider was quickly dismissed by Mrs. Lummis, when she testified that her sister and Big Howard had no more children after Sonny. "In fact," she revealed, "she was told when he was born that she couldn't have any more." Howard, Jr.'s, birth in 1905 was attended by Dr. Oscar Norsworthy, a prominent Houston physician, now deceased. Though Dinkins' team could not locate his records to confirm Mrs. Lummis' hearsay testimony, Allene and Howard Hughes were high-profile residents of Houston; and popular belief serves to substantiate the fact that the Hugheses had no children other than Howard, Jr., during their marriage. This knowledge, coupled with Mrs. Lummis' assurances that her sister did not give birth to a child before Sonny (Howard, Sr., was her first and only husband; she was twenty-one when they married) narrowed the search to Howard Hughes, Sr., and the period before he married Allene Gano. Hughes was thirty-five years old when he wed Allene, and a social outsider, facts that offered many anonymous bachelor years for the ad litem team to explore.

The Black Sheep

Collecting all the information on Hughes, Sr., readily available, the court-appointed heir searchers began to piece together his past. The first step was to scour the prominent Houstonian's obituaries for clues to his life history that might lead to other sources of information on his background. Though indelibly etched in the public consciousness as an oilman and a Texan, Howard, Sr., actually hailed from the Midwest.

Like his older sister and two younger brothers, he was born in Lancaster, Missouri (on September 9, 1869), and spent his boyhood in the Mississippi River town of Keokuk, in the southeastern tip of Iowa, where the state adjoins Missouri and Illinois.

Hughes' later reputation as a suave ladies' man and astute business leader would belie it, but visits to his hometown revealed that the young Howard Hughes, Sr., was remembered as something of a rascal. One prominent Keokuk citizen, a contemporary and former classmate of Hughes', characterized the young Howard as a "ruffian" who once pulled a knife on a chum in the school playground. Local rumors persist that Howard was known to put spurs on cocks and stage brutal cockfights, much to his younger brother Rupert's chagrin. "Howard's father, Howard Robard, Sr., was a kind of a black sheep of the family," according to the resident Keokuk historian. "He had an inventive mind—he was a genius in a way–but he . . . got into trouble, even as a boy." Doubtless the Keokuk legends have swelled in proportion to the Hughes fame, but puffery notwithstanding, a picture emerged of a young man with a restless nature. He may have been tame by today's standards, but compared to the provincial models in homespun Iowa, a lad with a touch of devilry. By his own admission, Howard, Sr., had been a "wild and untamable boy," expelled from every school he went to. Appropriately enough, the two preparatory schools he attended were both military academies: the St. Charles Military School at St. Charles, Missouri, and the Morgan Park Military School of Morgan Park, Illinois.

Having formed an idea of Hughes' temperament, the ad litem research team was surprised to learn that Howard, Sr., had later attended Harvard University, studied law at the University of Iowa, and eventually gained admittance to the Iowa bar. But Dinkins' staff determined, upon closer examination, that although he was a student at Harvard from 1893 to 1895, he never graduated, and his foray into the legal profession was extremely short-lived. The time he did spend as an attorney was apparently a concession to his father, a noted barrister and former judge.

Hughes' parents had lofty ambitions for all their children, and Howard, Sr., was no exception. "After leaving Harvard in '94," he wrote, "I found myself in the Law School of the Iowa State University. It was my father's wish that I succeed him in his practice. Too impatient to await the course of graduation, I passed the examination before the Supreme Court of Iowa and began the practice of law." His haste to complete the requirements was an early signal of Hughes' impatience with a legal career. "I soon found the law a too-exacting mistress for a man of my talent," he later wrote, tongue-in-cheek, "and I quit her between dark and dawn, and have never since been back."

The ad litem sleuths came to regard Howard Robard Hughes, Sr., as a man of great style and charm, with a cavalier approach to life. He immediately became a favorite of genealogist Mary Fay. Mrs. Fay saw Hughes as a dashing and romantic figure in American history, and she took great delight in peeping through the keyhole of her research at the man she affectionately described as "quite a rake."

Tracing Hughes' footsteps turned out to be a gypsy endeavor. He still had one foot in Keokuk until the late 1890s, but it was clear Howard had other things in mind. The city directories for the years 1887 to 1899 show his various occupations as "collector," "car accountant," without occupation, and briefly, as a "lawyer." Between his admission to the bar in 1896 and his marriage to Miss Gano in 1904, Howard Hughes, Sr.'s, life resembled Huckleberry Finn's. Unlike Huck, however, Howard had an indulgent and well-fixed father to bankroll his wanderlust. "As a matter of fact," reflects a Keokuk newspaper editor and Hughes chronicler, "his father . . . was rather happy to see (him) leave town." Howard, Sr., was "kind of a hippie with money in his jeans, and he left home to see what was on the other side of the hill. And I don't think his parents fought this too hard."

Bits and pieces of Hughes' escapades after he left home gradually emerged. As Rupert Hughes tattled in a magazine piece about his family, "My brother Howard was of an even more adventurous soul. He enjoyed gold mines, and cost my father much money, which he amply repaid in later years."

After traveling extensively through Germany, England, and France on his father's generosity, Hughes embarked on the sort of life Walter Mitty only fantasized, working by turn as a telegraph operator in the Midwest, a newspaper reporter in Denver, and prospecting and mining for zinc in Oklahoma and Missouri. In mining he at last found an occupation that suited him. "I decided to search for my fortune under the surface of the earth," he later reflected. "Colorado mining for low-grade silver followed for two years," he continued, "then two years more sinking shafts, driving drifts and drilling holes in the zinc fields of Indian Territory. If I accomplished nothing more, I, at least, learned something of the art of drilling wells with cable tools."

Then Dinkins and his colleagues began the real work. They requested massive document searches and, wherever possible, city directory information on Howard Hughes, Sr., from all the places he may have hung his hat on his circuitous journey to Texas—Iowa City (where he went to law school); Keokuk and the state of Iowa generally; Cambridge, Massachusetts (home of Harvard); Denver, Colorado, and Colorado Territory (from his reporting and mining days); Oklahoma and Missouri (the zinc mining interval); Beaumont, Texas, and Shreveport, Louisiana (early oil exploration). Dinkins wished to eliminate the possibility that Hughes was ever party to a marriage or divorce in any of the towns or cities he inhabited en route to Spindletop and his courtship of Allene Gano. He also queried whether Hughes had fathered any children in his travels.

Sending off these inquiries was like purchasing a lottery ticket. The odds against finding Hughes' name in any of the vital statistics bureaus were just as staggering as the chance one individual's lucky number might be pulled in the Irish Sweepstakes. Yet in Dinkins' office there were great expectations. Here lay the unpredictable element in Dinkins' task. Despite the odds against it, the discovery of a secret event could lead to an unknown heir and to dramatic changes in the lives of a number of people.

As the replies from statistics bureaus and libraries trickled in, Dinkins also began to hear from other ghosts of Hughes' past. Unbelievably, the St. Charles County Historical Society Archives had retained a "programme" of a dramatic performance given at the St. Charles Military School in which both Howard and Rupert Hughes had taken part as children. According to the playbill, entitled "Annual Entertainment given by the students of St. Charles College, Saturday night, Jan'y 22, 1887," the Hughes brothers both appeared in a drama called "Barr's Boarders; or That Pesky Widow;" and Rupert Hughes appeared as Ruth Lawrence in a miniature melodrama with the prophetic title, "The California Uncle." Most amazing, however, was the title of the second of the evening's theatricals, "How to Find an Heir." In Mrs. Fay's genealogical estimation, the discovery of this dramatic program alone made the monumental search worthwhile.

For weeks, however, this was the most exciting mail Dinkins received, as each of the document and directory searches he commissioned turned up negative. On a chance statement in a Rupert Hughes magazine article that mentioned Howard's onetime work "in the lead mines at Joplin, Missouri," Dinkins' team added Joplin to the list of target cities, and Mrs. Fay asked the Joplin librarian to verify his residence sometime between 1897 and 1904. As with all the others, Fay received a polite but negative reply. The Denver directories were likewise devoid of entries for Hughes, and the *Rocky Mountain News* and *Denver Post,* Denver's two newspapers, had no record of his supposed employment as a reporter. Somehow Hughes had disappeared without a trace from town to town on his winding pilgrimage to Houston.

A Mystery in Carthage

As exciting a life as Howard Hughes, Sr., undoubtedly led during these years of experimentation, each day's mail supported the theory that he avoided both matrimonial and paternal entanglements along the way; consequently, the ad litem team was about to accept as fact that Howard Hughes, Jr., had no siblings. Then, in July 1977, twelve months into his investigative effort, Dinkins received a reply that changed all that. In an envelope from the office of the circuit clerk of Jasper County, Missouri, there appeared a certified copy of a marriage license dated October 16, 1900, issued in Carthage, Missouri. The groom's name, larger than life, was Howard R. Hughes, "of Joplin, Missouri." His bride-to-be was one "Francis Geddes," also of Joplin. The license was signed by the deputy, with her seal of office, as well as by the recorder of deeds, and read: "This license authorizes any Judge of a Court of Record, or Justice of the Peace, or any licensed or ordained preacher of the Gospel who is a Citizen of the United States, to solemnize Marriage between Howard R. Hughes . . . and Francis Geddes."

The only oddity was the blank on the bottom of the marriage license, to have been filled in by the person who solemnized the marriage ceremony. Instead, the words "not used" were handwritten in red ink, with two diagonal lines drawn across them, as if to scratch out that portion of the license.

Howard Hughes, Sr.'s, past had at last caught up with him.

The excitement in Dinkins' office was palpable. After months of looking, they had at last found the needle in a haystack, and her name was Francis Geddes. Even the skeptical Dinkins was excited by this piece of evidence. His associates were less subdued. In their hands lay information that could possibly alter the course of Howard Hughes, Jr.'s, inheritance, and they recognized the impact of their discovery. Who was Francis Geddes, and what was her connection to Howard Hughes, Sr.? Did she and Hughes elope, and the Justice of the Peace neglect to return the marriage license? Did they go out of the county to marry? Did they choose to live together instead? (Hughes, after all, did not seem like the sort of man who would bow to convention.) Did they, like Howard, Jr., years later, marry elsewhere under pseudonyms? Or, finally, was the marriage license simply a red herring, a false lead?

This was the first evidence to suggest that there might actually *be* unknown heirs, legitimate relatives of Howard Hughes, Jr., who had not emerged, whether by ignorance or by choice, to claim their birthright. The discovery of the true heirs—whether they be the individuals listed on the *Philadelphia Inquirer* chart or an altogether different set of names—became an obsession to the ad litem team.

For the moment, Francis Geddes provided the only likelihood of an alternate line of inheritance; Francis Geddes, a name that appeared on a marriage license dated 1900. Whatever occurred between Geddes and Hughes took place over three-quarters of a century ago, and Hughes may have taken the explanation to his grave. Pursuing the story behind the returned marriage license would pose a formidable challenge.

To confront it, Dinkins dispatched one of his sleuths to Joplin to investigate further, certain that little would come of the trip. After all, the Joplin librarian had already notified Mrs. Fay that Howard Hughes did not even appear in the city directories of the early 1900s. More disheartening was the fact that no one with the surname "Geddes" was listed in a contemporary Joplin telephone directory. Perhaps Francis, too, was a drifter, which would make the search next to impossible.

Joplin and Carthage are neighboring towns on the western plains of Missouri, near Kansas and not far from Oklahoma. Joplin is the larger, but Carthage is the county seat, and hence the center of registry for events such as marriages and divorces. Wandering the streets of Joplin today, one would not find it difficult to imagine the town as it was at the turn of the century, when Howard Hughes, Sr., passed through. There is little to distinguish it from the hundreds of other small towns that dot the Midwest. Changes come slowly to these townships on the Great Plains, a fact that could not have escaped Hughes' attention as he searched for his fortune in Joplin, Missouri.

Since nothing was known of Howard Hughes' mysterious fiancée, the ad litem hoped an advertisement in the local newspaper might catch the attention of a native octogenarian acquainted with Francis or her family, who could put the investigation on the right track. Consequently, Dinkins' associate placed an ad in the *Carthage Press.*

Perhaps the ad was not conspicuous enough, or the local residents valued their privacy too much, or the encounter of Francis Geddes and Howard Hughes had simply been too brief for anyone to notice or remember. Whatever the reason, no one came forward with information. The Francis Geddes story would have to be put together, if at all, by tedious fact gathering.

To begin, this meant reviewing old newspapers for clues either to Francis' identity or to Howard Hughes' sojourn in Joplin. Each issue had to be studied for some reference to Hughes or Geddes. Conveniently, the turn-of-the-century *Joplin Daily Globe* did feature a weekly list of marriage licenses issued in the county seat, but their names did not appear for the week of October 16, 1900, though the issuance of their marriage license on that date was demonstrable. The newspaper's society columns were equally discouraging. The *Globe* printed many chatty descriptions of the comings and goings of local lights during the period, but no gossipy item mentioning the couple, either singly or together, could be found in any column for the years 1899 or 1900. Hughes seemed to have a knack for keeping his name out of print.

Francis, too, eluded the researchers. Her name did not appear in the register of deaths from 1900 to 1977, and no tombstone bearing her name could be found in a Joplin or Carthage cemetery. (Of course, she might not have died under the name "Geddes" or in Joplin.)

At the county recorder's office in Carthage, Francis Geddes' past began to unravel. To determine whether she had had a child by Hughes born in Joplin, the index of births was studied for the years 1897 to 1900, without success. However, the recording of births was not mandatory in Carthage at that time, and it would have been possible for Francis to have had a baby without notifying the registrar. The divorce records proved no more helpful—Howard and Francis, if they ever married, did not divorce in this area of Missouri. As a last resort, the original of the returned marriage license of October 16, 1900, was examined for some clue not apparent on the certified copy sent to Dinkins. There was none.

Finally, driven by a combination of instinct and desperation, Dinkins' clerk decided to skim through all the marriage licenses filed at or near the date of the Hughes-Geddes document, not looking for anything in particular. The first hint of possible success was the discovery of a marriage license taken out in the names of Nancy Geddes and Frank R. Harrington, dated October 26, 1901. The last name was either pure coincidence, or Nancy Geddes was related in some fashion to Howard Hughes' onetime love. Either way, it encouraged the researcher to continue looking. The discovery of the Nancy Geddes license was auspicious, for a few minutes later another marriage license was located. This time, the bride was Frances Geddes herself, spelled with an "e" rather than an "i," but surely the same person once engaged to Hughes. The groom was Arthur E. Bendelari (also of Joplin); the date, December 21, 1901, a little over a year after Howard's license to marry Francis. The Bendelari license had been returned, however, and indicated that the marriage was solemnized at St. Philip's Episcopal Church in Joplin.

It was now clear that at least two Geddeses were living in Joplin in early 1900, and that Francis/es was free to marry another man a year after her romance with Hughes. This new piece of information prompted a return to the society pages of the *Joplin Daily Globe,* which printed this account of the Bendelari wedding in the December 22, 1901 edition:

> The announcement of the marriage of Miss Frances Geddes and Mr.
> Arthur E. Bendelari comes as something of a surprise to even their

closest friends as the date was only decided upon by them 10 days ago. The engagement of these two popular young people has been an open secret in Joplin's most exclusive society for some months. Last evening at 5:30 o'clock at the home of the bride's parents, Mr. and Mrs. James I. Geddes on Jackson Avenue, their daughter, Miss Frances, was united in marriage to Mr. Arthur E. Bendelari, Rev. W. R. McCutcheon of St. Phillip's Episcopal Church offici-ating. . . . Just before the bridal party came downstairs, Mrs. Frank Harrington, the bride's sister, sang DeKoven's ''O Promise Me,'' Mrs. W. H. Wade, of Springfield, aunt of the bride, presided at the piano and played Mendelssohn's wedding march. . . . Miss Geddes has always been counted a beautiful young woman, and as a bride she looked indeed queenly, despite the girlish simplicity of her sheer swiss gown. . . . Mr. and Mrs. Bendelari left last evening for St. Louis. From there they will go to Cleveland to visit Mr. Bendelari's relatives. Their trip will include New York City and Toronto, Canada. They will be at home after January 20th at the home of the bride's parents, 511 Jackson Avenue.

With the discovery of this gushing column, Frances Geddes began to come alive. She was obviously a young lady of some social standing in Joplin, a woman of charm and beauty. Moreover, the news item tied in Nancy Geddes Harrington, the name on the October 1901 marriage license, as Frances' sister, and provided names and an address for Frances' parents. Finally, it vividly confirmed that the marriage between Frances and Arthur Bendelari had taken place. At the same time, however, it raised some questions: why did the reporter describe the Geddes-Bendelari engagement as an ''open secret'' and ''something of a surprise'' in Joplin? And whatever happened to Howard Hughes, Sr.— Frances' former suitor? There were still some fourteen months unac-counted for between the date of the Hughes marriage license and the Bendelari wedding, and Frances' activities during this interval were of great interest to Dinkins' investigative team.

From the background information present in the *Globe*'s coverage of Frances' wedding to Bendelari, more pieces were added to this intrigu-ing puzzle. The ad litem's assistant located yellowed, timeworn Joplin directories at the city hall and assembled a skeletal account of the Ged-des family. James and Dollie Geddes and their four children moved to Joplin, it appeared, in 1899, the year before Frances met Howard Hughes. According to the directories, James Geddes was an investment broker, sometime attorney, and mining operator. Both James and Dollie had died in Joplin by the mid-1930s. Bartley Geddes was their oldest child; he worked for a time with his father as an investment broker in the firm of Geddes and Geddes, followed by a position as superinten-dent of the Eagle-Picher Mining Company. At some point, he married a woman named Blanche, and they appeared in the directories until the 1940s.

Nancy and Frances Geddes were next to be investigated. Nancy's husband, Frank Harrington, worked as a mine operator. The couple left Joplin shortly after their marriage in 1901 and returned for several years in 1912. The youngest child, James Geddes, Jr., eventually wed "Florence E." and worked at the Eagle-Picher Company. By 1937 he and Florence were no longer in Joplin.

Arthur Bendelari, it seems, came on the scene about the same time as the rest of the cast; his name does not appear in a directory until 1904, by which time he and Frances had been married several years. Bendelari stayed in Joplin and worked his way up in the mining business through the 1920s to become vice-president of the Eagle-Picher Lead Company. The names of wives were first included in the directories in the teens, and the name "Frances" appeared after Bendelari's name in the books from 1916 to 1921. Frances Bendelari does not show up again after 1921, which suggested she had either died or had divorced Bendelari and moved away from Joplin. Arthur Bendelari appeared alone from 1922 to 1924, and in 1925 he was shown to be married to a woman named Grace. By 1926, Bendelari had disappeared from the Joplin directory altogether.

In 1921, the last year that Frances Geddes Bendelari was listed in the book, a "Miss Frances Geddes" first began to appear in the Joplin directory. She was listed every year until 1940, described sometimes as a student, a saleslady, a cashier, or with no occupation at all. The timing and circumstances made it seem unlikely she could be the same Frances Geddes who appeared on the marriage license with Howard Hughes, although with nothing more to go on, no possibility could be ruled out. Who, then, was she?

About this time, inquiries to the State Historical Society of Missouri met with unexpected success. The newspaper librarian there located a *Hoye's Joplin and Carthage Directory of 1900,* unavailable at either the city hall or library in Joplin. The directory was so fragile that photocopies could not be made from it, so the librarian copied by hand the following entry from page 193: "Hughes, Howard R. mines 408 Joplin rms Elks bldg."

By this listing, the elusive Mr. Hughes was at last linked to Joplin other than by casual recollection. Just as his brother Rupert wrote in *American* magazine, Hughes had indeed found himself in the lead mines at Joplin, Missouri, where he had taken a room at the Elks Building. And it was not too great a leap to assume, based upon the information in the Joplin directories, that he may have been introduced to the lovely Miss Geddes by any of the male members of her family, all of whom worked in the mining business, possibly side-by-side with Howard Hughes.

Even with these discoveries, however, Dinkins still had no more than a returned marriage license and romantic speculations to connect Frances and Howard. He needed a living individual with knowledge of the affair to help set the record straight. The most logical source of this information would be a member of Frances' family, but the fact remained that the last Geddes appeared in a Joplin directory in the late 1940s, and there wasn't a clue as to where the family members had scattered. And even if one were located, there was no guarantee that this individual would know about a romantic encounter that took place seventy-odd years ago. Then again, Frances' beau became the father of one of the world's most famous (and richest) men.

St. Philip's Episcopal Church provided the ad litem investigation with the breakthrough it needed. Since the Bendelari wedding was performed by a minister from St. Philip's, Dinkins' associate decided to visit the old church and search its membership records for the Geddeses. Not only were the Geddeses members of the church, but as luck would have it, the current rector could provide information that would lead to living Geddes family members who might know of the Hughes connection to Frances. He was also able to explain the identity of the mysterious "Miss Frances Geddes" who began to appear in the Joplin directories in the early 1920s. According to the reverend, she was the elder daughter of Bartley (and Blanche) Geddes, Frances Geddes Bendelari's older brother.

"Little Frances," as she was sometimes called to distinguish her from her aunt, was a widow and still lived in Joplin, as did her younger sister. Their parents, Bart and Blanche Geddes, had died, just as the Joplin directories had suggested. Little Frances, the rector volunteered, was born early in the 1900s. Her sister was born ten or twelve years later, and Bartley and Blanche Geddes had no other children.

The rector offered to locate baptismal information on the two "girls" in his general search for Geddes church records. To his puzzlement, he found the younger sister's baptism without difficulty, but was unable to locate any notation in the church books of little Frances' baptism. He was genuinely perplexed by the apparent fact that Frances was not baptized at St. Philip's. Her parents had been devout members of the congregation, and it had been the rector's understanding through the years that both their children were baptized at his church.

Little Frances (now in her seventies), was hospitalized and too ill to be disturbed for questioning at the time of the ad litem investigation in Joplin. In her place, her sister was queried, not only about the circumstances behind Little Frances' christening, but also about her aunt, Frances Geddes Bendelari. Regarding the former, she confirmed that her sister had been baptized "elsewhere." About her Aunt Frances she appeared to know very little, but suggested the ad litem contact the son of James Geddes, Jr. (Frances Geddes Bendelari's brother). James, Jr., was deceased, but his son retained the family Bible, which might shed some light on the early period in the family's history.

Ironically, this call revealed that, had the Hughes heirship investigation uncovered the returned marriage license a few months sooner, Dinkins and his protegés could have questioned Frances Geddes herself about her relationship with Howard Hughes. Frances Geddes Bendelari, her nephew revealed, had died in Los Angeles four or five months earlier, at the remarkable age of ninety-two. By a strange twist of fate, she had passed away at roughly the same time as Howard Hughes, Jr., the son of the man who might have been her husband.

In the course of the conversation, Mr. Geddes related that his Aunt Frances had divorced Arthur Bendelari in the early 1920s (just as the Joplin directories had implied) and had moved away from Joplin to New York City shortly thereafter. Like her former fiancé Howard Hughes, she found herself in Hollywood not too much later, where she worked in the movies. By the mid-1940s, when she was sixty-five years old, Frances married again. Her new husband's name was Dan Hubbell, and he was also her first cousin. They were wed in New York, one of the few states where first cousins can legally marry, and they settled in Cleveland. After Hubbell's death in 1956, Frances relocated to Los Angeles, where she spent the last twenty years of her life.

By this account it was clear that Frances Geddes Bendelari Hubbell was nobody's stereotype of a smalltown midwestern girl. In fact, it appeared that Howard Hughes, the wild and untamable boy from Keokuk, Iowa, had met his female counterpart during his lead-mining days in Joplin, Missouri. Aside from these basic facts pertaining to Frances' life *after* Howard Hughes, her nephew could provide little specific information of value to the heirship investigation. The family Bible in his possession proved to be another dead end. The notation of family events ceased in the late 1800s, before Frances' engagement to Howard Hughes.

More auspiciously, Geddes was able to direct the ad litem to two sisters-in-law of Frances Hubbell. Each had once been married to James Geddes, Jr., and each knew Frances at different periods in her life. If the returned marriage license of Howard Hughes and Frances Geddes had any significance to the search for missing heirs, these women were Dinkins' last hope to discover its origin.

Opal Geddes, James, Jr.'s, second wife, was the first to be contacted. Although she had not married Frances' younger brother until the 1930s,

Opal had been acquainted with Frances for over forty years. Circumstances brought the two closer together after the death of Dan Hubbell in 1956, when Frances, then in her seventies, packed her bags and drove from Cleveland to Los Angeles, where she moved into a duplex next door to Opal, who was a widow herself by this time. As Opal tended to Frances in her last two decades, she had the benefit of sharing in her sister-in-law's reflections on her very full life.

Dinkins' intermediary arranged an interview on the premise that Mrs. Geddes was to answer some questions about the Geddes family, particularly Frances, in connection with an unnamed "estate case" in Houston. However, the moment she learned whose estate proceedings it concerned, Mrs. Geddes immediately remarked: "I *wondered* whether this would have to do with Howard Hughes!" After weeks of gathering miscellaneous pieces of information, often with disheartening results, the ad litem's persistence had finally paid off. Just when the returned marriage license was about to be classified a dead issue, someone made the connection between Frances Geddes and Howard Hughes, Sr.

Amazingly, Opal Geddes did not seem the least bit surprised about receiving this call out of the blue. Indeed, she behaved almost as if it had been half-expected, which she later confessed was true. A short, feisty woman with a whisky-deep voice, Mrs. Geddes was a straight-talker with very definite opinions where her sister-in-law was concerned. In her years of caring for Frances Geddes she had developed a possessive attitude toward her, and she seemed to regard her sister-in-law with an admiration bordering on awe, combined with a trace of envy. ("She is what I would like to have been," she remarked wistfully at one point.) A loquacious woman, Opal Geddes was flattered by the attention the interview afforded, and she settled into a rambling and informative dialogue about Frances Geddes and her famous admirer.

Once she learned that the interview concerned Howard Hughes, Mrs. Geddes went straight to the heart of the matter:

Interviewer: So you have heard of this?

Geddes: Oh, I haven't heard anything about it, but I do know *all* about it. . . . Well, I know the estate has been going on, but I never dreamed anything like this would happen to Frances. Because really, I'm sure that as far as the estate is concerned—she never was involved you know. There was nothing consummated

69

from this romance. . . . She was eloping with Howard Hughes, Sr., and that—

Interviewer: This was in 1900, is that correct?

Geddes: Well, yes, because she was married in 1901. And he was a young engineer . . . I'm talking about Mr. Hughes . . . that came to Joplin. And he was approximately thirty-odd years old. Well, she was a young girl of probably sixteen or seventeen.

Interviewer: Oh, she was that young?

Geddes: Very young. Well, that's the reason her father interceded.

Interviewer: So it was Mr. Geddes who more or less obstructed this romance?

Geddes: Well, of course. And so, they were on their way to Carthage, Missouri—which is eighteen miles distance from Joplin—to the county seat to be married. And he overtook them. . . . And he said, "Frances, this is absurd. You're too young, my dear." So they came back, of course, you know. And therefore, he stayed around Joplin for some time. I'm not sure if her father allowed her to see him anymore. I doubt it, because he was quite a precise man.

Interviewer: Mr. Geddes was?

Geddes: Yes, her father. And so of course in the interim, she had known Arthur Bendelari. He was the president of the Eagle-Picher Mining Company. . . . So then after this episode with Mr. Hughes, then she married Arthur Bendelari in 1901. I think it was in the month of December. And she lived with him twenty-some years. But then Mr. Hughes then left for

70

Texas after a little period. I think he did do some mining, or prospecting mining in the interim. And then he went to Texas and he invented this . . . bit, or whatever it was, and made his fortune.

Mrs. Geddes then described her sister-in-law in 1900, the year she met Howard Hughes:

Geddes: Of course, at that time she was a beautiful woman. She was exquisite looking. When she was about sixteen years old, before she got married, she had on an apron and a sort of gingham dress, and her hair was done up here, and she was over a washboard—and that was put on the *Post*. Front of the *Post* magazine. . . .

Interviewer: Did she model, or was this a—?

Geddes: No! Frances had—she had talent, but of a singer. She had no talent—well, she probably was a blighted Bernhardt, but aren't we all at times? But she did have a beautiful voice, and so she sang, after later years. But when she was young, she flirted with her beauty. . . . No wonder Mr. Hughes fell in love with her. And this is about the age she was when he wanted to elope with her.

The interviewer then tried to pin Mrs. Geddes down on the family's objections to either Howard Hughes or the marriage:

Interviewer: You were saying that you felt that Mr. Geddes particularly was opposed to this elopement with Howard, because of her age. But then it was so soon thereafter that she married Mr. Bendelari.

Geddes: Yes, but he liked Arthur.

Interviewer: Oh, he did not like Howard?

71

Geddes: He didn't know him. No one knew him very well. He came into Joplin—he had been there several months—carrying a little satchel, you know, probably his work. And he was older, not the young sprouts that were in vogue at that time there. And especially with the Geddes girls—

Interviewer: They were, I'm sure, a socially prominent family.

Geddes: Oh, indeed they were. Her father was an attorney, her mother was a very aristocratic woman.

Interviewer: And you felt like perhaps he frowned upon Howard, Sr.?

Geddes: Well, he didn't want Frances to marry anyone that . . . had nothing. He really had nothing.

Interviewer: Howard had nothing?

Geddes: He had no money. He was just a young, thriving engineer. And he'd come there to probably make his fortune. And it wasn't that type of place to make a fortune. . . . Because, you see, Mr. Hughes was not there very long. He was less than a year in Joplin.

Interviewer: Less than a year?

Geddes: And you see, you have to stick around a mining town to get established, especially if you're an engineer. So he didn't last very long. I don't think he saw the potentials. . . . He had quite a struggle, you know. He borrowed on everything he had, as we understood.

Her vivid portrayal of Hughes continued:

72

Geddes: Actually, Howard Hughes was rather a mysterious man that came in town. He wasn't a man that, like all the young engineers that came in—you know, flamboyant and so forth, throwing themselves around and everything. He was older.

The background established, talk turned to the romance itself:

Interviewer: Do you know how long he'd been in town before they started dating, or any of the history of that?

Geddes: Ah, a very, very short time. He was introduced to the group. You know, the group—you know how all the young people get together . . . all the fraternity brothers and everything—engineers. And they're really all very clannish, you know. And so she was introduced to him and naturally he asked her for a date. And she started going with him. She went with him for some time . . . maybe a month or two.

Interviewer: Month or two?

Geddes: Thereabouts. And then, he saw that there was a lot of competition there, and he wanted to marry her.

Interviewer: Oh.

Geddes: Because he was older, you see. And that's the way it happened. But it didn't last long. It was very short-lived. . . . And when they would have dates, he'd drive up in a buggy, you know, and the horse. And he'd come to the door, and her father would say, you know, "All right, Frances." He'd let her go. But he thought, "This will pass, too."

Interviewer: It's just a phase.

73

Geddes: Yeah. But then, when they took off one day and were going to go to Carthage, Missouri, and be married, then he felt—he knew it was serious.

Interviewer: Do you know—did she ever say to you whether they went so far as to have the marriage license, or—

Geddes: Yes, they *did* have the marriage license! They had the marriage license and all they were going to do was go over to Carthage and be married by this Episcopalian minister.

Interviewer: This was on the sly?

Geddes: This was on the sly. And then they were on their way.

Interviewer: This was like maybe a day later . . . after they had taken out the license?

Geddes: Well, yes, because you see, in Missouri at that time, you could take a marriage license and marry that same day and didn't have to wait. You didn't have to take blood tests or anything. And you could get a divorce the same way.

Interviewer: So, they probably took out the license, and then they didn't marry the same day, they were going to wait?

Geddes: They were going, maybe a day or two later—and then they were intercepted by Papa, and he said, "No go. You're too young, Frances." So that's the way it was.

At least that's the way it was according to Opal Geddes, and her version is supported by certain established facts, such as the issuance of the marriage license, which she had not been informed of before the interview session. How much license she has taken with information she was given is unknown, nor is it possible to discern how much fiction was braided into the facts Frances related to her. Regardless of the source, Opal Geddes was seldom at a loss for words. Here, she offers her characteristically blunt appraisal of Howard Hughes at the turn of the century:

Interviewer: Did everyone know of their engagement . . . Howard and Frances' engagement?

Geddes: Oh, I'm sure they did. A lot of them did.

Interviewer: Do you think it would have raised a few eyebrows?

Geddes: Well honey, at that time, he wasn't anyone to raise an eyebrow to!

Interviewer: Well, that's what I meant . . . the fact that he—

Geddes: No. In fact, they sort of resented her going with him . . . because he was sort of underneath the rest of their prestige . . . he was really a nobody as far as the social people were concerned. They considered him a rather brilliant man. I presume he was, because I think he had some background of college and education, because he came as a mining engineer.

Interviewer: He was a Harvard man.

Geddes: So he had to have a little background and some credentials to show, which I'm sure he had. But no, no one felt left out if he didn't speak to them . . . he had to speak first, because, you know, these little towns are quite clannish . . . and they can be quite naughty to each other.

Stung by the rejection, Opal's version goes, Howard Hughes went to Texas. It is a documented fact that Frances Geddes married Arthur Bendelari approximately a year later in what was considered a "surprise" wedding, an "open secret," to quote the Joplin newspaper at the time. This is how Mrs. Geddes explains the transition:

75

Interviewer: In that period following Howard and Frances' little romance, did she stay in Joplin? Was she sort of hurt by the incident, or do you know what her feelings were?

Geddes: I don't know. I don't think she was too heart-broken, because her father was a very domineering person. And he gave her the alternative and she abided by it. And then she married Arthur, and naturally, a new romance coming in her life . . .

Interviewer: Right. That was about a year later.

Geddes: Yes, approximately.

Interviewer: But was she in Joplin that entire year, or did she maybe leave?

Geddes: Oh, no! She was there.

Interviewer: She stayed in Joplin?

Geddes: Ah (pause) . . . yes, she was there all the time . . . And, of course, I think Arthur started pursuing her right away to win her over, and once they were married then later in December 1901.

Interviewer: Did most of the people in Joplin know of their courtship?

Geddes: Oh, a lot of them did.

Interviewer: So it wasn't any kind of a secret?

Geddes: No, not really . . .

Although Mrs. Geddes played down Frances' engagement to Hughes as just a "stupid romance of a young girl" once or twice during the conversation, she also had this to say about her sister-in-law's marriage to Arthur Bendelari:

Geddes:	I don't think she, at that particular time, she wanted to marry Arthur.
Interviewer:	Is that right?
Geddes:	I just surmise that from what she told me. Because she had quite a lot of admirers, you know, and he kept persisting that she marry and finally she gave in. But I really doubt, at the time she married him, that she really loved him. I think it was on, you know, sort of a rebound or something.
Interviewer:	A rebound from not being able to marry Howard?
Geddes:	Yes! She really liked him.
Interviewer:	Did she? Did she speak of him very often?
Geddes:	Oh yes, she did, yes.

In summary, this is Opal Geddes' evaluation of the attempted elopement between Frances Geddes and Howard Hughes:

Geddes:	It was just a quick romance with Frances, and I think that the reason that she felt she would marry him is because—she wanted to just be a little smart-aleck, you know.
Interviewer:	Oh, this was a rebellious move?
Geddes:	Yes . . . She wanted to escape from a little town, I'm sure. Because I think Frances' mind and thinking was so much bigger than Joplin. She had ideologies of doing something and I'm sure she did, because her mind expanded so beautifully. . . . She felt that she had too much family. And her mother was a very, very domineering person, just like her father. Dollie was straight-laced, oh how straight-laced.

As fascinating a story as the Howard Hughes courtship of Frances Geddes undoubtedly made, its primary importance to Dinkins' investigation lay in its potential for unknown heirs. Obviously, this potential could exist only if the relationship between the two parties were consummated and a child born. This possibility was broached with Opal Geddes, who expressed unwavering opposition to the idea:

Interviewer: Quite frankly, the reason we're so vitally concerned with this is—if there were any possibility at all that there were a child born of this union, he would stand to inherit everything.

Geddes: There was no child born, because Frances never had any children. She never had any children, and when she married Arthur Bendelari she was a virgin . . . and she never had any children by Arthur.

Interviewer: Did she ever talk about that? That she did not want children, or—

Geddes: Oh no, she just couldn't have children.

Interviewer: Oh, I see.

Geddes: There was just—she never did anything *not* to have children, because I said, I've said to her many times when she was younger . . . "Frances, isn't it a shame you never had children?" And she said, "Well, I suppose that it's a blessing for the life I've liked to lead." You know, traveling and doing the things she wanted to.

But she didn't resent children. She was always good to little Jim (James Geddes, Jr.), and she was always good to little Frances . . . she was quite—*exceedingly* fond of little Frances. That's her—you know, her name.

78

"I want to be frank with the whole thing," Mrs. Geddes blurted at one point. "There was no intimacy with Frances and his father." She did not relate how she gathered such highly personal details, but added with certainty, "She never had any children, she never had an abortion, she never had a miscarriage . . . she just was not fertile." When pressed as to the source of this medical opinion, Mrs. Geddes faltered only slightly:

Interviewer: Did she ever check into it medically, why she couldn't have children?

Geddes: I don't know that. Actually, I don't think she did. I think she accepted it.

As Mrs. Geddes reflects, Frances was amazingly nonchalant about her presumed condition:

Interviewer: What did Frances say when you asked her about not having children, or expressed regret that she—

Geddes: Oh, she just said, "Well, it's one of those things." She said, you know, "Some people can, some people can't."

However, she emphasized this point:

Geddes: But she said, "I presume that this is the way it's supposed to be because I like to do what I want to do. Travel, sing, and everything."

As Mrs. Geddes tells the story, then, the Hughes-Geddes romance was little more than a harmless flirtation, designed to stir up Frances' straight-laced parents. According to her, it was the classic tale of two sweethearts, broken up by her outraged father, who thought his daughter was too young to be married (though Frances did indeed marry the next year). Or is this version what Frances wanted Opal to believe transpired? Was there more to the aborted elopement than Opal Geddes was led to believe? (Or did she, too, suppress salient details to protect the woman she revered?) Several actions taken by Frances Geddes later in her life suggest there may have been more to her "fling" with Howard Hughes than her sister-in-law repeated. First, as Mrs. Geddes

79

paged through a decaying photograph album of Frances' during the interview session, she mentioned in passing that Frances once tried to contact Howard Hughes, Jr., during his years of seclusion at the Desert Inn in Las Vegas. This is how it came about:

Geddes: About twelve years ago Frances had a picture that was taken in Joplin, Missouri, down in Shoal Creek of a group—and Mr. Hughes, Sr., was in that group. . . .Well, she sent this photograph—

Interviewer: This was in 1965, approximately, that she sent the photograph?

Geddes: Yes, approximately. So, we were sitting, and we were going through a lot of old pictures that she had, and she said, "You know, I've heard so much about this pathetic boy. You know, he'd never been born if I had of married his father." . . . And she said, "I think I'll send it to him." . . . And so she mailed it. And she put her address and I think she wrote a little note and she said she thought perhaps he might enjoy seeing this picture taken in Joplin on Shoal Creek of a certain era before he was ever born, and it might interest him. And she told him who she was.

Interviewer: Did she keep a copy of the letter, by any chance?

Geddes: No! She wasn't interested in anything other than giving this to him . . . you see, money meant nothing to her. She was—she liked love.

Interviewer: Did she explain what she said in this letter to—

Geddes:　　　　No, no. She just said, "Opal, I thought this would be something that Howard might want." She didn't say he would enjoy it. She said, "He might want it, and I have no further use of keeping this, and if it would give him any satisfaction to know that his father had good friends. . . ."

　　　　　　　　And so she sent it. And her picture was there, her sister's picture is there, Nancy Harrington, and Frank Harrington, and several men that I have heard of. Of course this is long before my era—I wasn't born then.

　　　　　　　　And so, anyway, she got no reply. She didn't expect one really, he being the eccentric person that he turned out to be.

Throughout the discussion, Mrs. Geddes insisted that Frances' behavior in sending the letter had no great significance. Still, it was this gesture on Frances' part that prompted Mrs. Geddes to think her unexpected call from Dinkins' law firm in 1977 pertained to Howard Hughes, Jr. As she explained, "I just thought, well maybe that Howard, young Howard, had shown this picture and had this letter or little note from Frances saying that she had known his father—and maybe he was, in his eccentric mind, acknowledging a little something."

Even more interesting is the exchange that followed:

Geddes:　　　　I'm sure that he knew about Frances, because—as I understood—years ago, he made a trip to Joplin.

Interviewer:　　Howard, Jr.?

Geddes:　　　　Uh-huh. To look on some of the mining claims his father had there. . . . Now, I'm not saying this is authentic, but some friends from Joplin—now this has been twenty-some years ago—told Jim, my husband . . . "You know I saw Howard Hughes." And Jim says, "You did?" And he said, "Yes, he was here."

81

> Being an engineer, (he) had surveyed . . . a
> lot of land; with all probability he knew and
> had surveyed some of his land. I'm not sure.
> And so, Jim said, "Well, what was he here
> for?" He said, "Oh, I think he was just
> prospecting."

After discovering that Frances Geddes had attempted to contact Howard Hughes, Jr., as recently as the 1960s, over a half-century after she knew his father, Mrs. Geddes' interviewer queried whether Frances ever talked about Howard, Jr., in the last years of his life, when his business dealings and personal lifestyle were the subject of worldwide speculation. Mrs. Geddes remarked, "She'd bring it up just as a conversation to me. Like for instance, 'Well, if I had married his father, he wouldn't have *been* here!' "

After concluding the interview, Dinkins and his colleagues were left with pages and pages of talk from the transcript, along with several nagging doubts and unanswered questions. Before "marking Frances off the books," as Opal Geddes half-facetiously suggested, it was decided among the Houston sleuths to question a few more of the Geddes survivors whose names had come up in passing.

They were bothered in part by the inconsistencies in Mrs. Geddes' explanation for the breakup of the Hughes engagement. Why would James Geddes, Sr., violently disapprove of Frances' marriage to Hughes in 1900, ostensibly because of her age, yet fail to obstruct her 1901 wedding to Arthur Bendelari? Moreover, Mrs. Geddes was almost too certain, too insistent, that Frances was infertile. And how could she assert without doubt that Howard Hughes and Frances Geddes were never intimate?

Also, Opal was not able to explain satisfactorily the "surprise" quality to Frances' marriage to Bendelari. In fact, she claimed it was no surprise at all. Finally, the Houston heir-searchers were intrigued by the role "Little Frances" played in all this. Mrs. Geddes stated that Frances Geddes Bendelari Hubbell was "exceedingly fond" of her.

This snippet of dialogue caught their attention as they reviewed the transcript:

Interviewer: Do you feel like he (Bartley Geddes) named
Frances just—in respect to the family name?

Geddes: I beg your pardon?

Interviewer: He named his daughter "Frances." This was a family name, and . . .

Geddes: No. I think our Frances wanted to give her that name—after *her*.

It seemed rather curious that Opal Geddes should choose to express herself as she did. Little Frances was supposedly the daughter of Bartley and Blanche Geddes (Frances' older brother). Why, then, should Frances "want to give her that name"? The decision should have been Bartley and Blanche's, one would think. And what of Nancy, Frances' older sister? Bartley, it will be remembered, had two sisters, Nancy and Frances. Wouldn't Nancy feel slighted to know Bartley named his daughter after her sister, and not her? Particularly since they did not name their second daughter Nancy, either. According to Opal, the second daughter was born seven years after little Frances and was Bartley and Blanche's only other child. "And of course, she knew nothing about her aunt," Opal Geddes said of Little Frances. "She knew nothing about her life." Why was that, Dinkins and his team wondered? Somehow all this didn't hang together for them. They wanted more information, another opinion.

Dinkins' team was also struck by the parallels between Frances Geddes' and Howard Hughes, Sr.'s, lives after they parted company in Joplin in 1900. After her marriage to Bendelari, Opal recounted, Frances made regular and frequent trips to New York, most often alone, living her life pretty much as she pleased.

In fact, it was her independence that finally caused Bendelari to divorce her. "Frances said to Arthur she wanted to go to Italy and study music," Opal related, "because she really loved music. And she said, 'Arthur, will you give me a year, and then I'll get this out of my system, and then I'll come home?' And he said no. And that was all there was to it. So she went and he went."

Frances fulfilled this particular dream and traveled to Milan to study music in 1921. When she returned to America, it was to New York City, where she did some singing for several years. Then, in 1927, she settled in Los Angeles, taught voice, and worked in the movies on occasion.

Dinkins and his group had just discovered that Howard, Sr.'s, brother Felix Hughes was teaching voice in Los Angeles at approximately the same time, and his sister Greta had been a music instructor in New York City for some years prior to 1920. As they already knew, brother Rupert Hughes was in Hollywood making films throughout the twenties. With such proximity of interest and geography, chances were excellent that Frances could have crossed paths with any or all of the Hughes siblings. Was this just a coincidence? "I know that she knew the brother" (meaning Rupert), Opal admitted, but she "never heard her speak" of the others, and she knew nothing about the nature of Frances' acquaintance with Rupert Hughes. She was similarly uninformed as to whether Frances kept in touch with Howard, Sr., after the breakup of their love affair. "There could have been correspondence or something," she acknowledges, "but it was never mentioned to me."

Certain facts kept haunting the researchers' thoughts: Little Frances not being baptized at St. Philip's like her sister and most of the Geddes clan, Frances' "surprise" marriage to Bendelari, Mr. Geddes' hostility toward Howard Hughes, and the latter's abrupt departure from Joplin. What did it all mean?

One more sister-in-law remained to be contacted, the last link. Her maiden name was Florence Eaves, and she was James Geddes, Jr.'s, first wife (from whom he was divorced when he married Opal). Florence was originally from Joplin and had known Frances back in her Bendelari days. According to the rector at St. Philip's Episcopal Church in Joplin, she was now known as Florence Ettinger, a widow in her eighties, residing in New England. He described her as "quite a character," and suggested that she would probably know more than anyone then living about Frances' past. Before talking to Mrs. Ettinger, however, Dinkins and company decided to call Little Frances directly, to see what she might have to say, both about her aunt and about herself.

"Little Frances," better known as Mrs. Frances Writer, was fairly cooperative about answering the ad litem's questions. She gave her date of birth as October 4, 1904, at the outset of the telephone interview, thereby appearing to nip in the bud any suspicions that might link her to the 1900 affair.

Nevertheless, the conversation progressed in a most provocative fashion:

Interviewer: Were you born in Joplin, or—?

Writer: Yes.

Interviewer: In Joplin? And, which hospital?

Writer:	I don't think they had hospitals then. I imagine I was born at home.
Interviewer:	Okay. Were you baptized in Joplin?
Writer:	Yes.
Interviewer:	At—do you recall the church?
Writer:	St. Philip's Episcopal Church.

This, of course, was in direct opposition to what her sister earlier told Dinkins' investigator (that little Frances was baptized "elsewhere"), and it was in conflict with St. Philip's records, which made no mention of her baptism.

Interviewer:	Do you have your birth certificate or baptismal—?
Writer:	I have my baptismal, yes.

At this point in the conversation Mrs. Writer understandably requested some explanation for these personal inquiries into her family history. When she was told it concerned the estate of Howard Hughes, she replied, "Yes, he lived here at one time," referring to Howard Hughes, Sr. The interviewer kept up the thread of conversation:

Interviewer:	He did. And from what I understand, he apparently considered eloping with your Aunt Frances.
Writer:	Considered what?
Interviewer:	Eloping with your Aunt Frances.
Writer:	Oh.
Interviewer:	Were you aware of that?
Writer:	Hardly! I remember there was a Hughes here that I've heard the family speak of, yes. That I know.

The dialogue thus far would suggest that Little Frances had not been enlightened as to the role Hughes played in her aunt's life. She was then queried in a roundabout way as to her own identity:

Interviewer:	I was just wondering, too, about your name. I realize that you are her namesake.
Writer:	Yes.
Interviewer:	How did you come to be named after Frances? Was this a family name?
Writer:	Well, I apparently was—I don't know whether it was a family name or not, but her name was Frances Geddes, and when my father married my mother, they named me Frances Geddes, also.
Interviewer:	Uh-huh. And do you feel like it was probably after your aunt?
Writer:	Well, I know it was, yes!

Next, her questioner tried to elicit from Mrs. Writer the names of any other individuals still living who might recall more about the Hughes business. "I'm afraid when my Aunt Frances died at ninety-two in February, that that kind of wipes out all the old people in Joplin," she said apologetically. "I'm sure it does." Her interrogator persisted:

Interviewer:	Wasn't there a lady (whom James Geddes, Jr.) was married to first who is now known as Florence Ettinger?
Writer:	She is in a nursing home.
Interviewer:	Is she?
Writer:	Uh-huh.
Interviewer:	Do you think that she might recall—?
Writer:	She doesn't know nothing from up or down.
Interviewer:	Is she . . . sick, or she just doesn't remember?

86

Writer: She's quite senile. . . . And, she's moved away from Joplin, and she was divorced from our family, oh, I would say a good thirty-five years ago.

Mrs. Writer also had this rather interesting comment to make about Opal Geddes:

Writer: Now Opal, I don't know how much she knows or *thinks* she knows, of our family background.

Interviewer: Was she probably the closest to Frances?

Writer: No, she was—lived out there in California when her husband died, and she continued to live in my aunt's duplex.

(Several weeks earlier, Opal Geddes told Dinkins' representative: "In fact, I think I'm the only one that really knows all about Frances' life, because I spent so many years with her. We were very close." Was this contradiction simple interfamily rivalry, or was there something more to it?)

The interviewer pressed on:

Interviewer: Do you know if—did you ever discuss with your aunt, or hear her discuss, whether she was perhaps unable to have children?

Writer: I have no idea about that. I never did ask her. She—she had a beautiful voice and she sang, and she was kind of ahead of her time in that respect. I mean, she was rather more interested in having a career. Now, as far as having children, I know they didn't have, but other than that I don't know.

Interviewer: Have you pretty much kept in contact with her over the years?

Writer: Oh, yes! Always.

Interviewer: And she never did mention anything to you about who she dated before she married Mr. Bendelari?

Writer: Oh my God, no! [laughter] I doubt if she dated many people, because as I remember, she was probably between seventeen and eighteen when she married him.

Interviewer: So as far as this romance that she had with Howard Hughes, that's just never been—

Writer: I haven't the vaguest idea about that. She was a very lovely looking person and . . . but this is all I know.

Interviewer: Had you even heard of it before I brought it up?

Writer: Heard what?

Interviewer: Heard that she even dated Howard Hughes— or was this not known to the family?

Writer: No, I'd never heard that discussed.

Interviewer: You'd never heard that before?

Writer: I didn't know anything about any of that.

For some reason, Little Frances was kept entirely in the dark about her aunt's relationship with Howard Hughes. Undaunted, Dinkins' associate kept asking questions, poking around in the past for nothing in particular. During this fishing expedition, Mrs. Writer made a casual comment that struck her questioner like an electric shock:

Interviewer: Okay . . . do you know what—any of the history of Frances' background before she married Arthur?

Writer: She went to a convent here in Joplin.

Interviewer: This was like a private school, or—?

Writer: Well, a Catholic convent.

Interviewer: Do you recall the name of it?

Writer: No.

Interviewer: Was she in Joplin the entire time before she married Mr. Bendelari, or did she—?

Writer: Yes.

Here was a missing piece. In that year's time between her broken engagement to Howard Hughes and her subsequent "surprise" wedding to Arthur Bendelari, Frances Geddes was in a Catholic convent. The picture of Frances Geddes that was emerging through the ad litem's research hardly suggested her to be the type to enter a convent, at least not of her volition. Furthermore, Frances was raised Episcopalian, and her family were high-profile members of St. Philip's Episcopal Church in Joplin. This startling piece of news made little sense. Unless—it did not take a particularly vivid imagination to put together a scenario to explain Frances' sudden enrollment in a convent. Putting aside these conjectures for the moment, Dinkins' assistant continued the telephone conversation with Mrs. Writer, bringing up the marriage of Frances' sister Nancy Geddes to Frank Harrington, which took place two months prior to the Bendelari wedding in December 1901:

Interviewer: Now Nancy married, didn't she . . . in the same period of time as Frances did?

Writer: I think yes, because her daughter was nine months younger than I.

Why would Frances Writer answer a question about her Aunt Nancy's wedding date in such a fashion, associating it with the comparison of her date of birth to Nancy's daughter's date of birth? This made no sense, following the accepted family history. It would be logical if Little Frances were Frances' daughter, however—the suspicion Dinkins' team kept coming back to. To try to clear up some of the confusion, Mrs. Writer was asked to produce her baptismal, which she agreed to provide. She was then asked whether she had a birth certificate. This question prompted another unexpected revelation:

Writer: I don't know if I did or not. I don't know where it was, and that's the way I got my Social Security, was through baptism in the church. And, I think it has my aunt's name on it.

Interviewer: The baptismal record does?

Writer: Uh-huh.

Interviewer: Why is that?

Writer: I don't know! Because you had godparents?

On that puzzling note, the conversation was terminated, and Dinkins awaited the arrival of Little Frances' baptismal record with great anticipation. In the interim, he and his staff pondered the telephone conversation with Frances Geddes Writer. Much more than the interview with Opal Geddes, this conversation raised a number of provocative questions. Dinkins' corps of researchers was beginning to suspect more and more that Little Frances might be more than a niece to Frances Geddes, and they had a pretty good idea who might be the father, despite the troublesome 1904 birthdate that Mrs. Writer offered for herself. To confront their suspicions, they compiled a working draft of "disturbing elements" in the telephone interview with Mrs. Writer:

1. Frances Writer claims she was born in Joplin, while her sister earlier informed us Frances was born elsewhere. Why the discrepancy?

2. Frances Writer, when asked which hospital she was born in, replied, "I imagine I was born at home." She doesn't know?

3. Frances Writer maintains that she was baptized at St. Philip's Episcopal. However, when we visited the church in July, the Father was unable to find any such record, although he did successfully locate her sister's.

4. The nine—or seven—year span between Little Frances and her sister, the only children of Bartley Geddes. Is it logical he would wait so long between children? And why the confusion about the age difference?

5. Frances has "heard the family speak of" Hughes' residence in Joplin, yet she knew nothing about the romance. Why was she kept in the dark? Even Opal said Little Frances "knew nothing" about her aunt. Was there a reason for this?

6. For a period after their marriage, Arthur and Frances Bendelari lived under the same roof with Bartley, Blanche, and Little Frances.

90

7. Frances' enrollment in a convent after her engagement to Hughes and before her surprise marriage to Arthur.

8. Frances had no birth certificate, and her aunt's name appears on her baptismal record. She doesn't know why.

A week or so after the phone conversation, a letter arrived from Frances Writer. It did not contain her baptismal papers, as expected. What it did say made the Houston ad litem team gasp with surprise:

> In reference to our telephone conversation of August 24, 1977, I will be happy to cooperate with you and furnish you the documents that you require. However, I would first like a letter from your firm stating that I will incur no financial obligation when I furnish you these documents. I am sure you are aware that there are many people looking into this matter and I want to be assured that your requests are ligitimate [sic].
>
> Yours truly,
> Frances Writer

"Oh, my!" was Mrs. Fay's startled reaction. Dinkins, always guarded in his response to the discoveries of his amateur detectives, grew thoughtful. The idea that ran through his logical mind as he read Mrs. Writer's letter was that she had sought the assistance of a lawyer after talking to his representative. The language clearly had a lawyer's touch, and he was quick to recognize it. Even Dinkins had to acknowledge that things were beginning to look serious. Darlene Cameron, his secretary, was more emotional. "I knew it!" she whooped, as she studied the correspondence. "I just knew there was something to this Frances Geddes thing!"

The letter from Frances Writer, all agreed, was a tantalizing bit of evidence. After all, Dinkins and his band of sleuths had conjured Frances Geddes out of nowhere, and here was a piece of correspondence from her namesake stating that "there are many people looking into this matter." Of course, Dinkins was acutely aware that there were a number of other heirship investigations going on simultaneously with his official search. With millions of Hughes dollars at stake and no will, fortune hunters across the country were checking their family trees for some link to Howard Hughes, Jr., and unofficial "heir-finders" offered to trace the lineage of individuals, for a price, to try to establish a Hughes connection. Moreover, the scores of lawyers representing the already-known cousins were no doubt conducting their own private investigations into Hughes' genealogy, anxious to confirm their clients inheritance position. The last thing they wished to uncover was a long-lost daughter of Howard Hughes, Sr., and a half-sister to Mr. Hughes, Jr.

91

Were such a person to surface, their clients would be booted out of the line of inheritance to make room for this closer relation. The unfolding scenario certainly created an atmosphere of melodrama among Dinkins' coworkers.

In response, Dinkins fired off a reply to Mrs. Writer assuring her his requests were "indeed legitimate," and explaining in greater detail his mission to discover unknown heirs of Howard R. Hughes for the purpose of inheritance. Then he waited.

During this anxious period, his assistant tracked down Florence Ettinger, James Geddes, Jr.'s, first wife, and spoke with her briefly by telephone. She seemed to be extremely clear-headed, and happy to cooperate in Dinkins' investigation. Interestingly, several of her recollections were in direct conflict with either Opal's or Little Frances'. Mrs. Ettinger, it turned out, had lived with Frances Geddes in New York for a year in the early 1920s and knew her sister-in-law quite well. She said that Frances talked quite openly about Howard Hughes, occasionally reminiscing during those moments when Howard Hughes, Jr., was doing something particularly newsworthy. (Why, then, did Little Frances know nothing about the relationship?) Asked whether Frances could conceive, Mrs. Ettinger chirped, "Sure she could! She just didn't *want* any! She didn't want to be tied down." At a point in the conversation when the subject was Hughes' courtship of Frances, Mrs. Ettinger said in an aside to her daughter, in the room with her at the time: "She might have been married to him."

After this phone call, several weeks went by and nothing happened. Dinkins received no reply from Frances Writer. He asked his associate to telephone her and inquire in a friendly, casual way as to whether she had received Dinkins' letter of explanation. As Dinkins' colleague wrote at the time of this conversation: "Mrs. Writer's reaction to what I had hoped and expected to be a cordial call was at best impatience, if not annoyance." The openness that had marked their earlier communications had been replaced by noncooperation. Mrs. Writer acknowledged that she had received Dinkins' letter, but stated, "I just don't care to go into this any further." She flatly refused to send the copies of her baptismal records, saying, "There's just [my sister] and me left, and we're tired of it. . . . I don't want to get involved." She didn't know whether her parents' names appeared on her baptismal certificate, and according to the notes made after the call, she "seemed perturbed" by the inquiry. She "supposed" her aunt Frances' signature appeared on the records because two women always "stand up" for a girl baby at St. Philip's. Finally, she denied her earlier comment that her aunt attended a convent. After fumbling around a bit for an explanation, she said, "Well, I suppose she went to a Catholic school."

At the close of the conversation, Mrs. Writer apologized for her irascible behavior, and repeated for the third or fourth time that just she and her sister remained of the family, and she just "didn't want to be troubled with it."

Faced with this turn of events, Dinkins finally acceded to his secretary's proddings to send someone to interview Florence Ettinger face to face. The door was obviously closed vis-à-vis Frances Writer, and Mrs. Ettinger was the last living member of the family grapevine. Having been divorced from the Geddesses for over thirty years, she might be less reluctant than a family member to shake a few skeletons.

Getting the green light, Dinkins' associate packed her suspicions and flew to New England to question the first Mrs. James Geddes, Jr. Quite the contrary to Frances Writer's warning that she "didn't know up from down," Florence Eaves Geddes Ettinger was a very alert, highly lucid woman with a shrill laugh and a spunky sense of humor. Midway into her interview, she was joined by her daughter, whereupon the two shared conjectures with Dinkins' emissary about Hughes' long-ago love.

Here, in part, is their meandering conversation:

Ettinger: Well, why would Frances be an heir?

Interviewer: We were doing some heirship research and discovered a—I have it with me—a marriage license that was taken out—

Ettinger: Oh, now that I know about. But it was never . . . used.

Interviewer: It was shortly before she married Arthur Bendelari.

Ettinger: Yes, Arthur was in the picture at the same time. She talked about it.

Interviewer: Did she say anything to you at all about this?

Ettinger: Oh, she kidded about it, you know . . . when Howard Hughes was in all the news, and when he did this and he did that . . . she laughingly said, "Do you know that I used to date his father?" And then she told me about this Mr. Hughes coming back to Joplin, you know, he was interested in doing some work in the mines, and he was an

93

engineer. And then she said, "He wanted to marry me," and she said, "I kiddingly said yes."

Interviewer: She "kiddingly" said yes?

Ettinger: Yeah. Frances was an awful kidder . . . and she didn't take men very seriously . . . she was very popular, she was a gorgeous looking person. Well anyway, he went over . . . to Carthage and got the wedding license and then he came back and told Frances that . . . he had the license and it was time to get married. And she was so flabbergasted that he took her seriously that she said no way was she gonna marry him.

Now what *he* said . . . anyway, she said that he was very angry and that he left Joplin and went down to Texas. And that's all she, pretty much, said.

Interviewer: She told you that particular story?

Ettinger: Yeah. I couldn't make it up to save my life, you know!

Not surprisingly, Mrs. Ettinger then offered yet another version of the romance between Howard Hughes and Frances Geddes. Gone is the interfering father who broke up the plotted elopement; in its place is Frances the "kidder" who, she would have Florence Ettinger believe, accepted a proposal of marriage on a lark, never intending to make it official. Following the apparent family custom of discrediting the veracity of the kinfolk, Mrs. Ettinger had this to say about Opal Geddes' reminiscences: "Opal . . . knew nothing about this. This has been years ago, and I don't think Frances ever talked to Opal. Now I don't know that, but I don't imagine that she did. Frances and I were very close, you know."

Mrs. Ettinger expanded on her acquaintance with Frances:

Interviewer: When did you meet Frances?

Ettinger Oh, I knew Frances before I married Jimmy. [They were married in 1920.]

94

Interviewer: You did?

Ettinger: Oh, yeah. You see, Arthur had a—they had a place down on Shoal Creek, and so I used to go down there with her, you know. So, I mean, I knew everybody a couple years before I married her brother.

Interviewer: Let's see, that would put it around 1915 . . . and then you lived with her, didn't you say, for about a year in New York?

Ettinger: Oh, I—no, it was about eight months. But that was—that was after we were married.

Interviewer: After you and James had married?

Ettinger: Yeah, yeah.

Interviewer: And she lived with you-all?

Ettinger: No . . . Frances was always interested in my voice, and she wanted me to do something with it. You wouldn't know it today, but anyway I used to sing. And so she wanted me to come to New York, so I went—and I stayed, well, I think it was about eight months.

Interviewer: And was she living there? Is that why she—

Ettinger: Oh, yeah! She—oh, she went to New York every winter. She only came home in the summertime. And Arthur—

Interviewer: Even while she was married to Arthur?

Ettinger: Oh, yeah! He didn't care. Well if he cared, he—

Interviewer: Didn't say anything?

Ettinger: He gave her money to live on, see.

Interviewer: Where did she stay when she was in New York?

Ettinger: Oh, we had an apartment. In fact, we had two different apartments.

Interviewer: Was she singing in New York?

Ettinger: Oh, she was studying.

Interviewer: Studying voice?

Ettinger: Yeah. Because then, later, she went to Italy. Oh, she knew everybody in the musical circles at that time.

Then Mrs. Ettinger touched on the subjects of Frances' fertility and the ill-fated romance:

Interviewer: I asked you before on the phone whether you thought that Frances was able to have children, and you said that she was able to—

Ettinger: Why, I wouldn't—now that would be absolutely sticking my neck out. I wouldn't *know*. I know she didn't want children—of her *own*. She was just crazy about children . . . but it just, for herself, she just didn't want to be tied down. I mean, she didn't want to be a housewife, let's put it that way. She wanted a career, and Arthur was willing to put up the money for it, so . . . and children do tie you down.

Interviewer: Did she say anything about her courtship days with Arthur and how all that came about?

Ettinger: No. I just knew that she was a very popular girl, and all these young men from the East, you know, would come back there, and—so she just had a ball, I guess.

But no, nothing was ever said . . . I don't think she was very crazy about Arthur, to tell you the truth, but he was crazy about her. I think the family prevailed upon her to marry him because he was

96

a very wealthy man. They were—they wanted her future, you know. I mean, I knew them well enough to know that they would definitely want somebody with money for their daughter.

Interviewer: I was asking if it was maybe a surprise, because there was an announcement in the paper . . . it said it had been a well-guarded secret—

Ettinger: Well now, all I know is that she dated him. I don't know that. I think she dated him exclusively, and I mean, maybe he was just one of the many. But I mean, now that . . . that's before I was born!

Interviewer: Sure. I just thought maybe she had told you about it.

Ettinger: No.

Interviewer: Did she ever say how she felt about Howard Hughes? Or did she say that it was just a passing fancy?

Ettinger: Well, she must have liked him well—she must have liked him well enough to think that maybe she might want to marry him! I mean, that's all I know.

Interviewer: But from what you understand, she never accepted his proposal . . . he just kind of went off on his own and picked up this license?

Ettinger: Oh, no, I think that she was—maybe at the time she was serious. I mean . . . I don't know that, I really don't. All I know is that she dated him and that he did go to Carthage. I know that. She told me so. But how crazy she was about him—I don't think she was ever very crazy about any man, to tell you the truth.

Dinkins' colleague then began to nose around for confirmation or refutation of the suspicions concerning Little Frances:

97

Interviewer:	Do you know anything about the fact that she attended a convent before she married Arthur?
Ettinger:	A convent?! No!
Interviewer:	That's what Frances Writer said.
Ettinger:	Well, then—Frances knows more than I do. I don't know that, I never heard that. Where was the convent?
Interviewer:	In Joplin, from what I understand.

And later:

Interviewer:	Do you know if Little Frances, Frances Writer, was born in Joplin, or—
Ettinger:	I think they, both of them [both sisters], were born in Joplin. I don't think they ever left Joplin—not that I know of.
Interviewer:	Because [Frances' sister] has said that she thought Frances was born out of Joplin.
Ettinger:	Well . . . I just don't know. If (she) said that—well, she ought to know where her sister was born!

As the questions became more pointed, Mrs. Ettinger's daughter guessed correctly what Dinkins' protégé was driving at:

Interviewer:	I guess sort of the bottom line on all this is—we need to find out whether there was any possibility at all that any children might have resulted from any sort of union between—
Ettinger:	Oh! I can't—I don't think so. I wouldn't know, but I don't think so.
Daughter:	Well, Mother—
Ettinger:	She's asking about if Frances could have had any children.

Daughter: Oh, I gathered from those questions, that it could possibly be either one of Bart's children could have been Frances'.

Whereupon, the three engaged in a free-for-all, tossing around theories and speculations concerning Little Frances' suspected identity.

The three then bandied about the possibility that Little Frances might have been Frances Geddes' daughter by Howard Hughes, resulting in her placement in a convent during the pregnancy, after which her brother took in the child as his own (this was small town America at the turn of the century), Frances being pressured into a hasty marriage to Arthur Bendelari, who promised her her freedom in exchange for her hand.

Mrs. Ettinger's daughter, however, summed it all up when she remarked, "Oh, it's too bad that [Frances Geddes is] not alive . . . only just to clarify it. Because it'll always be an 'if.' "

After the conversation with Florence Ettinger, there was no stone left to turn, no one else to talk to. Whatever transpired between Howard and Frances must remain buried in the past, leaving only suspicions to mark their relationship. Most of those centered on Little Frances, her namesake, and all the puzzling coincidences surrounding her identity. Were they just coincidences, or could Little Frances be the heir not apparent? Why, for example, did her aunt's name appear on her baptismal certificate? Why did she not know where she was born, and why did she have no birth certificate, to her own confusion? Why did St. Philip's Episcopal Church have no record of her baptism? Why the discrepancies over the age span between her and her sister? And why, finally, was Little Frances so ill-informed about her aunt's romance with Hughes? The Howard R. Hugheses, father and son, were both public figures on a grand scale, and a broken engagement with either one would surely be the stuff of a family legend. It is almost as if there were a conspiracy of silence within the family to protect her from the truth. As for Frances Geddes herself, she seems to have told bits and pieces of the story to each relative within her evolving circle of confidantes, careful not to disclose the complete story to any one individual, and telling each one that she "knew everything," and everyone else knew nothing. Did she have something to hide?

If Little Frances were not the victim of an intrigue nearly a century old, then what was the reason for her dramatic change in attitude after her friendly agreement to send Dinkins her baptismal papers? Did she discover something that she preferred to keep confidential? She explained her hesitation with the comment that there was no one left but herself and her sister, she had no children, no heirs, and she "didn't want to be bothered.'' Bothered by what? If there were nothing out of the ordinary in her past, then what did it matter, why did she change her mind? If, on the contrary, there were something unexpected . . . Joplin is a small town, and a revelation of that sort would likely have created a scandal, so why bother?

Even if Little Frances were excluded from speculation, there was still something "fishy," as Darlene Cameron put it, about the returned marriage license. There was still the matter of the convent to consider. (Dinkins' clerk discovered that there was indeed at least one such institution in Joplin in 1900: the Sisters of Mercy Convent. Predictably, they have very few records dating from this period, and cannot confirm or deny Frances' attendance.) And could Frances conceive, or could she not, and why was there such a division of opinion about it? The one thing that all agreed upon concerning Frances is that she did not under any circumstances *want* a child of her own. Since the Geddes family Bible stops before 1900, and recording of births was not compulsory in Joplin or Carthage at the time of Frances' affair with Hughes, whether she became pregnant and gave birth will always be unknown.

In his obligation to find the unknown heirs of Howard Hughes, Jr., Dinkins had nowhere else to turn in his quest to prove or disprove the suspicions about Frances Geddes. Moreover, he needed documentary evidence to establish any relationship in court, and that evidence was not forthcoming. During the deposition of Annette Lummis, he asked Hughes, Sr.'s, sister-in-law if she had any knowledge of the events in Joplin. "Did you know whether or not Howard, Sr., had ever lived in Missouri?" he queried. "No," she replied. "Have you ever heard of a lady named Frances Geddes?" he persisted. "How do you spell the last name?" she asked. "G-e-d-d-e-s" was his reply. "No." "Have you ever heard of a lady named Frances Bendelari?" he tried again. "No," was again the response. Whatever occurred between Howard and Frances, Hughes was enough of a gentleman to avoid bringing it up with his wife's family.

He did allude to the episode at least once, however. Mrs. Fay found a small mention of his Joplin interval in the biography he furnished his Harvard classmates in the *Fourth Report of the Class of 1897*. "In January, 1901, the great Lucas Oil Well came in at Spindle Top, near Beaumont, Texas," he writes. "I heard the roar in Joplin and made for the seat of disturbance." When Dinkins saw Hughes' explanation for his abrupt departure from Joplin, he laughed mischievously. "I'll bet he heard a roar in Joplin!" Dinkins snickered. "The roar of Mr. Geddes' shotgun!" Unfortunately, Hughes' discretion concerning his former ladylove offered no assistance in clearing up the intrigue.

Whether or not Hughes and Geddes ever had a child together,

Howard Hughes, Jr., certainly had this independent woman from Joplin to thank for his appearance in the world and, indirectly, for the fortune he inherited. Had she stayed with his father, Howard, Sr., might never have gone to Spindletop or entered the oil business, quite possibly never inventing the rotary bit that made them both rich and famous.

For Dinkins and his intrepid researchers, Frances Geddes introduced the first in a series of mysteries associated with the heirship investigation of Howard Hughes, Jr. With the discovery of the returned marriage license and the fascinating story that unfolded, they could not be certain, as Phase One of the heirship determination trial came to a close, that Howard Hughes, Jr., died without leaving a sibling to inherit the Hughes legacy. And yet the only evidence in the court records to demonstrate this episode in Hughes' life was Dinkins' introduction of the marriage license. It was offered to Judge Gregory without explanation, and none of the other attorneys present, representing the various cousins and interested parties, stopped to ask him, then or later, what it meant. To them, its anonymity was a distinct plus, clearly in their clients' best interest.

There is a fascinating footnote to the Howard Hughes–Frances Geddes saga. Nearly two years after the 1981 heirship trial, some startling new evidence surfaced via the family of James Geddes III (the son of Frances' younger brother Jimmy), who had been interviewed by Dinkins' associate in 1977, with little result. This unexpected eleventh-hour disclosure only added to the already considerable Geddes mystique.

Writing in 1983, Geddes' wife not only confessed to a full knowledge of the 1900 Hughes-Geddes relationship; she further indicated that a marriage actually took place. Indeed, she stated, "The doubt still lingers in our minds as to whether there was a consummation of the marriage between her and Howard Hughes, Sr. We believe the possibility is distinct because of the small information that we do have as to events that occurred in her life after the marriage license was issued." The exact nature of these events is not known, but it was revealed that Mr. and Mrs. Geddes suspect that Frances' fifteen-years-younger brother Jimmy (the husband of both Opal and Florence Ettinger) may in fact be her son by Howard Hughes, Sr. According to Opal, Frances was "exceedingly fond" of both Little Frances and Jimmy; she reportedly "gave her fortune away" to the latter: all of which makes sense in light of this discovery.

Geddes withheld the information for six years (before, during, and after the trial) because of a lack of "concrete evidence" and a desire to protect his aunt Frances' image. Among other things, the Geddeses have photographs from Frances' old album showing Howard Hughes and

Frances together, including several taken after her 1901 marriage to Arthur Bendelari, by which time Hughes had already left for Texas and begun courting Allene Gano. It is in fact probable that Hughes continued to see his Joplin love throughout his adult life, keeping the ghosts of his past secret from his family in Houston. It is clear from this development that the ad litem team's suspicions about Frances were on point all along.

It was ironic, really. to witness all the individuals clamoring for a piece of the Hughes pie, and then reflect on an obscure widow in Joplin, Missouri, who might have had it all, but turned it down because she didn't want to be bothered. Who knows? Maybe she was Howard Hughes, Sr.'s, daughter. Maybe James Geddes, Jr., was his son. Or maybe Frances Geddes' progeny was somewhere else, ignorant of his or her true identity. Florence Ettinger's daughter said it best: it will always be an "if."

A Millionaire Is Made

After Hughes, Sr., disappeared from Joplin, he kicked around for awhile in Independence, Missouri, before heading to Beaumont, where he smelled success in the black crude that surrounded him. "Beaumont in those days was no place for a divinity student," he wrote. "The reek of oil was everywhere. It filled the air, it painted the houses, it choked the lungs and stained men's souls. Such another excitement will not be seen in this generation. It will take that length of time to get together an equal number of fools and 'come-ons' at one spot." Hughes attacked his new profession with a vengeance. "I turned greaser and sank into the thick of it. Rough neck, owner, disowner, promoter, capitalist, and 'mark'—with each I can claim kin, for I have stood in the steps of each."

It was about this time, between 1901 and 1903, that Howard Hughes met Allene Gano, the woman who would one day become his wife and give birth to Howard, Jr. Allene was a Dallas socialite with a haunting and delicate beauty, named after Allen Gano, a distinguished forebear from Kentucky. Hughes fell instantly in love with her. Their courtship must have been the subject of many whispered conversations in the elite circles the Ganos frequented. Who could resist indulging in gossip about a midwestern wildcatter of no apparent means, keeping company with that most rarefied of species, a genuine southern belle? To make matters worse, Hughes was pushing forty, a reputed womanizer, and not particularly attractive. Howard Hughes, Sr., had been sowing wild oats and trying his hand at various occupations in a number of different states for almost ten years, all of which hardly made him a suitable candidate for the hand of Miss Allene Stone Gano.

Howard Robard Hughes, Sr., was an adventurer, a man of chance; and his fortunes changed with the seasons. "Though I never wrote a book, I furnished the local color for some of the stories in the *Saturday Evening Post* by my brother, Rupert Hughes," Hughes boasted in his Harvard resumé. His was not the sedate and secure life of the established families in the upper-crust society in which the Ganos moved. Reflecting on this period in her brother-in-law's life, Annette Gano Lummis paints a far different portrait of Howard Hughes. "Well, I know they all went down to Spindletop when all of us was together," she begins. "He was practicing law in Kentucky, a graduate of Harvard University. Spindletop was discovered, and Howard locked up his office, law office, and walked out . . . and they all met at Spindletop." Mrs. Lummis was either blissfully ignorant of Hughes' many adventures in the six years en route from Harvard to Beaumont—including his involvement with Frances Geddes in Joplin—or she chose to ignore them. "And it is your impression," Dinkins asked her at the time of her deposition, "that Howard, Sr., went to Spindletop, or the Spindletop area, directly from Keokuk?" "From Keokuk," she replied flatly.

Howard Hughes, Sr., was drawn to beautiful and well-born young women, and the debutante-types responded. To these sheltered creatures, Hughes must have cut a dashing and romantic figure, in stark contrast to the dully respectable gentry who generally came calling. In any event, Hughes' prospects improved when he made a small fortune at Spindletop, and he managed to persuade both Allene and her parents to accept him into the family. "In the thick of the fight I was successful one year, married, and travelled through England, Germany and France, but returned again to the oil game," he writes in his Harvard memoir. Hughes subsequently lost everything "almost in a night," when his field in Batson, Texas, turned to saltwater, whereupon he and the new Mrs. Hughes followed the oil industry from one field to another, dependent on the vagaries of petroleum prospecting, and the support of Hughes' parents back in Iowa for their livelihood. Allene Gano Hughes reportedly adjusted to her new style of living with few noticeable signs of strain. "All I know is my sister married Howard and she used to buy direct in St. Louis and charge them to Keokuk, Iowa," Annette Lummis recalled. "And she always spelled it: K-e-o-k-u-k. And finally, one time she was in St. Louis buying clothes, and they said, 'You don't have to spell Keokuk anymore.' " Though Hughes was forty years old, his parents continued to finance many of his ventures. "You gave Howard your life's blood," Rupert Hughes wrote in tribute to his mother in 1924, "your lifelong devotion to the last. . . . You got him his education at Harvard, the money to finance his many failures and his final tremendous success."

Success was still no more than a dream to Hughes about 1906, however. His further wildcatting in and around Texas proved so disheartening that he set his family up in Oil City, Louisiana (Sonny was born in December 1905), where Howard, Sr., got himself appointed postmaster. "I never held a public office," he wrote in his Harvard class report, "except that of deputy sheriff and postmaster at Oil City, Louisiana. Therein I lost my religion." Genealogist Mary Fay swiftly established a chummy correspondence with the 1977 postmaster, through whom she eventually confirmed this unusual interlude in Hughes' life. She learned from the postmaster general's records that Howard Hughes, Sr., became postmaster of this small Louisiana town on July 1, 1907, and held the post until early 1909. One of the older residents of Caddo Parish who reportedly knew Hughes at the time referred to Howard, Sr., as the first "self-appointed" postmaster of Oil City. "I do not know what he meant by that statement," Mrs. Fay's correspondent wrote facetiously. In one of his letters, he informed her that some of the locals had gone to school with Hughes' son and had played with young Howard, Jr.

Finally, in 1908, after fifteen restless and rootless years, Hughes hit it big. Still dabbling in oil exploration during his tenure as postmaster of Oil City, he and his partner in prospecting, Walter Sharp, abandoned a well at Pierce Junction, Texas, because the drill they employed could not penetrate the hard rock under the surface of the ground. They encountered the same difficulty at their next oil field in Goose Creek, Texas, leading to the invention of the rotary drill bit that eventually made Howard Hughes, Jr., reputedly the world's richest man.

Not surprisingly, the legend of its creation has many variations. Perhaps the most nearly accurate is the following account, which appeared as part of Howard Hughes, Sr.'s, obituary in the February 1924 issue of *Petroleum World,* a respected publication of the oil industry:

> Many thousands of dollars had been spent attempting to drill through this rock, and Howard Hughes' partner, Walter Sharp, suggested that Mr. Hughes take a vacation and try to figure out some kind of a drill to solve their difficulties. Mr. Hughes decided to go to his parents' home in Keokuk, Iowa, and, while on the way home, stopped off at St. Louis, purchased a set of drawing instruments, and after two weeks' work evolved the first cone-type rock bit.

Ruby Hughes, the widow of Howard, Sr.'s, younger brother Felix Hughes, claims Howard invented the drill bit one Christmas while sitting at the dining room table at his parents' house in Keokuk, and his brother Rupert Hughes lends credence to this story, as well. "Eventually running into a flint formation which could not be penetrated by the old fishtail bit with its two cutting edges," he wrote, "Howard went home to Keokuk, and invented the Hughes conical bit with one hundred and sixty-six cutting edges. My father backed him in patenting it and in its manufacture." One local historian of Keokuk claims that Hughes conceived the idea for his drill bit after talking with a dentist from Keokuk's dental school and being inspired by a dental drill.

Avis Hughes McIntyre, a daughter of one of Rupert Hughes' wives, offers yet another version. "Well, our English butler had a way with our own butter that was churned," her anecdote begins. "We had our own cows and our own dairy. And he had different ways of rolling the butter. But at one time when 'Uncle' Howard was visiting—we always had two pats of butter on the butter dish when we sat down to dinner, and they were large pats of butter—and this time they were cone-shaped points hitting each other, and then a ridge around. And I remember 'Uncle' Howard in later years . . . saying idly while sitting and toying with the butter balls one day, that, 'You know, your butter is what gave me the idea for the bit that I invented.' Because it was a rotary bit instead of a fishtail bit that went through all strata of shale and rock and everything."

Then there is the "old story" that the postmaster of Oil City related to Mrs. Fay, that a driller came into the post office during Hughes' tenure as postmaster, "and told Mr. Hughes of his idea on the drilling bit. . . . In due time then," the postmaster continued, "he would make a model of one out of wood and with a pocket knife." It was in fact during Hughes' stint as postmaster/deputy sheriff that he invented the drilling marvel. "I can't verify this story," Mrs. Fay's correspondent admitted, "but I don't doubt it." Nor can one forget Opal Geddes' emphatic assertions that credit for the invention was due at least in part to Arthur Bendelari, Hughes' rival for the affections of Frances Geddes.

There are no doubt others who dispute the official line, as well. The most serious threat to Hughes' credibility as inventor of the cone-shaped bit, ironically, may come out of the philanthropic endeavors of the widow of his former partner, Walter B. Sharp. In 1952, Mrs. Sharp sponsored a project to place on record the history of the Texas oil industry. In an oral reminiscence transcribed on July 7, 1953, now part of the Rare Book Collection of the Barker Texas History Center, University of Texas at Austin, Mr. Granville Allison Humason discussed at length the invention of the roller rock bit and the part played by Howard Hughes, Sr. It is full of surprises.

"Well, we started learning how to drill wells and all and I worked

105

in the field pulling rods and and tubing and everything like that and all, and got into the drilling," he recites. "I was with Lee Kinnebrew (?), a contract driller, and so I had discovered how to make a roller bit on account of I was having so much trouble with this packed sand . . . so we, I then had designed and made a little model out of spools and a roller bit that I thought would be fine to put. And I took this idea from grinding coffee when I used to have to put the coffee pot in my lap and grind the coffee for in the morning and everything, after it was parched. And I thought that would be a good idea, you understand, to puncture the ground, you understand, and do it. Well, all right. But I couldn't get nobody to assist me, you understand, and make it until Mr. Hughes came along and he bought the idea." According to Mr. Humason one thing led to another, and, "well, he bought my idea and paid me a hundred and fifty dollars for the idea in the bar one night. . . . I shall never forget it."

This is when Walter Sharp came into the picture, Humason suggests. "Mr. Hughes then went into the old Phoenix Hotel and Mr. Sharp was sitting there and he said, Howard said to him, he says, 'Sharp, give me fifteen hundred dollars. I'll give you half-interest into the—' And he said, 'What, into those spools?' He said, 'Yes.' Well, he talked with him and he made the deal. He gave him fifteen hundred dollars and he gave his wife five hundred and he took the thousand dollars and he jumped on the train and he went to Washington up there and had the patent, had it patented."

As Mr. Humason explains it, the chief drawback to his further success in the oil business was his inability to draw his designs according to engineering standards. "I had worked out ideas, you understand, that no one else could work out. . . . But it's no good until I get an engineer, you understand, to draw it out plain." Still, he contends the Hughes bit came from the spools he designed in and around Shreveport, Louisiana.

It is clear from his oral testimony that Humason knew Hughes and his partner Sharp during their months of frustration in Goose Creek and Louisiana. Of Sharp he said, "He was a fine, first-class gentleman. There wasn't a better oil man in the oil business. . . . He wasn't a cheap shrew, and that's the reason why him and Howard Hughes, when they were in Shreveport, they were what we called 'water drillers.' They drilled water wells, you understand, for the oil companies." His knowledge of Hughes is also apparent. "And Mr. Hughes, well, he lived up there in a tent. Mr.—and also he was promoted to be postmaster up there at Oil Center, Louisiana, Howard R. Hughes, Sr., not Junior, but Senior. Young Howard, I have nursed him on my knee a many a day. And they were a mighty fine set of people. They was a hundred per cent proof, son, all of those boys."

The rumor that Hughes "stole" the drill invention that made him a

106

millionaire reached all the way to Keokuk. "Well, that is—that's a sort of rumor that got passed around somewhat," admits William L. Talbot, a Keokuk native and historian.

Hughes himself was more discreet about the inspiration for his invention. "The chief drawback to the rotary system was its inability to drill with reasonable speed rock strata, interbedded with caving formation," he wrote in 1912. "From this need I invented a cone bit, in the manufacture of which all my efforts are . . . centered." Whoever or whatever may have helped Hughes conceive the notion of the cone-shaped bit, and wherever its inception, Howard Hughes, Sr., applied for the patent on November 20, 1908, and the invention of the bit was a source of pride as well as riches. "It is one of my fond plans," he once mused, "to drill the deepest well in the world. Amundsen has discovered the South Pole; Peary found the North Pole. The outermost ends of the earth have been found; the road towards the center is still virgin soil." Hughes viewed this lofty aspiration with characteristic good humor and self-mockery. "It has long been my wish to test the faith of our fathers that there is a region warmer than Texas, if a man will only go deep enough to find it," he wrote his Harvard classmates, "and thus it may be that the prophecy of a friend of mine will be fulfilled. He said 'This time you are on a fair way to your destination.' "

"I had been dragging my anchors for thirteen years, and it had come time to stop," wrote Howard Hughes, Sr., shortly after the invention of the cone-shaped bit. So Hughes and his partner, W. B. Sharp, set up the Sharp-Hughes Tool Company in Houston, and settled into the business of manufacturing and designing drill bits. Hughes soon tired of having a partner and bought out Sharp's interest in the company, leaving him the sole owner of a manufacturing gold mine. Prospects had improved considerably for the adventurous drifter who had captured the hand of Allene Gano, and Howard Hughes, Sr., assumed the role of millionaire-inventor as if he had been born to it. His domestic life took a dramatic turn for the conventional, also. Dinkins' research team could find little to indicate or suggest that Howard, Sr., after his marriage to Allene Gano, was anything but a model husband and father. No unknown heirs there, they concluded.

When Allene Hughes died in 1922, it was a real blow to Howard, Sr., as evidenced by his paranoid avoidance of the Yoakum family residence. He snapped back socially, however, and there is every indication that Hughes spent the two years between his wife's death and his own making the most of his widower status and his nouveaux riches. He took a sudden interest in moviemaking, began to spend a considerable amount of time in California near his screenwriter-brother Rupert, and was often seen arm-in-arm with Hollywood's most glamorous women. In fact, Howard Hughes, Sr., appears in both the 1923 and 1924 editions of the Los Angeles city directories, listed as the president of the Hughes Tool Company, residing in 1924 at the Ambassador Hotel in downtown Los Angeles. Like father, like son. Howard, Sr., in contrast to his more eccentric son, had a genuine charisma with women that was not altogether related to his wealth, though it was plainly not his looks that shaped his appeal. One relative described him as "short and Jewish-looking," and it is not entirely inaccurate. He did not have the dark good looks of his son, but he did possess an abundance of charm, and he knew how to indulge women. The claims against his estate at the time of his death in 1924 included gigantic sums spent weekly on jewels, flowers, and clothing. If his department and specialty store bills are any indication, Hughes was something of a dandy. He accumulated a huge running tab at Brooks Brothers, mostly for evening clothes, stayed at the finest hotels in New York and Los Angeles, and belonged to a number of social clubs coast-to-coast. Hughes, Sr., definitely lived in style and luxury. For all his socializing, however, he did not remarry, nor did he father any more children, so far as Dinkins and staff could determine, up to the time of his unexpected heart attack in January 1924.

With reluctance, then, Mrs. Fay crossed the name of Howard Hughes, Sr., off her list in the search for unknown heirs and turned her attention to other members of the Hughes family she considered less appealing, though, she and her colleagues would soon discover, no less flamboyant and certainly as mysterious. The investigation for Phase One of the heirship determination of Howard R. Hughes, Jr., had come to its inevitable end, and Dinkins had very little to show for it in court that uneventful Monday in July 1981. The exhaustive research he commissioned to search for unknown heirs to claim inheritance as a child, wife, brother, or sister of Howard Hughes, Jr., could produce nothing more substantive than speculations and startling coincidences; and unanswered questions are not admissible as evidence in a court of law. The law requires documentation to prove heirship. During his months as ad litem, Dinkins had not assembled any such tangible proof of a relationship for any of the individuals who might have fallen within this first category of kinship to Hughes. So Ted Dinkins sat in silence as Judge Gregory ruled that Howard R. Hughes, Jr., died without brother or sister, child or wife, leaving his two associates to wrestle with their doubts and misgivings as to whether this were not in fact, if not at law, the wrong resolution.

PART TWO
The Texas Aristocrats:
Hughes' Maternal Relatives

5

Mama's Boy

By the time Phase Two of the heirship determination trial of Howard R. Hughes, Jr., geared up on August 10, 1981—barely one month after the spectacle in which long-lost ''wives'' and ''children'' thoroughly tested Judge Pat Gregory's patience and good humor—the media and an intrigued public had braced themselves to expect almost anything from the tangled Hughes proceedings.

Instead, the August hearing proved to be a genuine nonevent. The trial to determine Hughes' maternal heirship was very much like the side of the family it concerned: reserved and unostentatious. The maternal branch of the Howard Hughes family tree avoids publicity just as assiduously as Hughes himself attracted it. It was appropriate that their section of the three-part trial should come off with a sense of decorum rare in the estate proceedings.

This controlled and slightly dull ambience was disturbed only once, before Judge Gregory entered the courtroom and called the assemblage to order. As a precaution, Gregory had required observers to sign their names, addresses, and affiliations at the door to Probate Court 2. This orderly procedure was interrupted by the arrival of Stella Mabry, a carry-over from the first phase of the heirship trials. Mabry bolted past the guard stationed at the door and into the packed courtroom, brushing aside the flustered bailiff who was attempting to hand her a pencil. Instead, she stridently announced her name, adding, "I'm hard of hearing!" She apologized to her captive audience for missing Phase One (the proper forum for stating her belief that she is Mrs. Howard Hughes, Jr.). "I've got the shingles, ya see," she blurted in explanation. For an awkward moment, the attorneys and spectators wondered whether to laugh or ignore her. Before they could react, Mabry flaunted a stack of loose sheets, proclaiming that she had the papers to prove her claim, "so everything will be all right." The bewildered bailiff ushered her into the courtroom, where she took her seat with an air of importance. Throughout the trial, she interrupted the proceedings from time to time with exaggerated coughs and indignant comments.

Several local television stations dispatched sketch artists to recreate the legal drama being played out that day, and representatives of the national news magazines dutifully attended, but there wasn't much to report. Tom Shubert, a partner at the Andrews, Kurth, Campbell, and Jones law firm and counsel for some of the maternal relatives, set the tone early on, when he propped a huge chart displaying the maternal heirs on an easel in front of Judge Gregory. This visual aid was the highlight of a tedious day. In the chart, Shubert graphically presented what a seemingly endless string of birth, death, and marriage certificates would legally confirm: that at the time of his death in 1976, Howard Hughes, Jr., left one surviving aunt (Mrs. Lummis), twelve first cousins, and four first cousins-once-removed to inherit his prodigious fortune on the Gano side of the family. (Another maternal aunt and uncle died before Howard, Jr., and one first cousin passed away in 1967.)

There was little else necessary to prove these family relationships to the satisfaction of the court, and no apparent controversy about them. The Ganos' heritage was part of the fabric of the Old South, and charting their family tree was a simple exercise toward the recovery of the windfall that was their birthright. To introduce into evidence the statistical documents that demonstrated this, Shubert called as his first witness Mrs. Mary Louis Ulmer, a retired genealogical librarian hired on behalf of the maternal side of the family shortly after Hughes' death.

Mrs. Ulmer was responsible for the Gano chart Shubert had enlarged for the trial. To assemble it, she testified, she made inquiries of family members and studied Bibles, correspondence, government records (marriages, deaths, wills, birth and death certificates, and census records), as well as a miscellany of other sources, such as tombstones, county and family histories—just as Dinkins, his associate, and Mrs. Fay had been doing for both sides of the family for over five years. Of course, Mrs. Ulmer's job was made easier by the fact that most of the maternal family members were still living, and there was no reason to dispute the data about those who were deceased. Her principal task was to collect vital statistics to confirm well-established dates of birth, death, and marriage.

Piece by piece, then, Mrs. Ulmer patiently read into evidence the relevant information present on the death certificates of Howard Hughes, Junior and Senior; Allene Gano Hughes, followed by Allene's parents; her brother and two sisters; and finally, their children and grandchildren. This was done to establish the line of inheritance on the Gano side of the family. She concluded by saying that the individuals portrayed on the chart correctly reflected the maternal grandparents, aunts, uncles, cousins, and first cousins-once-removed of Howard R. Hughes, Jr. She added that there were no children other than those depicted on the chart and mentioned that she had been given access to nearly six hundred pieces of correspondence, and in addition checked Dallas and Houston records for possible adoptions in her quest for an authentic list of heirs. In short, Mrs. Ulmer had not been denied access to any records by the Ganos or their progeny, and there was no question in her mind that this was the complete and accurate set of relatives on Hughes' mother's side of the family. Ted Dinkins, as the court-appointed attorney for the unknown heirs, echoed Mrs. Ulmer's belief that the chart correctly depicted the maternal heirs of Howard R. Hughes, Jr., and the Gano genealogist was excused from the stand.

By the time the maternal heirship trial took place in 1981, Annette Gano Lummis had died (in 1980). As the closest known living relative of Hughes at the time of his death, her spoken history of the family was critical to the heirship determination. In place of her live testimony, selected portions of Mrs. Lummis' deposition were read into evidence and taken down by the court reporter to establish the family history.

As his only other witness, Shubert called Mrs. Annette Lummis Neff, a daughter of Annette Gano Lummis, and a first cousin of Hughes. Mrs. Neff had become the custodian of the family photograph album, and she appeared on the stand to introduce such memorabilia as a photograph of Howard, Jr., and Mrs. Neff's "Aunt Allene," several pages from the Gano family Bible, a photograph of Allene and Annette Gano's parents

(Howard, Jr.'s, maternal grandparents), and letters as ancient as 1886 describing the birth of one of Allene Gano's brothers who died in infancy. Mrs. Neff, in contrast to the disturbed individuals who appeared for Phase One of the heirship trial, spoke with a deep, steady voice, projecting an image of quiet dignity during her brief testimony. A tall, handsome woman, she was dressed simply in a crisp white blouse and straight skirt and possessed a stately bearing not unlike photographs of her mother at the same age. Still, she admitted she had only seen her famous cousin Howard face-to-face once in her life, introducing a touch of irony to her testimony as family spokesperson in a trial to establish their right to inherit millions of Hughes dollars. The truth is that Howard Hughes, Jr., had been just as much a stranger to her and her family as he had been to the millions of Americans who read of his exploits with admiration and wonderment.

By midafternoon, the trial to determine Hughes' maternal heirs had inched its way to its inevitable conclusion. Judge Gregory ratified what the Ulmer chart set forth, and ruled that the individuals there represented were the bona fide maternal heirs of Howard R. Hughes, Jr. The few Gano relatives who turned up to keep Mrs. Neff company breathed an almost audible sigh of relief, noticeably cheered to have this unseemly bit of business behind them. Theirs had been an attitude of apparent disinterest, dismay, and possibly disgust throughout the five-year ordeal. Hughes' maternal relatives always seemed slightly embarrassed by the boon of their birthright, as if they were above the legal turmoil that brought them to their position of inheritance in August 1981. The Ganos were well-to-do in their own right and unaccustomed to the kind of attention the circumstances of Howard, Jr.'s, death focused on them. They led quiet, ordered lives. Yet did their smug, superior air belie a greater interest? Just who were these aristocratic Ganos, thrust into the limelight by the death of their eccentric cousin? And how did they figure in the legal maneuvering that took place following the search for a Hughes will?

Memories of Sonny

Howard Hughes, Jr.'s, mother, Allene Stone Gano, bore "perhaps the proudest name in the city's social register," according to the *Dallas Morning News,* at the time of Sonny's birth in 1905. Her grandfather, Richard Montgomery Gano, was a Confederate general and a legendary Indian fighter who moved his family from Kentucky to Texas in 1856 and settled in a place now known as Grapevine, a small town about fifteen miles from Dallas. The "Gano cabin," into which the family moved sometime after their arrival, was actually the first multiple-story residence built anywhere near the community and, according to a grandson-in-law of the general's, a "showplace in its day." The cabin was recently moved to the historic Old City Park section of Dallas, enshrined as a "living history" exhibit not far from Gano Street.

General Gano had twelve children. Three died in infancy, nine lived to maturity. Of those nine, there were three daughters and six sons. One of the sons became the father of Allene Gano and grandfather of Howard Hughes, Jr. He was known as W. B. Gano. "His name was William Beriah, but he hated Beriah, so he called himself W. B.," explained his daughter Annette Gano Lummis. W. B. was graduated from Harvard and earned his L.L.B. from Harvard Law School in 1877. On August 31, 1882, he took a bride in Georgetown, Kentucky, in a ceremony performed by his brother, the Reverend John Allen Gano (after whom Allene was named). "You won't believe it!" exclaimed Annette Lummis, when asked her mother's name. "Jeannette de Lafayette Grissom!"

Jeannette de Lafayette Grissom Gano, who possessed a French pedigree as impressive as her name, gave birth to Allene on July 14, 1883, a little over a year after her marriage to W. B. Gano. "Allene was the oldest," Annette Lummis once testified, "then my father . . . and my mother lost two children. My brother came next, and there was eight years between me and Allene. And then after me, I had a younger sister, Martha. So there was four of us that lived and two died as infants." The four children, then, of W. B. and Jeannette Gano were Allene, Richard Chilton (known as Chilton), Annette, and Martha: Howard Hughes, Jr.'s, mother, uncle, and two aunts, respectively.

The W. B. Gano family settled into a life of gentility just outside Dallas, where they remained until the turn of the century when Gano, a prosperous lawyer, moved his brood into the city proper. "We had moved from the country and sold our five-acre orchard of peaches, because Allene was nineteen and old enough to come out," Annette Lummis reminisced. It was shortly after Allene Gano's formal debut into society that she met and married the rakish Mr. Hughes, Sr., and embarked on her adventurous new life as the wife of a roving wildcatter-inventor. Her mother died the next year, 1905, about the time Sonny was born, putting an additional burden on Allene as the oldest of the four Gano children. By this time, Chilton was seventeen, Annette fourteen, and Martha thirteen. "My connection with Howard and Allene starts way back," mused Mrs. Lummis, "when my mother died and my sister Allene took charge of us all, and every summer we would go to Allene's, and she would fix our clothes for school, and she practically took the place of my mother to help my father, who lived with us in Dallas, still."

The year Sonny was born Howard and Allene Hughes were living at 1404 Crawford Street in Houston. "I was allowed to go down my Christmas vacation and see him before he was a couple of months old, on Crawford Street," Mrs. Lummis reflected. The next several years found Howard and Allene following the oil game from field to field throughout the Gulf Coast, and they moved from apartment to apartment in Houston (and Oil City, Louisiana, from 1907 to 1909) between 1905 and 1918. The Houston city directories show a different address for the Hugheses each year during that time. After Howard, Sr.'s, prospects brightened so considerably with the receipt of the letters patent on his drill bit in 1908 and the subsequent success of the Hughes Tool Company, he built the home at 3921 Yoakum. He began to revel in his swelling reputation as a business and social leader. "He had the first car in Houston," recalls Rupert Hughes' stepdaughter Avis, "a Pierce-Arrow." During these years, Annette Gano and her brother and sister visited Howard, Sr., Allene, and their son, Howard, Jr., infrequently. "Well, I saw him every summer when I came down," she stated. "My sister got my clothes ready for school. I saw him off and on."

W. B. Gano, Allene and Annette's father, died in 1913. By 1919, Annette was twenty-eight and unmarried, and it was decided that she would move in with Howard and Allene, who were by then settled in the Yoakum house. "After the war, in 1919, I came and was met by Howard and Allene, who said I was going to live with them until I felt like something," is Mrs. Lummis' description of the turn of events. Of course, by 1919 Sonny was away at school, so his aunt Annette saw little of him after her move to the Yoakum residence. (Sonny began his schooling at the Christ Church Cathedral School in Houston, later attended Professor Prosso's, a private school in the city, and briefly attended a public school, South End Junior High in Houston. By 1920, however, he had transferred to the posh Fessenden preparatory school in Massachusetts, a more suitable institution for a lad of his sensibilities and background.)

"He was perfectly beautiful," his aunt recalled fondly, when asked to describe Sonny at the time of these visits. "And he was a charming young boy." Though Mrs. Lummis is undoubtedly prejudiced in her opinion of the young Howard Hughes, Jr., it is a viewpoint apparently shared by most others who knew him as a teenager. Avis McIntyre, Rupert Hughes' stepdaughter, met Sonny in 1916, when he was ten or eleven. She remembers him as a "very attractive little boy," though "rather a solemn little fellow. Seemed to be quite good at golf . . . that's all I remember about him." Mrs. Lummis confirms Howard, Jr.'s, obsession with golf. "Every vacation Allene and I met him so he could play golf at White Sulphur, but he—he was crazy about golf."

The doctors and aides who were with Hughes in his later years all agree that Hughes seemed to have had a happy boyhood, filled with great admiration for his father, and adulation for his beautiful, doting mother. And why not? Sonny was the apple of their eye, a spoiled, pampered, and overprotected only child.

In 1922, the dream began to dissolve. Allene Gano Hughes was taken to the Baptist Hospital in Houston for routine female surgery, what was then called "curettment": a scraping of the uterus for dead tissue. Allene Hughes died during this simple procedure at the age of thirty-nine. The hospital is sensitive even today when asked about the event. "She was taken for a minor operation and they gave her too much anesthetic, I think," speculates Annette Lummis. "Anyway, she died on the operating table at the Baptist Hospital in Houston." On her death certificate, the attending physician, a Dr. Gavin Hamilton, stated that she died during administration of a gas anesthesia for curettment. (The question of Allene Hughes' inability to bear children after the birth of Howard, Jr., has never been fully explained. When asked during her deposition whether this was caused by some complication of childbirth, Mrs. Lummis replied, "I don't know anything about it. I was eight years younger, and I wasn't told nothing . . . all I know is the doctor told her.")

After the death of Allene Hughes, Howard, Sr., needed someone to look after Sonny, to free him to pursue his newfound interest in movies. Since Annette Gano was already staying in the Yoakum house, she seemed a logical choice for this task. "His father was possessed that I would live with them," she cites. "I had been living with them since 1919, and he was possessed that I would not get married, that I would stay and raise Sonny." When his mother died in 1922, Sonny was a student at the Thatcher School in Ojai, California, and this figured in Howard, Sr.'s, plans. "I was engaged," Mrs. Lummis continued, "and I told him that I would give him one year and live with Sonny in California, where he wanted me to, and then I was going to get married. I thought it was not good to have Sonny live with a little old maid." At that time the California arrangements were put together including Sonny, his aunt Annette, and Katherine Callaway, a first cousin of Allene and Annette's from Dallas. Kitty Callaway's mother was a daughter of General Richard M. Gano, sister to W. B.; family insiders say Howard, Jr., was probably closer to Kitty Callaway than any other relative, including his aunt Annette. "Katherine has kept up with, really, probably Nadine [Henley] and Howard, better than I," confessed Mrs. Lummis in her deposition. Mrs. Callaway's husband concurs. "Well, when . . . Mrs. Callaway's mother became, say, middle-aged, she became kind of the matriarch of the family," he offers in explanation.

117

"It was a very large family and it kind of split: half of them, approximately half of them, went to Houston, the others remained in Dallas and vicinity. So we always called them the 'Houston relatives' and the 'Dallas relatives.' . . . When Mrs. McLaurin died (Mrs. Callaway's mother), Mrs. Callaway became—assumed—the unofficial role of matriarch of the family."

Mr. Callaway tells a slightly different version of what transpired at the time of Allene Hughes' death. "When Mrs. Hughes died, Mr. Hughes phoned Mrs. McLaurin and asked her and Mrs. Callaway to come to Houston—not only for the funeral, but to stay down there and try to do something about Howard, during that trying time." According to Mr. Callaway, his wife stepped in to assume that responsibility. "She more or less took the place, as best she could, of his mother. And kept the house open and kept his little friends coming in, and kept parties going." Thus both Mrs. Lummis (then Annette Gano) and Mrs. Callaway (then Kitty McLaurin) accompanied Howard, Sr., and Sonny to California, where they took charge of Howard, Jr., leaving Howard, Sr., free to amuse himself elsewhere. "Well, he was keeping an eye on us," Mrs. Lummis acknowledged, "but he really was interested in the movies, movie people."

This babysitting service continued for the promised year, when both Kitty and Annette returned to their fiancés, and Sonny stayed behind in California with his father. When Annette married Dr. Frederick Lummis in 1923, shortly after her return to Houston, she asked Howard, Sr., to stand in for her father, who had died eleven years earlier. He didn't show. "I came back to Houston to get married, and I was married at Martha's house, and Big Howard was still in California and was supposed to come and give me away," she reflected. "Sonny was still in California, and Sonny flew back, and was in my wedding, and Howard didn't come. . . . My brother gave me away."

A few months later, Big Howard died, and approximately a year after that, Sonny was a married man. Sonny had spent the fifteen months after his father's death and before his marriage to Ella Rice at the Yoakum house with his aunt Annette and uncle Fred Lummis, during his short-lived studies at the Rice Institute. The following year, 1926, he followed his father's dream to Hollywood. By his own choice, he saw his aunt only once more before his death in 1976.

Yet it was to Annette Lummis, her children, and her brother and sister's children and grandchildren that more than half of Howard Hughes, Jr.'s, fortune was destined to go: relatives he hadn't seen or spoken to in over thirty years.

6

All in the Family

Throughout the heirship investigation of Howard R. Hughes, Jr. there was never any doubt that the maternal relatives were who they said they were; no dark clouds of suspicion hung over the family tree. As early as May 1977, Mary Fay dispelled whatever misgivings Dinkins may have entertained as she diligently went about her business of confirming the heirs on Hughes' mother's side. One month after she had been hired by Dinkins and approved by the court as the official Hughes genealogist, Mrs. Fay began to collect the certificates she would need to put her mind at ease concerning the Ganos. On May 23, 1977, she sent a progress report to Dinkins during a document-collecting trip. "I plan to check the Gano records in Dallas, Texas, on my way back to Houston," she wrote. "I feel sure these are straightforward."

119

Further research confirmed her predictions, and Dinkins largely put out of his mind the Gano side of the family. When the time came to prove Hughes' heirship and all the adjunct legal entanglements had been sorted out, he felt confident in the authenticity of the Gano family tree. If it came to a division between the maternal and paternal sides of the family, he could lend his stamp of approval to the chart Mrs. Ulmer had prepared and Mrs. Fay had verified. The question that plagued Ted Dinkins as he pondered the Gano family tree was not who's who, but who gets what? And once again he had Howard, Jr., to thank for his state of bewilderment. The possible legal scenarios brought about by Hughes' apparent failure to make a valid will and the uncertainty about his legal residence at the time of his death presented a study in confusion over inheritance rights, even within the maternal line.

The problem went something like this. During the last seven years of his life, Howard Hughes, Jr., zipped around the globe like a misguided missile, never lighting in one spot long enough to call it home, or such was the theory. From 1970 to 1976, he spent time in luxury hotels in Nassau, Managua, Vancouver, London, and Acapulco in a frantic effort to avoid the legal and tax entanglements that had shadowed him for years. When his life ended in April 1976 with the surprise announcement that no last will and testament could be located, a thorny legal problem arose. In order to administer Hughes' estate, it was necessary to determine his legal residence. Once established, that state would have the right to collect millions of dollars in inheritance taxes. The task was enormous.

The determination of Hughes' legal residence, or "domicile," as it is known in legal circles, was no small matter. As lawyers involved in the case were fond of pointing out, domicile is purely a matter of intent. One can live in New York one day, and become a legal resident of Connecticut the next—if the move was made with the *intent* to establish a permanent home. Without that intent, an individual may remain domiciled in the place of his or her birth, though he or she may have been physically absent from that state for years. One is called the *domicile of origin;* the other is known as the *domicile of choice.* Whether Hughes had abandoned his Texas domicile of origin and established a new legal residence elsewhere involved questions of fact and law still unresolved. Before his hotel-hopping of the 1970s, Howard Hughes had spent four unusual years at the Desert Inn Hotel in Las Vegas, where he also accumulated large holdings in real estate and invested in other Nevada-based financial ventures. Prior to that, he lived mostly in and around Los Angeles in rented houses or hotels, a pattern he established in 1926 after his marriage to Ella Rice. Of course, he had strong ties to the state of Texas, where he was born and raised, but he

120

fled the state at the age of nineteen, to return only a handful of times before his death in 1976. Of which state was Hughes a legal resident: Texas, California, Nevada, or one of the exotic locales to which he had wandered in his last years? That was the threshold question.

It made a great deal of difference to the Hughes heirs which state prevailed, and not out of a sense of allegiance. Rather, the outcome of the fight over Hughes' domicile would determine not only the size of their inheritance but, in some instances, whether they would inherit at all. Under the laws of the state of Nevada, for example, without a valid will or the discovery of any closer relatives (brother, sister, wife or child), Hughes' estate would pass entirely to Annette Lummis. By this scheme, the paternal relatives would not inherit anything, nor would the more distantly related maternal heirs—Mrs. Lummis' nieces and nephews. This was also the case in California. (Nevada, however, had the added attraction of taking less of the estate in taxes, leaving more for the heirs.) Texas, by contrast, would divide the estate in half: 50 percent to go to the paternal relatives, 50 percent to be divided equally among the descendants of W. B. and Jeannette Gano (Mrs. Lummis and the children or grandchildren of Chilton and Martha Gano).

Not surprisingly, the issue of Hughes' domicile became inflammatory. Theories about his legal residence were exchanged like baseball cards for some months, while the heirs and would-be heirs scrutinized each other and the opposing counsel, using the issue for bargaining power in the legal chess game that ensued. In the background, the competing states staged their own battle to declare Hughes a legal resident, eager to collect an estimated $300 million dollars in inheritance taxes. Since Hughes was brought to the Texas Medical Center in Houston on the last day of his life, and since his closest kin lived in the Bayou City, a temporary administration was established in Harris County, Texas. An ancillary administration was set up in California, and a third in Delaware to oversee the stock in Summa Corporation, Hughes' alter-ego. As one of his first orders of business, Houston judge Pat Gregory set the date for a jury trial to determine the legal residence of Howard R. Hughes, Jr. In the meantime, California had expressed some interest in pursuing the domicile question, and there was even some talk of the same in Mexico and the Bahamas. Each of these entities could conceivably declare Hughes a legal resident and seek to collect the inheritance taxes on his estate, giving rise to a bizarre scenario in which Howard Hughes' estate would be literally taxed out of existence.

The Heir Apparent

Out of this sea of confusion one relative emerged: William Rice Lummis, the eldest son of Frederick and Annette Gano Lummis. William Lummis, at the time of his cousin Howard's death, was a partner in the Andrews, Kurth law firm in Houston. It was Lummis who rushed to Methodist Hospital that fateful day in April 1976 to claim the withered body of Howard Hughes, Jr., standing in as next-of-kin for his mother. And it was Lummis who, from that moment forward, took charge of the myriad details attendant to his cousin's death, assuming in rapid succession the many positions of responsibility Hughes had vacated.

Acting in conjunction with Summa counsel Chester Davis, and with the help of his colleagues at Andrews, Kurth, Lummis persuaded the Chancery Court in Delaware to appoint him temporary sole stockholder in Summa, and he was named temporary coadministrator of the Hughes estate in Texas and Nevada. On May 15, 1976, one month after Hughes' death, Lummis took an indefinite leave of absence from Andrews, Kurth and moved to Las Vegas to run Summa Corporation (of which he is now chairman of the board). Within thirty days, William R. Lummis had assumed almost total control of his late cousin's empire. Reporters began to label him the "heir apparent," and much was made of the physical resemblance between Annette Lummis' son and her extraordinary nephew. Yet two people could not have led more dissimilar lives.

William R. Lummis, the man who assumed control of the Hughes domain, had seen his cousin Howard face-to-face only twice in his life. Lummis was four years old on the first occasion and can recall nothing about it. The second meeting was during the celebration of Hughes' spectacular 1938 round-the-world flight, when Howard returned in triumph to Houston (for the last time) to receive a hero's welcome from the mayor and hometown friends. (There was even some serious talk at the time of naming the soon-to-be-opened Houston airport "Howard Hughes International.") Lummis was only nine at the time and remembers that his cousin stayed at the Yoakum home for two or three days to attend parties and parades in his honor. Hughes sent a thank-you note to Annette Lummis some days later extending special greetings to "that adorable William" who, according to Hughes, "asked more questions" than the others.

William Lummis and Hughes had never exchanged cards, correspondence, or gifts of any kind through the years, nor had they spoken to each other by telephone. And, most amazing of all, though Hughes retained a number of Andrews, Kurth attorneys with whom he consulted right up to the time of his death (in fact, Frank Andrews, the founding partner, drew up his first will in 1925), he was never aware that he had a cousin who was a partner at the firm. (The Lummis connection actually goes even deeper. Lummis' father-in-law, Palmer

Bradley, was also an Andrews, Kurth partner, and supervised many of Hughes' legal transactions during his years with the firm.) Though there has been some testimony to the contrary, Lummis insists he did not handle any Hughes matters while practicing law at Andrews, Kurth.

The truth was that William Lummis had no deeper connection to Howard R. Hughes, Jr., than his other cousins, who knew him not at all. Furthermore, his mother, Annette Gano Lummis, was actually herself a virtual stranger to Hughes the last forty years of his life, though Lummis described them as "very close" during his deposition testimony. Was this strange turn of events that thrust William Lummis into control of the Hughes empire an appropriate denouement to Howard Hughes' life?

Family Ties

"Well, it's well known I think that . . . Howard Hughes, after he left Texas, kind of cut away from his family," concedes Carl Callaway, Kitty Callaway's husband. "It was my impression that Mrs. Callaway was closer really to Howard Hughes than any member of his family, even including his aunt, Mrs. Lummis." Of course, neither Katherine Callaway nor any of her children will inherit a part of the Hughes estate under any of the inheritance schemes, even the more liberal Texas intestate statute. Kitty Callaway is a daughter of W. B.'s sister, so she and her children do not fall within the line of inheritance—nor do they seem to care. Both Carl Callaway, a distinguished Dallas attorney, and his wife have kept a low profile in the tangled aftermath of Howard Hughes' death.

Still, as "close" as Howard, Jr., allegedly was to Mrs. Callaway, he last saw her in 1938, too. And the aides who attended him in the last twenty years of his life confirm that Hughes rarely, if ever, referred to his family.

The Houston celebration of Hughes' record-breaking round-the-world flight was really his last contact with any of his relatives, and even that seems to have been an awkward encounter for him. He stayed at the Yoakum home of his boyhood, occupied now by his aunt Annette and her family, where he was feted and fussed over for several days. He later confided to his aunt that the gala reception was a great surprise to him. "He came upstairs later," Mrs. Lummis recalled, "when they all left, and he said, 'I never had a bigger shock and surprise in my life. I didn't think any of my friends would speak to me after Ella and I got a divorce.' "

Despite the warm welcome, Hughes never returned to Houston and never saw any of his maternal family again. He moved in different worlds than they, and the difference in lifestyles was made dramatically apparent to him during his brief and unhappy marriage to Ella Rice. He later confided to an aide that he and Ella were "from different social planes," and Hughes probably felt as uncomfortable in the Junior League atmosphere of his mother's family as they felt in the movie colony he inhabited. Ella Rice's agonizing struggle to fit into Hughes' world was no doubt a painful reminder to him of the differences between himself and his Texas family. (Annette Lummis was in fact related to Ella Rice through her husband, Dr. Frederick Lummis.) When Hughes divorced Ella Rice, he also rejected the way of life she represented, and that included his mother's family.

When Howard Hughes initially broke away from his family to move to Hollywood in 1926, it became increasingly clear that he had put Texas behind him. And yet in certain ways he tried to preserve the souvenirs of his youth. During his marital problems with Ella, for example, he learned that Dr. and Mrs. Lummis were meeting with architects to design a new home for their family. The Lummises had been living in the Hughes home on Yoakum Boulevard since their marriage and quite naturally felt that it was time they got a home of their own. "Howard found out about it," Mrs. Lummis reflected, "and went berserk. He said, 'You have to live at Yoakum and I want to give it to you.' " Though Hughes himself had cut the Houston and family ties, he was determined that his aunt remain in the Yoakum home, preserving it as a memorial to his parents, his family, his background. He acceded to his aunt's request for more space and had a huge and beautiful library built as an addition to the family home—anything to keep her in the house. "He used that as bait," Mrs. Lummis smiled. "So, anyway, I accepted with pleasure, and we didn't build a house, and we lived many years very closely at Yoakum." Hughes deeded the house to Mrs. Lummis in 1926. She eventually sold it to St. Thomas University, which had taken over many of the houses in the neighborhood, with the express condition that the library remain untouched. "It is the loveliest room in Houston," she told university officials.

And yet, after the Houston celebration in 1938, Mrs. Lummis was never to see or talk to her nephew again. "I wouldn't know where to get him," she explained to lawyers who asked why she never tried to telephone him after 1938. By the 1950s, she stopped writing to him as well, closing off their communication completely. This was about the time Hughes began his system of screening correspondence and calls through an office located at 7000 Romaine Street in Los Angeles. "Well, I am amazed at how well I wrote him," Mrs. Lummis said indignantly. "I stopped writing to him when I had to send my letters to 7000 Romaine Street and they were read by Nadine—and I just wrote him that wasn't the way I was corresponding!" Carl Callaway confirms this unusual procedure. "Well," he acknowledged, "it was very difficult to tell when the correspondence would be from (Hughes) directly or through his private secretary, Miss Nadine Henley." Yet, knowing his aunt's disgust with the screening system, Hughes did nothing to make himself more accessible to her, nor did he compensate by writing to her more frequently; from 1938 to 1976, Hughes wrote Mrs. Lummis only twice.

In 1946, Hughes was in the plane crash that nearly took his life. When word of his accident reached her, Annette Lummis flew to the Good Samaritan Hospital in Los Angeles to be at her nephew's side, but Hughes would not let her in to see him, even though they had not met in more than eight years. "I flew out there, and he was very badly hurt, and they wouldn't let me see him," she recalled with disgust. "I came back and never had seen him. I blamed the doctor, but I am not sure I was right." She wasn't. Glenn Odekirk, Hughes' right-hand man, remembers how it happened. "[Hughes] had me go talk to her like I did to a lot of other people that came to visit him, and explain to her why he didn't want anyone to see him in the physical condition he was in." So Mrs. Lummis returned to Houston, thwarted by her nephew in her last attempt to see him. She never spoke to him or saw him again.

In 1971, however, she received a telegram from Hughes, the first communication she had received from him in more than thirty years. The occasion was her eightieth birthday, which Hughes acknowledged with this sentimental birthday greeting from his self-imposed exile in the Bahamas:

> Dear Annette:
> It doesn't seem possible that my favorite aunt is about to have her 80th birthday STOP You were always after me to come visit but since I never quite made it I still remember you as young and lovely and so kind STOP I am sure years have not really changed you and I hope you'll be around for many more STOP My warmest good wish to you and your family.

It is clear from this telegram that Hughes still remembered his aunt with great fondness.

Kitty Callaway didn't fare much better in her efforts to communicate with her famous relative. She, like Mrs. Lummis, last saw Howard, Jr., in 1938, and she never spoke with him by phone. "If Mrs. Callaway ever communicated with Mr. Howard Hughes by telephone, it was 50 years ago while he was in his teens," wrote Callaway in 1977. Years later, during Hughes' residence at the Desert Inn in Las Vegas, the Callaways had occasion to make a trip to that city. They stayed as Hughes' guests at one of his hotels, and in a gesture uniquely Hughes, they were assigned a limousine and one of his Mormon aides as a "companion" throughout their visit. This was at the height of the Hughes mystique, and Callaway himself is not sure how this celebrity treatment came about. "Well," he reflected, " . . . I think it came about because Miss Henley knew that we were going to Las Vegas, and Mr. Hughes asked her to make these arrangements. I think *she* made all the arrangements." It had been thirty years since Hughes had seen Kitty Callaway, possibly his favorite relative, and yet he made no effort to see her or her husband while they were in Las Vegas. Nor did the Callaways try to make contact with him, Callaway admits.

For all their professed affection and devotion, Kitty Callaway neither saw nor talked to Howard Hughes any more than did his aunt Annette. Unlike Mrs. Lummis, however, Mrs. Callaway did keep the relationship alive, using Nadine Henley as an intermediary. (Although it should be noted that Henley herself lost telephone contact with Hughes about 1966 and last saw her boss face-to-face in 1972. On the last occasion, Hughes was asleep and Henley never spoke to him.) "Mrs. Callaway and Miss Henley have kept rather close in touch with each other down through the years," Callaway concedes. "Now you'd asked how often (she) would hear from Mr. Howard Hughes, and I couldn't answer the question, because . . . some communications or something might come, but it might have been inspired by Miss Henley rather than Howard, I don't know." Kitty Callaway's only tangible evidence, then, of her relationship to Howard Hughes came once a year to her home. "Every Christmas," Callaway says with pride, "he always remembered her with a beautiful plant to be placed in front of our mantel." And when Hughes died, Nadine Henley notified Katherine Callaway first, according to Callaway.

The Maternal Heirs Cut a Deal

After the news of Howard Hughes' death broke and William Rice Lummis rushed to claim the body, he wasted little time reflecting on the past. In addition to fulfilling his new responsibilities as chairman of the board and sole stockholder of Summa Corporation, not to mention his serving as temporary administrator of the Hughes estate in Texas and Nevada (his cousin, Richard C. Gano, Jr., held that post in California), Lummis had numerous things to take into consideration as an heir apparent to Hughes' fortune. Not only would he inherit in his own right if the estate were ultimately divided according to Texas laws of descent and distribution, but he would also benefit indirectly if Hughes were found to be a legal resident of Nevada or California. In that eventuality, his mother would be Howard Hughes' sole heir, and Lummis would in turn be heir to his mother's greatly expanded fortune. In either case, Lummis would be a much richer man by virtue of his late cousin's carelessness concerning the disposition of his estate.

Because of the potential conflict between his mother and his cousins on the question of inheritance, Lummis immediately called a meeting of the twelve living maternal first cousins to designate a family spokesman who would, in the words of Lummis' lead attorney at Andrews, Kurth, "run the show." Lummis was the obvious choice. He then did a very novel thing. In concert with his Andrews, Kurth counsel, he conceived the notion of fashioning a "fair and equitable arrangement" to divide his cousin's vast estate privately among those individuals the group considered to be his heirs—taking into account the conflicting laws of California, Texas, and Nevada. This meeting led to the preparation of a sixteen-page "Settlement Agreement," a sophisticated legal contract filed in Judge Gregory's court in July 1976, only three months after Hughes' death. That document would prove to be exceedingly controversial.

The private speculation was that Lummis had orchestrated this agreement among potential heirs at his mother's behest to avoid an unseemly internecine power struggle. Certainly Annette Gano Lummis gave every indication that she was slightly appalled and disgusted by the predicament her nephew's death created for her. "I've talked to Mrs. Lummis now and then," remarked an intimate of both Annette Lummis and Ella Winston in 1978, at the height of the Hughes brouhaha, " . . . and she talks about how she's harassed by lawyers and so forth." In fact, as close as Ella Rice Winston and Annette Lummis were, and in view of their respective roles as Hughes' first wife and closest living relative, it is nothing short of remarkable that the two apparently never even discussed the legal maelstrom swirling around them. "No, I don't believe they have," pondered their mutual friend, "because . . . well, it's just not the kind of thing they would talk about." This sort of silence is part of an unspoken class code that still thrives in the Winston and Lummis social circles. As Carl Callaway remarked of his wife Kitty, "She is very emotional about her family, and she took Howard very seriously, and we don't mention it unless we have to."

So Mrs. Lummis' son William did the talking for the family, reacting with swift and sure instincts to a set of remarkable circumstances for which he could surely find no parallel in what had previously been a predictable, slightly dull corporate lawyer's existence. In a few short months, Lummis had been swept from an anonymous, rather dull career into a position of power, controversy, and even intrigue as chief executive officer of Summa. By May 1976, not only did William Lummis resemble his cousin Howard Hughes physically, but he had taken on his corporate identity as well. And although Lummis is usually described with adjectives such as "polite," "unassuming," and "diffident," few could deny that he played his new role as business mogul very convincingly. Despite his private protests that he and his wife hated Las Vegas and missed their quiet Houston routine, Lummis threw himself into the management of Summa 100 percent, even building a new house for himself and his wife in Las Vegas. The man who claims never to have participated in Hughes' legal affairs during his tenure at Andrews, Kurth (he once testified to the contrary in 1976, shortly after his cousin's death) was now "running the show." Life would never again be dull for Will Lummis, that much was certain.

Shortly after his settlement conversation with the other maternal cousins, Lummis learned for the first time of the existence of three relatives on the Hughes side of the family. Obviously, these paternal heirs had to be considered in the formulation of any settlement agreement pertaining to Howard Hughes' estate. It was here that the first sign of approaching controversy appeared on the horizon. Unlike the Gano family tree, the Hughes genealogy was an obscure, jumbled mess. Three alleged grandaughters of Rupert Hughes surfaced the month after Hughes' death, claiming to be the only paternal relatives in the line of inheritance. Not surprisingly, their attorney, Paul Freese, talked a lot about Texas domicile. Only if Hughes were declared a legal resident of Texas would his clients inherit a share of the Hughes estate, a full 50 percent. Lummis at the time was pushing to have Hughes declared a resident of Nevada. Were Hughes found to be a resident of either California or Nevada at the time of his death, Annette Lummis would inherit whatever was left of Hughes' fortune after taxes, and Freese's clients would walk away with nothing.

This was a problem that had to be faced head on, Lummis reasoned. Amidst much legal maneuvering and the filing of pleadings and cross-pleadings by all parties concerned, Lummis and his Andrews, Kurth counsel revised the settlement agreement to include the Hughes grand-daughters, an agreement that would be binding on all who signed, no matter what state was ultimately determined to have jurisdiction over the estate. Because Mrs. Lummis had the greatest bargaining power (as potentially the only heir, by the laws of both Nevada and California), the maternal heirs were to receive 75 percent of the estate under the terms of the settlement agreement. (Mrs. Lummis would get 25 percent herself, and 50 percent would go to the remaining maternal heirs, or approximately 4 percent to each cousin or first cousin-once-removed.) The three granddaughters settled for a guaranteed one-fourth of the Hughes estate, sacrificing the additional 25 percent they would have received by operation of law had they pursued a Texas domicile position and won. Of course, had they lost on the domicile issue, they wouldn't have been entitled to a penny.

In drawing up the agreement, Lummis and his cohorts were not unaware of the fact that much of their inheritance could be eaten away by costly litigation between rival family members. Hence the settlement contract was born. By its terms, the parties "may receive agreed portions of the estate regardless of the utlimate resolution of the question as to the Decendent's domicile . . . which all view as being to their substantial economic advantage." In addition, Will Lummis was named the "designating authority."

No sooner had the Hughes granddaughters been made parties to the settlement agreement than a pair of Rupert Hughes' stepchildren (Avis Hughes McIntyre and Rush Hughes) made their appearance in the Texas estate proceedings, claiming to have been "equitably adopted" by Howard, Jr.'s, uncle Rupert. Like Freese's client once had (before they signed the private settlement contract). Avis and Rush pushed for Hughes to be declared a resident of Texas where, if they prevailed, they would stand to inherit as much as a third of the Howard Hughes estate, as his paternal first cousins. In this regard, they faced strong opposition from Lummis. Acting in his dual capacities as temporary coadministrator of the estate *and* as a maternal heir, he continued to attempt to prove Hughes was domiciled in Nevada at the time of his death.

In what the state of Texas considered a conflict of interest, Lummis and the Andrews, Kurth law firm represented Lummis and his mother both in their individual behalf and as the administrators of Hughes' estate. The Texas attorney general contended that Lummis and the firm's stance on certain issues that would be most favorable to the Lummises and their kin personally might not necessarily be in the impartial interests of the estate—most notably Lummis' preference for a Nevada rather than a Texas domicile. Citing this supposed conflict, the state filed a challenge to Andrews, Kurth's first request for fees; but the state's argument was rejected by the court. Though the situation created by Lummis and the firm's dual appointments could be construed as problematic, it was within the bounds of the law.

To complicate matters even further, the three grandchildren of Rupert Hughes "didn't even know who Rush and Avis were," according to Barbara Cameron. The two stepchildren, for their part, raised questions about both Rupert Hughes and his so-called daughter Elspeth (the trio's mother). Each set of paternal relations appeared to cast doubt on the inheritance rights of the other. In essence, the Hughes granddaughters, led by Barbara Cameron, the youngest and the spokesperson for the group, questioned the sincerity and, more important, the legality of the adoption claim, while Rush and Avis closely examined the identity of the "Hughes girls' " mother.

Somehow, Lummis pulled this disparate group together and, a year after the consummation of the first settlement agreement, executed a "supplemental agreement" to include the two "informally" adopted children of Rupert Hughes. This was quite a legal coup for Rush and Avis, considering they had no papers to support their claim, and that they had made no attempt to inherit a portion of Rupert Hughes' estate some twenty years earlier. And yet, despite the fact that Rush and Avis had what many considered to be a very shaky claim, Barbara Cameron and her sisters agreed to concede 6 percent of their earlier 25 percent share to include Rupert Hughes' stepchildren in the private settlement contract. This left the granddaughters with 19 percent of Howard Hughes' estate. From the maternal heirs' share 3.5 percent was trimmed to cut in Rush and Avis. When all was said and done, these two never-adopted stepchildren of Rupert Hughes had negotiated an impressive 9.5 percent of the Howard Hughes fortune. How and why did this come about? In the language of the revised agreement, "the parties understand that the questions of domicile, adoption, rights to inherit and other questions of law and facts related thereto could take many years to resolve through litigation, that protracted litigation necessarily would involve serious adverse consequences to each of them, and it is in the best interests of all parties hereto to resolve these conflicting claims between themselves."

That was the official line. But does it adequately explain why the granddaughters of Rupert Hughes would voluntarily settle for 19 percent of the Howard Hughes estate to take part in such an agreement, knowing that the paternal heirs were entitled to a full 50 percent under the laws of the state of Texas? Thirty-one percent of a billion-dollar fortune is no small concession. And why did they agree to relinquish 6 percent from their share in the first settlement agreement to two stepchildren they had earlier discredited? Did it mean, as some said, that they had some doubt about their own relationship?

And why, in turn, would Rush and Avis settle for a mere 9.5 percent of the estate when, under Texas law, they would be entitled to almost one-third of Hughes' fortune as paternal first cousins if they could prove they were equitably adopted by Rupert Hughes?

Was there, as some have suggested, a conspiracy of silence between the alleged paternal heirs? Did the three granddaughters and the two stepchildren of Rupert Hughes "buy" each other's silence in exchange for a guaranteed percentage of the estate? These were the accusations hurled at them by their opposing counsel at the heirship trial in 1981. Did each suppress damaging evidence about the other's claim in exchange for the right to be included in the agreement, as their foes implied in court? Certainly the interfamily fighting stopped abruptly after the supplemental agreement was executed. Rush and Avis gave up their legal battle to declare Hughes a resident of Texas, and the rumors and innuendoes from all sides came to a screeching halt. Was the settlement agreement, as one adversary described it, a "cozy little party"?

Perhaps most important of all, how and why did the maternal heirs, represented by Andrews, Kurth and Will Lummis, determine that these five individuals were indeed the legitimate paternal heirs of Howard Hughes, Jr.? Why were they cut in on the settlement agreement?

The inheritance claims of Rupert Hughes' granddaughters and stepchildren were violently disputed by a number of people with varying degrees of proof. Why, then, would Lummis and his cousins choose to settle with a group whose family connection was so controversial? An attorney from Andrews, Kurth who represented the estate once testified that the firm had investigated these claims to their satisfaction. Yet Barbara Cameron and her two sisters were included in the first settlement agreement just three months after Hughes' death. The ad litem investigation, in contrast, continued for over five years. Was three months adequate time to resolve any doubts about the Hughes family tree? Ollie Blan, an attorney representing a different branch of the Hughes family, suggested otherwise. During the heirship trial in 1981, he questioned Andrews, Kurth partner William Miller about his firm's investigation of the Cameron claim. Though Miller was, by his own description, the "lead attorney" in charge of the Hughes estate administration, he admitted under oath that he had never even read the deposition testimony of Hughes granddaughter Barbara Cameron. By pointing out this omission Blan implied a general inattention to the investigation of the paternal heirs' claims by the Andrews, Kurth counsel. Because Miller never read Cameron's deposition, Blan continued, he was also unaware that she had testified that Rupert Hughes once told her "That's a damn lie!" when it was suggested that Rush Hughes was his son. This put Miller's firm in the unusual position of settling with two distinct sets of alleged paternal relatives of Howard Hughes, each of whom had at one time questioned the inheritance rights of the other. (Since the execution of the supplemental agreement, the granddaughters and Rush and Avis have supported each other's position, at least publicly, and deny they ever cast aspersions on the other's claim.) The circumstances behind the agreement are made even more complex by the fact that hundreds of individuals openly discredited both the granddaughters' *and* Rush and Avis' right to inherit, and instead maintained that an entirely different set of individuals—distant Hughes cousins—were in fact the bona fide paternal heirs of Howard R. Hughes, Jr.

131

All of this made Dinkins' heirship investigation and the upcoming trial to determine Hughes' paternal relatives even more intriguing. William Lummis and Andrews, Kurth had privately settled 28 percent of Howard Hughes' estate on five individuals whom they supported as Hughes' paternal heirs, and they were bound by the terms of the settlement agreement to pay this group their agreed percentages *no matter what the outcome* of the trial to determine Hughes' paternal heirs scheduled for August 27, 1981, in Judge Gregory's court.

Without a doubt Ted Dinkins was in a critical position. As the attorney ad litem, it was his official responsibility to present to the court a list of Hughes' paternal heirs, and to conduct a thorough investigation not only to attempt to locate any unknown paternal heirs, but also to prove or disprove the claims of the five who had been privately acknowledged as the legitimate and only heirs on the Hughes side of the family. What if Dinkins' investigation led to the discovery of another paternal heir? Or if he uncovered evidence to discredit any of the five alleged paternal heirs participating in the settlement agreement?

These were not idle speculations or fanciful possibilities. They were important, valid questions. It was altogether possible that Will Lummis had cut a deal with the wrong people. And it was up to Ted Dinkins to find out.

AUTHOR'S NOTE:

Going into the trial to determine Hughes' paternal heirs, a Texas jury had previously determined that Howard R. Hughes, Jr., was a legal resident of Texas at the time of his death. California subsequently sued Texas over the right to claim Hughes as a resident, as an original action in the United States Supreme Court. The Supreme Court refused to hear it but suggested that the estate file an "interpleader" action instead. An interpleader is a legal device to consolidate conflicting claims over the same issue into one lawsuit. Since more than one state claimed Hughes as a resident, an interpleader was an appropriate alternative.

The interpleader action was instituted in Austin, Texas, shortly after the Supreme Court's advisory opinion was issued. That case was on appeal at the time of the heirship trials. Consequently, Texas was the only state to have officially declared Hughes a legal resident at the time the heirship determination took place.

(Since the heirship trials, the domicile case again reached the United States Supreme Court. This time, the Court agreed to hear the case, and should render a decision by fall 1984.

This is a great victory for the heirs. By agreeing to rule on the domicile question, the Supreme Court will make one binding decision as to Hughes' legal residence. Consequently, only one state will have the right to impose death taxes on the estate, eliminating the fear that the Hughes estate might be taxed out of existence. ''The Hughes heirs apparently will not suffer unfair double taxation,'' wrote dissenting Justice Lewis F. Powell. ''Other heirs of other estates presumably will not be so fortunate.'' In making this point, Associate Justice Powell was referring to the fact that the Supreme Court is unlikely to accept all cases in which more than one state claims jurisdiction over an estate.)

PART THREE
A Family on Trial: Hughes' Paternal Relatives

7

Family Feud

"No, I've never met Howard, and believe it or not, I really don't care about his money. . . . I fully expect to be disinherited: after all, I don't know him. I really doubt he'd leave us anything. The Hugheses have never been a close-knit family."

—Agnes Lapp Roberts, Rupert Hughes' granddaughter; December 31, 1971

In 1971, Rupert Hughes' eldest granddaughter had no reason to believe she would be left one thin dime by her distant cousin. By 1977, Howard Hughes was dead, no valid will could be found, and the search was on for relatives to inherit his billion-dollar estate. And if Agnes

Roberts, "really [didn't] care about his money" in 1971, by 1981 she and her two sisters were involved in a bitter courtroom battle to prove their relationship to Howard Hughes in order to collect a sizable percentage of his estate. It was a relationship that had gone unnoticed and unacknowledged by Howard Hughes, Jr., all their lives, a relationship that, nonetheless, if legitimate, would make the three middle-aged housewives instant millionaires.

Suspicions

On August 27, 1981, Judge Pat Gregory's courtroom was filled to capacity. The court had already determined who would inherit half of Howard Hughes, Jr.'s, estate, and interested parties from across the country congregated for the last phase of the heirship trials to see who would be declared heirs on Hughes' father's side of the family. Once established, this would complete the three-pronged heirship determination and terminate the five-year struggle to distribute the estate to its heirs-at-law.

For Ted Dinkins and his associates, it was the culmination of a herculean investigation into the Hughes family history: an investigative odyssey that took Dinkins' colleagues across the U.S. and even to London and Paris in the search for answers to questions that still haunted them as the trial unfolded. For five years, they had skulked around cemeteries, scrutinized pictures, read and reread letters, papers, and records that had gathered dust for years, rattling more skeletons in closets than most genealogists find in a lifetime. Their efforts led each of them to the inescapable conclusion that something was very wrong in the Hughes family tree. Dinkins' protegés were convinced that the Hughes family concealed some dark mystery, some devious plot: some powerful secret that, discovered, could very possibly show that Barbara Cameron and her sisters were not, as they claimed, the "closest paternal relatives of Howard R. Hughes, Jr." Everywhere Dinkins and his staff looked, they found something unusual or unaccounted for. Each time they put to rest one suspicion about the Hughes lineage, several new, more disturbing ones crept in.

And so, that Monday in August, Dinkins made his appearance in court as the attorney responsible for presenting a list of Hughes' paternal heirs, not thoroughly convinced that the pedigree he was about to endorse was entirely accurate, yet missing the one piece of incontrovertible evidence that would prove it. As one attorney observed in his closing argument to the jury, "many things" in the case were "strange and unexplained," leaving the two researchers who had conducted Dinkins' investigation with the indelible impression that the

138

heirs on the Hughes side of the family might not be so apparent. Howard Hughes, Sr.'s, brothers and sister had many strange secrets in their past, some of which Dinkins' sleuths had uncovered, several of which they suspected but could not prove. In the end, for all his colleagues' doubts and uncertainty, Dinkins offered no objection whatsoever to the inheritance claims of Barbara Cameron and her sisters. At the close of the trial, a jury determined that Barbara Lapp Cameron, Elspeth Lapp DePould, and Agnes Lapp Roberts were the legitimate granddaughters of Rupert Hughes, the paternal heirs-at-law of Howard R. Hughes, Jr.— and Ted Dinkins supported that position.

Despite five years of extraordinary persistence and tenacity in the pursuit of information about the Hughes family, Dinkins spent only a few hours presenting his evidence, introducing perhaps a scant 5 percent of the material he and his colleagues had accumulated throughout their investigation. The jurors and the court therefore saw little of the information that might have caused them to dispute (or at least raise questions about) the granddaughters' right to inherit. What was the explanation? Why did the jury not see the stacks and stacks of papers and miscellany acquired during the heirship investigation to consider before returning its verdict?

The explanation, according to Dinkins, could be found in the rules of evidence. Despite the volumes of data he had accumulated, only a small percentage was legally admissible as "evidence" in a court of law (without some exception or a special ruling by the judge). The rest, he maintained, was barred by one or more of the rules of evidence. Most of the information that his associates had gathered and analyzed, he reasoned, was simply not admissible in court: newspaper articles, interviews, school records. The hodgepodge of information his team had studied and puzzled over for half a decade was either hearsay, or could not be admitted because of some legal technicality. Most of their suspicions and misgivings about the Hughes family were based on "circumstantial" evidence, and Dinkins chose to introduce only "documentary" evidence in his presentation to the jury. Though his two colleagues had formed the clear impression that there was something strange where Rupert's supposed daughter Elspeth (the Lapp sisters' mother) was concerned, they lacked the hard evidence to prove it—in court anyway—unless Dinkins opted to put together a case based on circumstantial evidence, which he did not. Since the ad litem chose not to introduce all the circumstantial evidence that cast doubt on Elspeth (and certain other members of the Hughes family), and since all the documentary evidence—birth, death, marriage, and divorce papers—supported her daughters' position, the jury was left with little choice but to return a verdict in their favor.

Still, enough had been unmasked in the investigation to cause genealogist Mary Fay to believe "without a doubt" that there was a flaw in the genealogy that Elspeth's three daughters presented in court that day—despite the succession of certificates in support of their claim. What Dinkins lacked was, as he put it, the "smoking gun": the missing piece of evidence that would confirm the suspicions that had hung over his office like a dark cloud since 1977.

The Controversy

Just what was the lineage that had sparked this spectacular controversy? It centered on Rupert Hughes, Howard Hughes, Jr.'s, uncle and lifelong adversary. Whether or not Rupert Hughes had a daughter named Elspeth was the key to all the dissension.

Just as they had with the maternal side of the family, genealogists turned to the aunts and uncles on the Hughes side in the search for Hughes' heirs in Phase Three. If living, Howard Hughes, Sr.'s, brothers and sisters would be the closest Hughes relatives. If not, their children, Howard, Jr.'s, first cousins, would be next in line to inherit the Hughes fortune.

According to the chart prepared by the *Philadelphia Inquirer* the month after Hughes' death, Howard Hughes, Sr., had two brothers and a sister: Rupert, Felix, and Greta Hughes, respectively. All three— Howard, Jr.'s, two uncles and an aunt—were deceased by April 1976, so none would inherit a percentage of his estate. Their children, however, would be first cousins of Howard, Jr., and could inherit in their place. Between the three siblings of Howard Hughes, Sr., it appeared from the *Inquirer* chart that only Rupert Hughes had any children: a daughter, Elspeth. If the *Inquirer* chart was accurate and Elspeth Hughes were alive, she would be the closest paternal heir of Howard Hughes, Jr.—a first cousin—and she would be entitled to a dazzling 50 percent of the Hughes estate under Texas law. Therein lay the controversy. Elspeth Hughes Lapp died in 1945. Her three daughters, however—Barbara Lapp Cameron, Elspeth Lapp DePould, and Agnes Lapp Roberts—would inherit in her place as the direct descendants of Rupert Hughes, Howard, Jr.'s, paternal uncle. These three first cousins-once-removed would divide among themselves one-half of Howard Hughes, Jr.'s, estate, according to the laws of the state of Texas. Hughes had never even met two of these ladies, and had no idea who the third (Barbara Cameron) was when they once met by accident at a party in 1945.

It is therefore easy to see why so much attention was focused on Elspeth Hughes Lapp. As the only first cousin on the paternal side of the family, her relationship was critical to the division of Hughes' estate. The question of who would inherit one-half of his fortune turned on whether or not Elspeth Hughes was the legitimate daughter of Rupert Hughes. If for any reason Elspeth were discredited, then Howard Hughes, Jr., would have no known first cousins on the paternal side. The three siblings of Howard, Sr., (Rupert, Felix, and Greta) would have no direct descendants, and the court would instead divide the Hughes half of the estate among the descendants of the elder Felix Hughes' siblings—skipping back a generation to Howard, Jr.'s, grandparents. That would mean that an entirely different set of people would be Hughes' paternal heirs. Felix Hughes, Howard, Jr.'s, grandfather, had many brothers and sisters, and their children and grandchildren, most of whom were plain folk from the Midwest, would replace Elspeth's children as the paternal heirs. If this happened, the paternal heirs' 50 percent would be scattered among literally hundreds of second and third cousins. Thus, for a great many people, Elspeth Hughes Lapp's identity was the real $67 million question.

Throughout the five-year heirship investigation, talk of scandal surrounded Elspeth Hughes at all times. Scores of individuals questioned her position of inheritance, and almost as many filed their own heirship claims against the estate, as the rightful paternal heirs of Howard Hughes, Jr. By the time of the heirship determination trial, however, these dissenters had essentially divided into two factions. Though their claims differed in certain important respects, they shared the belief that Elspeth Hughes was not the natural daughter of Rupert Hughes, and they requested a jury trial to prove it.

The first group was represented by Houston attorneys George Parnham and Jacqueline Taylor, and consisted of the second and third cousins who were descendants of Judge Felix Hughes' siblings. Parnham's clients had all grown up in the tri-state area—Missouri, Illinois, and Iowa—around Keokuk, Iowa, where Howard, Sr., Rupert, young Felix, and Greta Hughes were raised. Their fathers and mothers were first cousins of Howard, Jr.'s, father, and they had all played together as children. This group held the position that Rupert Hughes was sterile, that a childhood case of the mumps or measles or both had rendered him unable to father children, and that Elspeth was the product of an extramarital affair between Rupert Hughes' first wife and a lover.

This belief had been passed down from generation to generation in the Hughes family. The witnesses whom Parnham assembled from among his clients were all simple midwesterners—as ordinary and homespun as Howard Hughes, Jr., was extraordinary and eccentric. Many had been raised on farms, all in small towns or rural areas, and they seemed nothing if not sincere as they testified about their "Cousin

Rupert," the local boy who made good. "We were real proud of him being a writer," one distant cousin commented on the witness stand. The fathers or grandfathers of these witnesses had been acquainted with their relative Rupert through the years, and it was common knowledge in the family, they said, that Rupert Hughes could not have children "because of a childhood disease."

Several witnesses testified that Rupert himself told either their father, mother, grandfather, or grandmother about his affliction, and one elderly witness, Charles Ireland, remembers being taken to the movies by "Cousin Rupert" when Charles was thirteen. On the way home, Ireland testified, Rupert Hughes patted Charles on the head and said, "I wish I coulda had children." (By this time, Elspeth was a grown woman.) The measles incident occurred, the clan all agreed, when Rupert Hughes was attending the St. Charles Military School in St. Charles, Missouri, around 1887. He was admitted to St. Joseph Hospital, they all claim, and later stayed with an aunt of witness Dorothy Bacon Wilson to recuperate. According to Parnham's clients, this knowledge had circulated through the family for years—beginning long before the death of Howard Hughes, Jr., with its unexpected chance of an inheritance. As Dorothy Wilson noted, her grandfather George Askins was close to his cousin Rupert from childhood on. As an adult, Rupert Hughes returned to Askins' farm in Illinois from time to time for extended visits. The two would "sit out on a log in the chicken yard," Mrs. Wilson remembered, "and talk about the old times." Mrs. Wilson was thirteen or fourteen years old at the time of these visits, and she recalled her grandfather talking about Cousin Rupert. In fact, Askins and Rupert Hughes lived together for a year or so in New York City in the 1920s, when Askins was employed as a hotel dispatcher. (By this time, Elspeth Hughes was in her mid-twenties.) Her grandfather talked about Rupert constantly, Mrs. Wilson testified, and he told her a number of times through the years that Rupert was unable to have children because of a childhood disease.

Dorothy Bacon Wilson's testimony was typical of the recollections of Parnham's witnesses. None of them had even heard of Elspeth Hughes before the death of Howard Hughes, Jr., and the ensuing heirship determination. The family understanding was that Howard, Jr., was the only cousin on that side of the family. One witness, Philena Calvert, a third cousin, talked about the annual reunions held in Missouri or Iowa of the families of Felix Hughes' siblings. The other family members, most of whom came from a rural background, were "always proud" of the Felix Hughes family, she testified. They considered themselves to be the "poor side of the family," she noted, and viewed Felix Hughes' four children as "geniuses." These cousins and aunts and uncles often discussed how sad it was that there was only Howard Hughes, Jr., to carry on the line; that he was the only grandchild of Judge Hughes. Ms. Calvert even met Howard, Jr., at one of these reunions. She was six or seven at the time, and he was fifteen or sixteen. He accompanied his grandfather, "the Judge," on a summer afternoon. "He had about the only car in the whole country," she testified, her voice still touched with awe at the memory of the occasion.

The problems with Parnham's case, from a legal standpoint, were many. His evidence of Rupert Hughes' alleged sterility, however convincing from a human point of view, was entirely hearsay—the testimony of individuals who had been told by others that their cousin Rupert could not have children—and as such, legally insufficient. Though Rupert Hughes may indeed have told these witnesses' fathers, aunts, or other close relations that he could not have children, those individuals had all died by the time of the trial in September 1981, and only their children were alive to testify as to what had been "common family knowledge" for years. Not surprisingly, their opposing counsel ruthlessly attacked this family history. Wayne Fisher, who himself represented a pair of questionable paternal claimants (Avis and Rush "Hughes"—the children of Rupert Hughes' second wife by a former marriage), denounced Parnham's case in his opening statement to the jury as nothing more than "my mama told me that her grandma told her that. . . .Rumor based upon inference based upon hearsay," he sneered.

Parnham's clients, in short, had no legal proof of Rupert Hughes' alleged condition. Their argument, stated Paul Freese, the lead attorney for Barbara Cameron and her sisters (Elspeth's three daughters), "would rely heavily on contingencies and possibilities." As Freese was well aware, hearsay evidence is not admissible in court under most circumstances, and he fought to prevent Parnham's witnesses from being able to testify at all. "The other paternal claimants may argue," he wrote in a brief to Judge Gregory on the eve of the trial, "that *if* it can be shown that Rupert had the mumps, it is *possible* that he might have been rendered sterile as a result thereof, and that *if* Rupert were sterile at the time of Elspeth's conception, it is *possible* that he was not the biological father of Elspeth."

Yet for all Freese's and Fisher's jeering at the family-history nature of Parnham's case, it certainly offered room for speculation. Hearsay evidence may not be admissible in court as a general rule (though there are exceptions to this rule of evidence, and Judge Gregory interpreted them rather liberally, allowing several of the second and third cousins to testify as to what they had been told), and the family understanding that Rupert Hughes was sterile may have made a weak case *legally*. Even so, it certainly indicated that something strange was going on in the family. Why else would hundreds of Hughes cousins in and around Iowa, Illinois, and Missouri—all of whom grew up with the Felix Hughes family—have the very clear impression that their cousin Rupert was unable to have children? Simple logic suggested that there must have been something on which they based that belief. What could possibly have been the motive for spreading such gossip as far back as 1887? Howard Hughes, Jr., hadn't even been born yet. Whether Rupert Hughes did lose his fertility as a result of the mumps or measles will probably never be proven with certainty one way or the other. It is known, however, that he did have those childhood diseases. In the magazine piece "My Mother," which he wrote for *American Magazine* in 1924, Rupert Hughes had this to say about his upbringing: "(My mother) did not believe in exposing her children to diseases, as many did then, so that they could 'have it and get over it.' Too many children got over the River Jordan as a result of that policy. But she could not protect us from the mumps, the measles, and the typhoid fever."

Furthermore, it seemed odd that this whole set of cousins would never have even heard the name Elspeth in all the years before the trial. Rupert Hughes went back to visit his midwestern relatives from time to time (he died in 1956), and Judge and Mrs. Hughes lived in Keokuk until the twenties. Why, then, was her existence such a well-kept secret? Did Rupert Hughes have something to hide from the old hometown?

Parnham also relied heavily upon an application to join the Sons of the American Revolution filled out by Rupert Hughes in 1917, twenty years after the birth of his alleged daughter Elspeth. Parnham introduced Ruth Dietrich, a staff genealogist for the National Society of the Sons of the American Revolution, as his witness to explain the document to the jury. As Ms. Dietrich explained, the S.A.R. is a patriotic, educational, and historical society. To be eligible to join, an individual must be a lineal descendant of a patriot and must be able to trace his ancestry to the satisfaction of the staff genealogists who approve or disqualify each prospective entrant. The application is a sworn statement, she pointed out, taken very seriously by the society and its members. In his application, approved on December 11, 1917, Rupert Hughes left blank the line corresponding to children. As Ted Dinkins and his associate, both observing the proceedings from a separate counsel table, already knew, this was only one of a number of compromising documents bearing on the relationship between Elspeth and Rupert Hughes. Though Freese and Fisher tried their best to discredit Ms. Dietrich's testimony, emphasizing the fact that they had a birth certificate which proved that Elspeth was indeed the daughter of Rupert Hughes, the S.A.R. genealogist was still greatly influenced by his application form. She considered it to be "conclusive . . . since he swore to it," she testified, "and most people would be proud to list a son or daughter."

Finally, in his closing argument to the jury, Parnham pointed to Rupert Hughes' last will and testament. In this 1953 document, executed three years before his death, at a time when some considered him to be senile, Rupert Hughes specifically disinherited his three granddaughters, leaving his entire estate to his brother Felix and Felix's wife Ruby. Elspeth was already dead by this time. "I have intentionally and with full knowledge omitted to provide for my heirs," he wrote, "including but not limited to my granddaughters and their children."

As Darlene Cameron, Dinkins' secretary, was fond of saying, "something fishy" was indeed going on.

George Parnham's counterpart in his efforts to displace Elspeth's children was Ollie Blan, a highly respected lawyer from an established and conservative Birmingham law firm, who represented a group of Hugheses from Alabama. They were headed by Robert C. Hughes, a soft-spoken sixty-ish agribusiness teacher from Wilsonville, Alabama, with a B.A. and M.A. from Auburn University. Dinkins and his colleagues were very familiar with Mr. Hughes. Mrs. Fay spent several hours interviewing him in Alabama in August 1977, and Dinkins later sent his associate to Birmingham in company with Mrs. Fay to question Hughes further in 1978, so compelling was his claim.

Stated briefly, Robert C. Hughes hailed from a different branch of the Hughes family than the Iowa-Missouri-Illinois Hugheses represented by George Parnham. Parnham's clients are related to Howard Hughes, Jr., through the brothers and sisters of Felix Turner Hughes, father of Howard, Sr. The first point of controversy in Robert Hughes' story centers on the identity of Felix Hughes. Robert and his family claim that the man who went by the name Felix Turner Hughes, and who became Howard Hughes, Jr.'s, grandfather, was actually born Felix *Moner* Hughes. Felix Moner Hughes, the family contends, was a member of their branch of the Hughes family tree and grew up in Fulton County, Kentucky. During the Civil War, they assert, Felix Moner sided with the north , while his nine brothers were southern sympathizers. Felix Moner abandoned his family completely and aligned himself with the Joshua Hughes clan: the *Turner* Hugheses, apparently of more aristocratic Virginian lineage. As Felix Moner's eight brothers set off for the battle of Richmond in the summer of 1862, Felix Moner and his new mentor, Joshua Hughes, ambushed the group, ruthlessly killing Felix's siblings.

The widows of the brothers who had died, led by Daniel Freeman Hughes, Robert C. Hughes' grandfather (whose life was spared) organized the remaining family and prepared to move south to Georgia.

145

They collected what they could from their crops, sold their belongings, and pooled all their resources, which came to approximately $140,000. Along the way, the family contends, Felix Moner Hughes trailed them in secrecy. Before they reached Georgia, he held the family at gunpoint and stole their $140,000 in life savings. Felix Moner later moved to Missouri and Iowa and changed his name to Felix Turner Hughes, pretending to be a member of the Turner Hugheses from Virginia.

At this point, the saga takes an even more fascinating twist. After Felix Moner/Turner Hughes' dramatic betrayal, the Robert C. Hughes clan assigned a family member to keep him under "surveillance" for the rest of his life, and extended this scrutiny to his wife and children. They follow an old English custom known as the "calling of the clan," in which the family meets on a regular basis to discuss their history among themselves. As a part of this tradition, a "witness tree," or family historian, is appointed. Daniel Freeman Hughes' wife Nancy (Robert's grandmother) occupied this position for a number of years, from the time of the ambush, and she passed this knowledge on to her immediate successor, John Douglas Hughes, Robert's uncle. She also discussed these matters with Robert, when he was a child. "Uncle John," in his watch over the Felix Turner Hughes family, accumulated a wealth of newspaper clippings and other documentation about the brood through the years, which he kept in a trunk. Young Robert, as the heir apparent to the unique post of family witness tree, would study these clippings and papers at his Uncle John's side, to prepare for the position of honor he now holds in the family. It was through this unusual surveillance process that Robert C. Hughes came to know the intimate details of the lives of Felix Hughes' four children: Greta, Howard, Sr., Rupert, and Felix.

The essence of Robert Hughes' claim was that Rupert Hughes and his first wife, Agnes, had a daughter whom Rupert named "Leila," not Elspeth. Leila Hughes drowned in a swimming pool at Rupert Hughes' home in California in approximately 1921. At the time of Leila's death, Robert maintained, Rupert and his wife literally "substituted" another girl to take the place of his deceased daughter Leila. The young woman substituted for Leila was actually the daughter of Rupert's new wife by a previous liaison, and her name was Elspeth. Therefore, the Elspeth Hughes who went on to marry and have three daughters—Barbara Cameron, Elspeth DePould, and Agnes Roberts—was an imposter, not Rupert Hughes' real daughter at all.

If this remarkable story were true, then Elspeth's three daughters would not be Rupert Hughes' grandchildren, and they would not be entitled to a portion of Howard Hughes, Jr.'s, estate. Howard Hughes, Jr., would have no known first cousins, and the paternal one-half of his estate would descend, by the terms of the Texas statute, to his next closest kin: in this case, to his second and third cousins, the descendants of Judge Felix Hughes' brothers and sisters. Whether these second and third cousins would be George Parnham's clients or Robert Hughes' family turned upon the identity of Judge Hughes. If he were in fact Felix *Turner* Hughes, the son of Joshua W. Hughes, as he claimed, then Parnham's clients, as the descendants of Joshua Hughes' other children, would be the true Hughes heirs. But if, on the other hand, Robert Hughes could prove that Judge Hughes were actually Felix *Moner* Hughes, then the descendants of Felix's "real" brothers and sisters—Robert's branch of the Hughes family—would be the heirs apparent. Here was a case of mistaken and assumed identities worthy of Agatha Christie herself, only the stakes in this amazing whodunit were altogether real.

Robert Hughes had only one tangible piece of evidence in support of his extraordinary claim, and it came from Howard Hughes, Sr.'s, alma mater, Harvard University. In 1912, for the first time, Hughes provided an extensive firsthand autobiographical account for inclusion in the fifteen-year (fourth) report for the Class of 1897. It is here that Robert Hughes finds his support. By the fourth report, the class of 1897 had changed its format slightly, asking each alumnus to list his or her parents, spouse, children, etc., before offering a report of significant events. As his parents, Howard, Sr., listed "Felix *Moner,* Jean (Summerlin) Hughes." This information was picked up again in the fifth report of June 1917, and Hughes died before any further reports were published. Naturally, attorneys for Elspeth's daughters and Rush and Avis dismissed this entry in the report as a "mistake" or a "misprint," but if so, it was a very interesting mistake, to say the least. And highly coincidental.

Unfortunately for Robert Hughes, this was the extent of his evidence. The trunk in which his Uncle John kept all the articles and clippings related to the Felix Hughes family was allegedly destroyed in a fire in 1942, so he had no other papers to support his claim. Despite this setback, he continues to insist that he was instructed by John Douglas Hughes on the family history from the age of eight on, and that he has seen magazine and newspaper articles that describe the events concerning Judge Hughes' children, as told to him by his Uncle John. Since the death of Howard Hughes, Jr., he has attempted to relocate these clippings in the libraries at Auburn University and the Library of Congress, but he has met with little success. "I'm a working man," he testified, "and we did what we could." Robert Hughes' claim, therefore, was based almost exclusively on the testimony of Robert himself. As his attorney Ollie Blan stated to the jury in closing, "I do not apologize for it." His case, Blan admitted, was primarily family history, passed from grandmother to uncle to Robert, thwarted by the burning of a trunk that had stored information that would have supported his client's assertions. (Robert also claims he saw these articles at the Auburn University library while a student there years ago, but he "couldn't get his hands on them" in time before the trial.)

With his conspicuous lack of evidence and the embarrassing nature of his allegations about the Hughes family, it came as no surprise that Robert Hughes was questioned with thinly veiled disgust by Paul Freese, counsel for Elspeth Hughes' three daughters. Yet during Freese's examination, Hughes made it clear that he was not accusing Barbara Cameron and her sisters of lying about their mother's identity; that he in fact did not question the sincerity of their belief in their lineage. He pointed out that his testimony concerned events that took place long before "the three girls" were born, and about which he believed they were not informed. It was his opinion that Elspeth's daughters had not been apprised of the identity "switch." He was not so solicitous of Avis "Hughes" McIntyre, who had testified earlier in the trial that Elspeth Hughes was unquestionably the daughter of Rupert Hughes—despite the misgivings she expressed before signing the private settlement agreement. "Mrs. McIntyre is the one person in this whole case who could know all about this," Robert Hughes testified, "and her statements couldn't be anything but a lie." He was referring to the fact that Avis McIntyre is the only person still living who knew all the individuals in question at or near the time of the controversial events concerning Rupert Hughes. (She met both Rupert and Elspeth around 1906 or 1908.) If anything suspicious occurred in the family, it would seem likely that Avis was aware of it.

Wayne Fisher, Avis and her brother Rush Hughes' Houston attorney, in fact did the most damage to Robert Hughes' claim. In a legal maneuver designed to fluster Ollie Blan, Robert Hughes' quiet but competent attorney, Fisher called Mr. Hughes to the stand as an adverse witness during Fisher's case on behalf of Avis and Rush. Fisher knew that Blan, when his turn came, intended to call Robert Hughes as his only witness. By calling Mr. Hughes to the stand first as his own (adverse) witness, Fisher deprived Blan of the opportunity to set up his case as he had planned. In this way, Fisher got the first shot at questioning Hughes, presenting him to the jury in the most unfavorable light through intensive examination. After Fisher had interrogated Robert Hughes, the other counsel exercised their rights to question him. This put Ollie Blan in the awkward position of cross-examining his own witness, trying to both build his case and mitigate the damage that had already been done by Wayne Fisher on direct examination. It was a futile task.

Fisher attacked Hughes on point after point, emphasizing inconsistencies in his testimony, and driving home to the jury the fact that Robert had "no birth certificate, no newspaper accounts, no magazine articles, no letters, no pictures, no books, no Bibles . . . [just] a memory of family history from Uncle John's trunk." It was a brilliant piece of lawyering from a seasoned trial attorney, and it achieved its desired effect of making Robert Hughes appear to be an obsessed, possibly even deranged man pursuing a hopeless delusion. Dinkins and his associate, observing the theatrics, had their private opinions about Robert Hughes and his extraordinary story, based on many months of correspondence, repeated phone conversations and personal interviews, and independent research. Even they agreed, however, that by the time of the trial, Mr. Hughes had become emotionally unraveled, and his case collapsed with him.

By the time it was Ollie Blan's turn to put on his evidence, he simply restated his client Robert Hughes' tale for the jury "in capsule," and rested his case. He explained to the jury panel that there were other family members who knew and could testify as to parts of the family history, but he had decided not to call any other witnesses. Since Robert Hughes was the family historian, he reasoned aloud, any other testimony would just be "cumulative."

What of Paul Freese and Wayne Fisher's cases? one might ask. What did they do to prove their clients' claims? Freese, on behalf of Barbara Cameron and her sisters, introduced a collection of documents to show that Elspeth was Rupert Hughes' daughter: her birth certificate; her parents' marriage certificate; her parents' separation decree, mentioning Elspeth by name in 1904; and finally, a small number of letters from Rupert Hughes to either Elspeth or her daughters. The letters became the topic of much discussion during the proceedings. In putting together his case, Freese could find only six letters from Rupert Hughes to Elspeth, despite the fact that Rupert was an author and frequent letter-writer. Three of these letters concerned Elspeth's impending death in 1945. There are no known letters from Rupert to Elspeth before 1930, yet she was born in 1897, and the two did not live together after 1905, other than on occasional summer visits. In fact, the first letter from Rupert Hughes to any of Elspeth's family is dated 1931: ten years after the birth of his granddaughters, and thirty years after Elspeth's birth. Indeed, as George Parnham's associate Jackie Taylor pointed out, the only concentrated period of correspondence or communication from Rupert to his granddaughters was for a four-year period from 1945 to 1949, the years immediately following their mother's death.

Through the testimony of Barbara Cameron and her sisters, it became evident that Rupert Hughes rarely saw his granddaughters, not to mention his daughter. After her marriage, Elspeth, her husband, and the three daughters settled in Cleveland, Ohio. Over the next twenty-odd years, Rupert Hughes stopped in to see them perhaps eight or nine times while en route from his home in California to New York on business. Often these visits were limited to a few hours at the train station. One granddaughter, Agnes Lapp Roberts, did not even meet Rupert Hughes until she was seven or eight.

Freese's case revealed certain other unusual facts about Rupert Hughes' relationship with his daughter and her family. Both Barbara Cameron and Avis McIntyre testified, for example, that Rupert did not attend his daughter Elspeth's wedding in March 1921, even though two months earlier he had paid for a lavish wedding for his stepdaughter Avis and had given the bride away. And when Elspeth died in 1945, Rupert Hughes did not attend the funeral. Stranger yet, Elspeth's daughters have no idea of their mother's whereabouts for a number of years during her childhood—in fact, no one knows. According to Elspeth DePould, the three daughters possessed only one picture of their mother as a child. A few others were sent to them in the 1950s by a friend of their grandmother. How the friend came to possess them is something of a mystery.

Finally, Elspeth's age had been a continuing controversy up to and including the time of the trial. Avis McIntyre, who was born in December 1900 and who saw Elspeth every summer from 1908 through 1916, testified in two depositions (in 1976 and again in 1978) that Elspeth was "about a year" older than she. Elspeth's much-discussed birth certificate states that she was born in May 1897, which would make her almost *four* years older than Avis. As little girls playing together, the age difference should have been very clear to Avis—not only from her appearance, but in their discussions, introductions, comparisons of their respective grade in school, and the hundreds of other things little girls talk about. Dinkins' associate called his attention to the confusion about Elspeth's age after Avis McIntyre's first deposition in 1976. When her second deposition was taken in September 1978, Dinkins attempted to clarify the age problem in his examination of Mrs. McIntyre. Referring to her first deposition, taken two years earlier, he asked her:

Dinkins: I believe that you also said that Elspeth was about a year older than you?

Avis: Yes, yes.

Dinkins: Okay. Are you fairly sure that there was that one year disparity in age?

150

Avis: Yes.

Dinkins: Could Elspeth, say, have been three years older
                than you?

Avis: No, she was a year older than I.

However, when Avis was asked the same question on the witness
stand at the heirship trial in August 1981, she stated that she "now
believed" there was "three to four years" difference in age between
herself and Elspeth. Ollie Blan, counsel for Robert C. Hughes, immediately jumped on her change in testimony during his cross-
examination. He read aloud for both Avis and the jury what she had
repeated under oath several times in her deposition testimony of 1976
and 1978: that Elspeth was one year older than she. In the face of Blan's
attempts to impeach her, Mrs. McIntyre merely laughed and said, "I'm
not very good at historical facts." When Dinkins had his turn at cross-
examining Avis, he too asked about the sudden change from her deposition testimony relative to Elspeth's age. Avis tried to explain the turnabout by commenting that "later on she started thinking about it," but
this explanation made little sense. Avis McIntyre had persisted in her
sworn statements that there was a one-year age difference between
herself and Elspeth from 1976 to 1981, which gave her five years to
think about it and change her mind, yet she had not. In fact, she had
been most emphatic on this point during her depositions, becoming ir-
ritated when Dinkins or others attempted to get her to qualify her
response. The matter of Elspeth's age was hardly a trifling detail in the
case, for Elspeth's identity, with all the facts surrounding it, was the
pivotal issue in a multimillion-dollar lawsuit. The question of her age
was not a matter to be taken lightly.

Another surprising revelation with respect to Elspeth's age
developed at the trial through the testimony of her three middle-aged
daughters. Prior to the heirship hearing, Dinkins' associate had noticed
that Elspeth's husband, Ed Lapp, was born in May 1899. Born in May
1897 (as her birth certificate stated), Elspeth would have been two years
older than her husband. By Avis' deposition account, however, Elspeth
would have been a year younger—the more usual occurrence between
husbands and wives.

With this is mind, Dinkins asked witness Barbara Cameron who was
the older, her father or her mother? "That was a family joke,"
Cameron answered unexpectedly. "Mother was very coy about her
age." After questioning all three sisters on this point, Dinkins
discovered that none of Elspeth's daughters ever knew her age or

151

whether Ed or Elspeth Lapp was older. "Mother wouldn't tell," Cameron stated.

The family Bible that Cameron brought with her contributed to the mystery. Elspeth's date of birth had been written in the Bible as May 23, 1897, the same date that appeared on her birth certificate. What was strange was Barbara Cameron's disclosure that she had no idea who had made this notation. All the other entries in the Bible for family births, deaths, and marriages were in the handwriting of Cameron, Elspeth's mother, or grandmother, save this one. Barbara and her sisters could neither identify the script nor explain the reason for the discrepancy.

A third irregularity emerged quite by accident during the cross-examination of a later witness, as he described a 1924 letter from Elspeth to her mother on the occasion of Rupert Hughes' marriage to his third wife, a young actress. According to this witness, Elspeth wrote her mother to report that she (Elspeth) was "one or two years older" than Rupert's new wife, who was born in May 1902. This meant that, to her own mother, Elspeth identified her year of birth as 1899 or 1900—not 1897, as her birth certificate stated.

Why all this confusion? As Jackie Taylor, George Parnham's associate, asked the jury in her closing argument, "Who *was* Elspeth Hughes?" It was clear that the evidence presented in Gregory's courtroom did little to answer the question. Though attorney Paul Freese had a birth certificate on his side, the heirship determination trial on the paternal side was riddled with questions, inconsistencies, and altered testimony. As George Parnham noted to the bewildered jurors, "Take inference from what has *not* been said . . . the *circumstances* presented." No one could deny that the circumstances surrounding Elspeth were most unusual indeed. Even the judge later admitted privately that, based on the evidence and testimony put forth in court, there seemed to be "two Elspeths." Two different girls, of different ages: one who spoke French fluently, another who did not—along with a string of other nagging inconsistencies that created the impression that there were two different identities within the same person. It was a subtle impression, not assisted in any way by an orderly and efficient presentation of evidence, but an impression nonetheless. But impressions, however troubling, do not win lawsuits. Lawsuits are won by cold, hard evidence; and the evidence was on Elspeth's side.

Freese and Fisher, secure in the knowledge that they had a birth certificate to support their clients' position and that their opponents were inadequately prepared and had very little evidence, simply brushed aside the dangling questions and loose ends associated with their case, and instead attacked the motives of both Parnham and Blan's clients. Wayne Fisher, speaking on behalf of Rush and Avis, the allegedly

152

"adopted" stepchildren of Rupert Hughes, characterized each claim as an "abortive, ill-gained attempt to inherit money . . . crass as it sounds." Freese spoke disparagingly of "those who would bastardize my clients' mother," "casting a shadow of doubt on such a beautiful family relationship." Fisher went even further, scoffing at accusations that discredited what he called "one of the finest families that ever graced America." But behind all the rhetoric, the doubts and questions still lurked.

The Attorney Ad Litem's Case

What role did the attorney ad litem play in this unprecedented family drama? In his opening statement to the jury, Dinkins explained that he had accumulated an incredible amount of heirship information in his capacity as attorney ad litem, and he informed them that his function was to "insure that the jury be given a fair presentation of the evidence regardless of which side it affects." His sole objective, he stated, was that they "make an accurate determination of the heirship of Howard R. Hughes, Jr." To see, in other words, that the legitimate paternal relatives—be they Elspeth's children, Rush and Avis, George Parnham's clients, Robert Hughes' family, or an altogether different combination of individuals—assumed their positions of inheritance at the close of the trial.

Toward this end, Dinkins introduced two witnesses, Mrs. Mary Fay, the court-appointed genealogist who had assisted him so faithfully and competently for four unforgettable years, and the associate who had conducted the bulk of his massive investigation. Yet it was a curiously anti climactic presentation. Mrs. Fay was called as an expert witness merely to introduce into evidence the series of vital statistics relative to the genealogy of the Felix Hughes family (Howard, Jr.'s, grandfather). One by one she recited, without explanation, the known births, deaths, marriages, and divorces of Judge Hughes, his wife Jean Summerlin Hughes, and their children Greta, Howard, Sr., Rupert, and Felix, as reflected on the certificates and decrees that Dinkins quickly handed her. The testimony of Dinkins' associate, his only other witness, was restricted to a few arbitrary questions and answers, most of which concerned matters brought up earlier in the trial by Robert Hughes, and which served to discredit parts of his testimony.

Neither Mrs. Fay nor Dinkins' associate was asked to offer an opinion about the Hughes family tree, and little of the puzzling information they had gathered was offered into evidence. The many individuals they had interviewed during the prolonged discovery period were never called as witnesses, and the questions they entertained were never aired—all of which gave the jury the impression that Dinkins' investigators had every confidence in the genealogy endorsed by Freese and Fisher's clients. They had no way of knowing that Dinkins' researchers found the events in the Hughes family as strange and unexplained as Ollie Blan once described them.

So, in less than a day, Dinkins rested his case. In his closing statement, he again emphasized that he was impartial in the dispute, and asked the jury "simply to weigh the evidence" before returning a verdict. The irony, of course, is that the jury saw very little of the evidence Dinkins' staff had collected. Since by far the greater part of the data in his files was not documentary in nature, it was not generally admissible in court. How, then, could the jury possibly be expected to "weigh" the evidence? And was the string of certificates and licenses, introduced more or less at random, without much explanation and with no attempt to tie them all together, in fact a "fair presentation of the evidence"?

Some privately thought otherwise. As the attorney ad litem, Dinkins was by definition a truth and fact finder for the court in the matter of Howard Hughes' heirship. The dissenters believed that because of the unique and impartial nature of his role in the proceedings, any and all information Dinkins collected pertaining to heirship matters should have been open to all interested parties before the trial began, to use in the formulation of their cases. Since Dinkins had gathered this evidence in the pursuit of truth, "regardless of which side it affected," such a posture would have been in keeping with the spirit of the ad litem's role, they reasoned.

Dinkins only partially agreed. Though he opened his files to all parties for several months prior to the trial, he decided to display only the "public" documents. The "nonpublic" documents—interviews, internal memos, etc.—remained closed to scrutiny. Without the benefit of this additional information, and without explanation from the individuals who had conducted his research, the materials in Dinkins' files lost much of their value. It was a highly complex case, and only those who had been studying and analyzing the different branches of the Hughes family tree could hope to make any sense out of it. But Dinkins considered the nonpublic information to be privileged, so it remained under lock and key in the offices of Butler, Binion, Rice, Cook & Knapp.

This point of debate was particularly critical in the Hughes case. Since Dinkins' fees and expenses were paid out of Hughes' prodigious estate, he had abundant funds to pursue his independent heirship investigation. The Hughes relations from Missouri and Alabama who questioned Elspeth's parentage were not so fortunate. They were mostly individuals of modest means who had little time or resources to pursue their claims. This was complicated by the fact that the attorneys for the midwestern relatives who believed Rupert Hughes to be sterile, George Parnham and Jacqueline Taylor, were seriously outclassed by Wayne Fisher and Paul Freese. Elspeth's daughters and Rush and Avis were represented by shrewd and experienced attorneys from powerful and well-connected law firms in Los Angeles, Houston, and Florida. Parnham and Taylor were further handicapped by the fact that they were hired only a few months before the heirship trial, which gave them insufficient time to conduct their investigation. Consequently, they were annoyed at being denied access to Dinkins' many boxes of "privileged" heirship files, which might have contained information beneficial to their clients.

Elspeth's adversaries were similarly frustrated by Dinkins' decision to offer only documentary evidence in his presentation to the jury. It was Dinkins' opinion that there was no hard evidence with which to refute Elspeth's position of inheritance, and he chose not to put together a case based on circumstantial evidence. These decisions, which arguably served to strengthen Freese's and Fisher's cases while diluting the claims of Parnham's and Blan's clients, were nonetheless based on an adequate legal foundation. The function of an attorney ad litem is not clearly defined in the law, and Dinkins had little precedent to guide him in his responsibilities. Though his critics might argue with some authority that, as an officer of the court, Dinkins should have provided unlimited access to his files, or *attempted* to admit into evidence anything with possible relevance and allow the jury to decide its significance, the fact is that is that he was under no legal obligation to do so. These were judgment calls on his part. Thus by a combination of the law restricting admissibility of evidence and Dinkins' interpretation of his role as ad litem, the unsettling rumors, innuendoes, and inconsistent facts that Dinkins' investigation had dug up went undiscovered, unrepeated, and unreported. Ironically, in a legal proceeding designed to arrive at the truth, it was a rule of law that prohibited material that may have assisted in making that determination.

With the scales thus tipped in their favor it was an easy victory for Paul Freese's clients. Though they ruled that Elspeth was the daughter of Rupert Hughes, there is little doubt that the jury entertained certain suspicions about Rupert Hughes and his alleged progeny—not to mention the Hughes family in general—after hearing the evidence brought forward by all sides. Even based on the minimal and poorly organized information to which the jury was exposed, it must have been clear to them that there was something about the family history that, in the words of those close to the case, "just didn't hang together." The family understanding in and around Keokuk that Rupert Hughes had no children, that he was in fact sterile; the unusual nature of Rupert's relationship with Elspeth and, to a lesser degree, her daughters; the missing period in Elspeth's life; the contradictory nature of Avis McIntyre's testimony in general, and particularly concerning Elspeth's age; the dual nature of Elspeth's identity; the confusion over her year of birth; and the bizarre tale spun by Robert C. Hughes. Was Robert Hughes mentally unbalanced, as Fisher and Freese wanted the jury to believe, or was there something to his family's surveillance of Felix Hughes and his children? This parade of witnesses made one wonder whether Rupert Hughes and his daughter Elspeth's family indeed shared what Paul Freese had described as "such a beautiful family relationship." Was it really, as he characterized it, a "simple family story"? To Dinkins' colleagues, it was anything but simple.

And so Ted Dinkins' associate and genealogist sat in silent frustration as the jury deliberated, waiting for the verdict whose outcome was certain—knowing that the strange disclosures during this anticlimactic trial were just the tip of the iceberg as far as the Hughes family was concerned—and powerless to do anything about it. Perhaps the information they had puzzled over and tried so fervently to make sense of for five years did not meet the standards of admissibility in court, but that fact did not make their grave doubts about the paternal heirs any less real, or any less disturbing. They had been assigned the task of insuring that the rightful heirs-at-law of Howard Hughes, Jr., inherited his estate, and it was a responsibility they had come to take very seriously. As the verdict was announced, setting into motion the mechanism of inheritance rights to the Hughes fortune for Barbara Cameron, et al., they could not shake their belief, based both on instinct and fact, that the wrong people may have inherited the estate of Howard Hughes, Jr.

Rush and Avis: An Ironic Postscript

As a postlude to the trial, one issue of great importance remained to be resolved: the adoption by estoppel claim of Rush Hughes and Avis McIntyre. "Adoption by estoppel" is a little-known legal doctrine by which an individual who was not formally adopted by a stepparent may be recognized as "equitably" adopted (with the same rights and privileges as a natural or formally adopted child), if treated and regarded by the parent in question as his or her own child, and *not* as a stepchild. The process is often compared to a common-law marriage, and the concept is much the same. The equitable adoption theory is not recognized by every state, and it is applied discriminately in those states that do recognize it—hence its low profile both in and out of the legal profession.

156

Rush and Avis' attorney, Wayne Fisher, was quick to call his opponents' claims a "cock 'n' bull story" in court that autumn of 1981. What, then, of his own clients' less than airtight case? Insiders questioned whether Rupert Hughes actually considered the two stepchildren to be his adopted son and daughter, and privately speculated that the two could not overcome the flaws in their case and prove otherwise in court. Yet, judging by Wayne Fisher's bravura performance during the trial to determine Elspeth's legitimacy, one would never suspect there was a cloud over his own clients' claim of heirship. In his final argument to the jury, he announced that it was "with great honor" that he represented Rush and Avis, and supported the "three granddaughters of Rupert Hughes."

As it developed, Fisher's confidence was not misplaced. To the supreme bewilderment of the attorneys representing the midwestern and Alabama branches of the Hughes family who had struggled so hard to unseat Elspeth and demonstrate their own clients' kinship to Hughes, the claims of heirship of Rush and Avis were *never even litigated*. At several points in Phase Three of the heirship trials, George Parnham tried to introduce a motion to try the adoption by estoppel issue, but it was repeatedly denied. Judge Gregory explained his ruling by stating that the adoption issue was dependent on the outcome of the trial to determine Elspeth's legitimacy. If Barbara Cameron and her sisters were unsuccessful in their efforts to prove that Elspeth Hughes was the daughter of Rupert Hughes, Gregory stated, there would be no need to consider the adoption claim. This position was based on a complicated point of law. Judge Gregory believed that if it were shown that Rupert Hughes had no children of his own, then Rush and Avis would not have the option to prove that they were adopted by estoppel. He was following a line of cases that hold that, for an individual to be adopted "by estoppel," the adoptive parent must also have a natural-born child *to estop*. If there is no natural-born child, this line of reasoning continues, a stepchild cannot claim to be equitably adopted: the legal argument of estoppel would not apply. If Judge Gregory's analysis of the law is correct, it meant that, for their heirship claims to have a chance, Avis and Rush first needed to have Elspeth established as the natural daughter of Rupert Hughes—as much as Elspeth's daughters needed Avis' testimony on *their* behalf, some pointed out cynically. As a consequence, attorneys for some of the other claimants were heard to mutter about how the law creates strange bedfellows, pointing to Avis' turnabout endorsement of Elspeth and the daughters' support of Avis as a greed-motivated example of "you scratch my back, I'll scratch yours."

Once the jury returned its verdict legitimizing Elspeth on September 4, 1981, George Parnham again asked to try the adoption issue. And again, Judge Gregory denied his request. Instead, he set a hearing for September 16, 1981, at which time he would consider the claims of Rush and Avis Hughes, which he and Dinkins deemed to be "derivative" of the now-successful claim of Barbara Cameron, et al.

At the September 16 hearing, Judge Gregory ruled that only attorneys for Rush and Avis, the Barbara Cameron group, and ad litem Dinkins had "standing" to participate, blocking George Parnham and Jackie Taylor's attempts to introduce evidence in opposition to Rush and Avis' adoption claim. Wayne Fisher presented several hours' worth of evidence on behalf of his clients, consisting of portions of their depositions and several of their school records. Paul Freese then took over and said that he, speaking for Barbara Cameron and her sisters, had "no objection" to the claim that Rush and Avis were the adopted children of Rupert Hughes. In fact, he "strongly encouraged" the court to grant it, predicated upon the pretrial settlement agreement he and his clients had entered into with Rush, Avis, and the maternal heirs. Ted Dinkins, who had an obligation to protect the interests of the unknown heirs of the Hughes estate, announced that he was "not prepared to try Rush and Avis at this point," and asked the court whether he had an obligation to do so.

Apparently not. Judge Gregory, in what he described afterwards as a "formality," declared that Rush and Avis were the adopted children of Rupert Hughes, "based on the evidence and the agreement of the parties." The fallacy in that statement is that there was no one present to offer any evidence or testimony to the contrary, with the possible exception of ad litem Dinkins, who was instructed by the court that he was under no obligation to try the adoption by estoppel claim. Judge Gregory was then asked to approve the settlement agreement, in line with a final judgment that would be prepared by Dinkins, to distribute the Hughes estate in accordance with the "heirs' " earlier percentage agreement. The judge similarly approved the private agreement.

So it came to be that Rush Hughes and Avis McIntyre, born Rush and Avis Bissell, never adopted by their mother's second husband, Rupert Hughes, and unacknowledged in Rupert's own will, became legally entitled to 9.5 percent of the multimillion-dollar estate of Rupert's nephew, Howard Hughes, Jr., who demonstrated a well known and undisguised contempt for Rupert. It was a legal coup of unsurpassed audacity. Attorneys for the midwestern second and third cousins were up in arms over this latest development, frustrated in the extreme over their inability even to litigate Rush and Avis' claim. Those close to the estate saw nothing improper or unusual in this final twist to the heirship proceedings. "It's done all the time," said one probate attorney of the approved settlement agreement cutting in Rush, Avis, and the others. "An agreement to divide an estate," he maintained, such as the one entered into by the maternal and supposed paternal heirs of Howard Hughes, Jr., "is only improper if it affects anyone's interests other than those included in the agreement." And since the maternal heirs and the Barbara Cameron group had already been determined to be the bona fide Hughes heirs by judicial process, then according to this interpretation of the law, they were free to cut in anyone they chose, since the only interests they were diminishing in doing so would be their own.

How about the unknown heirs? Since it was at least possible, some would say probable, that Rush and Avis did not meet the legal standards of equitable adoption, didn't the attorney ad litem have an obligation on behalf of any existing unknown heirs at least to litigate both sides of the adoption issue? Those with the opposite view felt the "unknown heirs" had no interest in the matter because the 9.5 percent was money being paid "privately" to Rush and Avis by the court-determined heirs-at-law.

Isn't there still a hole in this argument? Does not Hughes' estate itself have an "interest": to see that only the rightful heirs share in the Hughes fortune? Insiders admitted that this was correct. With that in mind, one must wonder whether it would have been proper to let a judge or jury decide the factual question as to whether Rush and Avis were in fact equitably adopted by Rupert Hughes, based on all the evidence, not merely on unopposed testimony.

With the ever-shifting legal positions in counterpoint to the strange and conflicting facts that came to the surface about the Hughes family, it is easy to see why the third phase of the trial to determine the heirs-at-law of Howard R. Hughes, Jr., inspired such a torrent of controversy. Yet, as Dinkins' investigators knew, there was much more to the Hughes family tree than ever came out at the much-ballyhooed trial. The most disturbing and intriguing facts and circumstances never even made it to court. They remained hidden from view, locked in file drawers for safekeeping, or dancing in the heads of Dinkins' protegés.

8

To Find an Heir

When Ted Dinkins was first appointed the attorney ad litem in the Hughes case in 1976, neither he nor anyone else knew much about the Hughes family. And, based on the evidence and testimony brought out in court, the jury assigned the task of determining the paternal heirs were able to glean little more knowledge about the Hugheses of Keokuk, Iowa. The most they could hope to learn from the helter-skelter presentation of evidence during Phase Three was that, on the Hughes side of the family, Howard R. Hughes, Jr., had a grandfather named either Felix Turner Hughes or Felix Moner Hughes; that Judge Felix Hughes had a son named Howard Hughes, Sr., and another son called Rupert Hughes, whose marriages and alleged daughter were very much in question. Next to nothing was said at the trial about Felix Hughes' wife or his other children, Greta and Felix, Howard and Rupert's siblings. In fact, little came to light about Rupert's marriages or his life in general, despite the shadow of doubt cast on his line of descent. Finally, surprisingly little surfaced about Rupert's purported daughter Elspeth, the center of the heirship controversy.

Although not much more than this was made public at Phase Three of the heirship determination, in the intervening months between his appointment as ad litem and the trial to determine Howard Hughes, Jr.'s, heirs, Dinkins and his two investigators, genealogist Mary Fay and Dinkins' associate, came to know more about the Hughes family than they knew about their own.

The Story Begins to Unfold

Ted Dinkins and his aides began their investigation of the Hughes family by studying their well-worn copy of the *Philadelphia Inquirer* chart of potential heirs to get a rough idea of the Hughes lineage. The chart revealed that Howard Hughes, Jr.'s, grandfather Felix Hughes was married to a woman named Jean Amelia Summerlin, and that the couple had four children: Greta, Howard, Sr., Rupert, and Felix, in order of age (oldest to youngest). It also showed that Rupert Hughes had a daughter, Elspeth, who was born in 1897 and died in 1945. Aside from the years of these individuals' births and deaths, there was little on the chart to assist the ad litem: no information as to whom if anyone the four Hughes children married, or when and where the marriages occurred. Nevertheless, this slight information provided a convenient place for the ad litem team to begin in assembling the complete family tree.

Not long thereafter, a publication found its way into Dinkins' increasingly chaotic office that would be of great assistance to his heirfinders in their efforts to piece together the vital statistics and chronology on the Felix Hughes children. It was called "Howard Hughes: The 'Keokuk Connection,' " and was subtitled, "Tracing the Hughes family through Illinois, Missouri and Iowa." This chatty, gossipy forty-page booklet was put together after Hughes' death in 1976 by a genial former Keokuk newspaperman, Francis Helenthal, then the editor of a local "shopper's press." (He recently became editor of the Keokuk *Gate City.*) Helenthal was, by his description, "always aware" of Howard Hughes, Jr.'s, roots in Keokuk, and because of his notoriety, had "kept clippings and stuff" about his Keokuk family, occasionally writing an article or two for local publication.

After Hughes' death and the corresponding publicity about his relatives, Helenthal decided to "do something a little more thorough" and assembled his Keokuk anecdotes, collected a little more background on Hughes' midwestern ancestors, and compiled it all into "The Keokuk

Connection," which he distributed mostly in the region surrounding Keokuk. "The typical resident here didn't even know there were any Hugheses related to Howard around here," said Helenthal. Helenthal published the booklet when it became clear that the millionaire recluse had not left a valid will that could be found, and interest about his estate was at its peak. "The Keokuk Connection" was designed to call attention to the Hughes relations in the Midwest who had been living in anonymity for years and who, by a quirk of fate, might be in line to collect a share of their distant relative's estate. Helenthal had no idea that his small-town effort would prove to be a research tool for a team of lawyers and genealogists in Houston, Texas, and elsewhere. Since so little was known about the Hughes side of the family, and so much depended upon it, Helenthal's early research, though admittedly superficial, was seized upon by the disparate groups of individuals looking into Howard Hughes, Jr.'s, genealogy. ("This isn't a legal document," Helenthal later observed somewhat sheepishly. "It was just a little story, written for more or less local consumption, really.")

"The Keokuk Connection" is largely a collection of first-hand reminiscences and observations about being a "poor Hughes relation" by some second and third cousins sprinkled throughout Illinois, Missouri, and Iowa, tracked down by Helenthal for quotation and picture-taking—with a few "spicy tidbits" about Howard, Jr.'s, life thrown in for interest. As in any small town, the inhabitants of Keokuk kept a close watch on the comings and goings at every address— particularly at an eccentric residence such as the Hugheses'—and this small-town mentality, reflected in the pages of "The Keokuk Connection," was a definite plus in the ad litem's attempts to pursue rumors and innuendoes about the Hughes siblings, which were plentiful.

The booklet also printed some rare photographs from a Hughes album that originally belonged to Howard, Jr.'s, great-grandparents, Joshua and Martha Askins Hughes. Included were pictures of Joshua, Martha, and their five children: Joshua W., Jr., John Wesley (the sibling discussed earlier who had seventeen children), William P., Felix Turner (Howard, Jr.'s, grandfather), and Martha Ann Hughes. (It was Martha Ann's granddaughter, Florence Stevenson of Arbela, Missouri, who got custody of the family album, and Helenthal obtained the heirloom photographs from her.) Felix Turner Hughes' three brothers and one sister all married and raised their families in the same part of the Midwest, and their descendants (Howard, Jr.'s, second and third cousins) are still scattered throughout the tri-state area. This is the group that was represented by George Parnham during Phase Three of the heirship trials, and their recollections and comments fill the pages of "The Keokuk Connection." (As Helenthal observed of the subjects of his publication: "These people here . . . you're not talking about Houston here, or Las Vegas slickers; you're talking about common folks!")

As interesting or amusing as these insights might have been, it was Helenthal's discussion of the four children of Judge Hughes—their upbringing and marital history—that gave Dinkins' researchers a springboard to their investigation. "I would imagine you've had some problems on this," Helenthal acknowledged to Dinkins' associate, "because very little to my knowledge has been written about the paternal side of the family." About that Helenthal was not mistaken. The small amount of information contained in the two or three pages he devoted to the lives of Felix Hughes' children, though inaccurate in certain of its facts, details, and dates, was the most comprehensive data to be found on the four collectively. The booklet set Dinkins' sleuths off on an adventure into the past that met with unexpected results.

The comment most often made about the four children of Felix and Jean Hughes is how different from each other they were. Rupert Hughes reportedly often said, "It was almost unbelievable that four children having been brought up in the same environment and conditions were so unalike one another." Yet one thought was predominant to Dinkins and his two cohorts as they studied the Hughes genealogy: there was absolutely nothing in their background that would suggest the celebrity and notoriety each of the four Hughes children would attain as adults.

Howard Hughes' Paternal Ancestors:
The Felix Moner/Turner Hughes Mystery

Howard Robard Hughes, Jr., and his father and grandfather before him, descended from Joshua W. Hughes, a Virginian of humble origins and Welsh ancestry, and his wife Martha Askins, originally of Kentucky. Joshua Hughes served as a captain in the Black Hawk War in the 1840s, which eventually entitled him to a land grant of 160 acres, causing him to move his family from Kentucky (and later Illinois) to Scotland County, Missouri. There he raised five children under primitive conditions in a log cabin, supporting himself none too well as a blacksmith and a farmer. Felix Turner Hughes, Howard, Jr.'s, grandfather, was born to Joshua and Martha in 1838, while the family was still in Milstadt, Illinois, one of four sons and a daughter. It became genealogist Mary Fay's task to investigate and confirm the Hughes lineage roughly before 1880 (Dinkins' associate looked into events in the family that occurred after 1880), and with great diligence Mrs. Fay eventually found census reports, county histories, and military applications—tools of the genealogical trade—to support this much of Howard Hughes, Jr.'s, tangled paternal ancestry.

One of the heirship trials' most celebrated points of dispute was of course the identity of Howard, Jr.'s, grandfather Felix Hughes—be he Felix Turner Hughes or, as Robert Hughes claimed, Felix Moner Hughes. At the trial, Robert Hughes relied upon the Harvard alumni reports of Howard Hughes, Sr., in which he listed his father's name as "Felix Moner Hughes," to link Felix Hughes to the Robert Hughes branch of the family. In counterpoint to his evidence, Mrs. Fay located a United States Census Report taken in 1850 in St. Clair County, Illinois, where Joshua W. Hughes and his family resided at the time. In this 1850 Census, a "Felix, age 12" appears as one of the children of Joshua and Martha Hughes, along with William, John, and Joshua, Jr. The next federal census was taken in 1860. By this time Joshua Hughes had moved on to Missouri to take advantage of the government land grant, so Mrs. Fay ordered a copy of the census from Scotland County, Missouri. In the 1860 report, a "Felix J." appears as one of the sons of Joshua and Martha Hughes, now aged twenty-two.

Although no middle name appears for this Felix Hughes in either census record (though there is a middle initial "J" in the 1860 census), they both show that a Felix Hughes was a member of the Joshua W. Hughes family as early as 1850, when he was only twelve years old. A fundamental point of Robert Hughes' family saga is Felix Moner Hughes' dramatic betrayal of his clan during the Civil War in 1865, when he fought for the North and ambushed his kin, later changing his name to Felix Turner Hughes after a different branch of the family. Yet a Felix Hughes shows up in the 1850 census with the Joshua W. Hughes family *fifteen years before* this alleged incident, when Felix was a boy of twelve.

Late in 1977 Mrs. Fay received additional information that conflicted with Robert's family history. On October 8 she sent a letter to Dinkins enclosing not only the 1850 and 1860 United States census reports, but also, from the National Archives in Washington, the military records of Felix Hughes' service in the Civil War. "I would call your attention to the following . . . "she wrote Dinkins. "In 1903, one James Gillespie of Scotland County, Missouri, gave an affidavit that he had known Felix T. Hughes since he was ten years old and had lived within a mile of where Felix grew up and had enlisted with him in the same service in the spring of 1863." The letter continued, "On 20 February 1904, F. M. Cowell gave a General Affidavit stating he had known Felix T. Hughes since 1861 and had been with him in the service." In no way could the testimony of Gillespie and Cowell on these affidavits be reconciled with Robert Hughes' contention that Felix Hughes was born Felix Moner

Hughes and remained so until his split from the family in 1865. "It is my conclusion," wrote Mrs. Fay in closing, "that the attached evidence is damaging to Mr. Robert C. Hughes' claim."

Later in the investigation, Dinkins and his two researchers were struck by a paragraph in Rupert Hughes' 1924 tribute to his father in *American* magazine: "My father's father, Joshua Hughes, moved from Kentucky to Illinois, just across the Mississippi River from St. Louis. My father was born at Milstadt, Illinois, November 10th, 1838, and named Felix Turner Hughes, after an uncle." Rupert Hughes' behavior, of course, was subject to growing suspicion throughout the pretrial discovery period; therefore his opinions and statements about his family are open to considerable question. If his father were guilty of the treacherous acts described by Robert C. Hughes, then Rupert was no doubt in collusion with him by the time of this magazine article.

Nevertheless, the census reports and military records confirmed Felix Hughes' position in the Joshua W. Hughes family to genealogist Mary Fay's eventual satisfaction. This is not to say she was free from all doubts, however. In addition to the confusion over Felix Turner (alias Moner) Hughes' middle name, there was some degree of uncertainty over the middle name of the man whom Felix contended was his father, Joshua W. Hughes.

In most of Felix and his childrens' autobiographical information, it is listed as Joshua *Waters* Hughes, while Robert C. Hughes claimed the "W" in Joshua's name stood for William. To heighten the mystery, Joshua's middle name is reported variously as Waters or William, depending on the source of the data. Why this disparity occurs has never been explained. Nor has the Felix "Moner" Hughes entry in the Harvard Class Reports of Howard Hughes, Sr., and perhaps they never will be.

Despite these two troublesome irregularities, Mrs. Fay endorsed Felix Turner Hughes' position as the son of Joshua W. and Martha Askins Hughes by the time of the heirship trial, relying upon the census reports, military records, and certain other documents she had assembled over the course of the five-year investigation. However, in doing so, Mrs. Fay did not intend to rule out other aspects of Robert Hughes' claim, such as the alleged drowning of Rupert's "real" daughter and assorted other theories about the Hughes family. "I never would have worked so hard on the Robert Hughes thing if I hadn't thought there was an ounce of truth in it," she confided recently. Yet Mrs. Fay's feelings about Robert Hughes' claim were never explored when she was on the witness stand; her testimony, therefore, was taken as an unequivocal admission that his claims were entirely unworthy of belief, which is not the impression she had hoped to convey. As a consequence, the jury did not have the benefit of weighing the professional opinion of the genealogist appointed by the court for that express purpose, before rendering their verdict on the Hughes family tree.

Howard Hughes' Eccentric Grandparents

Putting their suspicions about the Felix Moner/Turner scandal aside, the ad litem team pieced together what they could of his adult life. From a humble background, Felix Hughes rose to a position of considerable esteem in the Midwest. After "such schooling as he could get," he became a schoolteacher, eventually being named superintendent of schools in Schuyler County, Missouri, where he served from 1865 to 1870. About this time he met Jean (often spelled "Jane" on official records for some reason) Amelia Summerlin of Memphis, Missouri. An old-time Keokuk resident described her as "unknown socially." If this is true, then her background would have been compatible with that of her husband-to-be. ("They were poor, poor people," observes Helenthal.) Jean's parents were Thomas and Bathsheba Robards Summerlin, which explains the origin of Howard Robard Hughes, Jr.'s, middle name. Jean Summerlin had an older brother named Elbert, an older sister Electra (or Electa), and a younger sister named Catherine.

Felix Hughes and Jean Summerlin were married in Memphis, Missouri, on August 1, 1985, and from this imperfect union there were to follow two generations touched by equal parts genius and madness. Shortly after they were wed, Hughes began to "read the law," in the vernacular of the times, and was admitted to the Missouri bar in 1866. He and his wife Jean then moved to Lancaster, Missouri, to a small white frame house where Hughes began to practice his chosen profession with skill and success. Within a short time, he was named local counsel for the railroad that ran through Lancaster, and his wife Jean was kept busy giving birth to their seven children. Their first child, a daughter whom they named Greta, was born June 4, 1866, followed in rapid succession by Howard Robard on September 9, 1869, Rupert on January 31, 1872, and finally Felix on October 1, 1874. (Three other children died young: a son, Reginald, described in the family as a "genius," was born in 1876 and died in 1881 at the age of five; a baby girl, Jean, was born in 1880 and died the same year; and a third child died in infancy in 1883, before it could be named.)

In 1880, when Hughes was forty-two, the family moved to Keokuk, when the children were fourteen, eleven, eight, and six years old, and there Hughes prospered. "The people had . . . a lot of wealth here," explains Helenthal. "There were seven railroads here at one time. This is what brought Hughes to Keokuk, because this was a railroad center and it really was the center of many things. In those days, it was either St.

Louis or Keokuk to headquarter.'' By all reports, Hughes was a shrewd and cunning attorney, and his talents were rewarded in the Mississippi River town. In 1885, Hughes was elected president and general counsel of the Keokuk & Western division of the Burlington rail system, and he continued to practice law outside his specialty as well. Hughes, a ''stalwart Republican,'' was elected mayor of Keokuk for one term (1895–96), and served as a judge for a time, preferring to be called ''Judge'' thereafter.

While mayor of Keokuk, Hughes was ''deeply involved'' in civic affairs. One of the more pressing issues of his day was the possible development of the Des Moines Rapids in the Mississippi River above Keokuk. For years, prominent residents and outsiders as well had expended much time and money in schemes to harness the Mississippi's water power, all without success. Hughes, an outspoken citizen, became ''intensely interested'' in plans that might lead to the construction of a power plant in Keokuk, which would make the community more prosperous. He conceived the notion of damming the entire width of the river from Iowa to Illinois with a single lock, instead of the three then in use, following a similar example in the Welland Canal between Lakes Ontario and Erie. Eleven years later, the ''Great Keokuk Dam'' was built, using Hughes' basic plan. When completed in 1913, it powered one of the largest hydroelectric plants and became, in the words of resident Francis Helenthal, ''the engineering marvel of the world.''

Though Felix Hughes is often described in glowing terms in the local county histories, there was another, perhaps dominant, side to his personality. He was hardworking in the extreme, driving himself to earn every available dollar, and he possessed more than the necessary quotient of ruthlessness to survive as an attorney in an era when frontier justice prevailed. Helenthal writes that Judge Hughes was a ''real showman'' in the courtroom, who would often ''wave his cane wildly'' during a trial, and sometimes ''point it threateningly at the opposing lawyer.'' These theatrics did not stop Hughes from ''walking down the street arm-in-arm'' with his adversary at the conclusion of a trial (which he usually won).

If ever there were a woman born who could handle the ''Judge,'' it was his wife, Jean Amelia Summerlin Hughes, known to all as ''Mimi.'' Throughout their married life, she referred to her husband as ''Mr. Hughes,'' a symbol of her autocratic disposition. Described as ''talented, temperamental, a money-spender, highly independent, and a strong individualist,'' the operative word would seem to be temperamental. If Howard Hughes, Jr.'s, eccentricities can be traced to any one ancestor, it would be his paternal grandmother, Mimi. A prominent local real estate man in Keokuk, Birdwell Sutlive, Jr., recalls that

168

Jean Hughes had a phobia about "flies, bugs, moths, and that sort of thing." Consequently, "there was no closet connected with any of the bedrooms—she preferred to use walnut wardrobes so that they could be emptied and taken out in the sun and air for purification."

A retired local newspaperman, writing in 1961 about the prominent families of Keokuk, had this to say about the Hugheses after their move to 312 North Fifth Street in Keokuk: "Life . . . at the beginning of the 1880s settled itself into a tragicomic pattern which was being constantly relieved by the humorous peccadilloes of the Judge's wife." From *Tales of Early Keokuk Homes,* published in 1959 by the same author, comes this disclosure: "Back at 312 North Fifth . . . the neighbors made no concealment of the fact they could hear the 'Judge' and his wife having words on a rather frequent schedule." Francis Helenthal, in gathering information for "The Keokuk Connection," concurs. "It was common gossip," he writes, "that Judge Hughes and his wife did not get along too compatibly, and it was always said that they maintained separate bedrooms—one upstairs and one down."

A greater oddity was that the Hugheses, though they lived in a town with a population of less than 15,000, eventually maintained two separate residences, both in Keokuk. Their second abode, a gift from son Howard Hughes, Sr., was located at 925 Grand Avenue, and referred to in the family as the "summer" home—because it boasted a view of the river. The house on North Fifth Street, only ten to twelve blocks away, was in turn used as the "winter" home, "or as a refuge for the Judge at times when Jean Hughes was 'cool' to the mayor," writes Helenthal. Ray Garrison, author of several books on Keokuk history, tells the story that Judge Hughes, returning to the house on North Fifth one evening, learned that his wife was at the "summer" house. "Valise in hand," Garrison writes, "he walked up there and knocked at the front door. 'Who's there?' came a familiar voice from within. 'Let me in,' said the Judge. 'Go back to the other house,' the voice ordered. 'This is mine.' Somewhat dismayed and a little put out, the Judge returned to the Winter Home." How much of this local gossip is true and how much hyperbole is open to speculation, but it does paint a revealing picture of life at the Hugheses'.

However much the Judge and Jean Hughes may have disagreed, they shared an almost smothering concern for their four children and spent lavish sums to educate and provide for them in a grand manner. Ruby H. Hughes, widow of the Judge's youngest child, Felix, has written that Jean Hughes was "always careful to foster the ambitions of her children," and this is a great understatement. Both Felix and Jean Hughes, but especially Mimi, were excessively devoted to the four Hughes siblings. "No sacrifice was too great for my mother or my father

169

to make for us, since nothing was quite good enough for the children they adored and were adored by," wrote Rupert Hughes in his 1924 paean to his parents. "My mother instilled the ambitions," he continues, "and my father found the funds." Time would reward their efforts, as each of their four children went on to success in different fields, and credit must go at least in part to the parents who raised this brilliant quartet who arose from the obscurity of Keokuk, Iowa, to lead lives of accomplishment and international recognition, leaving their bucolic kin to gape at the "family of geniuses" born to Felix and Jean Hughes. "We were always treated at home as if we were the world's best and greatest geniuses," observed son Rupert, and perhaps therein lies the secret.

Somehow Jean Hughes managed to ignore her less than elegant surroundings, and raised her brood as if they were born to royalty. "There, in the very heart of the Midwest, we were brought up to a knowledge of the world's art," remembered Rupert Hughes. "The names of Giotto, Cimabue, Andrea del Sarto, Raphael, and the others were household words." With this extravagant devotion and attention came unwavering loyalty. "Mimi has always insisted," noted Rupert, ". . . that her children, all of them, were the best and most beautiful specimens of the human race that ever existed." This unflagging maternal allegiance was carried to an extreme. "We got into fights and accidents incessantly," cites Rupert, "but when we fought with neighbor's children, it was always—according to Mimi—the fault of the neighbor's children." This is consistent with the recollections of Jean Hughes' grandniece, Frances Smith (Electa Summerlin's granddaughter). Mrs. Smith described Mimi as a "firecracker," and told Dinkins' associate that she raised her children in "laissez-faire fashion." "Anything goes" was her motto with her own children, she reported, yet Mimi was a "no-nonsense" type when it came to anyone else's brood. Mrs. Smith's mother lived with her aunt Jean's family in Keokuk for several years while attending college, and characterized the three "Hughes boys" as "obstreperous . . . always taking something apart." Electa would reportedly "lock everything up" if she expected her sister Jean's children to visit. Though Rupert Hughes denied it, his mother's blind devotion and unconditional loyalty must have had a profound effect on her children's self-image and perception of the world.

When she wasn't tutoring her "geniuses" at home, Jean Hughes was sending them to expensive boarding schools, Ivy League colleges, and European tutors. According to Rupert, Judge Hughes encouraged and fostered the same lofty ambitions for his children as his demanding wife. "Go ahead on your own lines," he reportedly told his middle son on many occasions, "and I will back you to my last dollar." Where Judge Hughes found his last dollar is an interesting subject for conjecture.

170

Practicing law in a city of only 15,000 population, accumulating such riches as were necessary to support the high-minded aspirations of his wife and four children would seem to be an impossible struggle. "Yet the money always came," marveled Rupert, "and I can never understand how he got it, as he was never accused of theft, forgery, or counterfeiting." Not until the 1970s, anyway. Rupert Hughes was unaware at the time he wrote this tribute, in 1924, that a group of Hugheses from Alabama would one day accuse his father of far worse as a part of the estate proceedings of his world-famous grandson, Howard Hughes, Jr. Robert C. Hughes maintains that the Felix Hughes "money tree" had its inception in the $140,000 in life savings he allegedly stole at gunpoint from Robert Hughes' war-torn family as Felix ambushed them on their way to Alabama, and Felix's remarkable facility for generating income makes this an intriguing possibility.

Whatever their source, Felix Hughes' funds appeared to be inexhaustible. "When we had finished our schoolings," chronicled Rupert, "our expenses seemed only to have begun. We had the habit of telegraphing home for money to get married on, or to put into investments that always failed, or to pay debts incurred by trying to hold up our end with our richer companions." Judge Hughes financed Howard Hughes, Sr.'s, many years of fortune-hunting, and continued to provide financial aid after his marriage to Allene Gano, even backing him in the patent and manufacture of his famous drill bit, all the while supporting Howard's sister and two brothers well into their middle age. Whatever else might be said about him, Judge Hughes was relentless in his pursuit of work. It was a source of great pride to his son Rupert that at the age of eighty-six, his father traveled to New York to "wind up a law case involving two million dollars"—which he won.

"The only evil consequence of this I can recall," wrote Rupert, "is that homesickness became a chronic and violent disease with all of us." Indeed, the Hugheses remained a close family throughout all their lives—with the possible exception of Howard, Sr., who seemed to maintain more emotional and geographical distance. Yet even Howard kept his ties with his parents. As Rupert wrote in tribute to his mother: "You got (Howard) his education at Harvard, the money to finance his many failures and his final tremendous success. He gave you rich gifts—a house, automobiles, anything you would accept; but he owed it all to you and to his father, and was glad to say so." In light of this, it was not surprising that, after Howard, Jr., was born, he was taken back to his grandparents' hometown to be baptized. There, at St. John's Episcopal Church of Keokuk, little Howard Robard Hughes, Jr., was officially christened.

The other three children of Judge and Mrs. Hughes were more

noticeably dependent on and devoted to their parents, and Mr. and Mrs. Hughes continued to exert a strong influence on their lives as adults. Felix and Jean Hughes in fact outlived two of their children, Greta and Howard, Sr. After the death of Howard, Sr., in 1924, they decided to move away from Keokuk to California, where their two remaining children were then living. Mimi and the Judge bought a house on North Rossmore Avenue in Los Angeles. "The first thing she did," wrote Jean Hughes' daughter-in-law Ruby Hughes, widow of Felix, "was to build a wing on the house so Felix and Rupert would always have a place to stay when they visited her and 'Daddy' (the Hughes children's name for their father)." Felix and Rupert were, by this time, fifty and fifty-two years old.

The Judge and Mimi led full, productive lives until well into their eighties. Even as octogenarians they made a singular couple. Felix Hughes had apparently mellowed slightly in his old age, as he was remembered fondly by Avis McIntyre as a "lovely, gentle old man with a white tuft." Jean Hughes, in contrast, was every inch the character she had always been. Described by Avis as a "straight as a ramrod type of person with a very determined air about her," she learned to play golf at eighty and read Spanish novels in the original—a language she began to study at sixty. When Felix and Jean Hughes finally died, he in 1926 at age eighty-eight, she two years later at eight-six, Rupert and Felix, their two devoted sons, had their remains interred, at their earlier request, in a family plot in Keokuk, where their three infant children were buried, and where their lives had left such an indelible impression on the community.

At a point in the heirship investigation, as Dinkins and his associate pondered the many questions surrounding the Hughes family—the doubts about Elspeth, and the mounting suspicions about Rupert, and later Greta—they thought about Felix and Jean Hughes, the parents or grandparents of the individuals under scrutiny, and their continuing influence over their children. With that in mind, Dinkins ordered copies of both Felix and Jean Hughes' wills, hoping that one or both might shed some light on what he considered a vague line of descent.

Felix Hughes' will arrived first, and it was something of a surprise to Dinkins' associate in several respects. First, though the Judge was a high-powered lawyer and a man of some means (judging by his expenses), his will was barely over a page in length, handwritten in a nearly illegible scrawl. It was executed on April 3, 1902, in Keokuk, Iowa. According to the traditional family history (as outlined by Barbara Cameron and her sisters and supported by Avis and Rush), all four of the Judge's children were grown by this time, and two—Rupert and Greta—were married. Howard, Jr., wasn't born yet (he came along in

1905), but Elspeth, the Hughes' first, and then only, grandchild, would have been five years old, having been born in 1897 (per her birth certificate). These were the alleged circumstances of his family at the time Judge Hughes made out his will in 1902. It reads, in pertinent part:

> First, I give and bequeath to my most dearly beloved wife Jean A. Hughes if she survive me my entire Estate real personal and mixed wheresoever situated and appoint her if she survive me my Executrix and direct that she be not required to give bond as Executrix—
>
> I recognize and most dearly love all of my children Howard Greta Witherspoon Rupert and Felix—in testimony whereof I have signed this instrument and caused it to be witnessed by two competent persons—this 3d day of April 1902
>
> Felix Turner Hughes

Though it was certainly not mandatory from a legal point of view for Hughes to mention his granddaughter in this instrument, he had made a special point to recognize his children, though they were not made direct beneficiaries of his estate, making Elspeth, his only grandchild, seem somehow conspicuous by her absence.

Jean Summerlin Hughes' will arrived several days later, giving rise to similar misgivings. Her last will and testament was executed years after her husband's—in 1928, nine months before she died, and two years after the Judge's death—and it was a more formally drafted document, though only three typewritten pages. Both Greta and Howard Hughes, Sr., were deceased by the time Mrs. Hughes made out her will in California, and her two grandchildren, Elspeth and Howard, Jr., were thirty-one and twenty-three years old, respectively. In Articles One and Two of her will, Jean A. Hughes left to her son Felix her home in Los Angeles, and all the household furniture and personal property upon the premises. In Article Three, she directed that the remainder of her property, both personal and real, be divided equally between her sons Rupert and Felix. Article Four reads as follows:

> I mention the name of my grandson, HOWARD R. HUGHES, JR., to show that I have not forgotten him and that I purposely have not given him anything in this my Last Will and Testament.

In Article Five, Mrs. Hughes appointed the Citizens Trust and Savings Bank of Los Angeles as executor of her will, after which it was sworn and signed.

Just as in the Judge's will, Elspeth is singular as the only Hughes not mentioned. As a "nurturing" woman, a "matriarch of the true sense, devoted to her children, husband and home,'' in the words of Ruby H. Hughes (Felix's widow), it seemed unusual to Dinkins' associate that Jean Hughes had not included, or at least acknowledged, her only grand-daughter in her last will and testament—particularly since she specifical-ly mentioned her grandson Howard, Jr., whom she had disinherited, ''to show that I have not forgotten him.''

Felix Hughes

So much dissension and controversy had arisen about Rupert Hughes in the course of the heirship investigation, its focus always being Howard, Jr., and Sr., that by the time Dinkins and his staff turned their attention to the other two children of Judge and Mrs. Hughes, Felix and Greta, several months and many more mysteries had come and gone. In Dinkins' office at any time, he and his assistant were pursuing at least twenty different aspects of the Hughes estate proceedings: preparing for and participating in the 1977–78 trial to determine Howard, Jr.'s, legal domicile (an unprecedented legal battle of four months' duration, preceded by two years of pretrial discovery); the ongoing efforts to locate a possible valid Hughes will (culminating in a six-month trial in Las Vegas to test the validity of a document offered for probate by ser-vice station attendant/game show contestant Melvin Dummar); in-vestigation into the more pressing of the heirship claims (Barbara Cameron, et al., Avis and Rush, possible wives, children, brother or sister); plus the uninterrupted train of letters and phone calls from potential heirs and certifiable lunatics. Attendance at the depositions noticed in the Hughes proceedings was in and of itself a full-time oc-cupation. With all this simultaneous activity, and so few to handle it, Dinkins' office was in a state of perpetual frenzy.

Amidst all this clutter, the ad litem began to put together the pieces of Felix and Greta Hughes' lives, leading to his eventual preparation of a complete family tree for the 1981 trial, showing the legitimate heirs on the paternal side of Howard Hughes, Jr.'s, family. Since nothing was said about either Felix or Greta at the heirship determination trial, one would assume that the two led lives of genealogical orderliness and clarity. Nothing could be further from the truth. Though it was not presented to the jury, their pasts—at least Greta's—were filled with the same sort of intrigue that pervaded Rupert's, and made the mystery sur-rounding the hidden years of their nephew Howard, Jr., seem pale by comparison.

Because their lives were not as public as Rupert and Howard, Sr.'s, there was less information readily available on Felix and Greta Hughes. But since no one had come forward to dispute their genealogy or claim to be their kin (as was the case with Rupert), there was less reason to suspect any irregularity. The *Inquirer* chart showed that Felix died in 1961, Greta in 1916, and that neither had ever had any children; at the outset of the investigation, Dinkins had no particular reason to question this information. It was, however, his appointed task to authenticate their marriages, divorces, and the like, and little was known about their lives.

Felix Hughes was born October 1, 1874, the youngest of the four Hughes children. In Francis Helenthal's words, he was the "least flamboyant, least controversial" of the siblings. To make matters even simpler for Dinkins, Felix's widow, Ruby Helen Hughes, was alive and well throughout the heirship investigation, and she was able to confirm the belief that her late husband had no children, more or less closing the door to any further searching for potential heirs via Felix. An aunt by marriage to Howard Hughes, Jr., Ruby Hughes was the closest living relation on the Hughes side of the family. Because the laws of inheritance do not extend to relationships by marriage, however, Ruby was not in line to inherit any of her nephew's estate. Ruby Hughes' deposition was taken early in the estate proceedings (September 1976), five months after Howard, Jr.'s, death, and for a time she seemed to be the final authority with respect to the Hughes family. Ruby Hughes, in fact, had proofread and corrected the statements about the Hugheses published in "The Keokuk Connection."

Yet as the investigation pressed on, Ruby Hughes became less and less a source authority for Dinkins' researcher, for several reasons. First, her deposition contained almost no information about the marriages of her sister-in-law Greta, brother-in-law Rupert, or even her own husband (who had been married previously). Second, and most important, Ruby Hughes did not meet her future husband Felix until around 1943, by which time Greta and Howard, Sr., had been dead for over twenty years, Rupert was seventy-one, and Felix himself was sixty-nine. Since she came into the family at such a late date, her knowledge of family events was all hearsay, and biased hearsay at that. As she wrote Helenthal during her editing of "The Keokuk Connection": "My source of this information was told to me by both Felix and Rupert." As Dinkins and company were only too aware, Rupert's motives and behavior were under close scrutiny, and by Ruby's description, he and Felix shared "a great admiration, love and devotion . . . as brothers." Ergo, whatever family information Ruby Hughes related had to be considered as less than objective where Rupert was concerned. At any rate, her knowledge of the dates and places of the multiple marriages and divorces of the Hughes siblings (including her husband) was vague at best.

However, with the assistance of Ruby Hughes' reminiscences about her late husband's life, genealogist Mary Fay was able to collect the records she needed to illustrate Felix Hughes' marital history and confirm that he had no children, so that by the time of the heirship trial Dinkins could scratch his name off the list with confidence. Felix was the only one of the four Hughes children of whom that could be said.

Although Rupert Hughes' first wife remembered Felix as the "family playboy," who often referred to himself as a "boulevardier," this description of Felix Hughes seems inappropriate. It is true he followed the tradition set by his siblings Greta and Rupert in marrying multiply (three times, to be exact). Yet Felix was by far the most conservative of the four Hughes children in his personal life, and the playboy epithet would be better applied to Howard, Sr. "Innately, he was very shy and sensitive," wrote Felix's widow, Ruby, and further study bore this out. To all appearances, Felix Hughes pursued a life devoted to music. As one of four talented children growing up in what one Keokuk resident described as "the most eccentric family" that he had known, Felix exhibited early his love of singing—much to the consternation of his neighbors. "One of the stories that was told to me," Ruby Hughes wrote in her florid 1977 memoir "Loving Memories of Felix Hughes," "was that when the family lived in the Fifth Street house, little Felix would get up early in the morning and go out on the front porch before the family or neighbors were awake and up for the day, and start to sing at the top of his voice as the sun was rising. Finally, one of the neighbors offered Felix a penny a day if he would curtail his musical renditions until later in the morning."

As an adult, Felix Hughes found a more appreciative audience. In 1895, after completing his studies at a private boarding school in Ohio, twenty-one-year-old Felix followed his older sister Greta to Europe, where she was studying voice with the great masters. ("My brother Felix was given a complete education as a singer, made a brief appearance in grand opera in Liège, Belgium, has sung much in recital, and is now prominent as a teacher in New York," reported Rupert Hughes in summarizing his brother's life in 1924.) Before his return to the United States, Felix spent eight to ten years studying music in Paris, Berlin, and London, learning to speak and read French fluently, all with the extravagant support of Judge Hughes. "Life in Paris was a glorious adventure for this 'young man from Keokuk,' " wrote Ruby Hughes in "Loving Memories." "The Louvre, Paris Opera House, Opéra Comique, and the other artistic and historical land-marks were visited frequently. Jean Amelia had instilled this love of beauty and Felix took advantage of this fascinating city." Carroll Tabor, the Hugheses' across-the-alley neighbor back in Keokuk, saw things rather differently. "Felix was the 'loafer' type," he told Raymond Garrison (author of *Early Keokuk Homes*) in

1950. "He lived the easy life." As Garrison noted after the interview:"Tabor once saw him in Paris where he was studying music. He wrote his father, the judge, Felix T. Hughes, for money to stay on, and he used the letterhead from L'Opéra Comique, which purported to show his father that he was doing well in music, and had a place in the Comique when his studies were over. The Judge sent him the money."

After returning to the United States, Felix sang in concerts and recitals, and eventually met Adella Prentiss, a Vassar graduate who was several years his senior. Described by Ruby Hughes as a "wealthy society matron," Adella Prentiss was the daughter of Loren and Ellen Rouse Prentiss, prominent residents of Cleveland, Ohio. On October 5, 1904, Felix, then thirty, married Adella Prentiss, aged thirty-four, in Cleveland, where the two set up housekeeping. Felix Hughes gave up his concert singing and began a career as a voice teacher, while Adella Prentiss Hughes pursued her own musical ambitions with phenomenal success, eventually being named manager of the Cleveland Symphony Orchestra, one of only a few women in the world to hold that position with a major symphony. Felix and Adella Hughes resided in Cleveland for almost two decades, interrupted by Felix's brief tenure in Washington, D.C., in 1918–19 as a captain in the Military Intelligence Division of the United States Army. At one point, Felix opened a voice studio in New York as well, and commuted back and forth between Cleveland and Manhattan.

It is common knowledge that Felix and Adella were divorced not too much later, but their divorce records could not be located by the attorney ad litem during his investigation, one of only two vital statistics on the Hughes family that eluded Dinkins' researchers. In her search for clues, genealogist Mary Fay eventually requested Adella Prentiss's alumni records from Vassar College. (Adella Prentiss Hughes died in Cleveland in 1950.) In filling out the 1947 Alumnae Address Register, Adella Hughes stated that her marriage to Felix Hughes was "dissolved in 1923," but she provided no information as to where the divorce had occurred. Requests for copies of the divorce proceedings were sent to Cleveland, New York, Washington, D. C., Keokuk, and Los Angeles— cities the Hugheses either frequented or lived in—all without success. The location of these divorce papers is still unknown.

Dinkins, of course, was more interested in whether Felix and his first wife had any children. The material in Adella Hughes' Vassar alumni file effectively removed any doubts that remained in his mind about possible offspring. Directed to list her children on the 1947 alumnae form, Adella Hughes typed in "None." Even more convincing, however, was an interview she had given to the *Cleveland News* late in her life, as part of a series on Cleveland newsmakers. Asked by the reporter, "If you had

had children, could you have worked so hard?'' Mrs. Hughes responded, ''No, not with justice to them. My life has been so exacting that I
would have had scant leisure and even less vitality to devote to such an
important task as rearing a family.'' Finally, the reporter wanted to
know, ''How do you wish to be remembered?'' ''As one who loving
music made music for Cleveland that all hearing it might be happier and
better and more useful citizens,'' was the lady's reply. In 1947, Adella
Prentiss Hughes wrote her memoirs, which she called, to the surprise of
no one on Dinkins' research team, *Music Is My Life*. Insofar as the heirship investigation was concerned, this title said it all. On discovering the
Vassar materials, Dinkins closed the door on the Felix and Adella Prentiss Hughes marriage, confident that whatever passion the couple shared
was reflected in their music alone.

After his divorce from Adella Prentiss, Felix Hughes, then about
fifty-one, relocated permanently to Central Park West, near his studio
in New York, where he had formerly been commuting on occasion from
Cleveland. According to his adoring widow, Ruby, ''Felix was a handsome, desirable, knowledgeable, and charming person, and soon
established an exciting social life along with his success as a teacher.
Among his friendships included some of the interesting and famous people of that time: John McCormack; Geraldine Farrar; Melba; Mary
Garden; and Enrico Caruso and his wife, Dorothy, who studied singing
with Felix after her husband's death.'' In 1924, his brother Howard, Sr.,
died, and his parents made the move from Keokuk to Los Angeles.
''Felix was then prevailed upon to close his studio in New York and
establish himself in Los Angeles,'' observed Ruby Hughes. ''This he did,
and made his home with his mother and father until their demise.''

During this period, the mid-to-late 1920s, Rupert Hughes was
writing and directing silent movies in Hollywood, and, the Hugheses being a close family, he hosted family gatherings regularly. Included were
Rupert, Felix, their parents, and, less frequently, Howard, Jr. (The Judge
died in 1926 and Mimi in 1928.) Somewhere in this time frame, Dinkins'
sleuths were told, Felix was married again. Details about this second
marriage were vague: Ruby Hughes wrote that her husband's second
wife was named Ruth Stonehouse; that she and Felix were married
''about 1925,'' and that Ruth Hughes died in ''approximately 1940.''
Colleen Moore, a star in the twenties and a colleague of Rupert's,
remembered that she met Felix and this wife at several of Rupert's parties, and that she was ''an old-time movie actress who died.''

With nothing more than this to go on, Mrs. Fay managed to find their
marriage certificate (no small feat). The bride's name was indeed Ruth
A. Stonehouse, but the marriage did not take place until 1931—five
years after Ruby Hughes had suggested. The license showed that Felix's

bride was the daughter of James and Georgia Wooster Stonehouse of Illinois and Iowa, respectively; that she was thirty-eight years old, and this was her second marriage. Felix Hughes was by then fifty-seven, and the marriage was performed in Santa Ana, California, outside Los Angeles—one reason it was so difficult to track down. Dinkins and his associate later noticed that "Ruth" began to appear in the Los Angeles city directories as his wife as early as 1929, three years before the couple was married. Perhaps this is how Felix earned his reputation as the "family playboy."

Felix's career prospered during this interval. "The studio in L. A., and later in Hollywood, became one of the most successful vocal studios in the city," Ruby Hughes recalled. Rupert Hughes commented on his brother's abilities as a vocal instructor, "Mary Garden told me that she considered Felix the best singing teacher in the world." A partial list of his pupils confirms Rupert's remark: Nancy Carroll, Anita Page, Hoot Gibson, Jean Harlow, Betty White, and others all studied voice with Felix Hughes.

On a trip to Los Angeles, Dinkins' associate thought to look up Felix's wife Ruth Stonehouse at the Academy of Motion Picture Arts and Sciences, thinking that if she were indeed an "old-time movie actress," as Colleen Moore testified, she might be represented in their files, which could in turn help resolve any doubts about her identity, and might possibly lead to the circumstances of her death. A Ruth Stonehouse indeed surfaced in the Academy's library. In her file was an obituary, with the headline, *Silent Film Star's Last Rites Awaited,* with her date of death listed as May 12, 1941, just about the time Ruby Hughes indicated. Here was one loose end tied. Probably Felix met his second wife at one of his screenwriter-brother's Hollywood parties, Dinkins' associate speculated. It all made sense as the obituary unfolded the events in Ruth Stonehouse's life:

> Funeral services were to be held today at the Wee Kirk o'the Heather for Mrs. Felix Hughes, 48, who as Ruth Stonehouse, starred in hundreds of silent movies in the old Essanay studios.
>
> Mrs. Hughes, who lived at 204 N. Rossmore Ave., died in the Queen of the Angels Hospital Monday with a cerebral hemorrhage.
>
> She was born in Chicago and started her career at the age of 8 as a dancer in Douglas, Arizona. Later she became a partner of Billy Anderson in the ownership of the Essanay Studios in Chicago and became one of the company's top feminine stars. Her contemporaries were Gloria Swanson, Dorothy Phillips, Agnes Ayres, Virginia Valli and Helen Ferguson.
>
> Among the hundreds of pictures she made were a series of Westerns with Tom Santschi and Bessie Love; the first screen play

179

starring Harry Houdini and scores of others in which such players as Norma Shearer, Pauline Garon, Dorothy Revier and Dorothy Reed rose to stardom.

In recent years she was active in club work and was former chairman of the Woman's Auxiliary Council of the Children's Home Society.

Entombment will be in Forest Lawn Memorial Park, under direction of Bresse Bros. and Gilette Mortuary.

Besides her husband, who is a brother of Col. Rupert Hughes, author, Mrs. Hughes is survived by her parents, Mr. and Mrs. James W. Stonehouse, and a sister, Mrs. Hazel E. Heager, Akron, Ohio.

The newspaper obituary did not mention any children born to Ruth Stonehouse Hughes, nor did any other source of information available to Dinkins and his investigators. Mrs. Hughes' death certificate bore out the facts as stated on her obituary, with the additional interesting piece of trivia that her mother, Georgia Wooster Stonehouse, was born in Keokuk, Iowa. After securing her death certificate, Dinkins closed this chapter in Felix Hughes' life. It was unlikely that Felix and Ruth Hughes had any unknown children together, natural or adopted, since during their marriage Felix aged from fifty-seven to sixty-seven, and his wife from thirty-eight to forty-eight, hardly conventional years to begin to raise a family.

The remainder of Felix Hughes' life was of little concern to the ad litem's investigation, for much the same reasons. Two years after his second wife, Ruth Stonehouse, died, Felix Hughes met widow Ruby Helen Parrott McCoy, a secretary in a geophysical company, and they married on October 22, 1943. Hughes was sixty-nine, his new wife thirty-eight. "I was younger in years than Felix," Ruby Hughes wrote in her testimonial to her late husband, "but ours was one of the most beautiful, contented, inspirational, and happy marriages any one could desire or hope to have in their lifetime." On September 9, 1961, eighteen years after his marriage to Ruby, Felix Hughes passed away in the home on North Rossmore purchased some forty years earlier by his parents. He was eighty-seven years old. Felix Hughes was interred in his third wife's family plot in Forest Lawn Memorial Park in Los Angeles.

As a final confirmation that Felix Hughes had no children, Dinkins requested copies of his probate proceedings from Los Angeles County. Just as the ad litem expected, he left his entire estate to his widow, Ruby—no surprise children, and no mention of his famous nephew, Howard, Jr.

9

Greta Hughes: A Woman of Mystery

Greta (pronounced Gree-tuh in the family), eldest of the four Hughes children and the only girl, was perhaps the most mysterious. According to Felix's widow, Ruby Hughes, Greta was "worshipped" by her brothers, and Dinkins' research would later bear this out, revealing a strange bond between Greta and her middle brother Rupert.

The word most often used to describe Greta by those who knew her is "lovely": "She was a perfectly lovely person," was Avis McIntyre's recollection at the time her first deposition was taken in the estate proceedings. "She and Aunt Allene were two standouts in my young life as lovely, lovely women." Annette Gano Lummis, who had occasion to meet Greta after her sister Allene Gano married Howard Hughes, Sr., said simply, "Beautiful woman." And indeed, this is as much information about Greta as was made public at the trial to determine Howard, Jr.'s, paternal heirs. When Avis McIntyre, Rupert's purportedly adopted stepdaughter, was asked on the witness stand by her counsel Wayne Fisher to tell the jury about Howard, Sr.'s, sister, she responded, "Aunt Greta was a lovely, very beautiful woman. Tall and slim . . . dark red hair. Lovely person."

As Dinkins and his associate knew at the time, listening from their counsel table to Avis' testimony, there was much more to Greta Hughes than met the eye.

As the pair reflected on the early stages of their investigation, they remembered that this description represented nearly the full extent of their understanding about Howard, Jr.'s, aunt for some time. As the attorney for the unknown heirs, Dinkins needed more. He needed, in fact, to document Greta's marriages and divorces—all the significant events in her life—in order to substantiate that she had died, as the *Philadelphia Inquirer* chart suggested, without children. If the *Inquirer* chart were wrong, and Greta did have a child, then Howard, Jr., would have another first cousin, and a new heir apparent.

The Tragic Heroine

When "The Keokuk Connection" first appeared in the office of the ad litem, its pages were immediately and thoroughly scoured for mention of this mystery figure. Helenthal's information was typically vague, but intriguing:

> Greta Hughes was the eldest. She grew into a tall, stately, beautiful woman with a shapely figure.

> Although highly talented, beautiful, and with every opportunity to become a world renowned success in her own right, Greta's life was not a particularly happy one. Her first husband was Fred Howell, son of a prominent Keokuk newspaper family, but this marriage soon ended in divorce.

> Greta had studied voice both in this country and Europe. Upon entering school in Paris, qualified observers there predicted "that within five years Greta Hughes will be acknowledged as the world's greatest singer." Taking her mother's name, she did sing professionally and well as "Jeanne Greta."

She had an English tour, with command royalty performances scheduled, but while in Paris she met and engaged in a whirlwind romance with Herbert Witherspoon, internationally known opera singer and star basso for the New York Metropolitan Opera Company. Greta gave up her career and they were married in Paris on September 25, 1899. Swollen with the success he enjoyed, the marriage soon became a one-sided love affair, and her husband began to more and more devote his attention to that other than the charms of his wife.

Once in a visit to Keokuk by Mr. and Mrs. Witherspoon, a "notable musical evening" was held at the Hughes home, with the "parlors and library filled with guests." The noted opera singer divided honors with his wife, Greta, and thrilled all in attendance with a musical program that would "remain forever unexcelled."

Within hearing range of local people, Witherspoon ridiculed Keokuk, however, and stated bluntly that he felt her family and friends here were a bunch of country bumpkins! The marriage soon headed for the rocks, and the experience caused Greta great disapointment. Although it was often reported locally that the sister of Howard's father committed suicide, the long standing belief along with some other stories about the Hughes family were corrected recently by Greta's sister-in-law, Ruby (Mrs. Felix) Hughes of Los Angeles.

Included with this brief biographical sketch was a photograph of a fetching Greta, taken from the Hughes family album passed down from Greta's grandfather, Joshua Hughes. In his customary purple prose, Helenthal included this caption: *"Greta Hughes Loved Seductive Poses When She Was Photographed. Her Two Marriages, However, Both Ended In Divorce And She Died Without The Love She Craved."*

As Greta's life unfolded, her story seemed more and more like the plot slowly unraveling for a Gothic romance. From the synopsis of Greta's life in "The Keokuk Connection," Dinkins distilled the facts he needed. Greta Hughes was married twice: first, briefly, to a "Keokuk newspaper editor" named Howell; second, to Metropolitan Opera star Herbert Witherspoon in Paris on September 25, 1899, a marriage that also ended in divorce. The piece further stated that Greta was rumored to have committed suicide, but this report was edited before publication by Ruby Hughes, who wrote Helenthal to say, "Greta died of tuberculosis of the spine and did not take her own life," and cited both Felix and Rupert Hughes as her sources.

The disclosures in "The Keokuk Connection" sent Dinkins' investigators on a treasure hunt for Greta's death certificate, marriage licenses, and divorce papers. To complicate the search, they still hadn't a clue as to when and where she had married and divorced Howell, or the year and location of her divorce from Witherspoon. The *Inquirer* chart noted that she died in 1916, and this was the full measure of their collection of material on Greta Hughes.

The depositions of Annette Lummis, Avis McIntyre, and her brother Rush Hughes, taken shortly after Howard, Jr.'s, death, did not help much, nor did the early interviews conducted independently by Dinkins' associate. Avis and Rush's mother, whose stage name was Adelaide Manola, married Rupert Hughes in 1908, and Avis, then eight years old, met Greta shortly thereafter. "I adored her," Avis testified. "She was married to a man named Herbert Witherspoon, who had to do with the Metropolitan Opera. I don't know whether he was impressario or what, but he had a lot to do with opera, I remember that." Mrs. McIntyre also testified that the Witherspoons "lived in an apartment in New York," and would visit Rupert and his family at their country home in Bedford Hills, a township in nearby Westchester County. "She would come out with—well, mostly she'd come out alone, but Herbert Witherspoon would come occasionally." Unfortunately, she told Dinkins she knew nothing about any previous marriages of Greta's. She did, however, have a vivid recollection of Greta's death, as reflected in her deposition testimony from September 1976:

Interviewer:	Greta, for the record, was Rupert's sister who died in 1916, I believe, in New York?
Avis:	1913, I believe.
Interviewer:	1913?
Avis:	1913, my first year in school.
Interviewer:	What was Rupert's reaction to his sister's death?
Avis:	Mother wrote that they had a rather terrifying experience with him because he passed out and slept for thirty-six hours. They couldn't arouse him.
Interviewer:	Couldn't arouse Rupert?

Avis: No. He went into shock. And of course in those days I don't suppose they had the sort of thing that would have brought him around. They seemed to think it was better to let him sleep. He was devoted to his sister.

Aside from this dramatic revelation about the effect her death had on Rupert, Avis had no pertinent information about Greta Hughes Witherspoon. Already, Dinkins' assistant began to sense something disturbing about Howard, Sr.'s, older sister. The deposition testimony of Annette Lummis did little to dispel those uneasy feelings. Asked what she knew about her sister Allene's sister-in-law, Greta, Mrs. Lummis responded: "She had a beautiful voice and she was sent to Paris to cultivate it, and was accepted by the Metropolitan to come to New York to sing in the Metropolitan. And she came on the boat and got laryngitis and lost her voice, and she married Witherspoon, who was one of the leading tenors in the Met, but she never sang." To Mrs. Lummis' knowledge, Greta was never married to anyone other than "Mr. Witherspoon."

With each new piece of testimony, the impression of Greta as a tragic heroine in a Gothic novel grew stronger. Deserted by a faithless husband, her voice lost on the threshold of stardom—what more cruel fate could befall her? Frances McLain Smith, whose mother lived at the Hughes home in Keokuk while attending college, knew of Greta, and her depiction of Howard, Jr.'s, aunt merely enhances this star-crossed image. Interviewed by Dinkins' associate, Mrs. Smith claimed that Greta had "died of a broken heart" when her husband "Bertie" Witherspoon "took up with another woman." Though Mrs. Smith's mother stayed at the Hughes home for several years when Greta was still a girl, she was not aware of any previous marriage.

In the meantime, Dinkins' research associate at Butler, Binion and his genealogist Mary Fay were striking out in their efforts to document Greta's two marriages, not to mention her death. They could find no marriage license or divorce decree for Greta and anyone named Howell in Keokuk, and they had no idea where else to look for this first marriage, since all they knew was that, according to "The Keokuk Connection," Howell was a "newspaper editor from Keokuk." Not only were they stumped as to where the event might have occurred, they were equally ignorant as to when, except that it must have occurred before 1899, since that was the reported date of Greta's marriage to Witherspoon. The ad litem team began to suspect that the Howell marriage was a figment of someone's imagination. To make matters even murkier, their correspondence with the Conservateur of the Paris Archives produced no marriage license for the Witherspoons in 1899, as "The Keokuk Connection" reported. Then one day, while pursuing an altogether different path in the investigation, they got the confirmation they needed, from a most unexpected source. While tracing one of many leads on the Rupert and Elspeth imbroglio, Dinkins requested a copy of the Register of Marriage at the church where Rupert Hughes and his first wife (Elspeth's mother) were wed on December 12, 1893. The register revealed "Greta Hughes HOWELL" acted as a witness to her brother's wedding ceremony. That meant that, at least in 1893, Greta was using the name Howell—implying that she had indeed married Keokuk resident Fred Howell, as Helenthal's publication suggested. Six years later, if this information held up, she was to become Mrs. Herbert Witherspoon, though apparently not in Paris.

With this new piece of information, the sleuths pressed ahead in their investigation. Some time later, Mrs. Fay stumbled onto an obscure book by a Keokuk author that contained some interesting and important trivia about the Hughes family. In July 1977 she wrote to the University of Iowa, routinely requesting verification of Howard Hughes, Sr.'s, brief studies in their law department, as indicated in his biographical sketches. Perhaps to compensate for a lack of material on Howard, Sr., the librarian enclosed several biographical portraits of his father, Felix Hughes, taken from certain Iowa county histories. He also enclosed a one-paragraph excerpt on the Hughes family taken from Raymond E. Garrison's book, *Early Keokuk Homes.* It was a highly fortuitous enclosure.

A Questionable Past

After being introduced to Garrison's work, Mrs. Fay was able to locate another of his efforts, *Goodbye My Keokuk Lady,* an anecdotal work portraying the more prominent families in Garrison's hometown. *Goodbye My Keokuk Lady* was published in 1962 and contained a comical seven-page sketch on the Felix Hughes family of Keokuk, called "Fame and Fortune At The Hughes House." Although no one took it too seriously, parts of Garrison's portrait of the Hughes family were read with special interest, particularly the paragraphs concerning Greta:

> Greta, eldest of the Hughes children, seemed fated for sorrow and tragedy. She grew into a tall, stately, beautiful young woman with a wealth of copper-colored hair, fair complexion and a handsome figure. In her life time she had 3 husbands, the first a Californian, Moore by name, the second, Fred Howell of a Keokuk newspaper publishing family, and brother of socially prominent Lida Gordon Howell.

186

Greta Hughes Moore-Howell divorced her first 2 mates and, on September 25, 1899, in Paris, married Herbert Witherspoon, star basso of the New York Metropolitan Opera Company.

Greta is said to have been madly in love,—something it turned out, Witherspoon was not, for he was reportedly having a clandestine affair with another woman at the time of the wedding.

Witherspoon, a native of Buffalo, New York, born July 21, 1873, and a Yale graduate, studied with voice teachers in New York, London and Paris, and was in English grand opera under direction of Henry W. Savage in the 1890's. He toured with the Theodore Thomas orchestra for 5 years as a vocalist, and the Pittsburgh and Boston symphonies in other seasons. For a year or 2 he managed the Chicago Grand Opera Company.

Eventually, it became the old, old story of too much talent and temperament on the part of both bride and groom, with jealousy rearing its ugly head. Recriminations begun were hard to stem.

Greta, too, had studied voice in this country and abroad. She was singing professionally and well under the name Jeanne Greta. In Paris she met Witherspoon and a whirlwind courtship followed.

Some of the critics in this country said Greta's voice was of fine quality but too light for operatic work.

Impression has grown through the years that Witherspoon, swollen with his own successes—which were substantial—had found greater attraction elsewhere than in the company of his wife. She became despondent after separation from her husband and there were reports that she ended her life in New York. Firsthand proof of this is lacking, though the story has been accepted as whole cloth in some quarters for years.

Witherspoon married Florence Hinkle, an opera singer in June, 1916. She died at age 58 in 1933, Witherspoon two years later at 62 in 1935.

At the time, no one in Dinkins' office put too much stock in the accuracy of Garrison's information. His sketch of the Hughes family did, however, provide a few entertaining moments:

Brighter and happier anecdotes about Greta Hughes and her pulchritude linger on from other days. Photographer Herman M. Anschutz had a superb likeness of her in his gallery window on North Fourth Street that was an eyecatcher, the diva being pictured reclining on a couch, a diaphonous drape covering the form divine. In the early 1900's this bordered on the sensuous if not the naughty.

Even though Garrison's portrayal of the Hughes family was largely anecdotal and written as local history for Keokuk residents, it still merited the ad litem's attention. It included several new and conflicting pieces of information about Greta's life, and those bits had to be explored. The most striking was Garrison's statement that Greta was first married to "a Californian, Moore by name," whom she later divorced. Then there was his report, consistent with Francis Helenthal's aside in "The Keokuk Connection" that Greta committed suicide in New York, despondent over her husband's infidelities.

Collecting all the available information on Greta in the ad litem's swelling files, Dinkins' associate now faced the seemingly impossible task of trying to locate not two, but possibly three marriage licenses and divorce decrees for Greta Hughes—with no further clues as to where or when these events occurred, and no more than a last name to go on for the first husband. (The only date advanced for any of Greta's nuptials, the September 25, 1899, marriage to Witherspoon in Paris, had already proven to be a false lead.)

About the same time as the discovery of "Fame and Fortune At The Hughes House," Dinkins' assistant was interviewing Ruby Hughes, Felix's widow, to clear up some of the more problematical questions about the Hughes siblings. One of the principal points of their discussion was the marital history of Ruby's sister-in-law Greta. Mrs. Hughes essentially repeated the information that had been published in "The Keokuk Connection, " reciting that Greta left Keokuk about 1895 to study voice in Chicago, New York, and Paris, where she remained for eight years; that she was married twice, first to Fred Howell, a Keokuk publisher she later divorced, and second to opera star Herbert Witherspoon, whom she married in Paris in 1899. She did not know where the Howells or the Witherspoons divorced, and she stated that Greta had no children. She also emphasized that Greta died in 1916 of spinal tuberculosis, dismissing Garrison's suicide reports, and generally discrediting the information he printed in his piece on the Hugheses in *Goodbye My Keokuk Lady*. Ruby Hughes also said she had never heard of a Mr. Moore, and that both Rupert and Felix had told her Greta was married twice, to Howell and Witherspoon.

After conducting the interview with Ruby Hughes in August 1977, Dinkins' associate more or less dismissed the allusion to the mysterious "Mr. Moore," and concentrated her efforts in respect to Greta on finding the Howell and Witherspoon marriages and divorces and locating Greta's death certificate. As diverting as "Fame and Fortune At The Hughes House" was, Dinkins attributed much of the information contained therein to hyperbole, small-town gossip or misreporting—too much emphasis on collecting "spicy bits" and too little on accuracy. Rupert Hughes' 1924 magazine articles about his family, "My Father" and "My Mother," essentially confirmed this course of action. Writing about his sister Greta, Rupert related:

> My sister Greta, who was one of the most beautiful women of her time, became briefly one of the most beautiful of vocal artists. Paderewski, hearing her in Paris, introduced her to his manager, who told me in Paris: "In five years the world will acknowledge Jeanne Greta as its greatest singer."
>
> This was no surprise to my father and mother. From her first pipings as a little girl about the house, *they* always had acknowledged her as the world's greatest singer! From childhood she had sung like a nightingale, with a high and flexible soprano of an almost uncanny appeal. The great specialist of the Metropolitan Opera House, Dr. Holbrook Curtis, showed me her throat once in his laryngoscope and said, "There is the most perfect pair of vocal cords in this world, and I've seen all the best."
>
> The teachers in Keokuk had found her beyond their skill, and advised Chicago. So my father sent her to Chicago. Then New York was advised, and my father sent her to New York. But in that day an American without foreign prestige simply was not considered. So my father sent her to Paris, and with her my brother Felix, who, though only a boy, had developed a glorious voice.
>
> After years of training, my sister was launched in London with sensational success. She toured England with such triumph that she was commanded to appear before royalty. Against the doctor's advice to spare her inflamed vocal cords, she kept her promise to sing for a royal charity. But her voice was silenced for months; and by the time she regained it, she had lost both her self-confidence and her interest in a personal career. She married another singer, to whose success she devoted her wonderful gifts. Her death was a grievous loss to art and heartbreak to her family.

Collecting all the data pertaining to Greta Hughes contained in the ad litem's elaborate heirship files by the latter part of 1977—fifteen months after Howard Hughes' death—Dinkins' associate put together a sort of minichronology on Greta, hoping this would facilitate the team's efforts to locate her vital statistics. Well into the second year of the heirship investigation, her life was still a disappointing blur.

Greta Hughes

1868? (maybe)	Born
?	Married and divorced Moore of California?

189

?	Married and divorced Fred Howell of Keokuk.
Pre-1895	Sent to Chicago and New York to cultivate her voice.
1895–1903	Studied abroad in Paris and London.
1899	Married Herbert Witherspoon September 25 (in Paris?).
?	Divorced Witherspoon.
1913/14 or 1916	Died. (Avis vividly recalled Greta's death in 1913 or 1914, the year she started at the Foxcroft School; Ruby and the official reports stated 1916.)
	Suicide? Tuberculosis of the spine? Or something else?

Shortly after this chronology was patched together, the investigation got its first break, when Mrs. Fay tracked down Greta's death certificate. Consistent with the official reports, the certificate reflected that Greta died on February 21, 1916. The certificate was filed in New York City, where it stated "Greta H. Witherspoon" had been a resident for ten years. Though no date of birth was filled in, the death record listed her age as forty-five years, which would mean that she was born in 1871. This was obviously incorrect, since Howard, Sr., was born in 1869, and Greta was the oldest child in the family. The cause of her death was stated to be "tuberculosis peritonitis" (tuberculosis of the abdominal lining). Finally, the ad litem's research team had some tangible evidence of Greta's existence, albeit through her demise.

The investigation into Greta's background receded for some months after this discovery, as Dinkins and company devoted their time and attention to the more pressing questions concerning Rupert and his tangled personal life, the unexpected marriage license between Howard Hughes, Sr., and Francis Geddes, and the myriad other heirship, domicile, and estate administration problems connected with the byzantine Hughes estate.

Dinkins in fact did not work on the Howard Hughes case exclusively after his appointment as attorney ad litem. He continued to handle his usual case load of probate and estate administration work as a partner in the tax and estate section of Butler, Binion, Rice, Cook & Knapp. In heirship matters, he supervised the investigation conducted by his one associate, who in turn coordinated the activities of genealogist Mary Fay.

Andrews, Kurth, in contrast, the law firm hired by its former law partner William Lummis (who was on an indefinite leave of absence after his May 1976 assumption of duties in connection with both his late cousin's estate and his corporate domain) to handle the estate administration and to represent Lummis and the other maternal heirs, maintained a fluid staff of as many as twenty-five attorneys, five or ten law clerks, and twenty to forty paralegals working on various aspects of the case throughout its evolution. Though Ted Dinkins, as the attorney ad litem, was responsible not only for heirship matters, but also for monitoring the rival aspects of the estate proceedings (actively participating in the Texas proceedings)—a daunting assignment most attorneys referred to as a "career case"—he managed to master the responsibilities of his appointment with the assistance of only one Butler & Binion employee, who worked on the case sporadically. That he accomplished what he did and somehow kept his sanity and sense of humor intact is truly remarkable.

Throughout the five-year Hughes debacle, attorneys participating in the case on three coasts went through dramatic upheavals in their personal lives, brought on by the peculiar pressures and intense demands of the monstrous legal case: Dinkins and his associate witnessed divorces and separations, a trial attorney who dropped out of the legal profession for a year, several cases of nervous exhaustion, couples brought together by their involvement in the case, the death of one attorney of cancer, and on and on. As it ground its way to a resolution, the Hughes case took its toll.

With so many facets of the complex estate proceedings bidding for Dinkins' attention simultaneously, it was small wonder that the investigation into Greta Hughes' life was carried on by fits and starts. On a fact-finding mission at the University of Texas Library in Austin in summer 1979, for example, Dinkins' law clerk picked up a new thread with which to weave together the patchwork quilt of Greta's life, which had been put aside in deference to more compelling matters for some months. Gathering newspaper clippings about the noteworthy events in the lives of all the Hughes family members, Dinkins' assistant found a *New York Times* obituary for Greta Witherspoon. The article stated that Greta died in New York City at the age of forty-six, employed as a music teacher at the time of her death. It went on to report that she was "educated in Paris, France," and sang for a time professionally in New York and Los Angeles as "Jeanne Greta." The obituary made reference to her marriage and divorce from Herbert Witherspoon, without mention of any previous spouses. Of particular interest to Dinkins' investigator was the statement in the obituary that the Witherspoons had been married in New York, not Paris, as Ruby Hughes was told. With this fresh lead, the ad litem's clerk once again picked up the trail of Howard, Jr.'s, mysterious aunt. A request for the Witherspoon marriage license from the New York City clerk was honored, and slowly the events of Greta's past began to fall into place.

The marriage license verified what the *Times* had reported in Greta's obituary. On September 25, 1899 (the same date Helenthal and Ruby Hughes had given), Herbert Witherspoon married Greta Hughes *Howell,* in New York City. The groom was stated to be twenty-six years old and a resident of the Yale Club in New York; the bride purported to be twenty-seven, and a resident of 180 West 81st Street, New York (Dinkins' clerk was later to discover that this was actually Rupert Hughes' residence). Assuming the information Greta furnished the New York City clerk was accurate, her year of birth would be 1872, a year later than reported on her death certificate. Both Mrs. Fay and Dinkins' associate knew Greta had to be at least thirty-one years old at the time of her marriage to Witherspoon, not twenty-seven as she told the registrar (and quite probably her groom, who was only twenty-six at the time). The two chuckled over the discrepancy, attributing it to vanity. More important to the investigation was the data on the certificate that followed: "first marriage for groom; second marriage for bride." With this confirmation that Greta was married to Howell and Witherspoon only, Dinkins was more convinced than ever that the Mr. Moore in Garrison's portrait of the Hughes family was a red herring. Genealogist Mary Fay was inclined to agree. Asked to put together a preliminary chart on the Hughes family in preparation for the upcoming heirship trial, Mrs. Fay included only two marriages for Greta—Howell and Witherspoon—her only documentation being the 1899 marriage certificate for the Witherspoons.

As the date of the heirship trial closed in on them, bringing their investigation of the Hughes family to its conclusion, Dinkins' associate, assisted by Mrs. Fay, began a feverish effort to gather the vital statistics necessary for Dinkins to make his presentation to the court. While keeping a watchful eye on the inquiry into Elspeth's parentage, the pair went full throttle to wrap up Greta's life history. Dinkins' colleague ordered her probate proceedings from Manhattan, finding nothing unusual in either her will or the accompanying documents. In its entirety, the instrument read:

> I, Greta H. Witherspoon, of the City of New York, do make,
> publish and declare the following as and for my Last Will And Testa-

ment, hereby revoking any Will by me at any time made.

First: I give all my property, real and personal, of every kind, to my mother, Jean A. Hughes. If she die before me, I give the same to my father, Felix T. Hughes. In case they both die before me, I give the same to my brothers, Howard R. Hughes, Rupert Hughes and Felix Hughes share and share alike.

Second: I appoint George Alger of New York City, Executor of this my Last Will And Testament.

In witness thereof, I have hereunto subscribed my name and affixed my seal this 20th day of July, 1914.

The simple will had been properly witnessed by two Philadelphians and a New Yorker, and duly filed.

In the petition filed by Alger proving the will is a paragraph that states "that said testator left her surviving no husband, child or children, no adopted child or children, no issue of any deceased child or children . . ."—standard language in petitions of this kind. With this will came the satisfaction that the information Mrs. Fay had included about Greta in her preliminary chart of the Hughes family was correct: twice married, no children. Or so Dinkins and his colleagues believed. What they didn't know at the time was that both Greta's will and Mrs. Fay's conclusions would later come back to haunt them.

Still anxious for further clues about Greta's marriage to Fred Howell, Dinkins' associate made inquiries requesting copies of any obituaries printed about her in the Keokuk newspapers, thinking these might be more informative than the *New York Times* perfunctory report. In the Monday evening edition of the *Daily Constitutional Democrat,* February 21, 1916, ran the headline, "Noted Keokuk Singer Dead/Greta Witherspoon, former Keokuk Girl." The obituary that followed provided the ad litem investigation its most comprehensive report of her girlhood to date:

Mrs. Witherspoon was about 50 years of age at the time of her death. She was born in Memphis, Mo., so an intimate friend of the family states, in the year 1866, and lived there until 10 years of age, when she came to Keokuk. She attended the common schools at Memphis for a short time previous to coming to Keokuk and later was a student in the public schools here.

Later she went to St. Louis and entered a select finishing school for young women, the Mrs. Cuthbert's school, which was at that period one of the most fashionable and exclusive education institutions in the middle west.

Shortly after leaving school she moved to California, and from the time of her removal to the Pacific coast she had only been to this city for an occasional visit.

Early in her life Mrs. Witherspoon evinced marked musical talent. This finally led her to seek to display her ability before the public. With that intention she went to New York and spent several seasons studying voice under Agrimonte, at that time and today the premier voice builder of America. It was while a pupil of Agrimonte that she won the gold medal in open contest for possessing the finest voice in the city. She also at that time made a number of public appearances in New York and was received with great favor.

Goes to Paris

Wishing to further herself in voice work, Mrs. Witherspoon went to Paris, where she studied in company with her brother, Felix Hughes, under such teachers as Marchesi, De Buhl and De LaGrande. It was during her stay upon the continent that she met her future husband, Herbert Witherspoon, now a tenor in the Metropolitan opera Company in New York.

Mrs. Witherspoon had her debut in European concert and operatic work and was very favorably received. Later she joined a grand opera company and sang in London, and afterwards went on a tour of the English provinces. Ill health forced her to cancel her engagements and return to New York. In New York she took up concert work and coaching singers for grand opera, being highly successful and winning a great reputation as an operatic coach.

Mrs. Witherspoon was a sister of Rupert Hughes, the author, of international reputation. Felix, another brother, is a noted singer, and a third brother, Howard, is an inventor of mining drills. During her preparation for the stage and a subsequent career, she crossed and recrossed the Atlantic some eighteen times.

Mrs. Witherspoon was a very beautiful woman, and time in passing had dealt lightly with her. Besides being a beautiful singer, she was an accomplished pianist. She was also a very brilliant conversationalist and highly intelligent.

Just as Dinkins' colleague expected, the Keokuk paper was much more descriptive in its account of Greta's life. However, there was still no discussion of her marriage to Fred Howell, which seemed particularly odd in light of his identification by other sources as a Keokuk newspaper editor. There were only two newspapers in Keokuk, and he was not mentioned in either obituary. Even without the newspaper connection, it seemed peculiar the local papers would not list Greta's marriage to a hometown boy, whether it ended in divorce or not. What they lacked in marital information, the Keokuk obituaries made up for in description of Greta's schooling and early career days. From this, Dinkins' law clerk cataloged the fact that Greta had attended Mrs. Cuthbert's finishing school in St. Louis. The obituary also mentioned that she "moved to California" after finishing school and before going to New York to study with Agrimonte. Tenuous as it was, this offhand remark was the first independent corroboration of any kind to Ray Garrison's reference to Greta's "first marriage" to a "Californian, Moore by name," in *Goodbye My Keokuk Lady.*

Increasingly frustrated in the continuing efforts to find documentation for anything but Greta's marriage to Witherspoon, Dinkins authorized searches in any and every likely place, as his associate cast about for clues in the miscellaneous assortment of information about Greta contained in the ad litem's elaborate heirship files. City clerks hunted without success for the Howell marriage or divorce in Keokuk, New York, and Chicago, every city Greta was known to haunt, covering as broad a range of years as probable, beginning when Greta was sixteen, up to 1899—the year of her marriage to Witherspoon. Similar searches were conducted in appropriate cities for her divorce from Herbert Witherspoon, anytime between 1899 and 1916 (the year of her death), all ending fruitlessly.

A Fortuitous Discovery

Just when it began to look as if the records might never be located, Mrs. Fay saved the day, producing three records that proved to be a catalyst to the rest of the investigation of Greta's background. Coincidental to the city-wide searches being conducted in New York and other likely cities, Mrs. Fay enlisted the aid of a Keokuk genealogist to assist in the search for records in that area. The Keokuk genealogist located not only Greta's marriage and divorce papers with respect to Fred Howell, but her divorce from Witherspoon as well! Lee County, Iowa (in which Keokuk is situated), has two courts, as it turns out: one in Keokuk, the other in Fort Madison, Iowa. The missing records were filed in Fort Madison, which explained why Dinkins was unable to find documentation of these events in response to his earlier search requests in Keokuk.

Based on the information sent to Mrs. Fay in 1980, which she passed on in a report to the ad litem dated March 26, 1980, Dinkins learned that Greta married Frederick J. Howell (son of James B. and Mary A. Howell) in Milwaukee, Wisconsin, on May 22, 1889, in a Methodist-Episcopal ceremony. Howell, though born in Keokuk, resided in Colorado, and described himself as a "broker," not a newspaper editor. Of greater interest, one of the blanks on the marriage record asked for the "full name of wife previous to marriage," after which the name "Greta Hughes" had been filled in. Had she married anyone named Moore prior to this,

Greta's name would have been reflected on the certificate as "Greta Hughes Moore." Since Greta was twenty-one at the time of her marriage to Howell (assuming she was born in 1868, as the ad litem then believed), it made perfect sense that it was her first marriage. If she were born in 1871 or 1872, as her death certificate and the *New York Times* obituary stated, she would have been seventeen or eighteen, making it even more unlikely that she had had an earlier marriage—to Moore or anyone else.

The Howells were divorced in Lee County, Iowa, on February 6, 1899, ten years later and seven months before Greta's marriage to Witherspoon. "J. F. Howell" sued for the divorce, and stated, in pertinent part:

> 1. That he is now and has been for the last seven years past a resident of the state of Iowa, and residing at Keokuk, in Lee County, and that he has resided at said place continuously during all of said time, except during the past 6 months, while in the Military Service of the United States Government.

> 4. That plaintiff and defendant were married in Milwaukee in the State of Wisconsin on the 22d day of May 1889, and lived together as husband and wife until about the 30th day of July, 1896 [three years before the divorce].

> 5. That during all the time plaintiff and defendant so lived together as husband and wife, this plaintiff at all times conducted himself towards his said wife as a dutiful and loving husband.

> 6. That on or about the 30 day of July, 1896, the defendant in violation of her marriage vows and without any fault of plaintiff, wilfully [*sic*] deserted this plaintiff and has ever since absented herself from him without any reasonable or just cause therefor.

The one-page deposition of J. F. Howell was attached to the divorce papers. In it, Howell basically repeated the points enumerated in his original petition, and added the following:

> On or about July 30, 1896 my wife deserted me and has remained away without reasonable or just cause and contrary to my wishes. During the autumn of 1897 my wife did return to Keokuk, Iowa, but refused to live in the home provided for her by me, and resided with her parents. She affirmed that her return was not in response to my desires, but for other personal reasons, and in December of the same year she returned to Paris, France, contrary to my desires, and has ever since remained away from me, and for several months past has

kept her whereabouts unknown to me. My wife has affirmed that she will not now or ever return to me as my wife, intending to follow a professional career on the stage.

In the Decree of Divorce, "J. F. Howell vs. Greta Hughes Howell," signed February 6, 1899, Greta's father, F. T. Hughes, appeared on her behalf as her counsel, asking that she be allowed to resume her maiden name, Greta Hughes. This request was granted and the divorce consummated, leaving Greta free to carry on with her career and other aspirations.

The last enclosure in Mrs. Fay's report was a handwritten facsimile of the divorce record for Greta and Herbert Witherspoon. Once again, as Dinkins' genealogist noted, "her father was her attorney." Copying the information located in Fort Madison's book of divorces for Lee County, Mrs. Fay's Keokuk correspondent made this notation:

Herbert Witherspoon - White - age 42 - American - Married 9-25-1899 - No. of Prior Marriages - None - Cause of divorce - Desertion.

Grita Witherspoon - White - age 40 - American - Divorce - 5-15-1915 - No. of Prior Marriages - two—Divorce granted to wife.

Scanning the information contained in this final enclosure to Mrs. Fay's letter, Dinkins' associate caught her breath. First, Greta's age had changed again. She was, in this 1915 divorce action, claiming to be forty years old (two years younger than Witherspoon; on their marriage certificate, she was one year younger), meaning she was born in 1875. If she were born in 1866, as the "intimate friend of the family" told the author of her Keokuk obituary, then by this time she was trimming nearly ten years off her age, which varied from five to ten years in every document. This discrepancy was eclipsed, however, by a far more dramatic disclosure.

Why, in the divorce record from Witherspoon, did it state that Greta had *two* prior marriages? Mrs. Fay's obliging Keokuk researcher had apparently noticed the same thing, as she noted in her cover letter: "Not so detailed as the earlier (Howell) divorce either, but it does report Greta as having been married twice before, but perhaps they consider Herbert as one prior marriage?" Dinkins' colleague was not so easily convinced, and bolted into the ad litem's office with this new evidence in hand. Dinkins, wary of the individual and collective suspicions of his secretary, genealogist, and associate regarding the Hughes family, awaited the news with the calm reserve of one who had come to expect such interruptions. However, even his customary recalcitrance was shaken by this piece of information—particularly since Greta's father had acted as her attorney in connection with the divorce, and it was presumably he who had furnished the information printed in the records. "Well," Dinkins drawled as he discussed the renewed possibility of a third marriage for Greta with his colleague, "go find it!"

This was easier said than done. Even though the notation in the Witherspoon divorce indicated Greta had been married three times, it could have been a misprint, a mistake, or—as the Keokuk genealogist observed—a difference in interpretation. Perhaps, after all, the clerk had considered Howell one marriage and Witherspoon the second, making it "two prior marriages" total. Furthermore, the evidence to the contrary was compelling.

First, on her 1889 marriage certificate to Frederick J. Howell, believed to be her first husband, Greta was listed as Greta *Hughes* in response to the request for the "full name of wife previous to marriage." Had she been married to anyone before Howell, this surname would have appeared on the certificate after the name Hughes.

Second, in her divorce proceedings from Howell, the action is listed as "J. F. Howell vs. Greta Hughes Howell." Again, no other last name for Greta.

Third, on her marriage certificate of registration to Herbert Witherspoon in 1899, it recites "second marriage for bride." If the information on the Witherspoon divorce were correct, it would have been the *third* marriage for the bride, not the second.

Fourth, both Rupert and Felix Hughes—Greta's own brothers—told Ruby Hughes that Greta was married twice: to Howell and Witherspoon. This fact alone was nearly impossible to get around.

Finally, from a practical point of view, if Greta had actually been married three times instead of twice, when and where would the marriage fit in? As Dinkins' clerk played around with the known events in her life, there seemed to be no available time. With the information Greta furnished on every official document concerning her age, she would have been seventeen or eighteen when she married Howell, making it unlikely she would have married anyone previously (which would jibe with her "full name" being listed as Greta Hughes on the Howell marriage license). Perhaps Garrison simply had his sequence mixed up in *Goodbye My Keokuk Lady,* and Greta actually married the elusive Mr. Moore *after* her marriage to Howell? (Maybe, in fact, the groom's name wasn't even Moore, and he wasn't from California.) Yet that also seemed improbable. Greta married Herbert Witherspoon a mere seven months after her divorce from Howell became final, and that would hardly give her time to marry and divorce in between. Moreover, her marriage certificate to Witherspoon states that it is her second marriage, not third.

A second theory presented itself. Could Greta have married Moore after she divorced Witherspoon? No, Dinkins' clerk reasoned, that was even more unlikely. It was the Witherspoon divorce record, after all, that stated that Greta had two prior marriages, so that didn't make sense, either. Furthermore, Greta is listed on her death certificate as Greta Witherspoon, implying she died as Witherspoon's divorced wife. Finally, she died shortly after the Witherspoon divorce, which left her little time to marry someone else in the interim. (This last hypothesis also conflicted with the recurring suggestions that Greta was acutely depressed over her breakup with Witherspoon, possibly even committing suicide as a result.) A husband following Witherspoon made no sense in any context.

In spite of the inherent problems associated with a contemplated third marriage for Greta, Dinkins' clerk, buoyed by the supporting evidence in the Witherspoon divorce record, began to search for it with missionary zeal. The clock was running out on the ad litem investigation, as the trial to officially determine Hughes' heirs approached. A trip to Keokuk to study the complete Witherspoon divorce records firsthand reinforced this aggressive new approach, as it eliminated the possibility that the entry copied by the Keokuk researcher showing that Greta had two marriages prior to Witherspoon was mistake or misinterpretation. Mrs. Fay's hired genealogist had copied the notation of the Witherspoon divorce found at the courthouse in Fort Madison, Iowa, in a huge book called "Record of Divorces for the County of Lee." As she pointed out, however, Lee County has two courthouses: one in Fort Madison, the other in Keokuk. In the case of the Witherspoon divorce, although the trial took place in Fort Madison, the complete file was kept in Keokuk, which led to a great deal of confusion in tracing these records—very possibly Judge Hughes' original intention.

After studying the complete divorce file in Keokuk, there was no doubt in Dinkins' associate's mind that Greta Hughes had another marriage somewhere. In her petition for divorce from Witherspoon (filed April 24, 1915), Greta recites that she and her husband were married in New York on September 25, 1899, "and lived together as husband and wife until the (left blank) day of April, 1912." The petition goes on to recite that "on the (blank) day of April, 1912," Witherspoon "wilfully deserted" his wife, leading her to her request for a divorce. Also included in the file is Witherspoon's answer, the final decree of divorce (granted to Greta May 5, 1915, and awarding her $20,000 as permanent alimony)—and the original information sheet prepared at the direction of Greta's attorney, with information about the couple seeking a divorce. This form asks for the husband and wife's full name, color, age, nationality, and "number of prior marriages." Once again, the word "two" has been handwritten after this last blank for Greta. The word "none" follows Witherspoon's name. Obviously there was no mistake here.

Even with this indisputable evidence that Greta had a missing third marriage, the ad litem investigation was at much the same impasse as before, with not a clue as to where to find a record of it. Greta Hughes was a worldwide traveler. Who but she knew when and where this event occurred, or if indeed it had? Greta had studied "abroad," and gadded about for several decades. Most of her life was a complete mystery to Dinkins' investigative team. Furthermore, there seemed to be no plausible interval in which she could have been secretly wed: her life was crowded with marriages as it was.

Against such insurmountable odds, Dinkins' assistant reinstated the sweeping document searches, requesting marriage checks for Greta Hughes/Howell/Witherspoon and a Mr. Moore, first name unknown, or Greta and anyone, for broad swings of years—beginning in 1883 (when she would have been anywhere from eight years old to seventeen, depending upon which official records one consulted for her year of birth) and ending with her death in 1916. The target cities were Keokuk, New York (all five boroughs), Chicago (where she had reportedly studied music for a time), Los Angeles (where the *Times* obituary said she had sung briefly as "Jeanne Greta"), California generally (since Moore was, according to *Goodbye My Keokuk Lady,* a "Californian"), St. Louis (where her Keokuk obituary stated she had attended Mrs. Cuthbert's finishing school), Paris, and London (where she had sung and studied). The ad litem's chances for success in this venture were slim. In conjunction with these searches, his protégé sought any school records available on Greta. This proved a fruitless effort: the St. Louis city directories had no entries for a Mrs. Cuthbert's School from 1883 to 1888, and no records were found anywhere else. One by one, the results trickled in, all with the same report: no marriage records for Greta under any of her last names, to Moore or anyone else. By mid-October 1980, Dinkins was about to give up his efforts to locate the purported marriage altogether, when the morning mail changed the course of his investigation and irrevocably altered his associate's perception of the accepted Hughes lineage.

A Secret Marriage

Just as had happened several years earlier with the unexpected arrival of the Howard Hughes, Sr.–Frances Geddes marriage application, the envelope was postmarked Missouri. This time around, however, the city was St. Louis, not Joplin. To Dinkins' amazement, his colleague's relentless search for Greta's secret marriage had indeed paid off.

The envelope contained a certified copy of a marriage license taken out in St. Louis on August 31, 1887. The bride's name was Miss Greta Hughes of Keokuk, Iowa; the groom, one Alexander S. More of Santa Barbara, California. As his associate handed him what would have to be described as a buried treasure if the union had issue, Dinkins examined and reexamined the document, making sure the certificate wasn't some sort of practical joke. Finally satisfied it was genuine, he chuckled and said, "Huh! Well, I'll be darned!"

Raymond Garrison had been right. Greta had been married three times, "first to a Californian named Moore." Though the last name was spelled differently, no one could quibble. The license went on to record that More was over the age of twenty-one, and Greta over the age of eighteen. That meant Greta was born no later than 1869, as Dinkins' sleuth suspected all along. Apparently, Greta was born in 1866, just as the "Keokuk intimate" had related at the time of her death. The return was filled in by a Reverend J. W. Lewis, 3521 Lucas Ave., a minister of the Methodist Church South in St. Louis, on August 31, 1887, the same day the license was issued.

Once the initial shock had worn off, and Dinkins and his colleague realized they had actually found the phantom Mr. More, they didn't know what to do with him. It was, after all, a highly significant discovery. The More marriage had obviously been a closely guarded secret in the Hughes family. When Greta married Frederick Howell approximately a year and a half later, in May 1899, she married as Greta *Hughes*. In her marriage license to Witherspoon in 1899, she stated under oath it was her second marriage, and in all subsequent documents (save the divorce record from Witherspoon that opened this Pandora's box and that, it should be noted, was filled in by her father's *law partner*, Mr. McCoid) she swore she had been married only two times. More incriminating was the fact that both Rupert and Felix Hughes, Greta's brothers, told Ruby Hughes their sister was married twice, to Howell and Witherspoon. Why would Felix Hughes lie to his own wife about Greta's first marriage? What was the Hughes family trying to hide?

Such were the questions running through their heads as Dinkins and his associate pondered the St. Louis marriage license. Some quick detective work revealed that the Methodist Church South was in existence in 1887, and a Reverend Joseph W. Lewis served as its minister, just as the license indicated. The church survives today under a different name, but its records reveal no membership for either a Hughes or a More, and there was no record in the church register of the marriage. Obviously

Alexander and Greta were not members of long standing, and the church was a matter of convenience for them. In support of that conclusion, they learned that Greta Hughes did not appear in any of the St. Louis city directories from 1884 to 1887, meaning she was presumably not a resident. Nor was there a listing for Alexander More.

Dinkins' assistant had originally thought to request the marriage search in St. Louis after noticing in her Keokuk obituary that Greta had attended Mrs. Cuthbert's finishing school in that city. Yet the school is not listed in the city directories from 1885 to 1887. Moreover, if Greta was born in 1866, which Dinkins' associate was more and more convinced was the case, then she would have been twenty-one at the time the license was issued in 1887—slightly beyond finishing school age. If she wasn't in St. Louis to attend school, then what was Greta doing in that city, who was this Alexander S. More she married, and how did he get from Santa Barbara, California, to St. Louis, Missouri? (For that matter, how did Greta ever connect with Frederick Howell, whom she married a year and a half later, in 1889, since Howell was identified on their marriage certificate as a resident of Colorado?) It was a confusing array of facts, with little hope for resolution.

To confront these ghosts from the past, Dinkins' protégé utilized the conventional research methods. Dinkins authorized further record searches, hoping to find a divorce proceeding for the Mores in St. Louis, Milwaukee, Los Angeles, New York, Colorado, or in the dual recording system in Lee County, Iowa. None appeared. Included in the far-ranging document searches were efforts to locate a birth certificate for a baby More, born anywhere between 1886 and 1889. No birth certificate was found in Santa Barbara, St. Louis, Keokuk, Chicago, Milwaukee, or New York. These results were not conclusive, however, since in most of these cities recording of births was not compulsory at the time.

By telephone, Dinkins' associate was unable to obtain Santa Barbara city directory information before the year 1895, which helped little in the efforts to trace More's connection, if any, to that city, which he listed as his residence on the marriage license. The only More listed in 1895 was a "P. H. More," who may or may not have been a relative. Meanwhile, the Los Angeles directories were scoured for mention of the Mores, Greta Hughes, or even Jeanne Greta, since the *New York Times* obituary discussed Greta's short singing career under that name in Los Angeles. No one turned up.

As an alternative, a Los Angeles-based researcher was hired to look for deaths, births, and divorces in Santa Barbara proper, under the direction of Dinkins' associate, who in turn traveled to Keokuk to interview the widow of Raymond Garrison, the newspaperman who wrote *Goodbye My Keokuk Lady,* and to look through the notes he used to compile his book of Keokuk reminiscences some thirty years earlier. Dinkins' assistant had corresponded with Garrison back in 1977, when *Goodbye My Keokuk Lady* first made its way into the ad litem's office, asking for "more specific information concerning the Hughes family in Keokuk." Garrison wrote back in September 1977 to report, "My material for 'Early Keokuk Homes' (1959) was obtained through years of contact with Keokuk families and, as a newspaper reporter for the Daily Gate City (local publication) also for my book, 'Goodbye My Keokuk Lady,' published in 1962. I knew none of the Hughes family personally, with the exception of Judge Felix T. Hughes, a stern barrister where news reporters were concerned." Garrison went on to cite his sources for "Fame and Fortune At The Hughes House":

> After early retirement from Chicago newspapers, I slowly and thoroughly researched the history of old Keokuk homes for one of my earlier publications tracing ownership records thru Keokuk City Directories, Lee County Iowa records and many personal interviews with elderly citizens. Thus family items and stories came to my attention from newspapers, society reports, business men, men and women friends as well as rumors and tales from various of these. A newswriter who is worth his salt respects these sources which respectful news writing demands.
>
> In conjunction with this procedure I wrote of the Hughes family . . . from factual material. In the typical small community, the family produced believable and accurate material for my use. The Hughes family was active in the various phases of small town life and were available for book material.
>
> The family had both summer and winter homes, moved several times in the late 1800's, had four talented children who left Keokuk early in life to follow cultural and business careers. Thus neighbors, friends, and business people had frequent personal contacts with members of the family. Hence every one had varying opinions of the Hughes family.
>
> What notes I retain in my writing files are a mixture of public and acquaintance impressions. But all whose opinions I respected because of these personal impressions. None of these people are living today, having died in their 80's and 90's. Thus the facts cannot be verified today.

In a postscript, Garrison added: "I do not relish doing this material—particularly at nearly ninety years of age . . . R.E.G."

Because he was never taken too seriously by Dinkins, et al., further attempts to communicate with Mr. Garrison were eventually abandoned altogether, particularly when his credibility and accuracy were put in question by sources close to him and the Hughes family. "Ray has been a fine old gentleman over the years," cites one local colleague. "He used to work for the *Chicago Tribune* and was a good reporter. But everytime I quote, or use Ray Garrison's material for fact, I find it inaccurate. . . . So I don't lend a lot of credence to his work." With the discovery of the More marriage license, however, Garrison's notes took on increased importance for research into Greta's life.

By 1980 Ray Garrison had died. However, his widow, Lois Garrison, had graciously consented to open her late husband's files to Dinkins' associate, and agreed to assist the ad litem team in its efforts to trace the Hughes family. Mrs. Garrison invited both a local librarian, Doris Foley, and a self-styled Keokuk historian, John Talbot, to sit in on the interview session to provide clues, information, or direction. Naturally, the recent discovery of the More marriage license was a central topic of conversation. As Mrs. Garrison rummaged through her late husband's writing files, the four exchanged information and theories on the multiple aspects of the heirship investigation as it related to the Felix Hughes family.

It soon came out that Garrison's source of Hughes material was an across-the-alley neighbor of the Hugheses in Keokuk, E. Carroll Tabor. Dinkins' representative requested permission to study the notes Garrison made from the 1952 conversation with Mr. Tabor, hoping they would provide some further clue as to More's identity, or about Greta's life in general:

Interviewer: May I look at the notes from Mr. Tabor?

Garrison: Well, let me read them to you, because they're kind of hard. He says, "Greta Hughes. Greta Hughes was the eldest of the Hughes children. . . . Greta was tall, shapely, slender, light brown-haired, tended toward blonde, attractive of face and figure. She 'really loved Herbert Witherspoon.' Her voice had finish but was too fine, too light for operatic work.

"She played 'wonderful accompaniments when she and Witherspoon gave a concert one early year in the parlors of Westminster Presbyterian Church.' "

And Mr. Tabor attended that concert. Now that concert, according to the paper, was October 18, 1900.

Interviewer: Okay.

Garrison: "Witherspoon was manager of the Chicago Opera Company for a year or two and was a top artist. When married to Greta he was living with another woman. Greta . . . " (That's all according to Mr. Tabor) "Greta was first married to a man named Moore in California. . . .Fred Howell was her second husband (brother of Adelove). . . .Herbert Witherspoon was her third mate. Greta (believed to have) ended her life in NY, an overdose of sleeping pills."

The interview continued for some time, with discussions about the other three children of Felix and Jean Hughes, Greta's second husband Fred Howell, and others, supplemented by occasional references to Garrison's notes, files, or Keokuk memorabilia. The notes from Carroll Tabor, however, quoted in full above, turned out to be nearly the complete extent of Garrison's source material on Greta.

In retrospect, the interview with Raymond Garrison's widow (and friends) did little to assist Dinkins' investigator in following the trail of the More marriage, since his remaining notes offered no additional information about Greta's first husband. It did, however, provide some useful insight into Garrison's modus operandi in writing the "Fame and Fortune At The Hughes House" section of *Goodbye My Keokuk Lady*. His facts and data about the four Hughes children were gleaned from interviews with neighbors and friends of the Judge's who were still alive at the time Garrison composed his book on Keokuk homes in the 1950s. The gentleman who apprised Garrison of Greta's top-secret first marriage to "a Californian, Moore by name," had in fact lived across the alley from the Hughes family on North Fifth Street in the late 1800s and early 1900s and had obviously gossiped about the comings and goings of his eccentric neighbors with great interest.

Though such rumor and innuendo may not meet the exacting standards of admissible evidence in a court of law, common sense and human nature would affirm that it is often the most reliable authority. Records can be changed, individuals can lie under oath on their official documents (Greta is certainly dramatic proof of this); this kind of evidence, in short, is not infallible. In the case of Garrison's chapter on the Hughes family, his factual information is based largely on the personal observations of Keokuk folk who grew up with the Hugheses, lived down the street from them, and observed their lifestyles—long before Howard Hughes, Jr., was a famous name, and long before his estate became a cause cèlébre. Whatever might be said about Garrison's reporting style or percentage of accuracy, the fact remained that he—and he alone—got the scoop on Greta.

As suspicions about Greta Hughes' secret marriage were building within the ad litem's circle in Houston, enhanced by the lack of further information in Garrison's writing files, great progress was being made in Santa Barbara by the California researcher hired and supervised by Dinkins' associate to look into Alexander More's background. Though her early efforts to trace a More family in either Los Angeles or Santa Barbara were discouraging, by late October 1980 the California investigator, working in conjunction with the Santa Barbara Historical Society, had located not only the Mores, but information about Alexander's death and his divorce from Greta Hughes. The ad litem could hardly have been more pleased if they had found the Lost Ark of the Covenant.

In a phone conversation with Dinkins' associate on October 24, the California researcher reported that Alexander More came from an "important family" in Santa Barbara, and that his father was one of five infamous More brothers who migrated to California from Ohio around 1850. She further stated that Alexander More filed for divorce from Greta More in Santa Barbara in October 1888 (fourteen months after they were married), "because she refused to sleep with him." This action was withdrawn in November, but More refiled, and the divorce was decreed against Greta's wishes on December 31, 1888. More chilling was the news that followed. Alexander More, so it seemed, died six months after the divorce at the age of twenty-three, under what the researcher described as "bizarre circumstances." She could find no death certificate. She did locate a contemporaneous newspaper article describing More's death, which she reported occurred "while he was on a hunting trip . . . alone at the time . . . fishing on a river bank . . . found dead with a fishing pole in his hand." Somehow, an Indian guide was mixed up in it, as well. The "reason for his death," she concluded, was "unascertained." The date of More's death, May 31, 1889, Dinkins' clerk noticed with a shudder, was almost a week to the day after Greta's subsequent marriage to J. Frederick Howell.

Intrigued in the extreme, the ad litem's associate immediately ordered copies of all the pertinent papers relating to More's death, divorce, and estate proceedings. The Gothic-romantic quality of Greta's life had by this time reached epic proportions. The arrival of the package of More material did little to allay the feelings of suspicion and intrigue that had taken over the ad litem investigation.

The More divorce action was filed in the Superior Court of Santa Barbara County, and was handwritten in the manner of the times. In his original complaint for divorce, More stated:

I. That plaintiff and defendant intermarried at the City of St. Louis in the State of Missouri on the 27th day of August 1887 and ever since have been and now are husband and wife.

II. That plaintiff is, and has been, for a period of more than 1 year immediately preceding the commencement of this action, a resident of the State of California.

III. That ever since the date of said marriage and continuously until the present time the defendant has persistently refused to have reasonable matrimonial intercourse with plaintiff as her husband; and that neither the health nor physical condition of the defendant made such refusal reasonably necessary. That in the month of September, 1887, the defendant came to the City of Santa Barbara in this State to reside with plaintiff; but from the time of her arrival in said City as aforesaid defendant refused to have continuous matrimonial intercourse with plaintiff, although neither the health nor physical condition of defendant rendered such refusal reasonably necessary; and defendant although often requested to consent to such intercourse persisted in the refusal of it until her departure from said City of Santa Barbara in the month of December, 1887.

That on or about the twenty-sixth day of December 1887, the defendant departed from the said City of Santa Barbara and went, as plaintiff is informed and believes, to reside in the City of Keokuk, State of Iowa with the intent to desert and abandon plaintiff; and that defendant has ever since said 26th day of December 1887, continued to be absent from the State of California and separated from the plaintiff with intent to desert and abandon plaintiff although requested by the plaintiff to return to him.

IV. That there has been no issue of said marriage.

V. That there is no community property of plaintiff and defendant, no property having been acquired by either of them since their marriage.

Wherefore plaintiff demands judgment, that the bonds of matrimony between plaintiff and defendant be dissolved.

October 12, 1888
Alex S. More (signed)
R. B. Canfield (signed)
Attorney for Plaintiff

207

In her answer to More's original complaint, Greta More admitted the two were married in St. Louis on August 27, 1887,[6] but otherwise generally denied More's claims that she "persistently refused or refused at all to have reasonable matrimonial intercourse" with him after "the date of said marriage or at any time since." She similarly admitted that she departed from Santa Barbara on December 26, 1887, to reside in Keokuk, but denied that she did so "with the intent to desert or abandon" More. She further prayed that Alexander More's petition for divorce be denied.

Sometime afterward, More withdrew his original complaint for divorce. Two months later, however, on December 31, 1887, he refiled. In his new complaint, he dropped the charge of refusal to have matrimonial intercourse and petitioned on the grounds of desertion and abandonment only, citing the December 26, 1887, date mentioned in his original petition. He once again stated that "there has been no issue of said marriage" and no community property. Greta More denied all of More's allegations, "except the allegations as to the marriage of plaintiff and defendant, that the plaintiff and defendant are now husband and wife, and that there is no issue of said marriage." Greta again petitioned the court to deny her husband's complaint, "but if the decree be granted . . . prays that she be restored to her maiden name of Greta Hughes." (Signed by Fernald, Cope & Boyce, Attys.—*not* her father, who was not licensed to practice in California.)

On December 31, 1888, Judge R. M. Dillard entered a judgment granting Alexander More's divorce, and allowing Greta More to resume her maiden name, Greta Hughes.

Also enclosed in the package of material sent by Dinkins' California researcher was a copy of More's obituary, printed in the June 1, 1889 edition of the *Daily Independent,* Santa Barbara's local newspaper. This is its lurid account of his death:

SUDDEN DEATH

Alexander S. More Found
Dead While Fishing

A Young Man Suddenly Called to
the Great Beyond Without
Warning. Details.

Three or four days since Alex More, George A. Culbertson and James Hope left Santa Barbara for a month's fishing and hunting near the source of the Santa Ynez River. On Thursday night they arrived at their destination, and pitched their tent. One night was spent in pleasant talk and anticipation of the pleasures of the days that were to follow. . . . These three, together with an Indian they had employed along the route, thought they alone were present at that camp during the night. But there was an unknown and unwelcome guest there. . . . It was the Spirit of Death.

Upon the first flush of manhood's days, Alexander S. More had learned sorrow, and tasted some of the bitterest of life's disappointments. His experiences had not been all those of pleasure, but deeply had the hand of affliction been laid upon him. It matters but little now, if by a wiser source he might perhaps have avoided some of the rocks upon which his young life was wrecked. He is dead, and we can but remember that he had many attributes which under different circumstances would have made him a more useful and honored member of society.

Yesterday morning at about daybreak, George A. Culbertson started from the camp hunting, and returned at night to find More still in bed. Soon after More arose, and later in the day More, Culbertson and the Indian left camp, and separated after reaching the stream. Culbertson going on with his gun to hunt game, and More and the Indian remaining to fish in the stream. The last time that Culbertson saw More alive he was fixing his fishing tackle. Still later the Indian rushed excitedly to Culbertson, telling him that the other man was dead. When they returned to the place where they had left Alex, they found him lying with his face partly submerged in the water, and his hands still holding his fishing rod. Apparently death had come very suddenly. The bank was shelving to the water, and More must have been standing near the edge with his hook and line in the water. When the awful call came he fell forward. There was no sign of any struggle. No contortion of the body or limbs to indicate that death was painful. Death had come to him as he stood, and when he fell with his face to the water, it was the hand of a corpse which grasped the rod.

Much more than her cousin once imagined, Greta's life was like a bad Gothic romance. In line with that, Dinkins' California researcher ultimately produced a certified copy of Alexander More's death record, which turned out to be as cryptic as he. His date of death is listed as June 1, 1889; place of death, Santa Ynez, California. His parents' names are not shown, nor is his date of birth. He is reported as married, but his spouse's name is not stated. No cause of death appears on the certificate.

It was eventually discovered that Alexander S. More was the son of T. Wallace and Susanna Hill More, a family of "high position," reported as "extensive purchasers of the old landed estates of the Spanish families" in and around Santa Barbara. T. Wallace More appears in a book on Santa Barbara's prominent men and pioneers, as "one of a numerous and remarkable family. . . including in its members such men as Sir Thomas More and others of note." The elder Mr. More was ruthlessly murdered in 1877, when Alexander was eleven years old, over a land skirmish of great celebrity in the Santa Barbara area.

At the Santa Barbara Historical Society, Dinkins' California researcher met a woman who was compiling a book on several prominent families of Santa Barbara, including the More family. She had become intrigued with Alexander More and collected background information on him in the course of her research. She reported that he was never employed, but "sold land right and left," accumulating large real estate holdings during his lifetime. She described Alexander and Greta as a "colorful couple," based on personal correspondence she had read. Both she and Dinkins' hired California assistant were asked to look for any evidence in Santa Barbara of a child or children born to the mystery couple during their year or so of marriage. "Neither she nor I have found any indication of a child born to Greta and Alexander More," was her concluding report. However, the woman conducting the genealogical work on Santa Barbara families noted that the only survivor of the More family was "an old woman who won't speak to anyone, " that birth records at that time are inconclusive, and that second- or even third-hand accounts of Alexander More's life were rare. She concluded that the specific details of the More marriage will probably always be unknown.

The final papers delivered to Dinkins with respect to More were his probate proceedings. Like Howard Hughes, Jr., Alexander More apparently died without a valid will. Alexander's brother, Thomas M. More, was appointed administrator of his estate, and in his petition stated that Alexander's "heirs-at-law" were himself, another brother, Wallace, and a sister, Mattie More Law. "Due search and inquiry have been made," More recited, "to ascertain if said deceased left any will and testament, but none have been found."

Not convinced by any means that the mystery of Greta and Alexander S. More was resolved, Dinkins' associate nonetheless moved on to other aspects of Greta's life. Now that the ad litem investigation had certain key dates in her life with which to work, it was possible to engage someone to review the "personal" columns of the Keokuk newspapers for some chirpy mention of Hughes' activities throughout the periods surrounding these key dates. Using the August 31, 1887, marriage license to More as a handle, the hired researcher discovered a flurry of entries about Greta in the *Daily Gate City*. On August 24, a week before the More wedding, the Keokuk newspaper noted that Greta was the "guest of friends in St. Louis with her mother," Jean A. Hughes.

By August 28, she had "returned from her St. Louis trip," with no mention of her impending change in marital status. The wedding announcement does appear in the August 31, 1887, edition of the Keokuk *Constitution-Democrat:*

> Miss Greta Hughes, married in St. Louis, August 31, at the residence of Rev. Dr. Lewis, her mother and other friends present, to Mr. Alexander Moore, a wealthy ranchman of Santa Barbara, California, left Saturday evening for her new home, accompanied by her mother and brother Felix . . .

It was clear from these published announcements that the Hughes family was definitely aware of Greta's first marriage to More. In fact, her mother attended the ceremony in St. Louis (the only family member to do so, oddly enough), and she and young Felix had traveled on to California with Greta and her new husband. (How all that came about is probably unascertainable.) More's divorce petition states that Greta "abandoned him" to return to Keokuk in December 1887, four months after the marriage, but there is no mention of her in the social columns until February 5, 1888—more than a month later. This entry noted, "Mrs. Alexander More, of Santa Barbara, California, visited at the home of her father during the week." If Greta had indeed moved back to Keokuk for good as of December 26, how does one explain this personal item in the newspaper? Greta is mentioned only one other time in the Keokuk social column for the remainder of the year 1888. On March 25, it is noted: "Mrs. A. More will return to her home in Santa Barbara about the first of April."

The question implicit in these entries in the Keokuk newspapers is this: Where was Greta Hughes More from December 1887 (when, by her own admission, she departed Santa Barbara permanently) and December 1888 (when More's divorce from her was granted)? She was obviously not in California with her husband, and she was by implication only in Keokuk for a week in February and part of March; yet the More divorce proceedings attest that she was in her hometown the entire period. There are at least ten or twelve months in her ill-fated marriage to Alexander More when Greta is simply unaccounted for.

Dinkins' investigative team was never able to answer that question, nor could they explain why the More marriage was such a secret in the Hughes family. It certainly wasn't the stigma of divorce: between them, Felix and Jean's four children had at least five divorces and twice as many marriages. Nor could it have been embarrassment over More's social status. No, there was some other reason—some dark secret, perhaps?—to explain why every Hughes family member conspired to

211

cover up Greta's marriage to Alexander More. Did he and Greta have a child during (before or after) their brief and unusual marriage? Did Greta marry More to legitimize a child she was carrying by someone else, then abandon him after the ceremony, possibly explaining why she allegedly refused to have intercourse with him? Why did Greta, the beautiful and only daughter of a prominent Keokuk family, eschew a big society wedding in favor of a secret ceremony in St. Louis attended only by her mother? These questions brought to mind the deposition testimony of Annette Gano Lummis, taken before the More marriage was discovered by the ad litem's associate. When Dinkins asked if Greta Witherspoon "ever had any children," Mrs. Lummis responded, "No. I know she didn't. I mean, at least her mother said she didn't. I really know nothing." Whatever mystery is associated with Greta's marriage to Alexander More, Jean Summerlin Hughes was obviously a party to it: Jean Hughes attended the ceremony in St. Louis; Jean Hughes accompanied Greta to Santa Barbara immediately afterward; and Jean Hughes supplied the explanations about Greta's life to those who asked.

Finally, there was the mystery of More's death. Was it in any way related to his marriage to Greta? How did the rancher die? Suicide? Murder? Natural causes? Since no one in the Hughes family ever broke their code of silence, the secrets of More's mysterious marriage to Greta Hughes died with him on the banks of the Santa Ynez River.

Fred Howell: A Key to the Confusion?

With theories and possible intrigues about Greta and her mysterious marriage to Alexander More still haunting the investigation, Dinkins' associate's thoughts naturally turned to Frederick J. Howell. Greta married Howell just seven months after her divorce from More, and it was a week later that the California rancher died suddenly under suspiciouis circumstances. Whatever the compelling reason to keep the More marriage top-secret, Howell must have been apprised of and possibly even party to it. While chances were slim that Howell himself was still alive to tell the story, he might have kin who knew the particulars and who could fill in some of the blanks about Greta. Moreover, Howell himself was something of a shadowy figure in the heirship investigation. Ruby Hughes, Felix's widow, had described him as a "Keokuk publisher." (She also identified him as Greta's first husband.) "The Keokuk Connection" denoted him as the "son of a prominent Keokuk newspaper family"; and Ray Garrison's description of him in "Fame and Fortune . . ." was similarly unhelpful: "of a prominent Keokuk newspaper publishing family, and brother of socially prominent Lida Gordon Howell."

Yet Howell's name is not mentioned in either of Greta's two Keokuk

Starlet Terry Moore, who claims to have been married to Howard Hughes, Jr., in 1949 by the captain of his yacht. They were never divorced, despite Hughes' subsequent marriage to Jean Peters and Moore's three later trips to the altar. *Courtesy of Terry Moore.*

Sonny (Howard Hughes, Jr.) crowned King of the May Fête, Christ Church Cathedral School, Houston, Texas, around 1915. *Courtesy of Christ Church Cathedral.*

Frances Geddes, as she appeared on her honeymoon with Arthur Bendelari in 1901, shortly after her engagement to Howard Hughes, Sr. *Courtesy of James I. Geddes.*

Taken on Shoal Creek. Frances and sister Nan, Paul sisters and Howard Hughes.

Howard Hughes, Sr., and Frances Geddes *(back row, center)*, pictured on Shoal Creek in Joplin at the turn of the century. With them are Frances' sister Nancy *(holding basin)* and friends. This picture is from Frances' original album; the handwriting below the photograph is hers. *Courtesy of James I. Geddes.*

Ruth Stonehouse, former silent film star and second wife of Felix Hughes.
Courtesy of the Academy of Motion Picture Arts and Sciences.

Greta Hughes. *Reprinted by permission of Francis J. Helenthal from* The "Keokuk Connection."

Fred Howell, Greta Hughes' second husband. The photograph was taken in Keokuk, Iowa, around 1889, possibly on the occasion of his marriage to Greta. *Courtesy of Liz Howell.*

Elspeth Hughes, pictured with her mother, Agnes Hedge Hughes. This photograph is one of the few pictures of Elspeth as a child, part of a small collection sent by Tashleene Robertson to Elspeth's daughters in the 1950s. *By permission of Barbara L. Cameron.*

Tashleene Merry Little Brown
Earley Jarvis Robertson ("Teddy"),
shown with her sons Carroll Brown
(standing) and John Robertson.
Courtesy of Sidney L. Brown.

Elizabeth Patterson Dial
Hughes and her nephew, Alston
Cockrell, Jr., in a photograph taken
in Los Angeles in 1926. Patterson
Dial should have been twenty-four
at the time. *Courtesy of Stephena
Cockrell Scott.*

Actress Leila Hughes, alleged to have been the "real" daughter of Rupert and Agnes Hedge Hughes. *Courtesy of Robert C. Hughes.*

Author Rupert Hughes, Adelaide Manola *(then his wife; holding dog),* and Adelaide's daughter Avis, photographed in Los Angeles around 1920. *Courtesy of Robert C. Hughes.*

RUPERT HUGHES

Rupert Hughes, *National Magazine,* August 1919.

Marion Manola (Adelaide's mother). Marion was once Rupert Hughes' mother-in-law and possibly his mysterious second wife. *Courtesy of the Billy Rose Theatre Collection, Library for the Performing Arts, Lincoln Center.*

Evelyn Gates, the daughter of Marion Manola's maid, born during her mother's employment in the Rupert Hughes household. Her father's identity has never been revealed. *Courtesy of Evelyn Gates.*

obituaries: an odd omission for the supposed scion of a local newspaper family. Furthermore, in the 1889 marriage license to Greta Hughes, Howell is described as a resident of Colorado, employed as a broker; and the marriage occurred in Milwaukee. The facts did not seem to mesh. The only confirmation of Howell's Keokuk "connection" to date appeared in his 1899 divorce proceedings from Greta, in which he is identified as a "resident of Iowa for the past seven years."

What became of Howell after the divorce? Where did he go? Did he, as one might confidently presume, stay in Keokuk, where his family was by all reports a prominent fixture in society—leaving Greta to pursue her career and Herbert Witherspoon? For that matter, what was known about his marriage to Greta? The couple was together for ten years, from 1889 to 1899, yet nothing had been written or said about their life together. Dinkins needed to confirm, above all, that Frederick and Greta Hughes Howell had no children together.

In search of the real Frederick J. Howell, Dinkins' associate traveled to Keokuk, Greta's hometown and by reputation, Howell's as well. There, the ad litem was able to attach an identity to Howell's name, but the story of his past, it developed, had only begun. A conversation with Francis Helenthal provided little insight or instruction. Helenthal reiterated that Howell came from a socially prominent Keokuk family and that he joined the board of directors of a local company and "continued to edit the paper" after his divorce from Greta in 1899. Why, then, was Howell's presence in Keokuk so inconspicuous?

At the Keokuk public library Howell's past finally began to take shape. Dinkins' assistant knew by the Howell marriage certificate that his parents' names were James B. and Mary Bowen Howell and with this information was able to trace his family's development in Keokuk through old copies of the city directories. Young Howell (referred to variously in the directories as "J. Fred," "Fred," and "J. F."), in the years immediately preceding his 1889 marriage at the age of twenty-nine to Greta Hughes, had led a drifting sort of existence, not unlike the young Howard, Sr. From 1879 (when he was nineteen) to the year 1887 (when he was twenty-seven), Howell appears in the Keokuk city directories on and off, employed by turn as a traveling agent, freight clerk, and auditor with the M.I. & N. Railway; or with no occupation. It also appeared from the directories (though this wasn't clear) that he had two brothers: Jesse B. and D. Lane Howell; and a sister, Lida Gordon Howell. In 1887-88, and 1888-89, the period of Greta's marriage to Alexander More, Howell is missing from the Keokuk directories. On May 22, 1889, Howell and Greta married in Milwaukee, and for the first four or five years of their married life (up to 1892), the couple does not appear in the Keokuk city directory, suggesting they lived elsewhere—probably

Colorado, where Howell was presumably employed as a "broker." (This is substantiated by their wedding announcement in the Keokuk paper, which stated that the couple was to reside "on Sherman Ave. in Denver.")

For the duration of their marriage (from 1893 to 1899) Howell is listed as a Keokuk resident, employed continuously as "ticket agent for the Union depot." The year Fred and Greta returned to Keokuk, 1893, they are listed at the same address as the Felix Hughes family in the city directory. The next five or six years of their married life, 1894 to 1899, "Mrs. Fred Howell" does not appear in the directories next to Fred's name. One can assume, based on Rupert's magazine article "My Father," Ruby Hughes' comments, and much other source material, that Greta was abroad during this period "studying voice," both with and without her brother Felix. This is, of course, confirmed in Howell's divorce petition, in which he states that his wife "abandoned him" for Europe on July 30, 1896. The Keokuk directories would suggest that her desertion of Howell actually took place several years earlier. A fascinating aspect to this residential portrait of a marriage is that while Greta Hughes Howell was flitting about Europe alone from 1894 or 1895 on, her husband Fred was back in Keokuk living in the same residence as her family! Only in 1898-99, the year he filed for divorce from Greta, does Howell show up at a different address.

Greta's European travels during this period are chronicled from time to time in the personal column of the Keokuk newspapers. In the summer of 1895, for example, several entries record that Howell and Jean Hughes (Greta's mother) sailed to Paris together to join Greta and young Felix, who had been "pursuing studies" in France. On September 26, Howell "returned alone" after spending five months in Paris and the summer in Switzerland with Greta, who was to remain abroad in Paris "until December." Yet in the folowing spring(May 1896), Greta is noted as performing at "Queen's Hall in London," and by July of that same year, she and Howell officially separated, according to his petition for divorce, which was filed several years later, in February 1899. Why Howell lingered another two years in an apparently unsuitable marriage is an open question.

As informative as these directory listings were in a superficial sense, they still told nothing about the intricacies of the Howell marriage. To discover the particulars, it was necessary to find Howell or someone who knew him or was related to him. At first, this did not seem difficult, since he was reputedly from one of Keokuk's more prominent families; local historian Francis Helenthal, among others, contended that Howell continued to edit the paper in Keokuk after his divorce from Greta and was later named to the board of directors of a local corporation. This picture of Howell, however, did not fit in with the series of unimpressive occupations held by J. Fred Howell before his marriage and who was employed thereafter as a ticket agent. The most overwhelming evidence to the contrary, however, was that Howell dropped out of the Keokuk city directory permanently from 1899 to 1900, the year he divorced Greta, and the Keokuk recorder had no notation of a death certificate on file for a Frederick J. Howell. Plainly, this did not fit the image of a "successful Keokuk newspaper publisher."

Puzzled by this paradox, Dinkins' associate decided to dig a little deeper into Fred Howell's Keokuk past, thinking it might provide some clue as to what became of his future. Armed with the skeletal information already gathered about his family, Dinkins' emissary journeyed to the Keokuk library in search of data about the other members of the Howell clan, who might have left more of an imprint in Keokuk than J. Fred had.

This strategy opened the door to Fred Howell's past. The library maintained a small envelope of clippings on James B. Howell, because of his status as a prominent former citizen of Keokuk, Fred's father had started the Keokuk *Gate City* newspaper and had later served in the United States Senate for one term. His obituary (June 17, 1880) recited that he left three sons, Jesse, Lane, and J. Frederick, and a daughter, Lida, all of Keokuk. The eldest of James Howell's sons, Jesse, apparently took over the editorship of the paper upon his father's death in 1880. Jesse Howell died in 1896. According to Jesse's obituary notice, he left two daughters, Adelove and Mary Howell; two brothers, Lane and Fred; and a sister, Lida. His death announcement also mentioned that Jesse moved to Denver in 1887 "for his health."

These newspaper clippings explained several things about Fred Howell's past. First, they illustrated his connection to a "newspaper publishing family," which had been mentioned by several sources in the course of the heirship investigation. At the same time, however, they dispelled the notion advanced by both Ruby Hughes and Francis Helenthal that Fred himself served as editor or publisher of the paper. That position was held first by his father and later by his brother Jesse. The clippings also served to demonstrate how and why Fred Howell ended up in Denver at the time of his 1889 marriage to Greta: his older brother Jesse was in Denver for health reasons at the time. More critically, the clippings envelope unquestionably placed Fred Howell in the James B. Howell family dynasty, Dinkins' best hope of ultimately tracing one of his descendants.

Yet the file on James B. Howell still failed to answer the question that vexed the ad litem investigation: what became of Fred Howell? The clippings in the "Howell" file at the Keokuk library stop abruptly with his brother Jesse's death in 1896, at a time when Fred was still married to Greta and living in Keokuk. It was obvious from the information already available to Dinkins that Fred Howell did not succeed to the family publishing business, nor did he stay on in Keokuk, where his family had a prominent position in society.

Later, the same day that Dinkins' associate stumbled upon the Howell file in the Keokuk library, she met with the widow of Ray Garrison to discuss the recently discovered Alex More marriage license, among other things. Since Mrs. Garrison had assembled a Keokuk librarian and a local historian, John Talbot, to sit in on the conversation, Dinkins' law clerk took advantage of the opportunity to quiz them about Fred Howell and his family, having reached a dead end in her research at the library.

With the assistance of Mrs. Garrison and her two companions, Dinkins' researcher determined the dates of death for both Lida Gordon Howell (Fred's sister) and Mary Bowen Howell (his mother). Using this information, she located their obituaries. The strategy was to ascertain Fred's whereabouts as of the date of his mother and sister's death. In 1903, the year of his mother's death, Howell was mentioned as a lieutenant in the United States Army Artillery stationed at Fortress Monroe "on the Atlantic Coast." That explained where he went immediately after his divorce from Greta in 1899: he joined the Army.

Lida Gordon Howell's obituary was even more enlightening. Lida died in 1946. Surviving her were, according to the announcement of her death, "a brother, James Frederick Howell of Brightwater, New York: three nephews and three nieces." Bingo! This was the first solid lead on Howell in the ad litem's investigation. Lida Howell's obituary also raised the possibility that Howell had a child or children. Dinkins already knew that Lida's brother Jesse had two children. That left three nephews and a niece unaccounted for. Either all four of these children were Lane Howell's (Lida's other brother), or Fred Howell had one or more children. And since Fred was thirty-nine years old at the time he divorced Greta, and it was not known whether he married again, it increased the chances the pair might have had a child at some point in their ten-year marriage.

Dinkins' clerk also carried with her from this expedition to Keokuk a lead on Fred Howell's relations. Mrs. Garrison and her cronies were acquainted with the two children of Jesse Howell, Mary and Adelove. Jesse Howell was Fred's older brother, so Mary and Adelove were Fred's nieces. Mary and Adelove were no longer living in 1980, but Mr. Talbot and the Keokuk librarian remembered that Mary Howell had married, given birth to two children, and eventually moved to China. Mary had died young, and her sister Adelove raised Mary's two sons. Adelove

216

Howell never married, and continued to live in Keokuk to raise her two nephews. The two sons of Mary (Adelove's nephews) moved away from Keokuk as adults, but through certain of Talbot's recollections Dinkins' colleague was eventually able to trace them, which was a great coup for the investigation. Not only did the ad litem have a date and place of the last known residence of Fred Howell; he now had the opportunity to question two of Howell's grandnephews: the children of Fred's niece, Mary. From them Dinkins hoped to learn where Howell went after his divorce from Greta, what line of business he had entered, whether he had remarried, if he had had any children (by Greta or anyone else), grandchildren, and so on. At last the mystery of Fred Howell's life appeared to be solved.

As had become the pattern in Dinkins' investigation, however, each time one puzzle was put together, three more took its place, and Fred Howell was no exception. Talking to his two grandnephews only increased the confusion. When asked about their great-uncle Fred Howell, each of the two men contacted "recalled the name," but neither had any idea what became of him. The older of the two seemed unwilling to discuss his great-uncle at all, saying curtly, "He was a different animal." His brother, although more cooperative during the short interview, could add little to this description. He admitted that Fred Howell was a "mystery figure" in the family, and seemed confused about his family connection. When asked by Dinkins' associate if he knew anything about Fred Howell's last known residence in Brightwater in 1946, this source stated that he didn't think Howell was even alive in 1946. Neither of the pair could offer any suggestions as to how to trace their great-uncle, and each said there were "no living relatives" in the Howell family, and no record of anybody. "It's very strange," confessed the younger, more cooperative of the brothers.

Once more, it seemed that Dinkins' investigation had taken one step forward to go two steps backward. It made next to no sense that the two men questioned should have so little information to offer about their great-uncle. After all, the two had grown up in Keokuk in the 1930s and 1940s, raised by their aunt Adelove Howell (Fred's niece). Throughout this period, Lida Gordon Howell (Fred's sister) was the grande dame of Keokuk society, and the pair of brothers associated with her up to the year of her death, 1946, when Fred Howell was presumably alive and living in Brightwater, New York. One would think that Fred might be a topic of conversation among Lida Howell (his sister) and Adelove (his niece) when they got together in Keokuk, with and without Adelove's two nephews. Yet the two men professed to know nothing about Fred Howell, and the older of the two noticeably bristled at the mention of his name. Why was Fred Howell, by the younger of the brothers' description, a "mystery figure" in the family; and why did the older brother, who seemed to know more but was less willing to speak, describe him with near contempt, as a "different animal"? Did Howell, too, have something to hide? Why did everyone connected with Greta Hughes carry this shroud of mystery?

Howell's Second Family

Dinkins' associate wasted little time in contemplating these questions, and instead followed the next path in her trail of research. She located a "Bright*waters*" in Suffolk County, New York—one of a cluster of villages crowded along Long Island—and made inquiries by telephone to determine whether a J. Frederick Howell appeared in the city directories or telephone books in 1946 (the year Howell is listed in his sister Lida's obituary as a resident of Brightwater, New York). The Brightwaters librarian found no listing for a J. Frederick Howell from 1944 to 1950, although there was a "Jasper F. Howell" who appeared until 1953. Dinkins' associate was disappointed but not surprised. Howell would have been eighty-six years old in 1946, and the Brightwaters connection was a long shot at best. Undaunted, she followed an instinct and requested copies of the probate proceedings for any "J. F. Howell" in Suffolk County for the period 1946 to 1953 (the year "Jasper F." ceased to appear in the Brightwaters phone books). If Howell were living in Brightwaters in 1946, chances were good he would have passed away by the early 1950s (when he would have been over ninety years old). If he died in Brightwaters, his probate papers should list his next of kin and determine once and for all whether Howell had any children.

It was a lucky hunch. Several weeks later, a package arrived from the Surrogate's Court, Suffolk County. Inside were the probate proceedings and last will and testament of one James Frederick Howell! "Amazing!" exclaimed Dinkins when presented with the latest piece in the Hughes jigsaw puzzle. Howell's probate file revealed that he died in Walter Reed Hospital on September 2, 1951, at the age of ninety-one. He was a resident of Islip, New York (another village in Suffolk County), at the time of his death. In his will, dated February 3, 1937, Howell recited that he was a resident of the village of Brightwaters, New York, and left his entire estate to his "wife, Adele." Listed as his next of kin were:

Adele W. Howell	Wife	Bay Shore, New York
James F. Howell, Jr.	Son	A.F.B., Colorado Springs
Carleton B. Howell	Son	Islip, New York

They had traveled a long way to get there, but Dinkins' suspicions were not unfounded: Fred Howell indeed had two children. The question was: were they Greta's or Adele's?

The discovery of Fred Howell's new life was a puzzling one. Why had his friends and family back in Keokuk been kept in the dark about his whereabouts? Why did his grandnephews either express ignorance about him or refuse to discuss him at all? More to the point, why did they both insist there were "no living relatives" in the Howell family, when this new evidence gave every indication that Howell had two children and possibly even grandchildren? It was, as the younger of the two said, "very strange."

Eager to tie the ribbon on Fred Howell's life, Dinkins' associate tried in vain to trace the individuals named in his probate proceedings. Neither Adele nor Carleton Howell appeared in the 1980 Islip-Brightwaters-Bay Shore directories, nor did the attorneys or witnesses mentioned in his will. James Howell, Jr., was no longer at the Air Force base in Colorado, though he did appear in the 1952–1955 telephone books. Dinkins agreed to request probate proceedings for Adele Howell, Fred's widow, from Suffolk County in the event she had stayed on in Islip and died there. This request provided the next link in the chain. Adele Howell had died in 1956, five years after her husband, and in her 1956 will left all her property to her "beloved son Carleton." Her next of kin were listed as Carleton Howell of Bay Shore, two granddaughters, and a grandson. Noticeably absent was James F. Howell, Jr., who had appeared five years earlier in Howell's probate file, identified as his son. Did this mean James, Jr., was not Adele's son—meaning he could be Greta's? Or did he die in the five-year interim between Fred's and Adele's deaths? That was the question that preyed on Dinkins' mind.

Through the information in Adele W. Howell's probate proceedings, Dinkins' associate eventually located Fred Howell's daughter-in-law, Velma Howell. Velma was the widow of James F. Howell, Jr. Velma Howell was able to answer the more vexing questions about Howell to Dinkins' complete satisfaction, with one intriguing twist.

Contacted by phone, Velma Howell explained to Dinkins' clerk that Fred (as she called her father-in-law) was stationed in Honolulu as an Army man sometime before the turn of the century, where he met his wife-to-be, then Adele Widdifield. Howell was then sent to the Philippines during the Spanish-American War in 1899–1900, and Adele joined him in Manila, where they were married soon afterward. Their first child, she revealed, was a daughter named Mary, born in Manila in 1900 or 1901. The Howells stayed in Manila about two years, then moved to Fort Monroe, where James, Jr., was born in October 1902. From Fort Monroe, they moved to New Bedford, Massachusetts, then Washington,

D. C., followed by a stint in France, later back to New Bedford, then on to Brightwaters, New York (in approximately 1924), where Fred retired from the Army and became "manager" of the village. Mary Howell, Fred's daughter, died of the flu when she was seventeen, probably in Washington.

This account of Howell's life for the most part allayed any suspicions the ad litem team had entertained concerning the parentage of the two Howell sons, although the dates and years seemed uncomfortably close: Fred and Greta Howell divorced in Keokuk in 1899, and by 1900 Fred was remarried and the father of a baby girl. It was the remainder of the conversation with James, Jr.'s, widow, however, that captured the undivided attention of Dinkins' associate.

Velma Howell maintained that her father-in-law kept up with the Keokuk folk somewhat, particularly his sister Lida, who was "very rich." She described Howell as "one big peach." She knew that Fred had been married once before, "to the sister of a writer," but Mrs. Howell did not know this wife's first name, and amazingly was not aware of the Howard Hughes connection. In contrast to his "very open" nature, Howell was "very secretive" about his first marriage, Mrs. Howell pointed out. No one, in fact, was allowed to bring the subject up. She described her father-in-law's marriage to Greta as the "big mystery of the Howell family."

In line with that, Mrs. Howell recalled that Fred made periodic but regular "secret trips" to Philadelphia of two or three days' duration throughout his marriage to Adele. It was the family understanding that these trips "had to do with his first wife." Both Velma and her husband, James Howell, Jr., were very curious about this practice, and occasionally discussed it. Adele never accompanied Fred, and they had what Velma called a "perfect understanding" about it. Velma Howell "feels in her heart" that Fred and Greta had a child kept in Philadelphia whom he would visit during these travels. He was, she reported, "crazy about children," and she found it impossible to believe he did *not* have a child during his ten-year marriage to Greta. She concluded in saying that it was family legend that the Philadelphia connection concerned Greta. It was once speculated, for example, that Greta was in a Philadelphia mental institution and Fred Howell made these visits out of a sense of obligation. On reflection, however, Velma Howell was "convinced" the mystery involved a child of the couple's.

Understandably, Dinkins' curiosity was more than a little piqued by this unexpected revelation. If what Velma Howell suspected was true, then Howard Hughes, Jr., had another first cousin somewhere, a truly "unknown heir." Greta's secret child, if he or she existed, would be on a par with Elspeth as one of only two first cousins on the Hughes side of Howard, Jr.'s, family. Indeed, if Elspeth was not Rupert Hughes' daughter, as many were trying to prove, then this child would be the *only* paternal cousin, possibly the sole paternal heir, entitled to one-half of Hughes' estate under Texas law (since Rush and Avis' right to inherit as equitably adopted children, questionable in and of itself, was arguably dependent on Elspeth's legitimacy, due to a legal technicality).

It would mean, of course, that the settlement agreement master-minded by William Lummis dividing the estate privately between the maternal heirs and those they considered to be the bona fide paternal heirs—namely Elspeth's daughters, Rush, and Avis—was perhaps drafted a bit prematurely. Any child of Greta's would unquestionably be a Hughes heir and would be entitled to some percentage of his estate, which would in turn reduce the pro rata proportion previously allotted to the other relatives. Moreover, if Greta actually had a descendant somewhere, then even if George Parnham or his peers successfully discredited Elspeth's status as Rupert Hughes' legal daughter, Parnham's clients (the midwestern second and third cousins) would still be left out in the cold, since the paternal one-half would instead go to Greta's child, a first cousin, and not back a generation to his more remote kin. From Dinkins' vantage point, the inheritance scenario resembled an elaborate game of musical chairs: each time the music stopped, a different group lost its place in the game. To extend the metaphor, it was Dinkins' hand that controlled the music.

Before Dinkins let his associate loose on the streets of Philadelphia in search of Greta's "secret child," she tried to locate Fred Howell's other daughter-in-law (Carleton's widow), to see if she corroborated Velma Howell's astonishing story of clandestine trips to Philadelphia, a secretive first marriage, and mental institutions. Following a mazy trail in a manner that would have made Dick Tracy proud, Dinkins' assistant managed to find Mrs. Carleton Howell. As his colleague expected and Dinkins feared, her story, although different in certain respects, supported the main points of Velma Howell's strange tale of Frederick J./ J. Frederick Howell.

Elizabeth (Mrs. Carleton) Howell remembered that Fred and Adele Howell married in Manila around 1900. General Bell stood up for them and then-Governor (later President) Taft gave her away. Similarly, Mrs. Howell recalled talk of Mary Howell (the daughter who died), but thought she was named Adele.

Like Velma Howell, Carleton's widow knew that Fred (whom she called "Pop") had been married to Rupert Hughes' sister. She did not know this wife's first name either, only that she was a "concert singer or pianist" who "would not be a proper wife and was always traveling," leading to their divorce.

Elizabeth Howell further informed Dinkins' associate that her father-in-law was the "youngest executive of the Pennsylvania Railway" and later edited a newspaper in Keokuk. In Denver, she went on, he "made and lost a fortune" in real estate. Howell joined Teddy Roosevelt's Rough Riders in 1898 during the Spanish-American War. He met his second wife Adele in Honolulu ("It was love at first sight," she said), and the two were married one year later in Manila.

Consistent with Velma Howell's recollections, Carleton's widow confirmed that Fred Howell took "secret trips" alone to Philadelphia, where he would generally spend the weekend. These unexplained visits continued until the 1940s, when Howell became too old to travel. According to Elizabeth Howell, Fred and Adele "never discussed" the arrangement, but there was never any discernible resentment on Adele's part. Howell, in fact, would send his wife a flower while he was away, and on his return would bring her a box of candy.

Elizabeth Howell reiterated Velma's earlier comment that there was a "family understanding" that the Philadelphia trips had to do with "Pop's" first wife. She "would not be surprised" to learn that the weekends were arranged so that Fred could visit a child by Greta. Howell, whom she described as a "very dignified person," kept this part of his background "completely" to himself.

Finally, expanding on Velma Howell's suppositions, Elizabeth Howell had an "intuition" that the mystery somehow involved a portrait of Howell painted during one of his weekends in Philadelphia by an artist named Moorehead Philips, the son of an old friend.

Based on these two conversations, it was clear that there was more than one mystery associated with Greta Hughes More Howell Witherspoon, and that one of them somehow concerned her second husband, a possible secret child, or confinement in a mental institution. And it was all connected to or associated with the city of Philadelphia. The Philadelphia connection rang a distant bell for Dinkins' associate. Although Greta, by all the source material located by the ad litem, had never lived in Philadelphia, his assistant dimly recalled an arcane reference to the city in connection with Greta somewhere in their files. After deliberation, the thought came to the surface—it was in Greta's will! Dinkins' associate remembered being mildly interested in the fact that two of the witnesses to Greta's will (whose names were strangers to the investigation) were residents of Philadelphia. At the time she made out her will Greta was married to Witherspoon, presumably living in New York and teaching voice, therefore it had seemed a trifle odd to Dinkins' clerk that a pair of Philadelphians should turn up as witnesses, but this fact, in the larger scheme of things, was dismissed at the time as unimportant. With the information provided by the Howell daughters-in-law, the Philadelphia reference took on new significance.

In Philadelphia on other business in 1981, a few months before the heirship trials commenced, Dinkins' associate tried to determine if indeed Fred and Greta had a "secret child" in that city, or if there were some other obscure reason each might return to visit. But there was not a trace of Fred Howell, Greta, or Moorehead Philips to be found, nor was there any documentation for an individual who would meet the statistical description put together for a possible child. Dinkins' colleague eventually successfully traced one of the two Philadelphia witnesses to Greta's will, but the other Philadelphian, an electrician, had died in 1935.

In the end, Dinkins' associate admitted defeat. There was simply too little information to go on to find an alleged child of Greta's in Philadelphia or anywhere else. Several loose ends were tied when Dinkins' researcher located the Fred Howell-Adele Widdifield marriage certificate (Manila, 1900), as well as the birth and death certificates of their daughter Mary, who reportedly died of the flu. Much as the Howell daughters-in-law had suggested, Mary was born in Honolulu in 1901 and died in Winthrop, Massachusetts, in 1918 of pneumonia.

The remainder of what Fred's older daughter-in-law called the "big mystery of the Howell family," like the peculiar circumstances of Greta's earlier marriage to Alexander More, has never been solved: Howell's clandestine trips to Philadelphia, his "perfect understanding" with his wife, Adele, about the lost weekends, the "family understanding" that it involved his first wife, Velma Howell's sincere belief Fred and Greta had a child in Philadelphia, Greta's rumored institutionalization, the elusive artist Moorehead Philips and his possibly related portrait of Fred Howell—the suspicions were endless, the explanations few. Once again, that phrase from Annette Lummis' testimony that Greta had no children surfaced in Dinkins' associate's mind—"or at least her mother said she didn't." Whatever the dark secrets of Greta Hughes' past—the explanation for her secret marriage, a possible secret child, emotional disorders, rumored suicide, broken love affairs—every member of her family played a pivotal role in the cover-up: the Judge, who handled her divorces and set up a labyrinth for anyone who might attempt to trace them; his wife, Jean, who was with Greta when she married Alexander More in St. Louis, accompanied her to Santa Barbara and was later to speak for her daughter on the subject of children; both the Judge and Mimi, who lived with Fred Howell in Keokuk for five years while Greta traveled about Europe; her brother Howard, who apparently said nothing to anyone; and her brothers Rupert and Felix, with whom she had an exceptionally close relationship, who told everyone, including their own wives, that their sister Greta was married only twice.

Increasingly, the attorney ad litem's investigation to find and confirm the heirs of Howard R. Hughes, Jr., came to represent Gertrude Stein's aphorism: "There are no answers, only questions."

The Final Curtain

The ultimate mystery of Greta Hughes, like her nephew Howard, Jr.'s, years later, concerned the circumstances of her death. At a point in the investigation into Greta's past when the ad litem was still in the process of piecing together the major events in her life, his associate, guided as if by some strange force, studied Greta's death certificate with particular care. What she noticed was unusual even by the standards of the heirship investigation, and led to perhaps the most startling revelation of the investigation.

Although Greta's death certificate appeared normal in every other respect, Dinkins' associate was struck by what she considered a significant paradox. Greta's date of death, as noted on the certificate, was February 21, 1916—a fact that in itself had eluded both Mrs. Fay and the ad litem's office for some time. Studying the death record more closely, Dinkins' associate noticed that the date of Greta's burial, handwritten on the death certificate by the undertaker, was April 23, 1911—nearly six years before her date of death!

Haunted by Avis McIntyre's earlier, extremely vivid testimony regarding Greta's death "in 1913 or 1914" (the year Avis started at the Foxcroft school), Dinkins' assistant decided to investigate further. Coupled with Greta's wildly variable age, she had never quite been able to shake an uncomfortable feeling with respect to Greta's demise. Avis' testimony, however, was the most eery: not only did her dates conflict madly with the date on Greta's death certificate, but it was accentuated by a particularly dramatic event involving Rupert and the thirty-six-hour state of shock into which he lapsed after his sister's death. Avis recalled that her mother, Adelaide, even wrote her a letter describing Rupert's frightening condition in great detail. Furthermore, there were the persistent rumors that Greta had committed suicide, possibly over her unhappy marriage to Witherspoon, related most notably by Ray Garrison, whose notes even indicated it was an overdose of pills.

It is here, in the investigation into Greta's death, that her life becomes intertwined with Rupert's in a strange and mysterious way, involving one or more of Rupert's wives, one of his mothers-in-law, and the young woman whom Robert C. Hughes contends was Rupert's real daughter. The drama unfolds, appropriately enough, in a cemetery.

10

Rupert Hughes: A Man of Many Faces

Although Greta was arguably the most mysterious of the Hughes children, Rupert was unquestionably the most inscrutable. As questions about his life intensified during the heirship investigation, and the body of material about him in the ad litem's files swelled correspondingly, a fuzzy image of Rupert Hughes began to emerge. To Dinkins and his two investigators, Rupert Hughes surfaced as a man of conflicting extremes: remembered as madly extravagant by some, "tight with a dollar" by others; loving, warm, and affectionate by some accounts, aloof, distant, and cold by others; a "close-knit" family man to his granddaughters, an apparent stranger to his alleged daughter; a proud midwesterner at certain times, scornful of his small-town background at others. The list of contradictions goes on and on.

225

For each glowing tribute the attorney ad litem collected on Rupert Hughes, there were as many hints of a darker side to his nature. Which aspect of his personality was the real one? Was he, as his granddaughters contended, a warm and generous human being, or was he, as a growing body of evidence suggested, a man of black moods and secretive, even ruthless behavior? Alternatively, was Rupert Hughes a man of truly schizophrenic tendencies, and did that explain the myriad of questions and suspicions that haunted his life, and everyone's close to him? As the counsel for Barbara Cameron and her sisters, Paul Freese, said to the jury at the conclusion of the heirship trial: let the facts speak for themselves.

Father Rupert?

From the moment of Ted Dinkins' appointment as attorney for the unknown heirs, Rupert Hughes' life posed problems for the ad litem investigation. The basic facts of his life, as set forth at this early stage, were these: Rupert Hughes, an author, was married three times. By his first wife, Agnes, he had a daughter, Elspeth (Howard Hughes, Jr.'s, first cousin). Elspeth Hughes Lapp was deceased, but her three daughters (Barbara Lapp Cameron, Elspeth Lapp DePould, and Agnes Lapp Roberts) emerged from the shadows to claim a percentage of the Howard Hughes estate in her place. According to this version of the family history, Rupert and Agnes Hughes divorced, and Rupert eventually married a woman named Adelaide. Adelaide Hughes died during the marriage, after which Rupert remarried. His third wife, Elizabeth Patterson Dial Hughes, died in 1945. Rupert Hughes did not marry again, and died in 1956 at the age of eighty-four. Rupert had no children by his second or third wife. Aside from this crude outline of his life, Rupert Hughes was a blank page to Ted Dinkins and his associates.

Before the ad litem or any of the others assigned to the case had a chance to assimilate or expand on this biographical information, two stepchildren of Rupert Hughes, Rush Hughes and Avis Hughes McIntyre (a son and daughter of Adelaide's by a former marriage) filed affidavits of heirship against the Howard Hughes estate. They claimed to be Rupert's "equitably" adopted children, entitled to a share of the Hughes fortune under the laws of the state of Texas, as Howard, Jr.'s, first cousins.

After Rush and Avis' unexpected entry into the estate proceedings late in 1976, as the common-law adopted children of Rupert Hughes, there was a period of frenzied deposition taking, as attorneys for Elspeth's daughters attempted to explore the authenticity of Rush and Avis' claim, which they disputed, while at the same time Rush and Avis' lawyers, led by Avis' Alabama attorney George Dean and his Texas co-counsel Wayne Fisher, set about to do the opposite: to prove through deposition testimony that their clients were in fact considered by Rupert Hughes to be his adopted children. From these depositions, the personality and lifestyle of Rupert Hughes first began to emerge.

Based on the testimony of those who were questioned in connection with Rush and Avis' claim, Rupert Hughes cut an enviable and somewhat romantic figure. During the period that he was married to their mother, Adelaide—1908 to 1923—Rupert led a glamorous, opulent life, hobnobbing with the rich and famous. He wintered in a house or apartment in New York City ("for the season," Avis noted) and summered at a series of rented country estates in Westchester County, forty-five minutes outside Manhattan. He eventually purchased a spectacular manor house on sixty acres of land in Bedford Hills, New York, thereafter leading the life of a country squire.

Rush and Avis were the first to be deposed in regard to their adoption by estoppel claim, and their testimony of life with "Father Rupert" (as they referred to Rupert Hughes as children) vividly portrayed a style of living rare today except among the very rich. Asked to describe the Bedford Hills house and the sort of life she led there, Avis responded:

> Well, the house that Rupert bought he bought from a German couple named von der Emde. They were relatives of the Ruperts, the Bushes and the Eberhard-Fabers in New York. And it was about 50 acres. Beautiful property. The Germans had planted it. It was just unbelievable. Hedges of three kinds of raspberries and walks as long as this house of lilac hedges. And anything that was imaginable that was indigenous to that part of the country they had. It was just beautiful.
>
> And trees. Mostly there were tulip trees in front of the house. And that's why Rupert named the place "Whitewood." That's another name for tulip trees. Marvelous apple orchards, cherry orchards. It was just a grand place, and it was quite self-sustaining.
>
> Rupert inherited the Polish foreman—Tony Polinski was his name—who always tickled Rupert to death, his accent and the way he did things and everything. And an old Italian gardener named Pop. He was called "Pop," "old toothless." He taught me to say "Bon giorno" and "Buona sera." And then he inherited—well, we brought an Irish cook from New York, and we had a German, very, very stylish, high-class German parlor maid as they were called. And then Rupert engaged an English butler by the name of Sully, and Sully was really something. I mean he was unbelievable in this day and age that we had anything like that. And he had a wife. What the devil was her name? Edie. Rush used to tease her and call her "Eenie, meenie, minee, moe" or something like that.

227

And then we got another German servant. We had a lot of servants running around there. Is that enough of the servants?

Linda Kelly, an associate of Dinkins' who attended Avis' deposition in Alabama the fall of 1976, reported that the witness was a living reminder of the era she depicted in her testimony. Kelly described Avis as "patrician . . . very horsey . . . like a character from a Katharine Hepburn movie"—and the description is an apt one. Mrs. McIntyre is an old-fashioned Southern gentlewoman, with all the style and panache the term connotes. Yet for all her considerable charm, she has also been described as arrogant, haughty, strong-willed, short-tempered, and impatient—traits that manifested themselves from time to time in her deposition testimony.

From the deposition testimony of Avis and her younger brother Rush, it was learned that their mother, born Adelaide Mould in 1884, was the only child of Henry Mould and his "musical comedy star" wife, "who appeared under the name of Marion Manola." Adelaide Mould became an actress and at some point adopted her mother's stage name, appearing in theatre and the movies as "Adelaide Manola." Adelaide married an electrical engineer named George Edgar Bissell in New York when she was "very young," eighteen or nineteen, and the Bissells had a daughter named Avis on December 19, 1900, while they were living on assignment in Kobe, Japan. Adelaide became pregnant with Rush a year or so later and, due to a bout with dysentery, moved back to Brooklyn (where Bissell's parents lived) to give birth. Rush Marion Hughes was born in May 1902. The Bissells separated that same year and divorced sometime before 1905, whereupon George Bissell was given custody of Rush, and Adelaide custody of Avis.

For the next several years, Avis lived with her maternal grandparents and great-grandmother (Marion Manola's mother) in Detroit, while Rush was farmed out to his paternal grandparents, the Bissells, in Brooklyn. At some point Adelaide met Rupert Hughes through actress Blanche Bates, a mutual friend, and the two were married in 1907 or 1908. "It's fuzzily vague that they might have been married in Atlantic City," recounted Avis, "but I'm not sure of that." Avis, by then a girl of eight or so, joined Adelaide and her new stepfather Rupert Hughes, and the three lived alternately in New York City and Westchester County, as Rupert pursued his literary career, mostly as a playwright. (Rupert was in his late thirties or early forties at the time.) Throughout this period, roughly 1908 to 1915, Rupert Hughes had several plays running on Broadway at the same time, a few of which flopped; but one, "Excuse Me," was a huge hit. He also wrote magazine articles and books. By Avis' account, the Hughes house was filled with the stars of stage and

228

screen at all times. "Oh, my goodness," she exclaimed. "There was a large theatrical gang in those very early days. Lillian Russell and Elsie Janis and Ethel Barrymore and all the leading men and women of the theater. There were Gouverneur Morris and Rex Beach . . . Booth Tarkington. There were so many people."

In May 1911, three years later, Rush Bissell was taken from his paternal grandparents' home, where he had been living since his parents' divorce, to reside with his father in Syracuse, where Bissell lived with a new wife. (Rush claimed he never saw his father prior to this.) By Rush's recollection, the new Mrs. Bissell did not accept him, and Rush was placed in a Catholic orphanage in Syracuse. In December 1911, eight months later, Adelaide Hughes removed her nine-year-old son from the orphanage and took him to Bedford Hills to live in the Rupert Hughes household. It is at this point that the apparent "equitable adoption" came about. This is Avis' explanation, upon which her claim to the Howard Hughes estate turns:

> Well, I remember that after Rush came and had become part of the family that Rupert had said he wanted to adopt us. And so I don't know what the machinations were or whether it was through lawyers or what the contact was, but they contacted my father and he said absolutely not. He would not under any circumstances permit us to be adopted. So there was no more talk of contacting my father. But from then on, Rupert asked if we would like to change our name to "Hughes" because that's what he would like and that we were his children, and that was that. . . .
>
> I have nothing to prove it. I have nothing written . . . I just know that it was said and that the family conversation in front of Rush and me was that he had been asked, and Rupert said that he wanted to legalize the fact that we were his children and that my father refused. And that was a family conversation, and after my father refused, then there was nothing more said, and we just belonged to Rupert . . . and my father was never mentioned by anybody again.

According to Avis, after Rupert married her mother in 1907 or 1908, she has no recollection of using the "Bissell" name again.

Their idyllic life on the Hughes farm continued until approximately 1918, as Rupert's career on the East Coast flourished. After a period of private tutoring in Bedford Hills, Avis and Rush were both sent to boarding schools. Avis attended St. Mary's in Raleigh, North Carolina, for one year in 1912, followed by her enrollment in the exclusive Foxcroft School of Virginia in 1913 ("I'm a charter member," she confided), where she remained until her graduation in 1917, and developed, according to her brother Rush, "one of the greatest Southern accents I ever heard." Rush, for his part, was schooled at St. John's Academy in Manlius, New York, from 1917 to 1920. "I remember we went through the school advertising section of *Cosmopolitan* magazine seeking the names and locations of various schools," Rush recalled nostalgically. "I chose Manlius Military Academy because I liked the picture of the drum major with the high shako." After leaving Manlius in 1920, Rush was tutored briefly at the Harstrom School in Connecticut ("It developed at Manlius that my mathematics was woeful," he explained), and later transferred to the Mercersberg Academy in Pennsylvania, which he attended for the duration of his schooling, until 1922. Both Avis and Rush's boarding school educations were paid for by Rupert Hughes.

During these years, Adelaide retired from the stage and began a modestly successful career as a poet and occasional collaborator to her husband. "The only extracurricular activity insofar as housework is concerned," recalled Rush, "wrapped around her writing, and she raised canaries. Loved to raise canaries." Adelaide Manola Hughes, by her children's admission, was a woman of extravagant tastes and artistic sensibilities. Both Rush and Avis were devoted to their mother, and the two described this time in their lives as a golden and halcyon period.

From their deposition testimony of life in Bedford Hills, the person of Elspeth Hughes makes her official appearance in the Hughes estate proceedings. Avis testified that Elspeth began to spend summers at the Rupert Hughes household in 1908 or 1909, shortly after Rupert and Adelaide married. Rush joined his mother and sister in Bedford Hills in 1911, and he too remembered that Elspeth summered with the family by arrangement between Rupert and his first wife, until about 1920. Each testified that they understood that Elspeth was Rupert's daughter by a prior marriage, and all were treated equally by Rupert. "Well, he treated us if anything better than Elspeth, as I remember," observed Avis. Their other recollections of Elspeth are not so clear. Avis knew of only one school Elspeth attended during this ten-year interval, Miss Madeira's, and had no idea what religion, if any, Elspeth was. She stated that Elspeth lived with her mother and stepfather, a "Mr. Reynolds," who was a naval officer of some sort, in Washington, D. C. Avis further testified that Elspeth was a year older than she, and Rush stated that he "thought Avis was younger than Elspeth," but wasn't sure.

Here, in the first depositions of the heirship investigation, the confusion about Elspeth begins, never to be resolved. During the years of her summer visits to Rupert's farm, from 1908 to 1919, Elspeth would have aged from eleven to twenty-two years old, assuming the May 1897 date on her birth certificate is accurate. Avis, by contrast, was born in December 1900 and would have been a girl of eight to nineteen years old within the same time frame. By the dates on their birth certificates, there was nearly four years difference between Avis and Elspeth. Rush was born in May 1902, making him exactly five years younger than Elspeth, a year and a half younger than Avis. None of this comported with either Rush or Avis' testimony. Rush noted hardly any difference in Avis' and Elspeth's ages; yet there was almost four years between them, and Avis insisted she was but a year younger than Elspeth. To harbor such a misimpression for ten years, during their adolescence, seems unusual in the extreme. Many attempts were made throughout both depositions to clarify Elspeth's age, all without success. Asked by Paul Freese if Elspeth dated during this period, or engaged in any activities that might identify her age, Rush replied, "No, no . . . she was rather a shy girl, and I don't think she had any interest in dating at that time." Yet Elspeth should have been twenty-two during the last of these summer visits.

Aside from perpetuating confusion about her age, Avis and Rush added little new information about Elspeth. The two knew only that she attended Miss Madeira's School and lived in Washington with her mother.

In 1917 or 1918, this magical family life began to dissolve. Rupert Hughes, a patriot and military man, was sent to Washington for several years, where he served as a major in the Intelligence Division of the U.S. Army during World War I. (A hearing deficiency disqualified him from combat duty.) On his return to Bedford Hills, Hughes was courted by movie czar Samuel Goldwyn, who ultimately convinced him to join a group of "Eminent Authors" (along with Mary Roberts Rinehart and others) to write scenarios for the infant motion picture industry. Henceforth Rupert and Adelaide departed for Hollywood, where they lived part-time in a series of rented homes, returning to Bedford Hills sporadically. The move was destined to be a permanent one. Rupert Hughes became not only a screenwriter, but also the director of his silent pictures, thus entering full-force into an entirely new phase of his career.

During the early years in California, 1919 to 1921, the family members scattered in various directions, and the relationship between Rupert and Adelaide began to deteriorate, according to Rush. The situation between them was complicated by a series of five operations performed on Adelaide, who was diagnosed to have colitis. "In retrospect," Rush reflected, "I believe the change came about . . . not only because of the deterioration of her physical condition, but because of the fact that she wanted . . . to take a cruise around the world on a tramp steamer, wanted to get away from it all, and this caused some conflict in the household." Avis, who did not like California, was attending a French school in New York at the time. She also made plans to wed John (Monk) Saunders, an Oxford graduate and aspiring writer. The two were married in a huge society wedding in New York City on January 8, 1922, with Rupert Hughes giving the bride away. (Elspeth was married a month or so later in Washington. Neither Avis, Rush, *nor Rupert* attended Elspeth's wedding. In fact, Avis and Rush never saw her again.) In the fall of 1922, while Rush was still a student at the Mercersberg Academy and Avis a newlywed, Adelaide traveled to the Orient by boat in the company of a nurse for several months. Later in this same time period—1922–23—Rush completed his studies at Mercersberg and joined Rupert Hughes in California. "He mistakenly thought I could be a motion picture actor," Rush noted good-naturedly, "by the simple expedient of casting me in all of his pictures."

By 1924—less than a year later—both Rush and Avis became permanently estranged from Rupert Hughes. By their explanation, this schism was caused by events within the family that occurred more or less simultaneously. The first, and most dramatic, concerned their mother, Adelaide. In August 1923, six months after her earlier trip, Adelaide embarked on a round-the-world cruise in failing health. Rupert did not accompany her. On December 14 of that year, while the boat was in Haiphong, China, Adelaide hanged herself on a boat strap. "There are actually conflicting reports as to what happened to her," Rush observed. "There was no medical officer on board. One story has it that she developed mastoiditis, and since there was no possibility of an operation behind the ear, she died. Another story has it that she hanged herself, again because of the frightening pain." All other reports indicate Adelaide committed suicide; most suggest it had nothing to do with pain from an ear injury.

Either before or immediately after Adelaide's tragic trip to China (Rush is not certain of the time sequence), Rush met a singer named Marion Harris, several years his senior, whom he wished to marry. "Rupert objected to the alliance," he noted. "He didn't want me marrying a professional singer." Rush married Marion Harris despite Rupert's dubious objections to her career and her age. (Rupert, after all, was married to an actress and was the brother of two singers, Felix and Greta.) Rush contended this contributed to the growing ill will between himself and Rupert. The final factor in Rush and Avis' resentment toward Rupert was his marriage to actress Patterson Dial in December 1924, a year after Adelaide's suicide. Rush explains: "Both my sister and I had developed a resentment . . . to the fact that Father Rupert had allowed my mother to go off alone on a trip around the world on a boat that had no medical officer. We resented that fiercely, and that contributed. And then the third factor stemmed from the fact that very shortly after my

232

mother's death, he made an association with another much younger woman.''

Avis' disgust with this turn of events is obvious in her description of Rupert's engagement: "Her name was Patterson Dial from Florida. And he wrote that 'Miss Patterson' had done him the honor of accepting his proposal of marriage in old Victorian terms. . . . She was younger than I. I guess I was about twenty-four at the time, maybe twenty-five.'' [Rupert Hughes was 52.]

"Well, I of course resented the fact that he would marry such a young woman. I didn't know her, and I didn't know anything about her. I thought he was making a mistake.''

After Rupert announced his engagement to Patterson Dial, both Rush and Avis "lost track" of him, and in fact Avis never saw him or spoke to him again, though more than thirty years elapsed before Rupert's death. "Our paths separated," she says simply. Rush was more explicit: "They dropped a curtain between us. We lost two factors in our relationship, two important factors between any two people. We lost the factor of companionship. We lost the factor of communication. I went my way and he went his.''

After the split, Avis and Rush each went on to marry several times: Avis three, Rush four. Rupert Hughes was not apprised of any of these events. Rush continued in show business, becoming a moderately successful radio announcer. He at one time acted as moderator of a program he called the "Hughesreel." At no time in their adult lives did either Rush or Avis try to locate their natural father George Bissell, or make any attempt to legalize the promised adoption by Rupert Hughes, though each had their own children. "We trusted him to do that," Rush explained feebly.

George Bissell resurfaced in their lives on one occasion, in 1942. At the time, Rush was master of ceremonies for the "General Electric Hour of Charm" in New York. As he explained it, he got a phone call one evening after the show. The caller said, "I heard you on the air. This is your father." Rush then asked, "Father Rupert?" The caller responded, "No. This is your real father, and I want to see you." Rush then traveled to Hartford, Connecticut, where Bissell was living in a "very nice apartment" with a new wife (different from the wife he had in Syracuse in 1911). According to Rush, "I only went to Hartford for one specific reason. I wanted to ask him why, why he had blocked our adoption." Their meeting lasted no more than twenty minutes. "When I asked him why he had blocked our adoption, he exploded, and he said some of the—well, he exploded," Rush recalled. "His reply was vitriolic against Father Rupert. He called him everything there is in the book. I retreated rapidly. There didn't seem to be any reason to con-

tinue the conversation.'' Only when pressed by adversary Paul Freese
would Rush repeat the substance of the conversation:

> After the initial greetings, he said, ''I hear—how are you doing?''
> I said, ''I'm doing all right. But there is a question I want to ask
> you that has bothered me for a long, long time. As you well know,
> Father Rupert, Rupert Hughes, has tried assiduously to complete
> adoption of my sister Avis and myself.''
> And he said, ''That no good son of a bitch.''
> You sure you want this?
> ''I wouldn't give him the sweat off my balls. He is a bastard. And
> there is nothing under any conditions that I would do to help him
> in his desire to adopt you.''

Bissell's impassioned response was the first hint in the heirship investigation of Rupert Hughes' darker side. In light of Bissell's apparent
willingness to forego the task of raising and providing for both Rush and
Avis, his contempt for Rupert Hughes and prohibition against adoption
is a puzzlement. Certain other unusual aspects to Rupert's personality
appeared in various places in the Rush and Avis depositions, as well.
''He was a complete atheist,'' testified Avis. ''He had read the Bible, I
believe he said, three times from cover to cover, and he just hadn't any
use for any of it. He was a complete atheist.''

Perhaps the greatest irony revealed in the testimony of Rush and
Avis is the set of events following Rupert Hughes' death in 1956. ''I
didn't know anything about it,'' admitted Avis. ''I saw no publicity
about it. Nobody notified me about it or anything.'' Neither she nor
Rush had been in correspondence with anyone who was even close to
Rupert, much less Rupert himself; hence the two did not attend his
funeral and cannot recall how or when they learned of his death. Once
apprised, they entertained no thought of claiming a right to his estate
as his adopted children. ''Oh, no,'' stated Avis. ''There was never any
discussion of inheriting anything from Rupert. I never even thought of
Rupert, you know.''

Within days after the genial Rush and domineering Avis were questioned by the Hughes attorneys, several other depositions were noticed
by Paul Freese, George Dean, and Wayne Fisher, in an attempt to prove,
in the case of Dean and Fisher, or disprove, in Freese's respect, Rush and
Avis' claim of adoption. Through the transcripts of this testimony,
somewhat conflicting pictures of both Rupert and his relationship with
his stepchildren were presented. Additionally, more was learned about
Rupert's life after Adelaide Hughes' suicide, during his marriage to actress Patterson Dial. One such deposition was that of Lee Harrell Palmer,

a witness discovered by Paul Freese, in his capacity as Barbara Cameron and her sisters' counsel.

Mrs. Palmer met Rupert Hughes in 1932, when she began to design clothes for Patterson Dial Hughes. She and Pat (as Mrs. Palmer called her) became "extremely close" friends and remained so until Pat's death in 1945. Through her friendship with Patterson Dial, Mrs. Palmer came to know Rupert Hughes quite well, attending birthday parties in his home and such through the years. She was particularly impressed with Rupert and Pat's mansion in Los Angeles, a house that would later have special significance in the heirship investigation:

> It was located on Los Feliz Boulevard, rather near Hillcrest—4751, I think. It was Moorish in style, which was most unusual in that particular era, but Rupert had somehow fallen in love with that type of architecture and he designed the house himself.
>
> And his library was the most interesting room in the house because it was tremendous. It was a two-story room with bookshelves to the ceiling, and it was so expansive that I think Rupert had five different desks where he kept different things going.
>
> He had a separate desk for each project. And that's really where most of the activity in the household took place. We almost never used the living room. And there was a very pleasant living room and a main entry hall and the dining room was off of that. A swimming pool was in the center. It was built on an atrium plan.

Throughout her fifteen-year friendship with Patterson Dial (1932–1945), and twenty-six year acquaintance with Rupert (1932–1956), Lee Harrell Palmer heard Rupert mention Rush Hughes "only on one occasion." At the time, Rush had a radio program in San Francisco. "A number of my friends had said that they heard the show and they were referring to Rush Hughes as Mr. Hughes' son, which puzzled me greatly," Mrs. Palmer recalled. "And I said that I had never heard him mention him, but sometime I would ask, you know, what the relationship was." Later, Mrs. Palmer and Rupert attended the same sports function, and it was then that she inquired about Rush Hughes. "I turned to Rupert and said, 'I have been hearing a bit about Rush Hughes and my friends have asked me if he is your son because there had been an implication of a filial relationship.' And I was startled by the reaction that I got because it was more or less explosive," Mrs. Palmer related. "He said, 'The young man is not my son. He is not my adopted son. In my opinion, he is an impostor who has always used my name as a stepping stone. And it would give me great pleasure if he never used my name in relation to himself again.' . . . He actually used the word 'imposter.' "

Asked by Paul Freese if criticism was typical of Rupert, Mrs. Palmer replied, "Well, he was not critical in the slightest. And I think perhaps the main reason why I remember this incident so clearly is that it startled me, and it almost embarrassed me that I had brought up a subject that upset him." Then she added, "I think on two other occasions in all the years that I knew him did I hear him say anything even slightly derogatory about any human being."

After Freese had completed his interrogation of Mrs. Palmer, George Dean, Avis' personal attorney, took over the questioning. Dean immediately attempted to discover the subject of Hughes' derogatory remarks on the two other occasions, but Palmer refused, saying, "I don't believe that is pertinent. I don't wish to answer that."

Dean did establish that Mrs. Palmer saw Rupert only a few times after the early death of Patterson Dial in 1945, and offered the first hint of its darker side:

Dean: Did her death come as a surprise or shock to you?

Palmer: Yes.

Dean: Had you known or was she in any sort of depression at the time of the death?

Palmer: I don't really feel I am qualified to answer that. I didn't see her when I thought she was in a depression.

Dean: Then her death came as a complete shock to you?

Palmer: I remember the circumstances. A friend of mine called me and said that she had read some news that she knew would be very upsetting to me and then she told me of Pat's death.

At the conclusion of Mrs. Palmer's deposition, after Freese and the ad litem fully questioned the witness, Dean came back to the incidents Mrs. Palmer earlier alluded to:

Dean: Mrs. Palmer, so that the record is clear, I have asked you for the other occasion on which you heard Mr. Rupert Hughes speak derogatorily or with some feeling or sharpness, I believe, if I may characterize it—

Palmer: Yes.

Dean: And did you refuse and do refuse to give me that answer; is that correct?

Palmer: I would prefer not to.

Persisting, Dean insisted that Freese speak to the witness off the record in order to obtain the information he sought. Again, Mrs. Palmer refused. Back on the record, Freese recorded the outcome of his private tête-à-tête with Mrs. Palmer:

Freese: You regard it as highly personal and irrelevant to what we have been discussing?

Palmer: That is the way I feel.

Freese: Do you have any further questions, Mr. Dean?

Dean: No. I would like to make this comment to you, if I might, Mrs. Palmer. It is that I am simply not snooping or trying to pry into people's personal lives. And I do understand how you obviously feel because of the way you have announced how you feel about this. But as a lawyer we have certain things that are given to us under the rules of discovery. . . . I want you to understand that I feel that this could be relevant under the rules of discovery but I certainly am not arguing with you. You have your position to take and we have our recourse to take if it becomes necessary.

From Mrs. Palmer's deposition, one begins to get a sense of Rupert Hughes' split personality, while at the same time it places Rush and Avis' equitable adoption claim in a highly damaging light, judging from Rupert's emotional outburst to the witness at the suggestion that Rush was his adopted son. There are also veiled allusions in the transcript by

George Dean as to the circumstances of Patterson Dial's death, and, not least, there are the derogatory comments made by Rupert on at least two occasions that Mrs. Palmer refused to discuss. This deposition also illustrates the adversarial nature of the relationship of Elspeth's daughters vis-à-vis Rush and Avis at this pre–settlement agreement juncture in the proceedings, as represented by their counsel, Paul Freese and George Dean. This legal posturing was further cemented with the testimony of Freese's client Barbara Cameron, in her deposition of September 27, 1976 (four months after Howard Hughes, Jr.'s, death), taken on the same day as Mrs. Palmer's.

Barbara Cameron was questioned by Freese, Dean, and a representative of Dinkins', to demonstrate her relationship to Rupert Hughes. In the pattern that was developing, the interviewers learned next to nothing about Elspeth Hughes, the witness's mother. Cameron testified that her parents were Edward John and Elspeth Hughes Lapp, and that she and her sisters, Rupert Hughes' three grandchildren, were born in 1924 (Agnes Christine Lapp, known as "Chris"), 1925 (Elspeth Summerlin Lapp, known as "Beth"), and 1926 (Barbara Patterson Lapp, known as "Bobby"). As a young child in the late 1920s, Barbara was shuttled between her parents' home in Cleveland, and her grandmother's in Jacksonville, Florida. (Her grandmother was Agnes Wheeler Hedge Hughes, Rupert's first wife.)

The greater part of Cameron's deposition testimony was a discussion of her relationship with Rupert Hughes, which essentially was confined to a two-year period from 1946 to 1948. She testified that her first recollection of her grandfather occurred when she was a young girl in Cleveland, where her family lived in a succession of houses. Rupert "tried to stop off" in Cleveland en route from his home on Los Feliz in Los Angeles to New York, if it was necessary for him to attend a meeting with his literary agent or editors in Manhattan. Neither Cameron, her sisters, nor Elspeth visited Rupert's home before 1945. In 1945, both Patterson Dial and Elspeth died within several months of each other, both apparently in their forties at the time. Less than a year later, Barbara moved from Cleveland into the Los Feliz house with Rupert Hughes, the only member of the family to visit it. He was then seventy-three; Barbara was twenty. "I really am not too versed on why," Cameron recounted, "except that he was alone and I was alone, and my sisters were married. . . . My mother was gone. She and Patty died the same year. And I was living with my father. So I was also entangled with a romance that my sisters didn't approve of, and they wrote grandfather as I understand it from Beth, and suggested that he tactfully invite me out to live with him in order to break up the romance."

238

Cameron lived with the elderly Rupert Hughes from December 1946 to December 1948, during which time she served as his occasional secretary, typing his manuscripts and the like. Cameron, too, was struck by Rupert's residence on Los Feliz, which was designed around an indoor pool in the center of the house.

Barbara met her future husband Wesley Cameron during this period in Los Angeles, and Wes would take the increasingly dependent Rupert Hughes to various club functions from time to time during his courtship of Barbara. The three also dined at the Brown Derby twice a week, schedules permitting. Throughout her association with Rupert Hughes, Barbara never heard him mention the name Avis Hughes or Avis Hughes McIntyre. She heard the name Rush Hughes only twice: "through a couple of occasions when we were dining." As Cameron explained:

Cameron:	Sitting in the booth at the Brown Derby one evening somebody—I don't know who—came up and mentioned Rush Hughes having made a broadcast or something about—and introduced himself as "the son of Rupert Hughes."
Freese:	Was there a reaction at that time that you recall?
Cameron:	Yes.
Freese:	What was that reaction?
Cameron:	He was not pleased.
Freese:	Did he say anything?
Cameron:	He said that was not true, that he was not his son.
Freese:	Was it a lengthy comment?
Cameron:	No. He just said, "That's a damn lie."

Barbara Lapp and Wes Cameron were married in Los Angeles in December 1948, after which they seldom saw Rupert Hughes, who later moved in with Felix and Ruby Hughes, where he died in 1956. Cameron's relationship with Rupert, therefore, is basically restricted to a two-year period between 1946 and 1948, and her deposition testimony is more or less confined to a discussion of that period in his life.

Mrs. Cameron is also the current custodian of the Hedge family Bible, which originally belonged to her grandmother, Agnes Hedge Hughes (Rupert's first wife). The Bible is dated February 8, 1869, and was originally given to Agnes' parents, Charles and Julia Wheeler Hedge, who in turn gave it to their daughter Agnes. After Agnes' death, it was sent to Elspeth in Cleveland, and from there it passed to Barbara Cameron. The remainder of Cameron's testimony is a recitation of certain events as recorded in the Hedge family Bible. Most of the handwritten notations in the Bible were made by Agnes Hedge, while the more recent dates were filled in by Barbara herself. These family events are recorded in the Bible under pages with the headings "Marriages," "Births," and "Deaths." The more significant of the dates noted therein include:

- Agnes Hedge's marriage to Rupert Hughes in New York City at St. George's Episcopal Church, December 12, 1893

- Birth of Elspeth Hedge Hughes, "daughter of Rupert and Agnes Wheeler Hughes born May 23rd, 1897—11 a.m. in New York at N. 202 W. 74th St., 'The —— (illegible)'"

- Agnes' divorce from "R. H.," March, 1904

- Agnes' marriage to William Herbert Reynolds, Lieutenant, U. S. Navy, New York, November 15, 1904

- Birth of William Herbert Reynolds, Jr., May 18, 1913

- Birth of Julia Field Reynolds, September 30, 1914

- Birth of John Chandler Reynolds, June 4, 1918

- Marriage of Elspeth Hedge Hughes to Edward John Lapp, March 20, 1922, at 2230 Q St., Washington, D. C.

- Death of Captain William H. Reynolds, November 29, 1937, Captain U. S. Navy, Retired, Jacksonville, Florida

- Marriage of William Herbert Reynolds, Jr., to Charlotte Selden Boush, July 29, 1940, Newport News, Virginia.

- Death of Agnes Hedge Reynolds, October 12, 1944

240

•Death of Patterson Dial Hughes, April, 1945

•Death of Elspeth Hughes Lapp, May 15, 1945—cremated

Beyond the dialogue concerning Barbara's temporary residence with Rupert Hughes in the mid-1940s and an examination of certain family Bible entries, her deposition testimony relating to her family, and specifically her mother Elspeth, is no more than a couple of pages in length. These two pages represent a discussion of Elspeth's relationship with Rupert during the early 1940s, just before Elspeth's death. To illustrate this testimony, Barbara briefly discussed Rupert's correspondence with Elspeth and her daughters during this period. (These are the letters Freese introduced during the heirship trial in support of his clients' case, as discussed earlier.) As Cameron testified in her deposition, her mother Elspeth suffered an ''illness'' for about a year prior to her death in 1945, and every letter but one Elspeth received from her father during her life is from this twelve-month period. The only other known letter from Rupert to Elspeth is dated 1938. Cameron noted in this discussion that Rupert sent Elspeth and her husband Ed Lapp a $300 monthly ''allowance'' for an undisclosed period during their marriage. When asked by Freese if Rupert was ''very fond'' of her mother, if there was a ''demonstration of affection'' from Rupert to Elspeth, Barbara responded succinctly: ''A physical demonstration was there, yes. Whenever he visited us there was a big embrace and a hug.''

This was the extent of Barbara Cameron's testimony. It clearly demonstrated that Rupert Hughes and his alleged granddaughters enjoyed a period of closeness for several years in the 1940s when Barbara and her sisters were adults, immediately preceding and following the deaths of Patterson Dial and Elspeth, when Rupert was ''all alone'' and in a state of emotional depression in the last years of his life. There is, however, nothing in the way of information or confirmation of family events or circumstances prior to the 1930s or 1940s in Cameron's deposition; indeed, Rupert Hughes appears to have been a stranger in the lives of Elspeth and her daughters up to the period of Elspeth's 1944–45 illness. Cameron's testimony is crystal clear on one point, however: Rupert Hughes, in the estimation of Barbara and her sisters, entertained no fatherly feeling whatsoever toward Rush Hughes, and by extension his sister Avis, and in fact that Rupert responded, ''That's a damn lie,'' when it was suggested in Barbara's presence that Rush was his son.

It was with this perspective that the deposition of Ruby Hughes, the widow of Rupert's younger brother Felix Hughes, and the last surviving member of the Felix and Jean Hughes extended family, was taken in the

241

fall of 1976. Like Barbara Cameron's testimony, Ruby Hughes' is confined to the last years of Rupert Hughes' life, and more specifically to his attitude, as she perceived it, toward Rush and Avis. Ruby first met Rupert (and Felix, her husband) in 1943, two years before the deaths of Patterson Dial and Elspeth. Felix and Ruby lived in the home on North Rossmore purchased years earlier by Judge and Mimi Hughes in Los Angeles, not far from the Los Feliz home of Rupert Hughes. As Rupert and Felix were exceptionally close as brothers, Ruby saw Rupert and Patterson Dial quite often. After Patterson's death in 1945 and Barbara Lapp's marriage to Wes Cameron in 1948, Rupert turned increasingly to Ruby and Felix for companionship.

In these declining years, Rupert Hughes' life again took a 180-degree turn. Rupert in 1950 was seventy-eight years old, and his literary career had taken a nosedive. He no longer wrote for the movies, his magazine work had fizzled out, and he flirted for a time with radio and television work, neither too successfully. His major avocation in his later years was speechmaking, at which he was highly acclaimed, but that too declined along with his health in the 1950s, as Rupert became senile. By 1951, he sold his fabulous home on Los Feliz and moved into a separate wing of Felix and Ruby's home. There Rupert Hughes, once an outspoken and controversial atheist, wrote a series of articles for inspirational magazines ("A Lesson from Mary's Lamb," "Be Thine Own Palace," to name a few titles). Avis McIntyre, asked during her deposition if she had reason to believe Rupert had converted to Christianity later in life or before he died, replied in her inimitable fashion, "I never heard of it. Most people when they see the end coming convert to something."

Based on conversations with her brother-in-law Rupert late in his life, which she characterized as "family history or family background," Ruby Hughes responded to questions about Rush and Avis. She further testified that she was acquainted with Barbara Cameron, whom she understood to be Rupert Hughes' granddaughter, the daughter of "his daughter, Elspeth." Questioned about Rush and Avis, Ruby stated that she had "heard about" the two through her association with Rupert from 1943 to 1956. "I was informed that Rupert had been married twice before he married Patterson Dial," she related, "and his first wife was Agnes and the mother of his daughter. And then he married Adelaide Manola Mould, Manola Bissell, and she had two children at the time of their marriage. And then his marriage to Patterson Dial whom I knew. Now, that is the way it was explained to me." She added that it was her understanding that Adelaide was a widow with two children, not that she was divorced from her first husband, George Bissell. Finally, Ruby testified that she never heard Rupert state that he had or ever intended to adopt either Avis or Rush, nor did she overhear anyone else mention the pair in connection with adoption.

This insight was the essence of Ruby Hughes' testimony. No other family matters were discussed during her deposition, and in fact Ruby admitted that conversations about Rupert, Felix, Howard, Sr., and Greta's lives prior to 1943 "were not important in our lives because our lives were being lived in the present, and it wasn't anything that was close in our lives."

Interestingly, attached to Ruby Hughes' deposition as an exhibit is a copy of a quitclaim deed to Rupert Hughes' Bedford Hills estate executed by Rush and Avis after their mother's suicide, found among Rupert's personal effects by Ruby after his death. The deed was kept in an envelope on which Rupert had written: "Deed to Bedford Hills property and General Release of all claims by Avis Bissell Golden and Rush Bissell—Nov. 1929." Not only does Rupert refer to the brother and sister as "Bissells" in his handwritten notation, but Avis and Rush have signed their names on the document in a similar fashion.

The Rumors Begin

As the early depositions were being taken to explore the legal merit of Rush and Avis' adoption claim, the first rumors, suspicions, innuendoes, and doubts about Rupert Hughes and his inner circle drifted into the ad litem's office back in Houston. As a consequence, added to the questions being raised publicly about Rush and Avis by Elspeth's daughters, there began to be questions proffered privately about Elspeth by sources close to Rush and Avis: dark hints that she might not be Rupert's daughter . . . suggestions that Barbara Cameron and her sisters "were not entitled to inherit under Texas law."

The most persistent and potentially damaging of these rumors emanated from a set of individuals identified at first as "the group from Alabama." This group believed that Elspeth Hughes (Lapp), the mother of Barbara Cameron and her two sisters, was not in fact the daughter of Rupert Hughes. They maintained that she was an impostor; that Rupert's "real" daughter drowned, and another young woman was substituted. This sketchy outline was the only information advanced at this early stage, with the additional tip that Rupert Hughes had written a play early in his career called *All for a Girl* which he dedicated to his "real" daughter, not named Elspeth.

Understandably, this startling theory made Ted Dinkins very nervous. If it, or perhaps an element of it, were true, it had the potential to alter drastically the line of descent on Howard Hughes' paternal side. Elspeth Hughes, Rupert's alleged daughter, was the only known first cousin in the Hughes branch of the family, and Dinkins profoundly understood the importance of her relationship to the total inheritance scheme. Were Elspeth somehow "knocked out," as he often put it, the court would have to look to a different set of individuals as heirs, and it was Dinkins' responsibility as the ad litem to draw up that list. It was furthermore Dinkins' official responsibility, as he well knew, to investigate thoroughly any serious claims of heirship, in addition to searching for unknown heirs.

All of this and more was going through his mind as he weighed the most extraordinary of the rumors about Elspeth. In combination with the other hushed talk circulating about Rupert Hughes from varied and well-connected sources, the latest theory caused Dinkins and his staff to feel uneasy about not only Rush and Avis, but about Elspeth's daughters, as well. The hints about Rupert Hughes that punctuated the first depositions taken in the heirship case began to take on new significance in light of the increasing suspicions about his past: George Bissell's vitriolic attack on his character; Lee Harrell Palmer's strange reluctance to disclose certain derogatory comments Rupert made; his apparent about-face with respect to Rush and Avis; his second wife's grisly suicide and the marital problems leading to it; the veiled allusions to his third wife's emotional problems, and her sudden "shocking" death. Finally, and most compelling, there was Elspeth herself. In the pages of deposition transcript about Rupert and his life, his daughter Elspeth is a complete void. The facts known about Elspeth were few indeed, and what was disclosed did not altogether make sense. The question at this point became not so much "Who was Rupert Hughes?" as "Who was Elspeth Hughes?"

Beginning with an effort to find the supposed Rupert Hughes play *All for a Girl,* Dinkins dispatched his intrigued assistant on the first of many missions in search of Elspeth. It was to be a fascinating journey.

Rummaging through various arcane theatrical magazines and anthologies, Dinkins' colleague indeed discovered a 1908 production at the Bijou Theatre in New York of a play entitled *All for a Girl.* It was, as the "Alabama group" suggested, written by Rupert Hughes, and it starred Douglas Fairbanks, Jr., and one Adelaide Manola, Rupert's second wife. The information in the theatre reference book also indicated that the 1908 play was produced in St. Louis in 1906 under the title, *The Richest Girl in the World,* also by Rupert Hughes. Unfortunately, there was no mention of the play's dedication. The play did, however, exist, and that was no small discovery.

At the library, the ad litem's assistant also found and made note of various entries for Rupert Hughes published in the *Who's Who* reference books through the years. In this collection, Rupert's marriages to Agnes

Hedge, Adelaide Bissell, and Elizabeth Patterson Dial are duly noted (though Agnes does not appear consistently). Conspicuously absent is Elspeth. Though the biographical reference books make it a practice to list the subject's children, Elspeth is not mentioned as Rupert's daughter in most of the yearly editions. The *Who's Who* listings do, however, offer specific illustration of Rupert Hughes' progress as an author, and they provide detailed biographical and career information on him. From them, it became apparent that Rupert was an amazingly prolific and versatile writer, beginning in the 1890s with various plays, followed by a children's book (*The Lakerim Athletic Club*), editorships at *Godey's, Current Literature,* and *The New Criterion,* a year or so spent as chief assistant editor of Encyclopedia Brittannica's *Historian's History of the World* at the turn of the century, a book of poems (*Gyge's Ring*), books on music, his series of successful and not so successful plays during the Adelaide-Rush-Avis period, hundreds of short stories, magazine articles, several biographies (including a highly acclaimed series on George Washington), novels, and later, screenplays. Small wonder, then, that in his obituary in *Time* magazine, Rupert Hughes was described as a "jowly Jack-of-all-literary-trades."

While Dinkins was still absorbing this information and somewhat casually looking for a copy of *All for a Girl,* the primary source of the drowning theory made himself public in an official way, and Dinkins was forced to pay closer attention to his extraordinary tale. The spokesperson in question for "the Alabama group" was Robert C. Hughes, the softspoken schoolteacher who testified at the heirship trial in 1980. By 1977, Mr. Hughes had engaged an attorney and officially filed a claim of heirship against the Howard Hughes estate, basing his inheritance position on the disqualification of Elspeth in the manner earlier alluded to. The rumors and innuendoes about Rupert Hughes—at least one set of them—now had the cloak of legal respectability. It was quite clear to Dinkins that Robert Hughes' claim was not a frivolous one and had to be reevaluated accordingly. Reinforcing this attitude was the fact that a well-established Birmingham law firm had agreed to represent Hughes in the matter—not the sort of firm to handle a "crackpot" legal claim by one of the usual species of crazy who rattled Dinkins' cage. Robert C. Hughes' attorneys, Ollie Blan and Sam Frazier, were conservative, competent, and thoroughly professional lawyers who by all appearances put great stock in their client's credibility.

As time passed, Dinkins learned that the fundamental point of Robert Hughes' family history was his belief that Judge Felix Hughes had wrongfully assumed the identity Felix "Turner" Hughes, though born Felix "Moner" Hughes, after his ambush of Robert's family in Civil War days, prompting a surveillance of the Felix Hughes family by a designated family "witness tree," leading in turn to the discovery of the allegedly incriminating data on Rupert and Elspeth. In support of this wild accusation, Robert Hughes' attorneys furnished the ad litem's genealogist with the Harvard Class Reports of Howard Hughes, Sr., in which Howard had listed his father's name as Felix "Moner" Hughes, just as Robert and his family suggested.

Impressed by this evidence, and certain other aspects of Robert Hughes' case, Dinkins sent Mary Fay to Alabama to interview Hughes and gather the necessary background information for the genealogist to investigate further his tale of family intrigue set against the War Between the States. While educating herself on the specifics of Felix Hughes' alleged betrayal of Robert Hughes' kin, Mrs. Fay was instructed to learn the details of his suspicions about Rupert and Elspeth, so that Dinkins' associate could explore their authenticity. Even if the Felix "Moner" alias "Turner" aspect to Robert Hughes' claim were unworthy of belief, all or part of his accusations about Rupert's life might still be valid. Finally, Mrs. Fay's Alabama interview would afford her the opportunity to evaluate Robert Hughes' credibility firsthand—possibly the most important of the multiple aspects to her trip.

Returning from Birmingham, Mrs. Fay filed a report. Since her genealogical work on the Hughes case was basically limited to events before 1880, most of Mrs. Fay's conversation with Robert Hughes concerned the Civil War phase of his story, and specifically Felix Moner Hughes' alleged betrayal and ambush of the family, all of which the genealogist related in detail to the ad litem. She added in closing:

> The Clan Hughes has since then retold the story among themselves, and has always had someone assigned to watch the progress of Felix Moner Hughes, who moved to Lancaster, Missouri. . . .
>
> "Uncle John" . . . was assigned to watch (and) had collected all the newspaper clippings, etc.; but these were all lost before they reached Mr. Robert C. Hughes who was appointed in 1936 to serve as Clan Witness. The grandmother who had gone through the Civil War and had helped keep the family together died in 1936. Mr. Robert C. Hughes recounts the information from memory, not having seen any of the clippings since 1936.

It was, to say the least, a fascinating family saga. Of greater interest to the ad litem, however, were Hughes' contentions about Rupert and Elspeth, based on his memory of the clippings and materials allegedly kept in his uncle's trunk as a part of his family's remarkable surveillance of Judge Felix Hughes and his descendants.

246

Robert Hughes contends that Rupert Hughes had two children by his first wife Agnes Hedge: a boy and a girl. The boy died as an infant or small child, possibly by Agnes' neglect. The daughter, with a name something like "Leonora" (at the time of the interview, Hughes was not certain of her first name, and could only recall that it began with an "L"), died in a swimming pool in Rupert Hughes' home in Los Angeles in 1920 or 1921. At the time of the drowning, Rupert was living with Elizabeth Patterson Dial (whom he married on December 31, 1924). She had had a daughter by a first marriage (to a man named Clayton Dial), whom she had named Elspeth. Elizabeth Dial, born Elizabeth Patterson, was also a writer, and Robert Hughes believed he recalled seeing a magazine article written by her in "Uncle John's" trunk in which she explained how she had named her daughter by using letters from her own name, "Elizabeth Patterson Dial," to make the name "ELSPETH," a sort of acronym.

Hughes maintains that Rupert came in contact with actress Patterson Dial while writing and producing movies, and that they lived together for several years before they were married. Rupert and Patterson Dial were living together at the time Adelaide took her trip to China, and that in part led to her suicide. At the time of the alleged drowning, Rupert's daughter Leonora was visiting for the summer by custody arrangements with Agnes. Rupert had given Leonora a farewell party, which both Elizabeth and Elspeth Dial attended. Leonora somehow drowned in Rupert's pool after the guests had gone home, whereupon Rupert and Patterson Dial literally "substituted" Elspeth Dial for Rupert's drowned daughter. From that day forward, Elspeth assumed the identity of Rupert's real daughter.

In support of his story, Robert Hughes asserts that the 1897 birth certificate of Elspeth Hughes is forged, and that he saw a copy of the birth certificate of Rupert's "real" daughter in his uncle's collection of materials. Since the trunk and all its contents were destroyed several decades ago, Hughes is forced to rely on his memory of the clippings and copies he can recall seeing as a young boy. "Uncle John" apparently kept copies of everything written by or about Rupert Hughes during his surveillance period, and several of the magazine articles, newspaper clippings and so forth that he had saved discussed various elements of Rupert's personal life as described by Robert Hughes.

Among the corroborating evidence he can recall seeing in the trunk were a copy of a play entitled *All for a Girl* written by Rupert Hughes and published in book form in a limited edition, which he had dedicated to his "real" daughter: Leonora, or something similar. Robert Hughes has a particularly vivid memory of seeing a magazine article about Rupert Hughes published shortly after his daughter's drowning, in which Rupert is pictured behind a rose trellis or the like, with the caption, "Mr. Rupert Hughes contemplates the swimming pool on the grounds of the Los Angeles estate where his daughter drowned on such-and-such a date." Robert Hughes has stated that his uncle John also had another magazine article written by Rupert Hughes titled "Elspeth, My Elspeth." The article was written about and dedicated to "his stepdaughter, Elspeth." Finally, Hughes recalls the series of magazine articles written by Patterson Dial prior to and after the birth of her daughter in which she describes how she named the child by using an acronym of her own name.

Mrs. Fay, who was initially skeptical of Robert Hughes and his amazing story, came away from Alabama with a different attitude. She was impressed with the occasionally specific and vivid nature of Hughes' recollections, the precise details he called to mind of magazine articles and such as that. She also felt that the sometimes fuzzy way in which he tried to put together images from his past observations of the clippings and other materials in his uncle's trunk was entirely consistent with that sort of memory recall—as in his inability to recall at the moment the exact name of Rupert's daughter. Being a genealogist, Mrs. Fay was extremely familiar with oral family histories, and how they are often confused, changed or slightly distorted as they are passed down from individual to individual or generation to generation; she attributed the occasional inconsistencies in his story to that.

After her long interview with him, Mrs. Fay pronounced Robert Hughes "sincere and worthy of credit." Though she could not and did not profess to vouch for all of his claims about the Hughes family, Rupert and Elspeth in particular, she did feel there was "something to" his story, that it was based on authentic family history. Though it may not be true down to the last detail, she believed there was an element of truth in it—an actual drowning in the family, for example—though the story might have undergone metamorphosis somewhat in its translation to Robert.

As Mrs. Fay left them, Robert Hughes and his attorneys were endeavoring to locate the magazine articles and other corroborating evidence to support his recollections about Rupert and Rupert's "daughters." When she returned to Houston, Dinkins and his staff set about to do the same. Hughes' fantastic tale of switched identities only added to the growing mystique about Elspeth, who was at best a remote figure in the ad litem's growing body of material. Combined with the occasional dark references to Rupert that had surfaced already, the ad litem and his team were prepared to believe any tale, even an apparently wild one such as this, to explain away the nagging doubts.

With Robert Hughes' details in the back of their minds, Dinkins and his colleague, assisted by Mrs. Fay, began to amass as much information as possible on Rupert Hughes in an ultimately futile effort to piece together what would hopefully be a comprehensive account of his life, to resolve the doubts and questions of nearly everyone involved in the heirship case, and to place his line of descent above question—which was, after all, Dinkins' official task as attorney ad litem. Throughout the remainder of the investigation, the three often went in circles attempting to check out seemingly false leads suggested by Robert Hughes. But they always remained faithful to Mrs. Fay's initial impression of Robert Hughes and his story: that there was some truth in what he said.

Robert Hughes was just one of a number of individuals who had cast aspersions on Rupert and his daughter Elspeth. Each tale was slightly different, but none of them—including, especially, the official family history related by Elspeth's daughters—could be fully reconciled with the known facts of Rupert's life. The truth about Rupert and Elspeth was a genuine mystery.

About the time that Robert Hughes made his official appearance in the estate proceedings, the last of the depositions in connection with Rush and Avis' adoption claim were taken. Nearly a year had elapsed since Howard Hughes, Jr.'s, death, and most of the energy expended in the Hughes case during this interval was directed toward preparation for the upcoming trial to determine Hughes' legal domicile, scheduled to begin in the fall of 1977. To recapitulate, the outcome of the domicile trial had its own set of implications in connection with the final determination of Hughes' heirs-at-law. Both the Barbara Cameron group and Rush and Avis had initially moved to have Hughes declared a legal resident of Texas as opposed to either California or Nevada, for the simple reason that each of their claims would be worthless in either California or Nevada. In the absence of a valid will, only Texas would divide Hughes' estate between the maternal and paternal sides of the family. In California or Nevada, everything would go to Annette Gano Lummis, as Hughes' closest known living relative. Hence Barbara Cameron and her sisters, and Rush and Avis—as alleged paternal relatives—would be out of luck in any state other than Texas. Rush and Avis would be further blocked in California and Nevada in that neither state recognized the doctrine of adoption by estoppel, the basis of their claim to the Hughes estate.

The two trials—domicile and heirship—were thus intertwined, and all legal strategies were affected by their interdependence. By the spring of 1977, however, Barbara Cameron and her sisters had been recognized as heirs by the maternal (Gano) branch of the family, and were, as a consequence, included in the Lummis settlement agreement to divide the Hughes estate privately. As one of the trade-offs, the three sisters agreed to drop their Texas domicile position. The maternal heirs favored a Nevada domicile position, and the settlement group wished to present a united front. By joining the agreement, the Cameron group was guaranteed 25 percent of Hughes' estate, regardless of which state was ultimately determined to be Hughes' legal residence. Elspeth's daughters chose to take a 25 percent sure thing, rather than risk losing everything in a trial to prove Texas domicile. If they won on the domicile issue, and Hughes were found to be a legal resident of Texas, then the three sisters could get as much as 50 percent of the estate (if they were shown to be the *only* paternal heirs). If they lost, however, they would get nothing. Hence by the time the last heirship depositions were taken, Barbara Cameron and her sisters were officially included in the private settlement agreement to divide Hughes' estate and were no longer promoting Texas domicile. Rush and Avis, not included in the agreement, were still hoping to have Hughes declared a resident of Texas, the only state of the three to recognize their adoption by estoppel theory. Barbara Cameron and her sisters were still refuting the equitable adoption claim, while Rush and Avis made subtle noises about Elspeth's position.

The battle lines thus drawn, the final pair of depositions in the heirship case were taken in March 1977. Rush and Avis' attorneys had located a couple of aging movie queens who had known and worked with Rupert Hughes in his early Hollywood days as a movie director and screenwriter and heard him mention one or both of their clients. The first of these depositions was that of Eleanor Boardman, a lovely actress once married to famous motion picture director King Vidor. Boardman, originally from Philadelphia, was signed to a seven-year contract with Metro-Goldwyn-Mayer in 1923. Her first picture was called *Souls for Sale,* written and directed by Rupert Hughes and filmed on location in Palm Springs.

Miss Boardman testified that Rush Hughes had a ''bit'' part in the film, and as she had never met him, he was introduced to her on the set by Rupert as ''my adopted son, Rush.'' Boardman saw Rush on occasion throughout the filming of the movie at Sunday afternoon luncheon parties given by Rupert's wife, Adelaide, at their ''Los Feliz home.'' Felix and Howard Hughes, Sr. and Jr., occasionally attended these parties, and Eleanor Boardman is rumored to have dated Howard, Sr., during this time period (and possibly before Allene's death). Boardman understood that Adelaide was an actress, but Adelaide ''stayed out of Rupert's working atmosphere'' and rarely visited her husband on the set. Boardman described Adelaide as very fragile and extremely nervous. ''There was something the matter with her,'' she noted. Adelaide

250

Hughes was, by Boardman's observation, always "popping pills," and her hands were often shaking.

Several months or perhaps a year after Boardman met Rush, possibly during the filming of *Souls for Sale,* Adelaide left for China with a woman companion, where she committed suicide. Boardman lost contact with Rush after the movie was completed, but she continued to see Rupert because, as she explained it, he had married a good friend of hers named Elizabeth Patterson. (Asked if she meant "Patterson Dial," Boardman said the name Patterson Dial meant nothing to her; she knew her only as Elizabeth Patterson.) Boardman continued to see the Hugheses socially until "Elizabeth's" death in 1945. Finally, Eleanor Boardman testified that she had never heard of Elspeth Hughes, and had no idea Rupert Hughes had a natural daughter.

The day after Eleanor Boardman's deposition was taken, actress Colleen Moore was questioned in connection with the heirship case at her ranch in Hidden Valley, California. Moore, a charming actress known for her china doll haircut, was a highly successful motion picture star in the 1920s and 1930s. "If I may be very immodest," she noted, "my first starring picture, *Flaming Youth,* was the first flapper picture, and it started a whole rash of them." Moore made her first motion picture in 1918 at the age of fifteen and retired from show business to marry one of the founding partners of Merrill, Lynch, Pierce, Fenner and Smith.

In 1921, she was given the starring role in what she identified as Rupert Hughes' first picture, *The Wallflower.* Moore recalled how that came about:

> Well, Sam Goldwyn, who owned the Goldwyn Company at that time—later it became Metro-Goldwyn-Mayer—Mr. Goldwyn decided what the movies needed was better stories, so he formed an idea called "The Eminent Authors" and he signed up a great many of the best-selling authors of the day. Now, Rupert Hughes, at that time, was a very important writer in America . . . and Rupert's first picture was *The Wallflower.* He had done the scenario for it.
>
> And they were looking for a girl to play the wallflower and they were testing all the little girls, and oh I wanted that part so badly, so my friend Marshall Neilan—I was under contract to Marshall Neilan at that time—talked to Rupert Hughes about me, and poor Mr. Hughes, I guess, thought he was getting a Sarah Bernhardt or something. Well, anyway, they hired me for the part and it was great fun.

Moore's collaboration with Hughes was successful. "Rupert was so pleased with my work that he wrote two other pictures for me and I appeared in them both," she noted proudly. It was during filming of *The Wallflower* in 1921 that Colleen Moore first met Rush Hughes. "Rupert brought a very good-looking young man on the set, and he introduced him to me as his son," Moore testified, "and he had a small part in the picture." Later, Moore had a conversation with a friend of hers named Carmelita Geraghty, and learned that Carmelita was dating Rush. "And I said something about Rupert's son having a small bit in the picture, and she said to me, 'He's not his son, he's Rupert's adopted son.' Well, I thought, 'That's interesting.' So I was talking to Rupert and I asked him—I said, 'I thought you said Rush was your son.' He said, 'No, he's my adopted son,' but he said, 'I feel for him just as if he were my own son.' "

Colleen Moore and Rupert Hughes apparently enjoyed a warm friendship during shooting of the three pictures they made together between 1921 and 1923, and Colleen considered Rupert a "father figure." Indeed, he gave her an autographed picture during filming, which he inscribed: "To Colleen Moore with admiration for the artist and fatherly affection for the girl."

Unlike Eleanor Boardman, Colleen seldom saw Rupert socially, so she was not well acquainted with his wife, Adelaide. "The thing I remember most about her was this flaming red hair," she reminisced. "I thought she was very striking looking, so did everyone else." Moore also met Avis once, but can recall little about her. "I just remember meeting her," she testified, "and she snubbed me a little bit, so I guess I didn't remember much about her." In contrast to Eleanor Boardman, who was under the distinct impression Rupert Hughes had no children, Moore "faintly" recalled asking Rupert whether he had any other children, and he briefly mentioned "a daughter back East somewhere."

After filming their third picture together in 1923, Moore never saw Rush, Avis, or Adelaide again. She saw Rupert only occasionally.

Colleen Moore and Eleanor Boardman's depositions in March 1977 were the last to be taken concerning Rush and Avis' equitable adoption claim, and they were also the only favorable deposition testimony to that claim. Ruby Hughes, Barbara Cameron, and Lee Harrell Palmer all provided damaging testimony against Adelaide's two childrens' claims, and certain aspects of Rush and Avis' own depositions could easily be construed against them: the fact that the pair did not see or speak to Rupert Hughes in the last thirty years of his life, did not know when he died, did not attend his funeral, and did nothing to pursue the adoption claim at any time in their lives.

The depositions of two of Rupert Hughes' male secretaries were also taken in connection with the heirship claim, and they did nothing to assist the adoption stance. Dale Eunson and Cornwell Jackson served as

Hughes' private secretaries from 1927 to 1948 between them. Based on their supervision of his correspondence in a secretarial capacity, they both testified that Rupert did nothing during those years to effect an adoption of either Rush or Avis, and that he never referred to the pair as his children or adopted children. Jackson, in fact, stated that he had been informed that Rush's "real" name was "Bissell," not Hughes. Both men remembered that Rupert Hughes was very generous toward struggling authors in the 1930s and 1940s and took a paternal interest in young people generally, actually putting Eunson's younger brother through college. (This is in contrast to Rush Hughes' earlier testimony, when he recounted Rupert's attitude toward young writers in the Bedford Hills period, 1911 to 1920. Then, Rush stated, Rupert normally did not help beginning authors. When manuscripts would arrive in the mail, Rush recalled, Rupert would send them back without even opening them.) Interestingly, Jackson also testified that in all his years as a secretary to Rupert Hughes, he never once observed his boss deal with attorneys. Rupert also wrote all his personal correspondence himself, in longhand, and would not allow his secretary to transcribe it. Rupert Hughes maintained a carefully delineated zone of privacy, apparently, even with his trusted personal secretaries.

Louis Kaminar, the attorney who drafted Rupert Hughes' 1954 will (in which Rupert disinherits his three granddaughters), was also deposed by Barbara Cameron's counsel in connection with Rush and Avis' claim. Kaminar testified that he first met Rupert Hughes in 1949, when Rupert was seventy-seven. Hughes strolled into Kaminar's office unannounced and asked him to handle the sale of his home on Los Feliz Boulevard. Apparently Rupert selected Kaminar at random, while taking a walk on the street where his office was located. Between the sale of Rupert's house in 1950 and the execution of his will in 1954, Kaminar did no legal work for Hughes, he testified. "The only activity that I would—well, I don't know whether you'd characterize it as 'business,' but he was still writing. And he would, as I say, telephone me and say, 'Now, I need your legal advice on how to get a particular character out of a situation that I got him in. What's the law on it, and how can I do it?' " In the months to come, Dinkins' associate would often call to mind this anecdote about Rupert Hughes.

While the depositions were being taken concerning Rush and Avis' claim of adoption, Dinkins and his colleagues were puzzling as well over their own independent investigation into all aspects of Rupert Hughes' life, with particular attention to Robert Hughes' allegations: the suspected drowning of Rupert's natural daughter and the suspicions about Patterson Dial. The combination of reported or reputed doubts and rumors about Elspeth's background and identity (from Robert

Hughes, Rush and Avis, and others), as well as the noticeable lack of information about Elspeth in the unfolding investigation, all gave Dinkins substantial reason to question the entire cast of supporting characters in Rupert Hughes' life. Rupert himself was emerging as a man of many paradoxes; his last wife, Patterson Dial, was an obscure figure about whom nothing was known, except for some strange rumblings about her early death, Rush and Avis' apparent dislike for her, and a confusion about her name; Elspeth was a complete mystery; and Adelaide had been portrayed in her later years as an emotional cripple whose marriage to Rupert ended with her harrowing suicide. Dinkins clearly had his work cut out for him in trying to put together the pasts of this odd assortment of individuals. Did Rupert's "real" daughter actually drown? Or was there some other family secret surrounding Elspeth? The testimony of Avis and Rush recalled two lakes on the Bedford Hills farm, and Barbara Cameron and others went into great detail about the unusual swimming pool in Rupert's Los Feliz home. If Elspeth—or Leonora—did drown, several of Rupert's residences provided the means.

In the midst of all this confusion came an unexpected development. After months of investigation came the June 1977 announcement that Rush and Avis were to be included in the private settlement agreement with Barbara Cameron and her sisters, along with the maternal heirs. Elspeth's daughters had agreed to give up 9.5 percent of their 25 percent share under the agreement to Rush and Avis, their bitter adversaries of the preceding months. Rush and Avis, for their part, agreed to drop their pursuit of the Texas domicile issue, as well as any possibly damaging evidence against anyone else included in the agreement—most notably Elspeth's three daughters—in exchange for a guaranteed 9.5 percent of Howard Hughes, Jr.'s, estate. By joining forces, Rush and Avis and the Barbara Cameron group lost their most formidable adversaries—the parties who could do the most damage to their claims of heirship.

Attorneys close to the estate noted that this private agreement between Barbara Cameron et al. and Rush and Avis came at a point in the estate proceedings when the conditions necessary to prove adoption by estoppel had come into sharper focus. When Rush and Avis first jumped into the proceedings, little was known about the equitable adoption theory. As the case intensified, so did the legal research into the particulars necessary to establish adoption by estoppel. This further legal study indicated to some that for an individual to prove in the Texas courts that he or she was "equitably adopted" by a stepparent, it might be necessary that the stepparent in question have a natural child of his or her own to estop. (This, in fact, was the legal position adopted by Judge Gregory during the heirship trial.)

If this line of cases prevailed, then Rush and Avis' claim depended on Elspeth. Since Elspeth was Rupert Hughes' only acknowledged child, if for some reason the many doubts that had surfaced about her relationship to Rupert were proven and she were deemed not to be his legal daughter, then Rupert Hughes would have no natural children, and the doctrine of common law adoption would not even be available to them. (Whether they could prove an equitable adoption actually took place was a separate issue.)

This state of affairs created an interesting legal scenario. Rush and Avis, who had implied in hushed tones that there was a fatal flaw in the heirship claim of Barbara Cameron and her sisters, now needed desperately to have Elspeth declared a legal child of Rupert Hughes: their claim was dependent upon it. Barbara Cameron and her sisters, who earlier expressed disdain both publicly and privately toward the adoptive claim (quoting Rupert as saying it was a "damn lie" that Rush was his adopted son), had to be aware that there were misgivings from many quarters about their mother's relationship to Rupert Hughes, and that Avis was in the best position to know the true nature of that relationship (by virtue of her age and proximity to the parties at a critical time in their lives). In short, each needed the other to prove his claim to Howard Hughes' estate.

It was this legal dilemma that many say led to the private agreement to divide the estate: by joining forces, each side was sworn to silence about the flaws in the other's case. Whether the whispered accusations of collusion between the Barbara Cameron group and Rush and Avis were true may always be a point of debate. The fact remains, however, that neither said anything damaging about the other's claim from the moment the ink on the amended settlement agreement was dry. The depositions to explore Rush and Avis' claim ended abruptly, and Avis and her attorneys had nothing but favorable things to say from that moment forward about both Elspeth and Rupert Hughes. They denied steadfastly that they had ever implied otherwise. (It was also interesting to speculate on why the two parties, Rush and Avis and the Barbara Cameron group, would agree to settle with the maternal heirs for a mere 28.5 percent of the Hughes estate collectively when, as bona fide paternal heirs, they would have been entitled to a full 50 percent under Texas law, if they could prove that Howard Hughes was a Texas resident, and if they could prove their claims of heirship. Did their private agreement to relinquish 21.5 percent of a billion-dollar estate indicate, as many suggested, that they had some doubts? Though each denies it, forfeiting a right to possibly hundreds of millions of dollars is eloquent evidence to the contrary.)

The Ad Litem's Role Takes on New Significance

By this point in the pretrial discovery period, a series of strange occurrences marked the ad litem's investigation. At the time, Dinkins' associate was juggling several competing but equally compelling mysteries involving the Hughes family: Howard, Sr.'s, notorious past and secret engagement to Frances Geddes had been discovered; the cryptic story of Greta's life was beginning to unravel; and Rupert's alleged daughter and two possibly adopted stepchildren were the objects of numerous allegations and suspicions. The trial to determine officially Hughes' heirs was still a distant thought, and Dinkins was independently studying the Hughes family tree to prepare his official list of heirs for the court. Behind the scenes, Will Lummis and the maternal heirs had plotted their own heirship strategy and entered into a private settlement with, first, Barbara Cameron and her sisters, apparently unconcerned about the persistent doubts surrounding their mother Elspeth's relationship to Rupert Hughes. Then, of course, Rush and Avis joined the private agreement to divide the Hughes estate.

With all this private settlement talk and legal negotiating going on, Dinkins' role as official heir-finder took on a faintly ominous and threatening tone. As those who had arranged to divide the Hughes estate privately must have realized, there was a clear and present danger that Dinkins could actually discover unknown Hughes heirs as a result of his independent heirship investigation—or, worse still, uncover evidence damaging to the claims of any or all of the individuals included in the private settlement contract. And since by the terms of the agreement the maternal heirs were bound to divide the Hughes estate with the alleged paternal heirs no matter what the outcome of the heirship trial, Dinkins' research posed a genuine threat. It opened the door to the possible discovery that Will Lummis and his family had agreed to divide the Hughes estate with the wrong individuals.

Dinkins' interests as ad litem were by definition nonadversarial: he was a court-appointed, impartial officer of justice, whose task it was to find the bona fide heirs of Howard Hughes, Jr., and then to present that information to the court at the time of the heirship determination trial. Though the maternal heirs may have satisfied themselves that Barbara Cameron and Rush and Avis' claims were valid, Dinkins' research continued regardless.

This set of circumstances set the stage for a strange turn of events in Dinkins' office. As he and his colleagues poked around for clues and requested copies of materials pertaining to Rupert Hughes and his various wives or alleged children—be they magazine articles, newspaper items, or entries from church records—it often seemed that, in Dinkins'

256

words, ''someone else got there first.'' Pertinent items would either be missing, or the page would be torn out, or a volume could not be located, or a fire had destroyed the records, or another law firm or individual had recently inquired about the same thing—a series of unexplained and highly coincidental happenings that frustrated the ad litem's efforts to gather evidence and information. Just when the ad litem appeared to have found the ''smoking gun,'' a critical piece of evidence would still be missing. It often seemed that others were following the same trails, possibly in an effort to suppress incriminating information.

Paranoid as this attitude seemed at first, the facts supported it. After all, millions of dollars were at stake. Dinkins' research could conceivably upset the plans not only of certain potential heirs, but their attorneys as well, whose contingent fees (if, as was generally supposed, that was the arrangement) rose or fell with their clients' fortunes. In this high stakes game, all the players held their cards close to their chests, and Dinkins was no exception. Though his motives as ad litem were above question, the results of Dinkins' research might conflict with the interests of the other heirship claimants, whose counsel he rubbed shoulders with daily.

Dinkins' inherent conflict of interest with the named heirs in the settlement agreement, and the series of strange occurrences in the course of his independent investigation of heirship combined to lend an atmosphere of espionage to his suite of offices. The material Dinkins was collecting was undeniably sensitive, and he was acutely aware of the need for secrecy. Indeed, on several occasions there was evidence that an intruder had actually been in Dinkins' or his associate's office and tampered with the Hughes files. Ultimately, Dinkins was forced to concede to this feeling of paranoia by setting up a true cloak-and-dagger type operation. He purchased a set of combination locks for his filing cabinets, removed both his and his associate's nameplates from outside their office doors, and circulated an internal memorandum at his law firm, instructing all receptionists to screen both telephone calls and visitors to the ad litem suite of offices. This CIA-type arrangement served two purposes: besides keeping the heirship materials safe from prying eyes, it also protected Dinkins and his staff from the more deranged individuals who wrote or appeared in person professing to be Hughes heirs. As the heirship investigation continued, and the questions about Elspeth and others intensified, Dinkins realized more and more that his role in the proceedings was potentially dangerous.

In the meantime, Dinkins instructed his associate to continue to gather evidence and information on the Hughes family as inconspicuously as possible, and this request was followed to the letter. Dinkins' suite was a hubbub of activity, as inquiries about the Hugheses were relayed by telephone, letter, or third party—any means imaginable of gathering information. Documents were studied, newspaper items examined, private researchers hired: the investigation of Rupert Hughes' life was a full-scale operation.

Most of these efforts in the first and second year were in pursuit of evidence to substantiate or refute Robert Hughes' allegations about Rupert, Elspeth, and Patterson Dial, which indirectly involved Adelaide Manola, and which in and of itself required a wide-ranging probe into Rupert's past. The first documents that made their way into Dinkins' suite were straightforward enough. Elspeth's birth certificate, probably the single most critical piece of evidence in the heirship case, was among these early papers. It appeared normal in every respect. Dated May 23, 1897, it was stamped and sealed by the health department of New York City, where she was born. On it, Elspeth's parents were stated to be Rupert Hughes, age twenty-five (occupation: editor), and Agnes Hedge Hughes, age twenty-two (born in Buffalo, New York). Their residence was listed as 202 W. 74th St., and the physician in attendance was said to be Walter Lester Carr.

Elspeth's death certificate was also located by the ad litem in Cleveland, where she lived with her husband Edward Lapp from the mid-1920s until her death in 1945. On it, her birth date is given as May 23, 1897; her parents as Rupert Hughes and Agnes Hedge. Dinkins also requested Rupert and Agnes' marriage certificate from the New York City clerk, and it too appeared to be in order. Rupert married Agnes W. Hedge (age nineteen, a resident of Syracuse) on December 12, 1893, when he was twenty-one years old—four years before the birth of Elspeth. So far, all of Elspeth's records seemed to be in order. Dinkins next secured what would prove to be a most controversial document. Hoping for a discussion of the custody arrangements of Elspeth, or some other confirmation of her identity, he attempted to order Rupert and Agnes' divorce proceedings in New York. His request produced only one document: a decree of judicial separation, dated November 1903 in the New York Supreme Court (New York's lowest, not highest, court.) This consent decree served to effect a "separation from bed and board" between Rupert and Agnes Hedge Hughes. It was not a final decree of divorce, nor was one included.

The second paragraph of this separation decree provided "that the custody, control and education of Elspeth Hedge Hughes, the issue of the said marriage . . . be and the same hereby is awarded to the defendant, Rupert Hughes." The third provision granted alternate custody such that Elspeth would be with Agnes for three months each year beginning in May or June. From this consent decree, it was evident that it was Agnes who had filed for divorce from Rupert in 1903, but that

Rupert was granted primary custody of Elspeth, with Agnes to keep her in the summer months.

Although the decree apparently answered some questions, it raised several more. In it, Elspeth is mentioned by name and acknowledged as Rupert and Agnes' daughter, a tremendous piece of evidence to support Barbara Cameron and her sisters' claim of heirship. (In fact, it, along with Elspeth's birth certificate, represented almost the full extent of their evidence at the trial.) Yet in the decree, Rupert Hughes was granted primary custody of Elspeth (nine months of the year), even though Agnes is the party who sued for the divorce. Why was that? More curious still, by the terms of the separation arrangement, Elspeth was to stay with Agnes during the months of May through July or June through August. Why, then, were Elspeth's visits to Bedford Hills to visit Rupert exclusively in the summertime? By their alternate custody arrangement, Elspeth should have been with Agnes those three months. Avis, however, testified in her deposition that Elspeth lived with her mother and a "Mr. Reynolds" in Washington for the remainder of the year. What was the explanation for this turnabout? Furthermore, why was there no final decree of divorce in the file? This last question would return to vex the ad litem, leading his investigation through the labyrinth of the court system in New York City, continuing to the very moment of the heirship trial.

Error or Heiress?

To try and relate with any degree of accuracy the precise order or manner in which what became a small library of information on Rupert Hughes accumulated in the ad litem's heirship files would be futile. Rupert Hughes materials would arrive in packages from Robert Hughes or his attorneys (who continued to search for the magazine and newspaper articles that Hughes recalled seeing in his uncle's trunk), in letters from Dinkins' deluded corps of correspondents, and in Mrs. Fay's occasional reports. It was Dinkins' associate's overwhelming responsibility to synthesize and distill these wildly random materials and documents about Rupert and his intimates in an effort to bring order out of the chaos. Most of the material in the heirship files, however, was generated by Dinkins' colleague from her relentless inquiries and research. Dinkins gave his assistant free rein to explore every avenue of Rupert Hughes' life to try and ascertain which, if any, of the madly varied stories about his marriages and children was true.

Quite naturally, Dinkins' team looked to the chatty "Keokuk Connection" for further insight about Rupert's background. Just as it had for Greta, Felix, and Howard, Sr., this publication provided a thumbnail biographical sketch of Judge and Mimi Hughes' other child, offering an overview of Rupert's life:

> A short, overplump, brown-haired kid, Rupert stood tall in the classroom. It is said that at the tender age of thirteen, he was speaking Latin fluently. His schoolmates nicknamed him "History" because he was so studious.
>
> After attending Keokuk schools, Rupert graduated from Adelbert College in Cleveland in 1892, with a Phi Beta Kappa key, followed by a masters degree in 1894. In 1899 he received his Master of Arts degree from Yale.
>
> Upon graduation from Yale, he studied music in London and had twenty-five or more songs published. . . . Rupert spent a few months as a reporter on a New York daily paper, but gave that up to serve as chief assistant editor of the "Historian's History of the World" in 25 volumes, frequenting both the British museum in London and the Bibliotheque Nationale in Paris.
>
> Rupert was very patriotic and was quick to praise the USA. He was a captain in the Mexican border service in 1916, and commissioned a captain of infantry in January, 1918. He was promoted to major in September, and was made major in the Reserve Corps in April of 1919, to later become a lieutenant-colonel on 3-10-23.

After Mrs. Fay discovered Raymond Garrison's book *Goodybye My Keokuk Lady*, his amusing and gossip-filled section on "Fame and Fortune At The Hughes House" was perused for information on Rupert's personal life. Rather than set the record straight, however, Garrison's account only added to the confusion:

> Rupert Hughes was a marrying man, with three, and probably four wives in his lifetime. His first was Adelaide Manola, whom he married in 1908 when he was 36, and by her he had his only child, a daughter, Elspeth. Hughes was divorced from this mate and, under arrangement, he and the mother were each to have care of the girl alternately for six months in the year. When it came his turn, Hughes placed Elspeth with his mother in Keokuk. But the grandmother "was mean to her," the neighbors said they "felt sorry for the child."
>
> Hughes' second wife was believed to have been Agnes Hedges of Syracuse, N.Y. who became enamored of another man after she came to Keokuk and the husband sought the courts for release.
>
> The third wife was Elizabeth Patterson Dial, who wrote fiction and was in the movies, the marriage taking place a half dozen years after the first World War. She died in 1945.

> The story has persisted through the years that one of Hughes'
> several wives was Marion Manola, daughter of his first wife by a
> previous marriage, which would have brought an interesting rela-
> tionship of his being both foster father and husband of his bride. Ad-
> ditional statement is advanced that this wife died in China.

When Dinkins first laid eyes on this excerpt from Garrison's piece
on the Hugheses he was understandably skeptical. *Goodbye My Keokuk
Lady* was the only source to suggest Rupert Hughes had been married
four times, and it was clear that its author, Ray Garrison, had at least
some of his facts about Rupert's marital history garbled. Garrison had
written in the piece that Rupert's first wife was Adelaide Manola, and
his second wife Agnes Hedge. It was evident to Dinkins and his associate
from other sources that the sequence was in fact reversed: Rupert's first
wife was Agnes Hedge, believed to be the mother of Elspeth. Adelaide
Manola was wife number two, and the mother of Avis and Rush. Furthermore, the idea that Rupert may have been married to Marion Manola
at one time was completely new to Dinkins and his staff. They were
familiar with Marion's identity from Rush and Avis' depositions. Contrary to what Garrison had written, Marion Manola was actually
Adelaide Manola's mother, not her daughter. According to Rush, Marion
was a former vaudeville star who was first married to Henry Mould
(Adelaide's father). Marion adopted the stage name "Manola," which
her daughter Adelaide later copied. Garrison was further inaccurate in
reporting that it was Marion Manola who died in China, rather than
Adelaide. Did Garrison confuse Marion Manola with Avis, who was
Adelaide's daughter, or did the confusion lie elsewhere?

Though Garrison's report of four wives for Rupert Hughes interested
Dinkins and his investigator, it was casually dismissed in the preliminary
stages of the investigation as wholly inaccurate, partly because it was in
this same piece by Garrison that Greta Hughes was reported to have
three husbands, instead of the traditional two attributed to her. ("Mr.
Moore's" identity had not yet been uncovered by Dinkins' colleague.)
Both Greta's rumored third marriage to Moore and Rupert's fourth marriage to Marion Manola were put in the same category as fanciful inven-
tions of the author.

Ruby Hughes' information about Rupert followed the traditional
line, and it was her version that was printed in "The Keokuk Connection," since she supplied the family background information for author
Francis Helenthal. Ruby was told by Rupert Hughes that he was married
three times. Her account is that his first wife was Agnes Hedge, by
whom he had a daughter named Elspeth. This marriage ended in
divorce. She had stated that Rupert's second marriage was to "Mrs.

Adelaide Mould in 1908.'' About Adelaide Ruby has written: ''She was widowed and had two children, Avis and Rush. They assumed the name of Hughes, but were never adopted by Rupert. Adelaide's stage name was Adelaide Manola. She was born in Cleveland on May 7, 1884; committed suicide in Haiphong, French Indo-China on December 14, 1923. Rupert had no children by this marriage. Adelaide's mother (Marion Manola) divorced Henry S. Mould in 1891. Married a stage actor by name of John Mason, divorced him in 1900. Died in 1914.'' Rupert's third wife, Ruby wrote Helenthal, ''was Elizabeth Patterson Dial, who wrote fiction and was in the movies. She died in 1945 from an accidental overdose of sleeping pills.'' Ruby once estimated that Patterson Dial was ''between forty-three and forty-five years old at the time of her death.''

In her letters to Helenthal to correct, edit, and furnish background information on the Hugheses for publication in ''The Keokuk Connection,'' Ruby Hughes dismissed completely Ray Garrison's suggestions that Rupert Hughes had been married four times, once to Marion Manola, just as she rejected his notion that Greta was married at one time to a Mr. Moore. Ruby also took issue with Garrison's comments about Elspeth being mistreated in Keokuk by Rupert's mother: ''To say that the grandmother, Jean Hughes, was 'mean' to her grandchild (Rupert's daughter) when left in her care is a story I cannot believe. Disciplining a child is quite different than 'being mean to her.' ''

Even though Garrison's allegations about Rupert Hughes were dismissed as erroneous by Ruby Hughes and taken under advisement by Dinkins and his associate, they did serve to put the pair on notice about Marion Manola. Her name was added to the growing list of individuals to watch closely in their unfolding investigation into Rupert's past. The list included all the women in his life: Elspeth, Patterson Dial, Leonora?, Adelaide, Agnes, and now Marion Manola, Adelaide's mother. On that score, information was steadily trickling into Dinkins' suite. Ruby's description of Patterson Dial as ''between forty-three and forty-five'' in 1945 was the first indication of her age, other than by Avis, who remembered that Patterson was younger than herself. (Avis was born in December 1900.) Ruby also indicated that Dial died from a drug overdose, which helped to explain George Dean's allusions to her emotional condition at the time of her death. This now marked the tragic deaths of two out of the three known wives of Rupert Hughes, and his first wife Agnes' ultimate whereabouts were still unaccounted for, all of which made Rupert appear to be at the very least a difficult man to live with.

Elizabeth Patterson Dial, suggested by Robert Hughes to be Elspeth Hughes Lapp's real mother, was made the focus of further study by Dinkins' associate. By both Avis and Ruby Hughes' accounts, Elizabeth (or Patterson) Dial was born sometime between 1900 and 1902. Obviously, if this were true, it would have been impossible for her to be the mother of Elspeth Hughes Lapp, as Elspeth (according to her birth and death certificates) was born in 1897. That being the case, Elspeth would be five years older than Patterson Dial, the woman Robert Hughes contended was her mother.

To substantiate Patterson Dial's age and learn more about her background, Dinkins' associate ordered a copy of her marriage license to Rupert Hughes. A request was also made for photocopies of her probate proceedings in Los Angeles, where she died in 1945. Not only would her probate papers reveal her age, but also they would indicate her named heirs, and possibly shed some light on a previous marriage to Clayton Dial. Fortunately, Elizabeth Patterson Dial Hughes made out a will before her death, and it was filed among her estate proceedings in Los Angeles County. The document was drafted in 1941, when she was stated to be 38 years old (meaning she was born in 1902 or 1903). Named as her heirs-at-law were her husband Rupert Hughes and a nephew, Alston Cockrell, Jr., then in the Army. She stated that she had "no issue of her body living." Her entire estate was left to Rupert Hughes. Interestingly, Elspeth Hughes Lapp is named as a beneficiary in the event Rupert predeceased Patterson, though she is identified in the will as "my husband's daughter." The remaining contingent beneficiaries were either personal secretaries or household help, with the exceptions of Patterson's nephew Alston Cockrell, Jr., and Mr. and Mrs. Marshall Ricksen of Berkeley, California, whose relationship to Patterson was not indicated. By the terms of the will, Mrs. Ricksen was to receive all of Patterson Dial Hughes' personal items.

Rupert and Elizabeth Patterson Dial's marriage license supported the information in her will. Dated December 31, 1924, Patterson was described on the license as twenty-two years old, born in Florida (no city mentioned) in 1902. The marriage to Rupert is noted as her first, and her name is recited as Elizabeth Patterson *Dial*, not Elizabeth Patterson. Her parents are listed as William H. *Dial* and Sarah B. Whitner. With this information, Dinkins' assistant ordered a birth certificate for an Elizabeth Patterson Dial born in the state of Florida between 1900 and 1905. Patterson Dial's birth certificate would clarify her age beyond question and put to rest Robert Hughes' belief that she was the mother of Elspeth.

The 1902 birthdate that continued to emerge for Patterson Dial was not the only discouraging news with respect to Robert Hughes' theory about Elspeth's "true" background. Dinkins could find no marriage license for an Elizabeth Patterson and a Clayton Dial, nor could he find a birth certificate for an Elspeth Dial, Patterson's alleged daughter by her

263

reputed first marriage to Clayton Dial—all elements of Robert Hughes' claim. There were, however, a cluster of somewhat corroborating facts to support his theory that Elspeth and Patterson Dial might be either mother and daughter or party to some strange deception:

1. Patterson's name: Robert Hughes claimed she was born Elizabeth Patterson, and later married Clayton Dial. Most other accounts indicated her maiden name was Dial, and for some reason she went by her middle name of Patterson, using it as her first name. Yet actress Eleanor Boardman, a good friend of hers before and during her marriage to Rupert, knew her only as Elizabeth Patterson, and had never heard of the surname Dial.

2. It was learned that Patterson Dial was a writer, just as Robert Hughes had informed Mrs. Fay, which made it at least plausible that she might have written a magazine article in which she described the birth of her daughter Elspeth, and how she had named the child using an acronym of her own name.

3. Elspeth was named as a contingent beneficiary in Patterson's will—though she is identified as "my husband's daughter."

4. Elspeth named her daughter Barbara (Cameron) in honor of Patterson Dial. Barbara's middle name is Patterson: Barbara Patterson Lapp. Somehow it seemed odd that Elspeth would name her daughter after her father's third wife. This would make perfect sense, however, if Elspeth were actually Patterson's daughter, as Robert Hughes contended.

5. Both Elspeth and Patterson Dial died in 1945, within several months of each other, both relatively young and under questionable circumstances. Could this mean there was a connection between the two in the manner Robert Hughes suggested? Did the perpetuation of a fraud (Elspeth posing as Rupert's real daughter, and Patterson arranging the deception) ultimately lead the two to early, tragic, and nearly coincidental deaths? The highly suggestive language in certain of the letters written by Rupert Hughes to Elspeth and her family just before her death in May 1945 would seem to bear this out:

•In July 1944, the year before Elspeth's death, Rupert Hughes wrote to her husband Ed Lapp, and noted: "As I understand it, you saw the doctor and he said that Elspeth had a severe nervous collapse and (illegible) to rest for two months—or longer. Poor Elspeth tried to talk to me but began to cry.''

•In February 1945, seven months later, Rupert again wrote Ed Lapp: ''The last letter I had from you was dated February 13th and it was not very hopeful. I judge from your silence that the poor thing hangs on suffering, perhaps more and more. Enclosed is a letter in which I have done the best I can to be cheerful. Nothing could be harder. There is so much to say that must not be said and everything else seems so unimportant.''

•In April 1945, Rupert sent a letter to Elspeth (one of the few in her lifetime), to inform her that he would be stopping in Cleveland on the way to New York City on business: ''It will give me a chance to see you after so long a time and after so many cruel sufferings for both of us.''

•On May 6, 1945 (just nine days before her death), Rupert wrote Elspeth a second time: ''For a long time it looked as if I would never get to Cleveland to see you. Then suddenly the opportunity and the necessity for this trip arose and I had the sweet privilege of an hour with you after long years of separation.
It grieved me deeply to find you in bed, undergoing so great a martyrdom, but I was immensely comforted to find you so brave and philosophical about your terrific ordeal.'' (Elspeth Hughes Lapp died on May 15, 1945; Rupert Hughes did not attend the funeral. The cause of her death, as stated on the death certificate, was cerebral apoplexy.)

•Rupert Hughes sent a letter of condolence to Ed Lapp after Elspeth's death, on May 20, 1945. He remarked in closing: ''I have always said that the crowning cruelty of life is to have some beloved soul endure such torment that death comes as a blessing. That was poor Elspeth's fate. . . . But what can we say?—or do?''

What did the strange allusions in these letters from Rupert Hughes to or about Elspeth signify? Her nervous collapse and untimely death; ''so much to say that must not be said''; the ''long years of separation'' between them (and still Rupert visited his dying daughter for *one hour* only, and did not return to Cleveland for the funeral); the ''so many cruel sufferings for us both''; Elspeth's ''great martyrdom.'' What did it all mean? What was the bond between Rupert and Elspeth that these letters suggested? And did Patterson Dial's death two months before

Elspeth's somehow fit in? Only further research would help tell the story.

Dinkins could find no birth certificate for Patterson Dial in the state of Florida to allay the suspicions about her age, and since nothing was really known about her background, his associate tried to collect whatever media information about her that was readily accessible. In this vein, the research staff dug up an article about her death printed as a special report in the March 24, 1945, edition of the *New York Times*. It is reprinted here in pertinent part:

MRS. HUGHES DIES:
WIFE OF NOVELIST

Overdose of Sleeping Pills is
Called Responsible for Her
Death in California

HOLLYWOOD, March 23—Mrs. Rupert Hughes, wife of the author and lecturer, and a writer herself under her maiden name of Patterson Dial, died today of an overdose of sleeping pills. She was 42 years old.

She was found unconscious in bed at her home this morning by a maid. An ambulance was summoned from the Hollywood Receiving Hospital but she died on the way.

Mr. Hughes, who followed the ambulance to the hospital in the car of a friend, was stunned by the tragedy, but rallied later to say that he believed her death was accidental.

"I returned home about 10:30 p.m. Thursday from a lecture. She told me she had been working in the garden and said she was going to take a sleeping pill to get a good rest. When I finished writing about 3:30 a.m., I looked in on her and noted she was sound asleep. I felt her pulse, because she looked pale, and noticed it was vibrant, almost racing. I thought nothing of it and retired."

He said his wife obtained the sedative about a year ago to induce sleep when she became overwrought from long hours of writing. "She had intense depression when she became morose because she felt her own writing was not up to the goal she set for herself." Mr. Hughes said. "Often she said life was a vanity, and that she could leave it any time."

It was the second time that a similar tragedy touched his life. His first wife, Adelaide Manola Hughes, writer and pioneer film producer, hanged herself in her cabin on a round-the-world steamer on December 14, 1923, at Haiphong, Indo-China. She had started the trip to try and convalesce from ill health.

Whether an inquest is to be held will not be decided until after an autopsy scheduled for tomorrow.

Frustrated in the persistent attempts to locate Patterson Dial's birth certificate, and still in the dark about her background, Dinkins' colleague tried to locate the beneficiaries named in her 1941 will. Possibly these individuals, if they were still alive and could be found, might provide some data on Patterson's life before Rupert. One of these was her nephew, Alston Cockrell, Jr. As a relative, he would be in the best position to answer Dinkins' questions about Patterson Dial's past. Unfortunately, Cockrell's address at the time of his aunt's death was "in care of the U.S. Army," and efforts to trace him through Army records were not successful. With nothing further to go on—no former residence or other identifying information about him—it was impossible to trace Cockrell.

Similar efforts to locate the household servants named in Patterson's will were eventually abandoned. Patterson Dial Hughes died in 1945, more than thirty years before the ad litem's investigation, and the chances that the individuals named in her will were still living were remote. That they might be residents of the same city as they were in 1945 was just as unlikely. Still, Dinkins' associate persisted. These efforts were rewarded with the discovery of Mrs. Marshall Ricksen. Mrs. Ricksen and her husband were both named as contingent beneficiaries in Patterson Dial Hughes' will. To Dinkins' great good fortune, Mrs. Ricksen still resided in Berkeley, California, her home at the time of Patterson's death.

Marshall Ricksen died in 1975, but his wife spoke to Dinkins' colleague about their relationship with both Patterson and Rupert Hughes. As she explained it, Rupert Hughes was made her husband's court-appointed guardian in 1924, when Ricksen was seventeen, the year Rupert married Patterson Dial. Marshall lived with Rupert and Patterson for several years thereafter while attending college. It was then that Marshall met Mrs. Ricksen, and she was introduced to Rupert and Pat in 1929. Mrs. Ricksen and her husband socialized with the Hugheses often up to the time of Patterson's death in 1945, and they continued to see Rupert until his death in 1956. According to Mrs. Ricksen, both Patterson and Rupert were "very dear" to the Ricksens. She stated that her husband Marshall and Rupert Hughes had a "very close father-son relationship'' through the years, and in fact the Ricksens named their son Rupert in his honor.

Close as the Ricksens were to Rupert, Mrs. Ricksen had only a vague notion that Hughes had a child, and even then she was ''less than certain.'' The name ''Elspeth'' at first meant nothing to her. On reflection, she ''seemed to think'' this was Rupert's daughter. The two, she stated, were not ''necessarily close.'' Mrs. Ricksen had no idea who Rush and Avis were. Oddly, she was just as ignorant concerning Patterson Dial's past. Mrs. Ricksen referred to Mrs. Hughes as ''Pat,'' and described her as ''delightful.'' Yet she knew ''nothing'' about her background, and remembered that Pat ''did not enjoy answering questions about her personal life.'' In line with that, Mrs. Ricksen explained, Patterson left a note with her will that Mrs. Ricksen alone would be allowed to search through and distribute her personal belongings. Mrs. Ricksen was not aware that Pat's first name was Elizabeth, and she estimated that she was born in about 1900. She did not believe Pat had been married previously, though she ''wouldn't swear to it.''

As with nearly every other person contacted by Dinkins' associate, the interview with Mrs. Ricksen both confused and clarified things. Patterson Dial was just as much a mystery to the ad litem as she had been before the conversation with her friend Mrs. Ricksen, if not more. Elspeth continued to emerge as an aberration in Rupert's life. It made no sense that Rupert would be appointed official guardian to Marshall Ricksen, a complete stranger, and continue to treat him with warm affection, while coldly ignoring his own flesh and blood. Rupert's court-appointed-guardian status with respect to Marshall also illustrated the fact that he was ready and willing to go to court to legalize his relationship as surrogate father—a fact that would not have cheered attorneys for Rush and Avis. Why would Rupert go through a court proceeding to become Marshall's official guardian in 1924 and never formally adopt Avis and Rush? This omission, in light of Rupert's actions on behalf of Marshall Ricksen, could certainly be construed as damaging to their equitable adoption claim. (Some might even suggest that Marshall's son, Rupert Ricksen, had an even stronger claim to the Howard Hughes estate than Rush and Avis, Marshall being Rupert Hughes' legal ward. Of course Ricksen made no claim to Howard, Jr.'s, fortune, and it is safe to assume that no one involved in the heirship case [aside from Dinkins and his associate] was even aware of his existence, much less his father's relationship to Rupert Hughes.)

The ambiguous nature of Rupert Hughes' relationship to Elspeth is nowhere demonstrated more clearly than in his alumni folder from his undergraduate alma mater, Case Western Reserve University. Rupert attended Case Western Reserve University (then called Adelbert College) in Cleveland from 1888 to 1892, where he graduated Phi Beta Kappa with an A.B. in 1892, and a masters degree in 1894. (Hughes was also given a masters degree from Yale in 1899 for work done at their graduate school in 1893–94). Hughes maintained close ties with his alma mater after graduation, and Case Western Reserve is the repository for many of Rupert Hughes' original manuscripts, by his choice. In 1907, fifteen years after his graduation from college, he was sent a biographical information sheet from a fellow alumnus, to be used in the official catalog of alumni. The alumni editor asked for Hughes' assistance in making it a "comprehensive and accurate source of information." Hughes complied, and filled in the data sheet himself. He cited his college work (including a list of college extracurricular activities), his career achievements (referring to *Who's Who* for more specific information), and his residences since graduation (Yale 1892–93; New York City 1893–1900; London May 1900 – November 1901; "since then" New York City). The line following "number of children" is left completely blank: no name, no number, nothing. It is clear that Rupert Hughes did not acknowledge any children in 1907. He filled out the Case Western information sheet completely and in his own handwriting, and obviously deliberately omitted this item.

The biographical information Rupert supplied in 1907 apparently persisted through the years, until 1949. Then, curiously, Rupert Hughes changed the data on his alumni records. The form he sent to the college Registrar in 1949 was also filled in by Hughes himself, although his handwriting had undergone a dramatic metamorphosis caused by his advanced age. On the 1949 form, after the blank for children, Hughes has written "Elspeth Hughes, (born) 1897." At this stage in his life, Elspeth was dead, as was Patterson Dial. Rupert was seventy-seven and in failing health. Elspeth's daughter Barbara had only recently moved out of Rupert's Los Feliz residence to marry Wes Cameron. In these declining years, Rupert Hughes chose to acknowledge Elspeth as his daughter, despite indications to the contrary in the past. Why this ambivalent attitude? Why did Rupert Hughes imply he had no children in 1907, and list a daughter in 1949?

In response to this unsettling new evidence, Dinkins intensified his search for data on Elspeth. His associate hunted diligently for some notation of her baptism, to confirm the information on her birth certificate (which Robert Hughes claimed was forged): that she was born in 1897 to Rupert and Agnes Hedge Hughes. Dinkins also continued to look for the final decree of divorce between Rupert and Agnes, inexplicably missing from their separation proceedings in New York City. The only record was the 1903 separation decree. In the Hedge family

Bible, Agnes Hedge Hughes noted that her divorce from "R. H." occurred in March of 1904, but she did not indicate the location. Consequently, Dinkins' clerk checked in Bedford Hills (Rupert's Westchester County residence), Syracuse (Agnes' hometown) and other likely places, thinking the Hugheses might have refiled elsewhere, all to no avail. The final divorce decree could not be found by Dinkins or any of the other parties to the heirship proceedings.

The separation agreement divided custody of Elspeth between Rupert and Agnes: Rupert nine months of the year, Agnes three months in the summertime. Dinkins knew that this custody arrangement was not put into practice, based on Rush and Avis' recollections of Elspeth's summer visits to Bedford Hills. There had to be additional divorce proceedings and possibly even a transcript of the divorce trial elsewhere. But where?

The ad litem team fared no better in a search for Elspeth's baptismal certificate. She was not baptized in the Episcopal church where Rupert and Agnes were married in New York, nor was she christened at the church in Keokuk where Howard, Jr., was brought by his parents. There was little to suggest where else this event might have occurred. The only information to date on Elspeth's background, aside from her summer visits to Bedford Hills between 1908 and 1919, was Avis' recollection that she attended the Madeira School throughout this period and lived in Washington. Where was Elspeth from 1919 to 1922, when she married Ed Lapp? Did she, as Robert Hughes believed, drown in Rupert Hughes' swimming pool in Los Angeles in 1920 or 1921, thereafter impersonated by Elizabeth Patterson Dial's daughter, or perhaps by someone else? Neither Rush nor Avis ever saw Elspeth again after 1921. And yet Avis, Rush, and certain others maintained that Rupert did not move into the Los Feliz house with the swimming pool until after his marriage to Patterson Dial in 1924. Since his previous residences in Los Angeles did not have a pool, how could the drowning have occurred in 1920 or 1921? (Although, strangely enough, actress Eleanor Boardman recalled the Sunday luncheon parties given by Rupert and *Adelaide* at their Los Feliz home. How could that be if Rupert built the house for Patterson Dial?) Why did none of the circumstances in Rupert Hughes' life hang together?

Dinkins' associate was also puzzled over Elspeth's whereabouts *before* 1921. Why did Agnes, rather than Rupert, assume primary custody of Elspeth, if indeed she did? And if she did not, where was Elspeth from 1903 (when Rupert and Agnes separated) to 1908 (the beginning of her summer visits to Rupert's)? Furthermore, where exactly was Elspeth during the other nine months of the year in the period from 1908 to 1919, when she spent the summers in Bedford Hills?

Dinkins' efforts were yielding more questions and fewer answers. To add to the continuing intrigue concerning Elspeth and Patterson Dial, disappointingly little was known about Adelaide Manola, Agnes Hedge, and Marion Manola, the other mystery women in Rupert Hughes' life. Was Rupert actually married at one time to Marion Manola, Adelaide's mother, as Garrison reported in *Goodbye My Keokuk Lady*? And was there yet another female figure in Rupert's life: a daughter who drowned?

Meanwhile, Robert Hughes continued his own search for the newspaper and magazine articles that he insisted supported his version of Rupert's life, which he had earlier studied from the copies retained in his uncle's trunk. Hughes also expanded on his family history from time to time, as certain memories "came into focus." He explained, for example, that Elizabeth Patterson was not born in 1902, as she and Rupert Hughes contended. She was actually, Robert Hughes asserted, born in Florida sometime in the 1890s, and later lied about her age. If true, that would explain the contradiction in Robert's claim that Patterson Dial was Elspeth's mother, impossible if Patterson were born in 1902, since she would then be younger than her supposed daughter.

Unfortunately, Hughes could not locate a copy of *All for a Girl,* the play Rupert Hughes presumably dedicated to his "real" daughter, nor could he find the magazine article "Elspeth, My Elspeth," written by Rupert for "my stepdaughter, Elspeth Dial." Likewise, he could not "get his hands on" the magazine series that Patterson Dial ostensibly wrote in connection with her pregnancy and the subsequent birth of her daughter, Elspeth. (Robert Hughes believed that Elspeth Dial was born in Florida between 1902 and 1906, and that it was she who impersonated Rupert's real daughter, married Ed Lapp, and gave birth to Barbara Cameron and her two sisters.) Hughes was similarly unsuccessful in locating the magazine interview with Rupert in contemplation of the swimming pool where his daughter drowned. No death certificate could be secured for the "real" daughter in Los Angeles, either. Still, Hughes was optimistic, and he and his attorneys continued their efforts to track down the material he needed to prove his case.

Now and then, Robert Hughes would send copies of related magazine or newspaper items about Rupert and others he copied in the course of his search for materials once kept in his uncle's safe. In one such collection, Dinkins' associate noticed a series of newspaper articles taken from the society pages in Washington relative to Elspeth's wedding, which took place on March 22, 1922. Her wedding announcement appeared in the March 6, 1922, issue of the *Washington Star*:

271

Mid-Lenten Wedding
Of Special Interest
To the Younger Set

Miss Elspeth Hughes to Become Bride of Mr. Edward
John Lapp - Other Matri-
monial Events of Record.

A mid-Lenten wedding of great interest to the younger members
of society, and especially the debutantes of the winter, will be that
on March 20 of Miss Elspeth Hughes, daughter of Mrs. W. H.
Reynolds, to Mr. Edward John Lapp of New York, at the home of
Mrs. Reynolds, 2230 Q street northwest.

The ceremony will be performed at 6 o'clock, and the bride will
be attended by a maid of honor as youthful as herself—her cousin,
Miss Elizabeth Rynell of Riverside, Calif., who is a student at the
Cathedral School.

The March 19th edition of the *Star* carried this more detailed report:

The marriage of Miss Elspeth Hughes, daughter of Mrs. Reynolds,
wife of Capt. William H. Reynolds, U.S.N., to Mr. Edward John Lapp
of New York will take place tomorrow afternoon. The ceremony
will be performed at 6 o'clock in the home of Capt. and Mrs.
Reynolds, 2220 [*sic*] Q street, by the Rev. Andrew R. Bird, pastor of
the Church of the Pilgrims, and will be followed by an informal
reception for the small company which will witness the ceremony.

Miss Elizabeth Rynell of Riverside, Calif., cousin of the bride,
will be maid of honor, and the bridesmaids will be Miss Cornelia
Magruder Bowie and Miss Charlotte Freeman Clark. Mr. Richard
Zantsinger will be best man and the ushers will be Mr. John Sprague,
Mr. Grant Lyons and Mr. Wents, all of Lehigh University and fraternity brothers of the bridegroom. Little Miss Mary Lapp, sister of the
bridegroom will be the flower girl and William Reynolds, Jr., will be
the train bearer.

On March 21, 1922, the Lapp wedding again made the society pages.
A photograph of Elspeth appeared, with the caption: "Mrs. Edward
John Lapp, daughter of Mrs. W. H. Reynolds, who until her marriage
late yesterday was Miss Elspeth Hughes, a debutante of this season." The
item then went on to repeat basically what was printed in the announcement of several days earlier.

These articles were significant in several respects. First, they supplied additional information about Elspeth and provided the name of

"her cousin" and maid of honor, "Elizabeth Rynell of Riverside," a student at the Cathedral School. An announcement in a rival Washington paper mentioned that Elspeth herself had attended the National Cathedral School in Washington at one time. This now gave the ad litem the names of two schools Elspeth had allegedly attended, both good leads for information concerning her adolescent years. What Dinkins and his associate did not notice at the time about the wedding announcements, but which they would come back to puzzle over later—when Elspeth's age became a genuine mystery—was the fact that Elspeth was described in several of these society reports as a "debutante" of the previous season. One of the wedding announcements, in fact, cited her wedding as being of special interest to the "younger members of society, and especially the debutantes of the winter." This same item referred to Elspeth's cousin Elizabeth Rynell as being "as youthful as herself." The oddity in all this is that Elspeth would have been twenty-five years old in 1922, well beyond the age when a young woman makes her formal debut into society. The social etiquette of the day prescribed that a girl "come out" between the ages of seventeen to twenty; "certainly not at twenty-five," to quote a former editor of Washington's *Green Book*. Why the emphasis was on youth in these society reports of Elspeth's wedding is a true puzzle: a twenty-five-year-old bride (as Elspeth would have been, assuming she was born in 1897) in 1922 was, if anything, dangerously close to old-maid status.

Dinkins' associate immediately set about to confirm Elspeth's attendance at both the Madeira School (mentioned by Avis) and the National Cathedral School (cited in her wedding announcement). Dinkins' assistant also inquired about Elizabeth Rynell, Elspeth's cousin and maid of honor, said to be a Cathedral student in 1922. Both queries were successful. The Madeira School confirmed the attendance of an Elspeth Hughes in the academic years 1911–12, 1912–13, and 1913–14. She withdrew in February 1914. National Cathedral, a posh private girls' school in Washington, likewise verified Elspeth Hughes' attendance, reporting that Elspeth entered the school in the fall of 1916, at the age of nineteen, and attended classes there through May 1917. Her father was indicated to be "Captain Rupert Hughes, Bedford Hills"; her mother, Mrs. (Lt. Com.) W. H. Reynolds, U.S.N.

The director of development at the Cathedral School also located the attendance records of an Elizabeth Rimell (thought to be the same person as the "Elizabeth Rynell" in the society reports of Elspeth's wedding), and furnished her current address. With this new information, Dinkins' associate was able to telephone the maid of honor at Elspeth's wedding: the first breakthrough in the ad litem's exploration of her past. Dinkins also now had information to suggest Elspeth's schooling between 1911–14 and 1916–17. Her whereabouts before 1911 were still a mystery, as was her status from 1914 to 1916, between her enrollments at the Madeira and Cathedral Schools. There was, however, something very strange about Elspeth's school records. Something that escaped Dinkins' associate's attention until late in the investigation. Something that has never been explained.

For the moment, though, the abnormality passed unnoticed, and Dinkins' assistant anxiously engaged in conversation with the former Elizabeth Rimell (now Mrs. Robert Westbrook) about her participation in Elspeth's wedding and about Elspeth herself. Typically, it was a conversation both enlightening and intriguing.

Elspeth Comes to Life

The telephone conversation with Mrs. Westbrook was brief, as not enough was then known about Elspeth and the others for Dinkins' associate to determine what questions were important. The first point of interest with respect to Mrs. Westbrook, naturally enough, was in what way Elspeth was her "cousin," as the wedding announcements described her. The only known first cousin to Elspeth should have been Howard Hughes, Jr., by Dinkins' assessment. In explanation, Mrs. Westbrook stated that she was the daughter of Jenny MacDonald Rimell. Her mother Jenny was Rupert Hughes' first cousin; Jenny MacDonald Rimell's mother (Mrs. Westbrook's grandmother) was Electa Summerlin, who later married Sterling MacDonald. Dinkins' associate recognized the name Electa Summerlin from the census reports sent by Mrs. Fay: she was a sister of Jean Summerlin, Rupert's mother. This genealogy made Rupert Mrs. Westbrook's first cousin-once-removed, the same degree of kinship between Barbara Cameron and her sisters and Howard Hughes, Jr. Elspeth was thus Mrs. Westbrook's second cousin: a "cousin," as the *Washington Star* depicted her, albeit a fairly distant one.

Asked what sort of contact she had with Elspeth during her lifetime, Betty Westbrook answered, "Well, I was the maid of honor in her wedding, for one thing." As the conversation developed, it became clear that that was about the only thing. Mrs. Westbrook first enrolled at National Cathedral School outside Washington in the fall of 1921. Elspeth was not then a student. "I think Elspeth was before me," she offered somewhat hesitantly, "because Elspeth was just a little older than I . . . about—maybe two or three years was all." This observation, largely unnoticed at the time of the telephone interview, would later be of great interest to the heirship investigation, when it was learned that Betty Rimell Westbrook was born in February of 1904, making her a full seven years younger than her cousin Elspeth, not two or three, as she always thought. (Assuming, again, that Elspeth's 1897 birthdate was accurate.)

The two were introduced that autumn of 1921 when Betty began her studies at Cathedral. (Mrs. Westbrook had never met or heard of Elspeth before this time.) Six months later, Mrs. Westbrook, then Elizabeth Rimell, was asked to serve as Elspeth's maid of honor in her March 1922 wedding to Ed Lapp. During their six-months acquaintance in the fall of 1921, Mrs. Westbrook saw Elspeth both on and off campus. "She'd come out to the school a lot," she recalled, "and on weekends I'd go in to visit her—see, her mother had divorced Rupert and remarried a man in the Navy. And so I'd go and spend weekends with them."

"So tell me," Mrs. Westbrook then asked Dinkins' associate, "is she alive or dead?" It was obvious from this question that Elspeth's maid of honor was as distantly acquainted with her as everyone else seemed to be. Just how slight their relationship was, however, came as a surprise. Elspeth was married in Washington in March 1922. "And then I came on home," Mrs. Westbrook explained, "back to Riverside (California). And I've never seen or heard from her since." From this conversation, it was apparent that Elspeth and her maid of honor were not close in any sense, and in fact hardly knew each other at all. To add to the mystique, there were no other bridesmaids. "No, no—just I," Mrs. Westbrook observed. Completing the strange portrait of Elspeth's wedding, her former maid of honor revealed that Rupert Hughes did not attend: the father of the bride. Elspeth was given away by her stepfather, Lieutenant William Reynolds.

Still hoping to learn something more about Elspeth's early years, which were a complete blank, Dinkins' associate asked Mrs. Westbrook if Elspeth ever talked to her about where she grew up, her childhood. "No, no," her cousin responded. "Elspeth was a very—I liked her, but she was not—she was very intense. She was not a fun person." In what would become a pattern in the investigation, Dinkins' assistant also asked Mrs. Westbrook about the origin of Elspeth's name: if there might be a story behind it. (Recalling Robert Hughes' theory that "Elspeth" was an acronym for Elizabeth Patterson Dial, whom he believed to be her mother.) Again, she knew nothing. Mrs. Westbrook was more familiar with Rupert Hughes. She remembered that Rupert would often visit her grandmother Electa, his aunt, at her home in Riverside, which is not far from Los Angeles, where Rupert lived from 1920 on. "When my grandmother was alive," she observed, "he used to come up quite a bit to Riverside to see her. They were very fond of each other." Interestingly, Rupert and his wife gave a dinner party to celebrate Betty Rimell's engagement to Robert Westbrook in the mid-1920s. Such gestures only served to highlight Rupert's peculiar attitude toward Elspeth.

275

Vaguely disturbed by Mrs. Westbrook's account of Elspeth and her wedding, Dinkins' associate nonetheless moved on to the next phase of the investigation, in the continuing hope that someone or something would finally complete the portrait of Rupert's alleged daughter. In that regard, the ad litem team continued to search for individuals who had known not only Elspeth, but also the other persons who figured in Rupert's life: Adelaide and Marion Manola, Agnes Hedge, and Patterson Dial. As the quest persisted, the collection of newspaper and magazine clippings in the heirship files increased accordingly. Since most of these individuals were either public figures or socially prominent, there were a number of stories written about them in the contemporary press. In the many articles about Rupert, both professionally and personally, his daughter—whether she was named Elspeth, Leonora or something else—is never mentioned. Rupert Hughes often wrote about or was quoted referring to his wife of the moment, his parents, or his brothers and sister. (Even Rush and Avis turned up on occasion, in several magazine features showing "the author at home" in Bedford Hills.) Yet he never mentioned a daughter. In his series entitled "My Father" and "My Mother," published in *National* magazine in 1924 as a tribute to his parents and his family, Rupert wrote in great detail about his parents, Howard, Sr., Felix, and Greta. There is no reference to Elspeth. The close bond between Rupert and his immediate family was always evident in his writing and in his interviews. Here, as always, Elspeth is conspicuous by her absence.

It was in one of the hundreds of newspaper clippings accumulating in Dinkins' office that his associate got the first glimpse of Rupert's life with Agnes Hedge, wife number one. It was not a favorable review. Dinkins' colleague found an item referring to Rupert's divorce proceedings from Agnes on the front page of the *New York Times*. Unlike the scandal sheets and tabloids of yesterday and today, the *Times* is not generally given to publicizing the private scandals of public figures. Exception was evidently made in Rupert Hughes' case, as the newspaper carried this somewhat lurid account of his divorce, on October 16, 1903:

USE VIOLENCE TO
DEFEND HUGHES JURY.

———————

Court Officers Rescue Them from Co-
Respondents and Other Too Eager
Questioners - Lawyer Strikes
a Witness.

276

When the jury, which retired yesterday afternoon to decide from the evidence that had been introduced during the past four or five days whether or not Rupert Hughes, the author, playwright, and sculptor, was entitled to a divorce from his wife, Agnes Wheeler Hedge Hughes, passed out of the Court House at midnight last night they were almost mobbed by two of the eight co-respondents named, representatives of counsel for both sides, and several other persons who were anxious to learn what was the prevailing opinion. Court officers who tried to protect the jurymen from the men had a tough time in doing it. The questioners were so persistent that the officers got into a hot fight with them and finally knocked one or two of them down.

That was the second exciting incident of the day in the divorce case. In the afternoon Lyman Spalding, Mrs. Hughes' lawyer, struck one of the witnesses, and spectators had to separate them. It was just after the jury had passed out of the courtroom that Herbert Witherspoon, Mrs. Hughes' brother-in-law, went up to Mr. Spalding, who was standing in the upper corridor near the courtroom door and said something to him in a low tone.

Mr. Spalding said Witherspoon said to him: "You are a mudslinging scoundrel." The lawyer struck the man on the left side of the jaw and sent him reeling backward ten or twelve feet. Several persons rushed between the two men, and Witherspoon left the building. He is a concert singer.

The jury went out about 5 o'clock. Among several persons who hung around the Court House waiting for the verdict were Arthur Vandover Conover, a member of the United States Lighthouse Service, and Lieut. Reynolds, United States Navy, two of the co-respondents named; Mr. Schofield, Mr. Spalding's partner, and a clerk in the office of Attorney Mathot, Mr. Hughes' lawyer. At 11:45 Justice Clarke, learning by telephone that the jurymen had not reached a verdict, instructed them to go home and report to him this morning at 10:30 o'clock . . .

A month later, on November 30, 1903, the *Times* ran a special report out of Syracuse, with the headline: "HUGHES DIVORCE IS SETTLED OUT OF COURT." The report outlined the terms of the separation decree that Dinkins already had in his possession: alternate custody of "the daughter," and an undisclosed sum of alimony for Mrs. Hughes. "The report became noised among Mrs. Hughes' friends here (in Syracuse)," the piece recited, "and they are expressing gratitude that the matter, which has been widely aired, has been adjusted. Mrs. Hughes is the daughter of Mr. and Mrs. Charles L. Hedge of Syracuse, and several of the co-respondents mentioned in the divorce action are prominent Syracuse persons."

The *New York Times* newspaper articles both amused and interested Dinkins' circle of investigators. It was apparent from them that the Hughes divorce was a cause cèlébre even in world-weary New York, which made Dinkins and his associate wonder all the more what might be printed in the trial transcript, if it existed. For obvious reasons, it also piqued their curiosity to learn that Rupert Hughes charged his wife Agnes with adultery, and named eight to ten co-respondents in his pleading—several of whom showed up to observe the proceedings! Dinkins couldn't help but observe that one of these co-respondents was William H. Reynolds, the man whom Agnes married a matter of months after her divorce from Rupert Hughes became final, which lent a certain amount of credence to Hughes' allegations. Also interesting was the fact that Greta's husband Herbert Witherspoon came to blows with Agnes' divorce lawyer, which proved in a dramatic way that the ties between Greta and Rupert were as close as earlier reports suggested.

Still missing after all this, however, was some word of where the final decree of divorce was filed. Dinkins already had a copy of the separation agreement dated November 1903. Where was the final judgment? More importantly, where might copies of the complete pleadings and trial transcript be? As sensational a divorce as the Hugheses had, the trial transcript had to make fascinating reading and might well contain more than a few clues regarding Elspeth, Leonora, and who knew what other lurid secrets about Rupert and his first marriage. At last Agnes Hedge became more than a name to Dinkins and his staff, and, like the other women in Rupert Hughes' life, she was not a disappointment.

At this point in the heirship investigation, Dinkins' associate ferreted out a trio of key individuals with links to Rupert Hughes' past. The first such person was made known to the ad litem via Mrs. Westbrook, Elspeth's former maid of honor. After talking to Dinkins' associate, Mrs. Westbrook thought further about her distant cousin, and wrote to Dinkins' colleague suggesting that the ad litem get in contact with another of Electa Summerlin MacDonald's granddaughters, a woman by the name of Frances McLain Smith. Mrs. Smith's mother (Rupert's first cousin) had lived with Judge and Mimi Hughes in Keokuk for several years while attending college, and Mrs. Smith and her mother were especially close to Rupert and the rest of the Hughes family. In her ensuing interview with Dinkins' associate, Frances Smith had a number of interesting observations about nearly everyone close to Rupert.

Mrs. Smith, born Frances McLain in 1900, grew up in Montana, where her grandparents (Sterling and Electa Summerlin MacDonald, Jean Summerlin's brother-in-law and sister) had settled after leaving Missouri in the late 1800s. During her adolescent years in Montana, Frances heard much about her mother's cousin Rupert but had never met him. In 1916, she was sent to the exclusive National Cathedral School in Washington, where she remained until 1918. Elspeth attended the school during Frances' first year (1916–17) as a "day pupil," not a boarder, and lived in Washington with her mother Agnes and her husband, a "Navy man." This was Frances' first acquaintance with Elspeth.

Mrs. Smith also met her mother's cousin Rupert at this time. Rupert Hughes was then dividing his time between Washington and New York, fulfilling his military duties as a major in the Intelligence Division of the U.S. Army. Frances spent nearly every weekend with Rupert and his then-wife Adelaide between 1916 and 1918 (her years of attendance at the Cathedral School), and she and Rupert became very close. Rupert, in fact, "made every effort" to have her move in with him and his wife, and even wanted to adopt Frances, who declined. Rupert also wished to groom his cousin's daughter to become a movie star, but Frances rejected this offer as well. She had already met her future husband, Merle Smith, and Smith would not allow her to go to Hollywood. Frances McLain moved to California after graduating from National Cathedral in 1918, and she and Merle Smith were married in 1920. (Rupert Hughes attended this wedding ceremony; Mrs. Smith still has the wedding gift-book, with the entry reflecting that Rupert gave her a "fine clock" as a wedding present.) After the Smiths' marriage in 1920, Frances continued to see Rupert and Adelaide, and later Rupert and Patterson Dial. Merle and Frances Smith moved from Los Angeles to Riverside, California, in the mid-1920s, and from then until Rupert's death, Frances' contact with him was limited to frequent letters and telephone calls.

With this background, Dinkins' colleague questioned Frances Smith more comprehensively about Elspeth, and more specifically about Elspeth's relationship with Rupert. Here, finally, Elspeth began to emerge as a person. Mrs. Smith related that Elspeth made a "desperate attempt" to win her friendship when they met in 1916 at the Cathedral School. Elspeth, she went on, was "friendless," always grasping at anything and anyone. Mrs. Smith found her "overpowering and smothering," and so resisted her overtures of friendship, to the extent that Frances would hide in a closet if she heard Elspeth approach her room at school. On the other hand, she noted that Elspeth was "brilliant," spoke many languages, and had a photographic mind. In appearance, Elspeth was short, with a "swarthy" complexion, and spoke with an impediment.

Mrs. Smith met Elspeth's mother, Agnes Hughes Reynolds, only briefly, and by her description Mrs. Reynolds was an "inoffensive, insignificant, rather small woman." Elspeth and her mother, Mrs. Smith observed, were not particularly close. Elspeth continually invited Frances to spend weekends with the Reynolds in Washington, and Mrs.

279

Smith consistently turned her down, mostly because Elspeth was so "possessive." She further recalled that Elspeth might have been "asked to leave" the Cathedral School before graduation, due to some infraction of the school rules. Whatever the cause, Elspeth was dropped from the register at the school in the spring of 1917. Mrs. Smith continued on for another year. After her marriage to Merle Smith in 1920, Frances Smith never saw Elspeth again. All told, Frances McLain Smith knew Elspeth between 1916 and 1920.

As for Elspeth's relationship with Rupert Hughes, Mrs. Smith was explicit. She told Dinkins' associate she could easily believe there was something "amiss" in that father-daughter situation. She observed that the two did not resemble each other in the slightest, "and neither had anything positive to say about the other." In line with that, Frances remembered Elspeth once saying something so atrocious about Rupert it prompted her to ask, "How can you say that about your father?" Rupert's behavior was equally strange. Frances would occasionally ask him why he didn't express more interest in Elspeth. According to Mrs. Smith, Hughes "wheeled around" and "gave her a look" that closed the subject completely. Mrs. Smith often wondered, she told Dinkins' emissary, "where Elspeth came from . . . she was so completely different and odd." There was "no closeness" between her and Rupert, yet Rupert was, by Frances' description, "an extremely warm and giving person." After "losing contact" with Elspeth between 1918 and 1920, Mrs. Smith rarely if ever discussed her with Rupert Hughes again. When asked why, she explained that Rupert "knew how she felt" about Elspeth, and she was aware of his feelings, "so there would be no reason to discuss her." She did not know why he did not attend Elspeth's wedding.

Queried about Adelaide, Mrs. Smith described her as "fascinating . . . rather small with bright red hair, quite dynamic." She was always surrounded by interesting people. Mrs. Smith stated that Rupert "adored" Adelaide, and that they had a "normal" relationship. It was Rupert, she related, who insisted that Adelaide make her fatal trip to China, as she was suffering from a "breakdown." Immediately after he received the telegram from Haiphong announcing Adelaide's suicide, Rupert telephoned Frances and her husband and invited them to his house. The two accepted, and Mrs. Smith recalled that he did not seem shaken in the least, and never even mentioned the incident. Mrs. Smith did not find this behavior unusual since Rupert had, as she put it, "a great deal of composure."

Mrs. Smith had also met Rush and Avis. "They were adopted children of Rupert's," she noted. She had been told they were Adelaide's children by a former marriage. Characterizing Rupert's attitude toward the pair, Mrs. Smith stated bluntly, "He put up with them."

Mrs. Smith also offered some additional insight about Patterson Dial. She met the actress only once, at a Thanksgiving dinner at Rupert's home on Los Feliz in 1924, shortly before her marriage to Rupert. "Patty," as Rupert called here, was "very pretty, with bronzy hair." Mrs. Smith referred to her throughout the conversation as Rupert's "proofreader," which she claims Rupert called his wife. Dinkins' associate informed Mrs. Smith at the time of the interview that Patterson's age was a point of controversy in the heirship proceedings, and asked her to recall to the best of her ability what age Patty appeared to be in 1924 when they met. After musing several minutes, she stated that Patterson Dial was "young," but placed her in her thirties in 1924. (If born in 1902, as stated on her marriage certificate, Patterson Dial would have been twenty-two.) Asked if she could have been in her twenties at this meeting, Frances Smith replied: "I would think not. Again, she was young, but appeared to be at least in her mid-thirties." If correct, Mrs. Smith's recollection would support Robert Hughes' allegations that Patterson Dial was actually born in the 1890s, and give rise to the possibility that she could have been Elspeth's mother.

Asked if Patty and Rupert were living together before their marriage, at the time of Adelaide's departure for China, Mrs. Smith thought that "could have been" the case. She did not know the particulars of the situation but thought it was possible that Adelaide was despondent over something of that sort at the time of her suicide. Mrs. Smith also stated that Patty never mentioned her background, nor did Rupert. Aside from this one meeting in 1924, Mrs. Smith did not see Patterson Dial before her death in 1945, although she did continue to telephone and write to Rupert. She added that Rupert wrote her a long letter after Patty's drug overdose, in which he confessed: "I blame myself because it was more than she could take." According to Mrs. Smith, Rupert was referring to the tedious proofing and long hours to which he subjected his wife. (Rupert, she observed, was a "nocturnal" person. He slept all day and wrote at night. His house was decorated with heavy drapes that he kept closed most of the time.) In closing, Mrs. Smith acknowledged that although she adored Rupert, he must have been "impossible to live with."

In addition to her valuable insight on Rupert and his various wives or children, Mrs. Smith provided an interesting piece of background on Howard Hughes, Jr. She related that after the death of his parents, Sonny was sent to Los Angeles to live with his grandparents in their new home on North Rossmore. As she tells the story, "Aunt Jean" (Jean Hughes) tried to persuade Frances, then married and living in California, to "take

Howard in,'' because Mrs. Smith ''felt sorry for him.'' Sonny was very interested in planes, and his grandmother disapproved of many of his interests, insisting for example that there be ''no airplane talk'' in her house. Characteristic of Howard, Jr., he continued to engage in his activities, behind his grandmother's back.

Mrs. Smith also acknowledged what had become a growing impression among Dinkins and his staff: that there was a great deal of animosity between Howard, Jr., and his uncle Rupert. She was aware of the friction and asserted that it began at the time of Big Howard's death in 1924. She vaguely recalled attempts to establish a guardianship for Sonny that same year and remembered that it was Rupert who acted as the family spokesman in negotiations for control of Howard, Sr.'s, estate. Howard, Jr., eventually won the battle, after persuading a Houston judge to remove his disabilities as a minor, thus allowing him not only to take over the Tool Company, but also to avoid the dreaded guardianship proceedings as well. Rupert was ''disgusted'' with his nephew, according to Mrs. Smith, and found him ''hard to manage.'' From every account available to the ad litem, Howard, Jr., returned this enmity. Rupert Hughes, Mrs. Smith explained, could be warm and charming if he liked you, and ''positively icy'' if the reverse were true.

Through conversations such as these, the multiple facets and dimensions of Rupert Hughes made themselves known to Dinkins and his associate: his astonishingly blasé behavior after the tragic deaths of both Adelaide and Patterson Dial, and the letter he sent Mrs. Smith after Patty's death in which he said ''it was more than she could take''; his enigmatic attitude toward Elspeth, in thought, word, and deed; his apparent contempt for Howard Hughes, Jr., and Sonny's reciprocated scorn for Rupert; the power play he headed to wrest control of his brother Howard, Sr.'s, estate; suggestions that he was difficult to live with; his seeming eagerness to adopt nearly everyone in sight (including Rush and Avis, Frances McLain, and Marshall Ricksen), contrasted with his disavowal of Elspeth; his divorce action against Agnes Hedge, leading to fisticuffs between Greta's husband and Agnes' attorney and several of her alleged lovers. What did these complexities suggest about the inner man? It was obvious that the ''warm and loving'' side that Rupert Hughes revealed to his granddaughters in his last ten years belied a lifetime of paradoxical behavior. Were there dark secrets as well? What roles did the phantom women he allegedly married or fathered play in Rupert Hughes' life? These were the questions Dinkins needed to answer.

The books and articles Rupert wrote were often as illuminating as the interviews he gave in his literary heyday. Dinkins' office continued to be a repository for prose by and about Rupert, and this literature reinforced the complex image of him conjured up by the depositions, interviews, and other material collected during the investigation. Robert Hughes, for example, in his continuing quest for the corroborating articles he once saw in the family trunk, called everyone's attention to a magazine article Rupert Hughes wrote for *Cosmopolitan* magazine in 1924, entitled "Why I Quit Going To Church." ("I quit," Rupert wrote, "because I came to believe that what is preached in the churches is mainly untrue, or unimportant, or tiresome, or hostile to genuine progress and in general not worth while.") Contemporaneous criticism reveals that this piece was, not surprisingly, extremely controversial when it appeared. At the time, Rupert Hughes was the highest-paid short story writer in America, and his opinions and beliefs were front page news.

Other pieces by Rupert Hughes were equally shocking in their time. In August 1924, Hughes wrote another article for *Cosmopolitan*, this one entitled, "I Am In Favor of Divorce by Mutual Consent." The essay revealed that Hughes had a lawyer's knowledge of the divorce laws in all (then) forty-eight states. There were, by his count, thirty-five grounds for divorce, and he was intimately acquainted with them all. "All this slow hell," he chastised, "could be done away with if the U.S. were civilized enough to permit divorce by mutual consent"—a rather outré concept for 1924. Several years before this article was printed, Hughes was interviewed by Adela Rogers St. Johns for *Photoplay* magazine, as he and his current wife Adelaide visited the set of the Goldwyn picture Hughes was then filming, *Dangerous Curves Ahead.* "Marriage is the greatest bunco game in the world," he told St. Johns in 1921. "If a man has a wife he doesn't like, he should get rid of her as soon as he possibly can." Hughes then compared the situation to a cinder in the eye. "The only philosophy I have about marriage is divorce," he stated flatly. "Divorce should be as simple, inexpensive and private as marriage."

It was plain from the tone and tenor of these articles that Rupert Hughes espoused some very controversial views for the times in which he lived. Obviously, this fact was significant to Dinkins' investigation. Undoubtedly Hughes' front page divorce from Agnes Hedge contributed mightily toward his bitter attitude toward marriage. These magazine articles also indicated that Rupert Hughes was a man of unconventional morals, and possibly unconventional behavior, facts that would become important to the unfolding investigation of his personal life. "People and character are not all good nor all bad," Rupert Hughes wrote in the late 1920s. "They should be presented as they are." This was precisely what Dinkins was endeavoring to accomplish with Hughes himself.

As the ad litem's research concerning Rupert and Elspeth expanded, it only contributed to the initial doubts expressed about her parentage. Though the documentary evidence all supported the fact that she was Rupert's daughter—her birth certificate, the 1903 separation decree between Rupert and Agnes Hedge Hughes—everything else Dinkins' associate uncovered seemed to dispute it. Dinkins' secretary put it bluntly: "Something is weird." Robert Hughes all the while persisted in his belief that Elspeth, the individual who married Ed Lapp and became the mother of Barbara Cameron and her sisters, was actually Patterson Dial's daughter, and that she was born in the early 1900s in Florida. His initial confusion about the name of Rupert Hughes' "real" daughter (by first wife Agnes Hedge) had been resolved; he was certain that Rupert's natural daughter was named "Leila B. Hughes," and it was she who was born in New York in 1897. ("Elspeth was somewhat younger than Leila," Robert testified in his deposition.) "I was unsure about the names of the children," Hughes told Avis' attorney George Dean. "It came back to me: the full name. I can remember my Uncle John using that name in his conversation with me now. I could not remember it sometimes. When you remember things over a long period of time you need something to nudge your memory to make you remember it. And this is what happened to me. It finally came around in my mind that that was the daughter's full name."

Robert Hughes contended that Rupert's daughter Leila Hughes became an actress and appeared for a time on the New York stage before her alleged drowning in the early 1920s. In his search for evidence to support his claim, he located a reference to her in a 1913 issue of *Theatre* magazine. The magazine pictured a "Leila Hughes," then appearing in a production of the play *My Little Friend* at the New Amsterdam Theatre in New York. This actress, Hughes told attorneys connected with the heirship case, was Rupert Hughes' "real" daughter (by Agnes Hedge). It was Leila who drowned in Rupert's swimming pool, and was subsequently impersonated by Elspeth Dial, the daughter of Elizabeth Patterson Dial. By Robert's account, Leila was the person born in New York in 1897. Elspeth was born in the state of Florida sometime early in 1900, making Elspeth "somewhat younger" than the person whose identity she later assumed.

With this updated information from Robert C. Hughes, Dinkins' associate had yet another individual to trace: Leila B. Hughes, the onetime star of *My Little Friend*. Along with his enclosure of the *Theatre* magazine piece about Leila, Robert Hughes furnished copies of a new collection of articles about Rupert, Patterson Dial, and Adelaide. In the developing custom of the investigation, Dinkins' colleague studied these articles carefully, adding them to the ad litem's burgeoning Rupert

Hughes library. One in particular caught their attention. Pictured on the front page of the *Los Angeles Times* of December 17, 1924, were Rupert Hughes and Elizabeth Patterson Dial: "Principals in Latest Romance of Cinema Land." The article read:

> Rupert Hughes, novelist, dramatist and motion picture director and executive, and Elizabeth Patterson Dial, known on the screen as Patterson Dial, will be married in Los Angeles early next year. After a three weeks' honeymoon trip to New York, they will return here to make their permanent residence.
>
> Mr. and Mrs. Alston Cockrell of Jacksonville, Fla., relatives of Miss Dial, have announced the engagement of the two.
>
> Miss Dial first met Mr. Hughes during the filming of the dramatic story, "Reno," a little more than a year ago. She has appeared prominently in "Married Flirts," "Tol'able David," as well as in lesser productions.
>
> Recently Mr. Hughes was advanced from director to production executive at the Metro-Goldwyn-Mayer studios.

At approximately the same time, Dinkins received a copy of a passport application for Rupert and Patterson Dial Hughes, dated April 15, 1930, preparatory to a trip to Europe. The application was filled in by Rupert Hughes, whose handwriting was by this time fully familiar to Dinkins' associate. On the passport form, Hughes noted that his wife was born May 19, 1902 (the same date reflected on her marriage license to Rupert Hughes), in Madison, Florida. If correct, how could one explain Frances Smith's recollection that Patty appeared to be in her thirties in 1924?

The passport application gave the ad litem investigation the name of a town in Florida as the birthplace of Elizabeth Patterson Dial, perhaps a valuable clue in the still unsuccessful search for her birth certificate. (The Florida Health Department plainly had no birth certificate on file for her.) The wedding announcement that appeared in the *Los Angeles Times* was equally helpful: it provided a city of residence, Jacksonville, for "Mr. and Mrs. Alston Cockrell," the "relatives" who announced Patterson Dial's engagement to Rupert Hughes in 1924. These were obviously the parents of Alston Cockrell, Jr., referred to as Patterson's "nephew" in her 1941 will. The discovery that the Cockrells (Sr.) were from Jacksonville gave Dinkins' colleague hope that their son may have settled there as well, after his enlistment in the Army. If so, and if he could be traced, he might well be able to clear up the confusion about his aunt Patterson (Elizabeth). The idea that Cockrell might be in Jacksonville was an interesting coincidence in itself. It appeared from

Barbara Cameron's deposition that Jacksonville was the city where Agnes Hedge Hughes Reynolds and her second husband William H. Reynolds ultimately retired, after moving away from Washington. Wouldn't it be interesting if Elizabeth Patterson Dial were from Jacksonville, too?

Patterson Dial

There was no listing for an "Alston Cockrell, Jr.," in the Jacksonville telephone directory, but Dinkins' associate telephoned every Cockrell in the city with a barrage of questions about Alston. Only one had ever heard of him, and the one who had, had no idea where he was or what he was doing. However, she gave Dinkins' assistant the name of an elderly Jacksonville attorney who handled legal affairs for "one of the Cockrells" in the past. The attorney in question passed on another name to Dinkins' associate, and this individual in turn produced a telephone number at which to contact Cockrell. It was like something out of a spy thriller.

When Dinkins' associate called the number, she heard something resembling the background sounds in a longshoreman's bar. The woman who answered the phone said Cockrell was not at that number, but she might be able to find the number where he was staying. If she could find it, she stated, it would be necessary for Dinkins' representative to ask whoever answered the telephone to go across the hall and find him. "Yeah," the woman went on, "he's got a place where he keeps all of his magic tricks across the hall, and he's always over there. And that's the only number I know that you can get him at."

Still game, albeit somewhat leery, Dinkins' colleague called the number she was given. A man answered the phone, saying, "92787." With some trepidation, Dinkins' associate asked him if Alston Cockrell, Jr., might be reached at this number. "One moment," he responded politely, "I'll see if he's here." A few minutes later, the man returned to the phone. "He's not here right now," he announced. "Do you know when he'll be back?" Dinkins' clerk asked doubtfully. "That I couldn't tell you," he replied.

After several more tries, Dinkins' associate finally reached Cockrell. It was well worth the trouble. Not only was the man Patterson Dial's nephew, but he was also intimately acquainted with Rupert Hughes and knowledgeable about many of the individuals who were the subject of Dinkins' investigation. In finding Cockrell, Dinkins' associate found the key to Patterson Dial. Cockrell also had some rather provocative things to say about some of the other cast of characters. When asked if he were related to Elizabeth Patterson Dial Hughes, he replied, "Yeah, that's right. That was my mother's sister."

In a matter of seconds he was able to clear up the confusion over the Dial surname:

Interviewer: And what was your mother's name?

Cockrell: My mother's name was Stephena Cockrell. Now her maiden name was Stephena Dial.

Interviewer: And her sister was Elizabeth Patteson Dial, I'm correct?

Cockrell: Well, I'm almost positive that that was her maiden name.

   Yeah, because you see, she was named for a cousin who was Elizabeth Patterson.

Interviewer: It was not Elizabeth Patterson, though: in other words, Patterson was not her maiden name?

Cockrell: No, no.

Cockrell then established that his aunt was born in Madison, Florida in 1900. Her parents were William Henry Dial and his wife "Burtie." (Just as Patterson's marriage certificate indicated.) After setting that much of the record straight, Cockrell asked: "Why do you want all this information?" Dinkins' associate began to explain Dinkins' involvement as the ad litem in the estate of Howard Hughes. Before she could go any further, Cockrell interrupted to say.

Cockrell: She wouldn't let the son-of-a-bitch in the house!

Interviewer: Is that right?

Cockrell: That's right.

Interviewer: She didn't care for Mr. Hughes?

Cockrell: No. They raised me—fortunately. But they wouldn't let—she wouldn't let Howard come in her house.

Interviewer:　Was this out in California?

Cockrell:　4751 Los Feliz Boulevard!

Interviewer:　Aha. During what years did you see your aunt?

Cockrell:　Since the time I was born until she died.

Interviewer:　And when were you born?

Cockrell:　1917.

Interviewer:　In 1917. And she raised you?

Cockrell:　She didn't raise me, no. She and my mother were very close. I lived out there with them—in Los Angeles.

Interviewer:　On Los Feliz?

Cockrell:　Yeah. I visited with them. My mother went to Europe one summer and I stayed with them. I lived out there and worked in pictures for about a year.

Interviewer:　You lived with your aunt and Mr. Rupert Hughes?

Cockrell:　That's right.

Interviewer:　I see. Did she have any children?

Cockrell:　No.

Interviewer:　She had no children?

Cockrell:　I am her only heir.

Certain by this time that Cockrell was legitimate, Dinkins' associate asked him about Elspeth, with surprising results:

Interviewer:　Did you know a lady by the name of Elspeth Hughes?

Cockrell:　Yeah.

Interviewer: Do you recall who she is?

Cockrell: At the time I knew her she was Lapp.

Interviewer: And was she related in any fashion to your aunt, Patterson Dial?

Cockrell: No.

Interviewer: She was not. How was that connection made?

Cockrell: Well, she was . . . ah . . . Rupert's daughter.

Interviewer: I see. Did she visit at the home in California? Is that how—did you ever meet Elspeth?

Cockrell: I met her here in Jacksonville.

Interviewer: Did she live in Jacksonville, or how did that come about?

Cockrell: Oh, I was probably around eleven or twelve years old. They visited down here—Elspeth and her husband.

Interviewer: Mr. Lapp. And did they come to visit your family, or what was their—

Cockrell: No, no. My aunt and uncle were down here one winter. They spent the winter down here.

Interviewer: This is Rupert and Patterson?

Cockrell: Yeah.

Interviewer: And at that time Elspeth and her husband visited with you-all?

Cockrell: Yeah. They came to dinner.

Wondering whether the "Patterson" in Barbara Cameron's name (Elspeth's daughter) was in fact in honor of Patterson Dial, Dinkins' associate inquired about the relationship between Elspeth and Cockrell's aunt, leading to a startling disclosure:

Interviewer: Were they that close? Did Elspeth—

Cockrell: They weren't close at all. They were extremely distant. Ah—

Interviewer: Patterson and Elspeth?

Cockrell: You know, there are things that—in the back of my mind, that I hesitate to say . . . I'm talking about Rupert and his so-called—his daughter.

Here was an independent source who stated what had become the overriding suspicion of Dinkins' investigation: that there was something terribly wrong in the relationship between Rupert and Elspeth. Others had merely implied it, and the circumstances compelled that conclusion: Cockrell simply went one step further. Dinkins' associate encouraged him to say more:

Interviewer: Did they not get along?

Cockrell: I don't—I don't know. I don't think they did. I'm sure they—they saw very little of each other, I mean—

Interviewer: Did they resemble one another?

Cockrell: I see what you're getting at. I don't think so.

Interviewer: You don't think they resembled one another?

Cockrell: No.

Interviewer: So are you saying you have some sort of inkling that perhaps they weren't related?

Cockrell: I'm not saying anything. Because I don't *know*.

Interviewer: You're too clever for me, Mr. Cockrell.

Cockrell: No, I'm not clever, but my father was an attorney.

Interviewer:	So, in other words, Rupert—you are saying that Rupert and Elspeth were not that close?
Cockrell:	I don't think they were—not unless it's something that—You see, he was—I was a small child.
Interviewer:	I understand.
Cockrell:	There was a good deal of difference between Rupert and my aunt—in their age.
Interviewer:	Yes, uh-huh.
Cockrell:	He had been married many times. . . . as I recall, he had one that committed suicide—hung herself over in China.
	Now, I don't know whether that was Elspeth's mother or not.
Interviewer:	From what we understand, it wasn't. I believe it was his first wife, Agnes.
Cockrell:	Agnes?
Interviewer:	Yes—who was Elspeth's mother. Is that not the story you heard?
Cockrell:	I don't—I just wonder . . . Adelaide, isn't it?

Cockrell persisted in his belief that it was Adelaide who was the mother of Elspeth. To add to the confusion, he added: "Well now, he had a sister with a name that was similar to that, too. . . . I just remember there was a sister. The sister was dead before I came around." Continuing his recollection that Rupert had "many" wives, Cockrell said in closing:

Cockrell:	And then—the other wives were nondescript—just meaningless to me, except I had heard stories about one who hung herself over in China.

Moving back to Patterson Dial, Dinkins' clerk learned from Cockrell that his aunt had moved to Jacksonville from Madison as a young girl

291

and had attended grammar school and high school in Jacksonville. Stephena Dial, her older sister, had married Alston's father and was living in Jacksonville as well. Cockrell recalled what he knew of his aunt's background:

Cockrell: (My parents) came to Jacksonville, I'm sure, shortly after their marriage and (she) probably lived with them. And she attended school here. And she was a pretty sharp cookie. She was ambitious and she had a lot of sense. And she would go to school and not go to school . . . she knew where she wanted to go. And pretty soon she was in New York working Broadway shows. You know—I think by the time she was like seventeen years old.

I think that's right. Now that might be entirely incorrect. My first recollection of anything like that was when she was, I think, in her early twenties. Everything had gone to hell, and she was coming back here to start a dancing school. And—

Interviewer: This was in Florida, she started the dancing school?

Cockrell: She was on the verge of doing it, and a telegram came and she went on to the West Coast and she was pretty successful in pictures after that.

And then when she married Rupert, why her acting career ended and she did nothing for quite some time, and then finally she started to write.

Cockrell then recalled that he and his mother visited Rupert and Patterson in California the summer before their marriage, in 1924. "Let's see . . . I was eight years old. And she and I and my aunt and Rupert took a trip to San Francisco." Alston's mother died several years later, and Patterson became his surrogate mother. Rupert, as usual, assumed the role of surrogate father.

Before terminating the conversation, Dinkins' associate again asked Cockrell to expand on his earlier comment about Elspeth. By this time, he was wary of saying too much:

Interviewer: Would you—could you maybe expand on what you were saying about Rupert and his daughter Elspeth . . . that there were some things that you had in the back of your mind or something?

Cockrell: No, I couldn't.

Interviewer: You'd rather not say?

Cockrell: Anything I'd say would be pure speculation, honey, and I'm not going to speculate about anything like that.

Interviewer: But they didn't have a warm relationship?

Cockrell: [Pause] Ah . . . I don't think there was a warm relationship there at all.

Finally, Dinkins' clerk inquired about Rush and Avis, thinking Cockrell might know whether Rupert considered the two to be, as they were claiming, his adopted children:

Interviewer: Do you know anyone by the name of Avis and/or Rush Hughes?

Cockrell: I've heard of a Rush Hughes, who was no kin in the world to Rupert.

Rush Hughes was the son, I believe, of one of his wives—who was no kin in the world to Rupert. You know, like I was no kin in the world to Rupert. He called me his uncle, but hell—my aunt's husband, who made him my uncle-in-law.

Interviewer: And Avis doesn't ring a bell for you?

Cockrell: I suppose Avis was Rush's sister.

With the discovery of Alston Cockrell, Jr., the suspicions about Patterson Dial seemed at last to be dispelled. Cockrell confirmed that his aunt's surname was Dial, not Patterson, and that his mother Stephena Dial was Patterson Dial's sister. If his family history was correct, then Patterson was born in 1900, and couldn't possibly be Elspeth's mother.

Yet the records on Patterson were still not forthcoming. The Jacksonville grammar schools and high schools came up without a trace of her, and Dinkins could not find a birth certificate for Patterson anywhere in Florida: he looked under the names Elizabeth Patterson and Elizabeth Patterson Dial, for a period from 1880 to 1905. Still no birth certificate. Was Alston misinformed?

Dinkins' associate began a series of telephone calls to libraries in Jacksonville and Madison for some confirmation of the Dials' residence in either city. Meanwhile, Mrs. Fay had secured a copy of the marriage license of William Henry Dial and Sara Burton Whitner. The Dials were married in Madison County, Florida, in 1890. About the same time as this license surfaced, Dinkins' associate's calls to libraries and public schools in Florida paid off. One of the school clerical workers found a 1915 item in the *Florida Times-Union* pertaining to Sara Burton Dial, Patterson's mother. Mrs. Dial, the article noted, recently moved from Madison to Jacksonville, where she had been elected chairman of the Equal Suffrage League.

With this pair of confirmations on Patterson's Florida past, Dinkins' colleague made a flurry of calls to Madison and eventually found several elderly women who remembered the Dials. The results, as always, were a mixed blessing.

One of the women contacted stated that she knew "Burtie" (Sara Burton Dial) and her daughter, who went by the name of Elizabeth Dial. She described Elizabeth as "tall and willowy with auburn hair." This source was born in 1903, and she judged Elizabeth Dial to be ten years older than she (born about 1893). This was consistent with Robert Hughes' theory, at least in regard to Patterson Dial's age.

Another Madison resident, born in 1909, "barely knew" the Dials. She knew they had a daughter Elizabeth, and guessed that Elizabeth was born in 1893.

A former neighbor of the Dials in Madison thought Elizabeth was born in 1902, and believed that "Patterson" was a family name. Elizabeth, who had red hair, attended Madison schools and probably never finished high school. She "wrote," the neighbor recalled, and later married Rupert Hughes. Her sister "Stevie" was "a beautiful person."

Faced with the persistent doubts about Rupert Hughes, and his marriages, the mixed reports about Patterson Dial (her name and age), and the overwhelming suspicions about Elspeth (not least from Cockrell himself), Dinkins decided an interview in Jacksonville with Patterson's nephew might be a good idea. Jacksonville was also the site of a related investigation by the ad litem's associate into the ultimate whereabouts of Rupert's first wife, Agnes Hughes Reynolds. Dinkins knew she and

294

William Reynolds had retired to Jacksonville, but he could find no death certificate for Agnes in that city. Her place of death was not written in the Hedge family Bible, merely the date: October 1944, five months before the deaths of Elspeth and Patterson Dial. Dinkins' associate hoped to find her certificate of death, or some other mention of her last years, in the Jacksonville record system. Perhaps Agnes' past could help to explain the bizarre mystery about her alleged daughter Elspeth, and the possible substitution of identities propounded by Robert Hughes.

Partly because of concern over the unusual system of communication necessary to reach Alston Cockrell, Jr. (the strange network of phones and the unusual characters who answered them), and partially because of the importance of Cockrell's recollections, Dinkins chose to accompany his associate to Jacksonville to interview Patterson Dial's nephew—the only such trip Dinkins made during his tenure as ad litem. It was a wise decision. If forced to make a choice, the interview with Cockrell would probably rank as his high point in a madcap five-year investigation.

With an equal blend of curiosity and apprehension, Dinkins and his law clerk boarded a plane from Houston to Jacksonville to meet the mysterious Alston Cockrell, Jr. To their happy surprise, they were treated to an unforgettable afternoon with a charming and colorful personality. Alston Cockrell, Jr., they discovered, was a magician by trade. (His stage name was ''Mars the Magician.'') That explained the unusual reference to the ''big room in a kind of office building where he was building magic tricks.'' Cockrell was in the midst of a divorce when contacted by the ad litem and was both living in and storing his equipment in a rented loft in a ''low-rent district'' in downtown Jacksonville. Because he was often on the road performing magic shows, he was almost impossible to reach by phone.

Once he had explained his ''precarious situation'' to the increasingly fascinated Dinkins and his associate, Cockrell settled into an informative discussion about his aunt and Rupert Hughes. He explained by way of background that William H. and Sara Burton Dial had two daughters: his mother, Stephena (born between 1885 and 1890 in Madison) and Elizabeth Patterson (born in 1902 in Madison). Mr. Dial died in 1913 at the age of thirty-five. Sara Dial, Alston's grandmother, was raised in Richmond by several aunts, and was extremely close to a cousin of hers named Elizabeth Patterson, in whose honor she named her youngest daughter, Elizabeth Patterson Dial. Stephena Dial married Alston's father, Alston Cockrell, Sr., in 1914, and the two resided in Jacksonville. Sara Dial and Elizabeth soon joined them, and moved into a house at 1838 St. John's Avenue.

Patterson Dial moved to New York from Jacksonville about 1920, starting as a dancer. She later appeared in a musical called *Aphrodite,* and worked in pictures with actor Richard Barthelmes and "the Gish girls." One of the films she made in New York was called *Way Down East.* Patterson lived in Manhattan, where her mother Sara B. Dial eventually joined her. According to Cockrell, Patterson stayed in New York a year or two, "until things went to hell." Sara Dial died in New York in the early 1920s, and Patterson moved back to Jacksonville and lived with the Cockrells for several months. (Alston was then five or six years old.) He claims she talked of starting a dancing school in Jacksonville, until she received a telegram from Hollywood with a contract enclosed. In 1920 or 1921, she left for Hollywood and immediately got a part in a film. "She didn't struggle," he recollected.

While making one of several films in California, his aunt met Rupert Hughes. Cockrell was told that she "stuck a pin in her finger" on the set, and Rupert Hughes offered his help. This began their courtship. He was not told which film his aunt was making when this introduction occurred, nor does he know the year. He remembered one film Patterson made before she married Rupert, in which she played a prostitute. As he tells the story, she purchased a pair of cufflinks for Rupert with the money she earned, "so she could say she'd walked the streets for him."

Alston met Rupert Hughes before Hughes and Patterson were married. The meeting was in 1923, during a trip to California with Stephena Cockrell. After the Hugheses were married, Alston returned to California to spend the summer with them in 1925 and again in 1931, when he was eight and fourteen years old, respectively. He remembers that his aunt and Rupert seemed very close. At some point in his adolescence, Cockrell attended a boarding school in Maryland, paid for by Rupert Hughes. (Alston, Sr., was not doing well financially.) In 1935, Alston's mother Stephena was diagnosed as having cancer and rented a house in Los Angeles a block from Rupert and Pat's to undergo medical treatments. Alston stayed with his aunt and Rupert for all of that year, during which he landed a few small parts in motion pictures. In 1936–37, when Alston was twenty years old, Rupert financed his studies at the American Academy in New York. Stephena Cockrell, Alston's mother, died in Jacksonville in 1938.

After completing his dramatic studies at the American Academy, Cockrell returned to Florida. Fighting a drinking problem,he enlisted in the Army for five years, and his aunt Patterson died in 1945 while he was in Germany. His father, Alston, Sr., wrote Cockrell with the bad news. (It is Alston's belief that Patterson Dial died from a mixture of whiskey and sleeping pills. "She wasn't a pillhead or an alcoholic," he noted defensively.) Alston wrote Rupert Hughes a letter of condolence after his aunt's death, and Hughes "insisted" Alston come live with him. Cockrell agreed and moved into the Hughes home on Los Feliz. Rupert told Alston he "was gonna do big things for him," that he'd be the "son he never had," etc. He entreated Alston to "quit drinking and stay here." According to Cockrell, this arrangement didn't last too long. Alston stayed out one night, and Rupert found him and ordered him back to Los Feliz. With no further discussion, Hughes told him to pack up and go back to Jacksonville. Although Alston apologized, the situation between the two of them was never resolved. As Cockrell described it, he got "bad vibes" from Rupert.

Alston stayed on in Los Angeles another six months (at a different residence). He visited Rupert Hughes at Christmas, but relations were still strained. By this time, he noted, "things had changed" for Rupert: his work was not selling, and his career and finances were on the decline. Cockrell moved back to Jacksonville, and never saw Rupert again. He did receive a small wedding present from him in 1947, and Hughes mailed a box of Patterson's memorabilia in the late 1940s, at the time he sold the Los Feliz house. The next news Alston received was of Rupert Hughes' death in 1956.

In addition to this chronology of Patterson Dial and himself, Alston Cockrell, Jr. had a number of other interesting observations about Rupert and his hangers-on to share with Dinkins and his clerk.

He said, for example, that Rupert Hughes believed that funerals were "barbaric," and insisted that he be cremated. (As did Patterson Dial.) This fact would later become relevant to Dinkins' investigation in a rather bizarre way.

On his birthdays, Rupert Hughes would pretend to be ten years old. His first pen name as an author had been "George Robinson," and Hughes would "become" George Robinson on his birthday. He also requested that his guests present him with "kiddie" birthday gifts.

According to Alston, Jr., Rupert Hughes and Alston, Sr., had a "closeness." After Patterson Dial's death of a barbiturate overdose, Alston Cockrell, Sr., would have "nothing to do with" Rupert, and he would never tell Alston, Jr., why. Alston still doesn't know. (Cockrell, Sr., died in 1961.)

Alston remembered "always hearing" that Adelaide Manola Hughes was a heavy drinker, and an "expensive" woman. She caused Rupert financial strain. When Rupert and Patterson Dial met, Hughes described himself as a "near millionaire"—meaning a millionaire in debts. This was understood to be the result of Adelaide's heavy spending, although Cockrell said that Rupert spent money lavishly as well.

On the subject of Avis and Rush, Alston noted that Rush was a radio announcer who "tried to pawn himself off as Rupert's son." Rupert,

Alston declared, "seemed to resent them."

There was tremendous friction between Rupert and Howard Hughes, Jr. Alston recalled that Howard, Jr., once lived on North Rossmore (the Judge and Jean Hughes' house in Los Angeles), and Rupert was acting as his "guardian." Howard, Jr., was getting $100 monthly allowance and resented asking Rupert for money. Patterson Dial also disliked Howard, Jr., Cockrell added.

Alston "first heard" of Elspeth on the occasion of the dinner party held at his parents' home on St. Johns Avenue in Jacksonville in 1928, even though he had then known Rupert for more than five years. There was "no closeness" between Hughes and Elspeth, he observed; the two did not even sit at the same table at the Cockrell home.

He described Elspeth as "medium to short, dumpy, dark black hair, swarthy complexion, buxom, not attractive."

She was not introduced as Rupert's daughter; Alston "just knew" she was. He never actually heard Rupert *deny* that Elspeth was his daughter, he just "heard rumors." "Her mother had other friends," Cockrell stated.

He insisted Elspeth was not his aunt's daughter, when presented with Robert Hughes' theory. The two were no more than cordial, he related: Patterson felt that Elspeth was a "moocher," and Elspeth thought Patterson stood in the way of getting something out of Rupert.

Alston did not know the origin of the name "Elspeth," and had never heard it was an acronym for Elizabeth Patterson.

After the interview, Cockrell invited Dinkins and his clerk to visit his loft, an invitation that Dinkins eagerly accepted. When Cockrell could wrest Dinkins away from his magic props, he showed the ad litem and his associate a collection of letters he had received from his aunt and Rupert over the years. It was clear from the correspondence that Alston and Patterson Dial were extremely close. Before Dinkins and partner left the loft, Cockrell happened to remember a short story written by his aunt years before. (Alston had occasionally typed her manuscripts when he was in California and in this way had become familiar with some of her fiction.) The short story that came to mind, he said, was called "The Secret Child."

Dinkins' associate took advantage of the trip to Jacksonville to do a little more sleuthing into Patterson Dial's past, to confirm what her nephew had related about her background. She rented a car and drove on to Patterson's home of Madison, Florida (population: 3737), about a ninety-minute drive west of Jacksonville. Madison was reported to be Patterson's home from 1902 to 1915, before her mother's move to Jacksonville. The Madison Courthouse had no birth, death, or marriage records pertaining to any of the Dials: William H., Sara B.,

298

Stephena, or Elizabeth Patterson. Nor did the Madison School Board: neither Stephena nor Elizabeth's names appeared in public school records between 1905 and 1915, under the surname Patterson or Dial. However, one longtime Madison resident recalled that grammar school students attended class in a courthouse until 1913. In one of the many flukes associated with the heirship investigation, all these records had been destroyed in a fire. The Madison Public Library, essentially a one-room affair, had no helpful information on the Dials, either; likewise the City Hall and Chamber of Commerce.

Finally, Dinkins' associate visited the offices of the *Madison Enterprise-Recorder*, the local newspaper. Back issues, what there were of them, were kept in the newspaper office itself (again, essentially a one-room building)—not, as is usually the case, at the public library. The old editions of the paper that had been retained were in their original form in large volumes, which the newspaper custodian was none too willing to share. Plainly, she was not accustomed to nor did she approve of requests to examine back issues of the paper. The pages of these books were in such fragile condition (yellowed and brittle) that simply turning a page could cause it to disintegrate. (In fact, many of the pages were torn or missing as it was.) This precarious situation was complicated by the spotty collection itself; many months, and occasionally entire years, of the *Enterprise-Recorder* were missing. Obviously, there was no index, so the books had to be perused one by one.

Dinkins' associate was undeterred by either the manager's attitude or the unpromising conditions for research, and searched what volumes were available for some mention of the Dial family to confirm Alston Cockrell's family history. The first sign of hope was an obituary for William H. Dial (whom both Alston and Patterson identified as Elizabeth Patterson Dial's father), dated January 3, 1913:

W. H. DIAL ANSWERS FINAL SUMMONS

On Tuesday afternoon, December 24, William H. Dial passed away at his home in this city after a short illness.

Mr. Dial was born in Madison March 3, 1870. . . . He attended college at the South Carolina Citadel in Charleston, and graduated there at the age of 18, being the youngest ever turned out from that institution.

On September 22, 1890, he was married to Miss Sarah Burton Whitner of Richmond, Virginia, who with two daughters, Misses Stevie and Elizabeth, survive him.

Mr. Dial . . . was when a young man Mayor of the town . . . Chairman of the County Commissioners . . . first Captain of the old Madison Guards. For several years he was engaged in the hardware business in this city.

The funeral services were held at the Oak Grove Cemetery on Wednesday afternoon, being conducted by the Reverend Curtis Grubb, rector of the Episcopalian Church.

By this account, Mr. Dial died just at the time that Alston Cockrell had said. The obituary also verified that Dial had two daughters, Stevie and Elizabeth: confirming what was increasingly clear—that Elizabeth Patterson Dials's maiden name was Dial, not Patterson. Unfortunately, the obituary did not state Elizabeth's age, and since the Dials (William and Sara) were married in 1890, it was at least possible that Elizabeth Patterson Dial was born earlier than 1902, as Robert C. Hughes had maintained.

Dinkins' clerk also found in the old volumes an announcement of Stephena Dial's wedding to Alston Cockrell, Sr. ("a prominent young attorney of Jacksonville and a popular member of Jacksonville's social circles"), taking place in New York City on September 17, 1914. There was no mention of her sister.

After locating these two articles about the Dials, Dinkins' associate began the tedious and time-consuming process of searching through the available newspaper volumes in the likely period of Elizabeth Patterson Dial's birth. Though birth announcements were far from standard in newspapers, this was the last hope for finding some semiofficial record of Patterson Dial's date of birth, since it was plainly not recorded in the state of Florida's official register: Dinkins simply could not locate a birth certificate for Elizabeth Patterson Dial. Unfortunately, the *Enterprise-Recorder* did not run a regular column or feature announcing births, from what Dinkins' associate could discern in her perusal of back issues. Thus it was necessary to scan every page of every edition for a possible reference to Elizabeth Patterson Dial's birth. Since Robert Hughes could not remember exactly when she was born (the 1890s, he thought), Dinkins' colleague began instead with the period surrounding the date that Patterson Dial noted on her marriage certificate and her passport application: May 19, 1902.

There was no reference to the birth of Patterson Dial in the newspaper on that day or several days thereafter. But on May 22, 1902, in a social feature called "Town Topics," was this entry: "Born to Mr. and Mrs. W. H. Dial, Jr., on Monday, 19th inst., a girl baby." What was perhaps more startling than the discovery of this notation of the birth of a little girl Dial on May 19, 1902 (the date of birth Patterson Dial gave

300

for herself), was the fact that there was a parenthesis in blue ink marked on the side of the entry. Judging from its appearance, and the condition of the ink, the mark had been made recently. Someone had obviously discovered this reference to the May 19, 1902, birthdate not too much before Dinkins' associate.

Before leaving Madison, Dinkins' assistant stopped by the local Episcopal Church. The reference to William Dial's funeral service indicated that the Dials were members of the Episcopal Church, and Dinkins' colleague hoped to confirm the birth of Elizabeth Patterson Dial in May 1902 (or whatever other "girl baby" was born to the Dials on that date), by checking on the baptismal records. The local vicar promised to conduct a thorough search and report his results. A week later, he wrote to Dinkins' associate to say:

> RE: William Henry Dial, Stephana, Elizabeth Patterson et al. I can find nothing in our registers regarding them. We have two registers on hand: one of these has a few entries which cover the dates in question (i.e. 1891 AD - 1913 AD) but there is clearly a missing book which would have had most of these items. I have twice asked the congregation and leaders about another register. No one knows of another book.

To complete the circle of genealogy on Elizabeth Patterson Dial, Dinkins' associate visited Stephena (Stevie) Cockrell Scott, Alston Cockrell, Jr.'s, daughter, and the custodian of the original box of Patterson Dial's memorabilia, sent after Patterson's death in 1945 to Alston from Rupert Hughes. ("I'm the family historian," she joked.) Stevie Scott, named for her grandmother Stephena Dial Cockrell (Elizabeth Patterson Dial's sister), is fascinated by her great-aunt Patterson (who died before she was born), and was "thrilled to death" to assist Dinkins' associate in the search for background information on her family.

Dinkin's assistant learned, for example, Stevie Cockrell's explanation for Elizabeth Patterson Dial's name: "Now she had . . . Patty, her name was Elizabeth Patterson Dial. But she went by Patterson. . . . I'll tell you why. She was named for a woman in Virginia named Elizabeth Patterson, who she absolutely despised . . . and she was called Lizzie. And Patterson Dial did not like Lizzie, so I think that's the reason she dropped Elizabeth. But I think ever since childhood she was called Pat."

Elizabeth Patterson was a cousin of Sara Burton Dial (Patterson Dial's mother). Elizabeth was raised on a large estate in Richmond, Virginia, called "Reveille." Sara Burton was brought up at Reveille as well and brought her two daughters, Stevie and Patterson, to visit Elizabeth Patterson in Richmond quite often.

301

Included in Stevie Cockrell's heirloom collection is a photograph album put together by her grandmother, Stephena Dial, before her marriage to Alston Cockrell, Sr. The pictures are mostly of Stephena and her sister Elizabeth/Patterson (also known, for some undisclosed reason, as "Miss Witz"), taken at Reveille when Stephena was seventeen and Patterson seven years old. The difference in their ages is indisputable from these photographs. "Pictures I've got, but it's the documents I don't have," Stevie Scott noted regretfully. There was, she admitted, no family Bible to confirm the dates of birth of the two Dial girls, nor were there baptismal certificates. What she did have, ironically, was a book on the Dial family genealogy published in 1931 and commissioned by Rupert Hughes and his last wife Patterson! The two of them, along with Alston's mother, Stephena Dial Cockrell, hired a genealogist to write a book eventually called *The Duval Family of Virginia*. The information on Patterson and her background was, therefore, furnished by Patterson herself—along with her husband Rupert, who took an active part in the formulation of the book in its various stages of research. Included in the "box" in Stevie's possession is a letter Hughes wrote to his sister-in-law Stephena in 1928 concerning the progress of the genealogy:

Dearest Stevie:

I have read with interest your letter and the letter from your genealogist, Mrs. Grabowsky, and she makes a better impression on me than she apparently does on the rest of you. My father spent years corresponding with scores of people and having records searched for wills and dates and it is an ungodly job. . . .

I do not believe in delaying too long in these matters as fire and apoplexy have a devastating effect on genealogy. . . .

The important thing is to trace the lineage incontrovertibly showing just who is who's father beyond dispute. . . .

Yours devotedly,
Rupert

The irony (and possible significance) of this letter was not lost on Dinkins' associate. It revealed several things. That Rupert's father, Judge Felix Hughes, took a great interest in genealogy and "spent years" pursuing family records—a highly interesting revelation in light of Robert Hughes' accusations about the judge and his assumed ancestry, switching from Felix Moner to the "more aristocratic" Felix Turner Hughes branch of the family. More relevant was Rupert Hughes' participation and interest in the genealogy project. It was obvious from the correspondence in Stevie Scott's box of memorabilia that Rupert Hughes was monitoring the progress on the Dial genealogy, and in fact assisting in the research. That Rupert Hughes should instruct Stephena Cockrell that the "important thing is to trace the lineage incontrovertibly showing just who is who's father beyond dispute" was ironic in the extreme, for it was Rupert Hughes' alleged daughter who was then the subject of a multimillion-dollar scrutiny concerning her paternity.

As scrupulous as Rupert obviously was about genealogical record-keeping, and as interested as he was in tracing ancestry, why in the world did he omit his natural daughter in his Case Western alumni information forms and in his *Who's Who* biography? More incriminating still, why did he not include Elspeth in his sworn application to join the Sons of the American Revolution (introduced during the heirship trial)? It is an indisputable fact that Rupert Hughes took great stock in tracing lineage and genealogy, leading to the inevitable conclusion that he simply did not recognize that he had a daughter in those instances. No other conclusion would be realistic. Rupert Hughes' letter to his sister-in-law also revealed his acute awareness of the effect of "fire" and such on genealogy. Did he perhaps use that knowledge to suppress facts about his own past that he wished to remain secret? And did his and his wife Patterson Dial's eagerness to compile a book on the Dial genealogy suggest a desire to set the record straight on her past—as they wished it to read? These were only suppositions, of course, but tempting ones at that. After all the research and correspondence, the date of Rupert Hughes' and Elizabeth Patterson Dial's marriage is incorrectly reflected in the Dial book of genealogy as 1925 instead of 1924.

Stevie Scott also had a collection of movie stills from Patterson Dial's acting career in the early 1920s and several pictures of her father, Alston, Jr., at the Los Feliz house in California. "My father used to tell me he used to dive from the roof into the swimming pool," she remarked. "Crazy! They were all crazy!" She also observed that Patterson Dial was like a surrogate mother to Alston. "Oh yeah, they were very close—*very* close. Yeah. He was like a son to her. He would go out there to visit." One of her pictures shows Patterson Dial and nine-year-old Alston together in California in 1926. As Stevie Scott and Dinkins' representative studied the photograph more closely, they both noticed something strange about it:

Interviewer: I guess if this was [taken] in '26, she would have been about twenty-four. [Pause] Does she look older than that to you?

303

Scott: Yeah, she does.

Interviewer: She really does look older.

Scott: 1902 would be right, and that would make her twenty-four. She does look older, she really does. Look at that. I don't know if its the sun or what, but she looks much older.

Interviewer: She looks almost like she's in her mid-thirties.

Scott: Uh-huh. At least.

Finally, although Stevie Scott's grandfather Alston Cockrell, Sr., was alive until Stevie was eleven years old, the two never discussed Patterson Dial; therefore Stevie had no idea why Cockrell, Sr., became estranged from Rupert Hughes after Patterson's death.

While the Florida trip closed a number of doors relative to Robert Hughes' theory about Elspeth/Leila/Elizabeth Patterson Dial, it opened several more: if not related to Robert's specific allegations, then related to the questions about Rupert in general, such as his marital history, Rush and Avis, and of course Elspeth. Dinkins now had a birth notation in a newspaper in May 1902 for a baby girl Dial born in Madison (unfortunately, she is not mentioned by name); confirmation that a Dial family resided in Florida (as opposed to a Patterson family); pictures of Elizabeth Patterson Dial and her sister at ages seven and seventeen; an explanation for the name "Elizabeth Patterson Dial" and Pat's use of her middle name; and her nephew Alston's belief she had no children, as well as his independent verification of the Dial family history.

Yet for all that, the ad litem also had the following to consider:

Why did Elizabeth Patterson Dial use the names Elizabeth and Patterson somewhat interchangeably, despite Stevie Cockrell's statement to the contrary, and why did several people remember her as Elizabeth *Patterson* (not Dial)?

Why did Patterson Dial appear to be in her mid-thirties in the picture taken with her nephew in 1926, when she should have been twenty-four? And why did Frances McLain Smith (Rupert's cousin's daughter) believe her to be in her mid-thirties "at least," at the dinner party at Los Feliz in 1925?

If Elizabeth Patterson Dial and Elspeth were "extremely distant" as Alston related, then why did Elspeth name her daughter Barbara Patterson Lapp in Patterson's honor?

304

Why the strange and suggestive letters from Rupert Hughes to Elspeth just before Elspeth's and Patterson Dial's deaths in 1945? What was the true story of Patterson Dial's death?

What caused the bitter estrangement between Alston Cockrell, Sr., and Rupert Hughes after the death of Cockrell's sister-in-law Patterson Dial in 1945, and that Alston Cockrell, Sr., wouldn't even tell his own son?

The "bad vibes" Alston picked up from Rupert Hughes after Rupert threw Alston out of the Los Feliz house in 1946.

Why was Rupert Hughes so eager to adopt the orphans of the world, while not recognizing that he had a natural daughter? (Witness Rush/Avis, Marshall Ricksen, Frances McLain, and Alston Cockrell, Jr.)

Alston stated Rupert Hughes had "many wives" before Patterson Dial—more than two?

Alston's guarded comments about Elspeth's parentage, and his statement that her mother "had many friends," coupled with his belief that Adelaide was her mother.

Rupert Hughes' intense interest in genealogy, and accurate family record-keeping, contrasted with his disavowal of Elspeth.

Alston Cockrell's feelings about Rupert Hughes' attitude toward Rush and Avis. (Was it a travesty of justice that their adoption claims were never litigated?)

Perhaps most germane to the underlying significance of Dinkins' heirship investigation was Alston's confirmation of the rumored ill will between Howard R. Hughes, Jr., and Rupert Hughes. Cockrell's comments were not the first the ad litem had heard on this subject. All indications were that the enmity developed after the death of Howard Hughes, Jr.'s, father in 1924, and the ensuing positioning within the family for control of Howard, Sr.'s, estate.

There are competing reports as to the particulars of these attempts: Betty Rimell Westbrook (Elspeth's maid of honor) remembered that it was Rupert who assumed the position of Sonny's guardian; Mrs. Frances Smith stated that Jean Hughes asked her to "take over" caring for Howard; a grand-nephew of Adella Prentiss Hughes was told it was Adella's husband, Felix; and Alston Cockrell, Jr., declared that Rupert Hughes not only acted as Sonny's guardian, but put him on a $100-a-month allowance. Lee Harrell Palmer, the friend of Patterson Dial and Rupert Hughes' from the twenties and thirties, gave attorneys in the heirship case Rupert's version: "(Rupert) told me at one time that when his brother died, that he and Pat called and offered him a home if he wanted it. They felt that he was a young man and might be terribly lonely, and they were offering their home and their love to him if he needed it. And Howard did not seem particularly interested in the offer."

No doubt Mrs. Palmer's version of Rupert's gesture is not entirely accurate. Frances Smith told Dinkins' associate that Rupert Hughes was "disgusted" with his nephew at the time, and that Sonny was "hard to manage." Combined with Alston Cockrell's comments that Rupert Hughes was "nearly broke" from Adelaide's excessive spending in 1924, it would suggest that Rupert's interest in Howard, Jr., were not entirely altruistic. (Dinkin's associate even found copies of correspondence from Rupert Hughes to various editors and cronies in the 1912–1917 period in which Rupert makes mention of his "millionaire brother" in Texas, indicating that Howard R. Hughes, Sr.'s estate was not foreign to Rupert Hughes' thinking—even while his brother was still a relatively young man. Ironically, when Howard, Sr., died in 1924, the only family member he had excluded from his will was his brother Rupert.)

The real story behind the threatened guardianship proceedings and the negotiations for Howard, Sr.'s estate, will probably never be known. The results of the power struggle, however, are quite clear: Howard R. Hughes, Jr., and Rupert Hughes were bitter enemies thereafter, all of their adult lives. Whether this was due entirely to the estate takeover is a matter of conjecture; possibly there were other reasons for Howard, Jr.'s, contempt for Rupert Hughes. Whatever its basis, it was no secret. Nearly every aide who was with Howard R. Hughes, Jr., in the last decades of his life testified in his deposition that "the Boss" hated his uncle Rupert. One of the aides even mentioned that Hughes told him Rupert was involved with drugs and lived a "bohemian" life in Hollywood. Rupert Hughes' contempt for Howard was equally publicized. In a famous 1954 three-part *Look* Magazine series called "The Howard Hughes Story," author Stephen White outlined certain of the "Hughes legends." Rupert Hughes figured in one of them: "Howard's uncle Rupert won his animosity during the struggle for control of Hughes' father's estate. The two men were enemies for decades. The novelist was once asked why he didn't talk to his nephew, and replied, 'When I get down on my knees I can talk to God, but there's no way to talk to Howard Hughes.' " Then of course there was Alston Cockrell, Jr.'s, comment, in response to Dinkins' clerk's suggestion that he was being contacted regarding the Howard Hughes estate: "(My aunt) wouldn't let the son-of-a-bitch in the house!"

The irony in this situation was unmistakable. Rupert Hughes' descendants were poised to inherit millions of dollars of Howard R. Hughes, Jr.'s, estate—the estate Howard, Jr., fought so feverishly to wrest away from Rupert decades earlier, at the time of his father's death. To add to this sardonic situation, it was highly questionable whether these five individuals were even legitimate heirs of Rupert's.

If Howard R. Hughes, Jr., was not dead in 1976, as a few of the more deranged of Dinkins' correspondents claimed, then this news would almost certainly have killed him. No inheritance scheme imaginable could have been further from his intentions.

Elspeth's Half-Brother Speaks Up

In Jacksonville, Dinkins' colleague picked up the trail of Agnes Hedge Hughes Reynolds (Elspeth's alleged mother) whose activities after her divorce from Rupert were mostly unknown. City directories revealed that William and Agnes Reynolds moved to Jacksonville (from Washington) in 1923, just as Barbara Cameron had suggested. By then, Elspeth was married to Ed Lapp, and William H. Reynolds had retired from the Navy. William and Agnes Reynolds moved into a house at 2223 St. John's Avenue—just three blocks from the Cockrell residence at 1838 St. John's Avenue. (Elizabeth Patterson Dial lived for a time with Alston and Stephena Cockrell at this home in the early 1920s, between her careers in New York and Hollywood). That meant that Rupert's first wife, from whom he was bitterly divorced, and his last wife's family (and occasionally Patterson Dial herself) were near neighbors in Jacksonville, Florida.

William Reynolds died in 1937, and his widow Agnes did not continue to appear in the Jacksonville directories. Though the Reynolds and the Cockrells moved several times between 1923 and 1937, their homes were always within close proximity of each other in a fashionable older Jacksonville neighborhood. Their paths must have crossed. Furthermore, Alston Cockrell, Jr., told Dinkins and his clerk that Rupert Hughes and Elizabeth Patterson Dial spent the summer of 1928 with the Cockrells—just down the street from Agnes Hedge Hughes Reynolds! In the context of Robert Hughes' strange theory that Elizabeth Patterson Dial was actually Elspeth's mother, that Agnes and Rupert were the parents of Leila Hughes (who drowned), and that all of the parties were in collusion to substitute Elspeth for the deceased Leila (Robert's explanation was that Rupert Hughes paid Agnes off to go along with the scheme)—the proximity of the Reynolds and Cockrells certainly added a strange twist to an already bizarre situation.

Dinkins' colleague consulted the Jacksonville newspaper index for the year 1944 (indicated in the Hedge Bible to be Agnes' year of death), on the chance that Agnes Reynold's obituary might appear, even though there was no death certificate on record for her in Jacksonville. Indeed it did. The *Florida Times-Union*, October 15, 1944, announced the death of "Mrs. Herbert Reynolds", former Jacksonville resident:

> Mrs. Herbert Reynolds, former Jacksonville resident, died Thursday in Virginia, friends here learned yesterday, and was buried in Arlington National Cemetery.
>
> Mrs. Reynolds and her husband, the late Captain Herbert Reynolds, moved to Jacksonville in 1923 following Captain Reynolds' retirement from the U.S. Navy. They were both prominent here for many years.
>
> Mrs. Reynolds was a member of the Riverside Presbyterian Church and served twice as president of the Woman's Auxiliary of that church.
>
> Surviving are a son, William Reynolds of Newport News, Va., a daughter, Mrs. Edward J. Lapp of Cleveland, Ohio, and four grandchildren.

With this announcement, Dinkins was able to do several things. He secured, at last, a copy of Agnes' death certificate from the Virginia (not Florida) state registrar. Mrs. Reynolds died at the age of seventy (born March 1874, two years later than Rupert Hughes), of arteriosclerosis. She was buried (not cremated) at Arlington Cemetery, next to William H. Reynolds. According to her death certificate, Agnes Hughes Reynolds had been a patient at the Eastern State hospital for the insane for almost four years before her death.

The arrival of Agnes' death certificate simply added to the mystique that was building about Rupert and Elspeth. It was now evident that of Rupert Hughes' three known wives, one hanged herself on a boat in China, another died of a drug overdose, and the third (reportedly the mother of his child) died in a mental institution. The romantic image of Rupert Hughes first presented to Dinkins and his associate—a warm and loving grandfather, then a rich and successful author living in bucolic splendor in Bedford Hills—was being challenged by a darker, almost sinister persona, whose personal and career triumphs were punctuated with ugly or mysterious incidents. For all the reports of Hughes' generous and loving nature, there were matching recollections of enmity, hostility, and estrangement. More disturbing, those who felt bitterest toward Hughes (Bissell, Cockrell, Sr., Howard R. Hughes, Jr., to name three) would never say why, implying perhaps that it was something too awful to talk about. Rupert Hughes' rumored drug experimentation, bohemian style of living, and the many other innuendoes hurled against him, could not be easily reconciled with the "loving" human being known to Barbara Cameron and her sisters in the last ten years of his life. To Dinkins and his investigators, Rupert Hughes truly seemed to be a man of many faces.

The information in Agnes Reynolds' Jacksonville obituary led Dinkins to a key figure in the heirship investigation, and later a star witness at the heirship trial. The announcement of her death in 1944 mentioned a surviving son, William H. Reynolds, Jr., then a resident of Virginia. Dinkins' associate found him, and in doing so opened the door to another piece of Rupert and Elspeth's past.

Young Reynolds was the son of Agnes by her second husband, Navy officer William H. Reynolds, Sr. William, Jr., was born in 1913 and proved to be an intelligent, softspoken gentleman with a historian's recollection of dates, names, and places. He referred to Elspeth as "Sister" ("I was taught to call her that," he explained), and expressed not even the slightest doubt that she was anything other than the daughter of his mother and Rupert Hughes—his half-sister. At the trial, his testimony would be a compelling element of Paul Freese's case on behalf of Elspeth's three daughters: Barbara Cameron and her sisters. Yet, amazingly, at the time Dinkins' associate located Reynolds, Jr., in 1978, he had not been contacted by anyone else involved in the heirship case, despite the fact that it was his half-sister Elspeth whose identity was at issue. More surprising than that was the fact that Reynolds had not seen Elspeth's three children to speak of since 1945, the year of her death.

Reynolds repeated the accepted Hughes genealogy that Elspeth was born in May 1897; that she was sixteen years older than he. Since William, Jr., was born in 1913, however, he was not really acquainted with his half-sister until she was a young adult. Even as late as 1920, Reynolds was only seven years old; therefore most of what he "knows" about Elspeth and Rupert Hughes is what he has been told by his mother Agnes. Reynolds is the only living child of Lieutenant and Agnes Reynolds; however, his mother had two other children by her second husband (in 1914 and 1918) who died within ten hours after birth. She also suffered several miscarriages.

According to Reynolds, his mother was a "brilliant" woman, a staunch Presbyterian, and a strict disciplinarian. ("Mother said she spanked Sister when she was sixteen years old. She believed in discipline.") His mother, Agnes, he explained by way of background, was born in Buffalo to Charles and Julia Hedge in 1874, an only child. The family moved to Syracuse, New York, in 1882, when Agnes was eight years old. "Grandfather Hedge was an insurance agent," Reynolds related. "I think he went there because it was a business promotion." In Syracuse, Agnes attended a private school run by "two maiden ladies." Her debutante years were spent touring Europe, first with the graduates of her finishing school, later with her father. ("She said that first trip she got all the culture, going over there with her father she said she had all the good time.")

After graduating in 1892, Agnes attended Evelyn College, a now-defunct woman's college associated with Princeton University, for a year and a half. It was during her second year at Evelyn that Agnes Hedge met Rupert Hughes, and she dropped out in 1893 to marry him. According to Reynolds, the two met through an older cousin of Agnes', Maude Field Clark, the widow of an officer. Mrs. Clark ran a boarding house on West 55th Street in New York City. "Yeah, Cousin Maude . . . I think Mother used to go and visit her on weekends, I think it was at her house that she met Rupert Hughes." Rupert Hughes, a recent graduate of Adelbert College, was just starting his writing career at the time and attending graduate school at both Adelbert and Yale simultaneously. Hughes was twenty-one; Agnes nineteen. They married at St. George's Episcopal in New York City. ("It has a nickname it's known by," remarked Reynolds. "It's called the 'Little Church Around the Corner.' . . . It's a favorite place for marriages down in lower New York City.") "Well, the Hugheses were Episcopal," Reynolds stated, "and I think Mother went to the Episcopal Church there in New York, mostly, because cousin Maude was Episcopal, too."

Reynolds' knowledge of his mother's ten-year marriage to Rupert Hughes is sketchy. "It was happy at first," he reflected. "Now, at first, a lot of that she went to Europe, they lived in Europe. After they got back maybe things fell apart, I don't know." (Research indicates that Rupert Hughes and Agnes were married from 1893 to 1904. They were only in Europe a year and a half, from May 1900 to November 1901, while Rupert Hughes was employed by the Encyclopedia Britannica.) Agnes never talked about Rupert Hughes to her son. "Well, Mother never, she always—if she ever mentioned his name in conversation, which would have been with my sister entirely, she always spoke of him as 'RH'." Reynolds confirmed what the *New York Times* newspaper divorce articles already suggested: that there was a great deal of animosity between Rupert Hughes and his first wife. "Mother never saw him after they were divorced," he observed. "The only correspondence, the only thing she ever had to do with him was when my sister was married, she sent him the bill for the wedding."

Agnes' attitude toward Rupert Hughes was obviously instilled in her son at an early age. "See, Rupert Hughes . . . was married twice after Mother left him," Reynolds told Dinkins' clerk, "and both of his other wives committed suicide. He must not have been easy to live with or something." In conversations with William H. Reynolds, Jr., it is obvious that his mother had a very dominant personality, and that she exerted a strong influence over her son, particularly in the way she presented the circumstances of her breakup with Rupert Hughes. She told William, Jr., next to nothing about her marriage to Hughes, and almost never mentioned Hughes in conversation. From the perspective his mother gave him on the divorce, the fault was all Rupert's. "Mother said that Rupert Hughes was carrying on with a neighbor at the time she divorced him," Reynolds noted. "I know I asked Mother what she did with his wedding ring. She took the ferry over to Staten Island and threw it in the Bay!"

Reynolds was aware that the divorce was "real sensational," but this information was not gleaned from his mother. "When I was married," he explained, "my mother-in-law felt that maybe I ought to know what happened . . . so they wouldn't throw it up to me or something. She got (my father-in-law) to go to the New York Public Library and research that divorce case and it was real sensational." Even then, Reynolds seemed somehow ignorant—by choice or by fact—of the scandalous accusations Rupert Hughes made against his mother, charging her with adultery with eight to ten different men. Asked by Dinkins' colleague if Reynolds accused Agnes of any indiscretions, he replied innocently, "Well, he might have, because they had a lot of young friends, young naval officers at the time—that's how my father . . . Mother's best friend in Syracuse had married one of these . . . They were all attached to the old Battleship Texas. There were all young lieutenants attached to it, and it was probably through this friend that was married to one of them (Molly Hinds)." Reynolds seemed to believe that the divorce allegations were a product of New York state's sole ground for divorce at the time: adultery. "In New York City there were lawyers and all kinds of people by the hundreds that just made a living framing up fake adulteries," he declared. "That was quite a racket in New York. I don't know whether it was one of those framed-up cases or not." Reynolds did believe, however, that it was Rupert Hughes who got the divorce from his mother.

About his half-sister, Elspeth, Reynolds had more to say. He mentioned, for example, that as a baby and little girl, Elspeth was tended by a British nanny by the name of Miss Page. When William, Jr., was born sixteen years later, in May 1913, Agnes asked Miss Page to come back to care for him as well. "When I came along, I don't know how Mother got hold of her again," he pondered. Even more interesting, Reynolds had an explanation for the name "Elspeth." "Mother," he explained, "read the story by James M. Barrie, a story called *Sentimental Tommy* . . . and he had a minor character in that, a minor character named Elspeth. 'Elspeth': it's just the Scotch form of Elizabeth. Mother, I think Mother picked that name for—she was carrying a child then." Reynolds could not be as explicit regarding Elspeth's baptism. He was convinced she was baptized, though, because *he* was, and because his mother Agnes was a regular churchgoer. "I remember Sister told me," he

311

remarked, "said Mother was always so strict about taking her to Sunday School, and I imagine Mother took her around the corner to the Church of the Pilgrims in Washington that they belonged to." The Reynolds did not move to Washington until 1906 or so, however, and William, Jr., did not know at which church Elspeth was christened in 1897, particularly since Agnes was Presbyterian and Rupert Hughes was then Episcopalian.

Reynolds was even more vague about Elspeth's custody arrangements. "I don't know," he said frankly, "I say, my father-in-law looked that up in New York Public Library, and I think he said that maybe he (Rupert) got the custody of the child. I don't know." Agnes and Rupert Hughes were divorced sometime in 1904. Agnes Hughes married William H. Reynolds, Sr., in November 1904. Soon afterward, the Reynolds moved from New York to Washington. Reynolds knew nothing about Elspeth's summer visits to Rupert Hughes' Bedford Hills farm. Asked about Elspeth's schooling, Reynolds recalled that she went to the National Cathedral School "when she was back living in Washington with my parents." He had also heard that she attended St. Mary's School—an Episcopalian boarding school in Peekskill, New York. "That's all I know about," he declared. "I don't think Sister ever went to public schools. I doubt it. Mother was a great believer in private schools."

Reynolds has a photograph album of his mother's, dating from approximately the time William, Jr., was born in 1913, in which Elspeth is pictured at the age of sixteen holding Reynolds as a baby. "Now, she looked pretty much like that all her life," he remarked. "She got heavier a little bit, but she was stocky, anyway." The pictures of Elspeth continue up to the early 1940s, before her death. Reynolds has no pictures of Elspeth taken before 1913, and has never seen any. "I don't know whether they got lost in the shuffle or one of the grandchildren might have them," he pondered, "I don't know." Reynolds saw Elspeth consistently from the time he was a little boy (he was born in 1913) until her death, and it was he who acted as train-bearer at her wedding in 1922, when he was nine years old. "(Rupert Hughes) didn't come to that," he remarked. Asked if Hughes was invited, Reynolds responded: "I don't know. I wouldn't know—you'd think they'd—well, he wouldn't need an invitation, really—he was the father of the bride. I think my father gave her away." Asked if Elspeth was upset by that, Reynolds replied, "No, I wouldn't know anything about that. I wouldn't know about any of their opinions, I was only seven or eight years old then." This is Reynolds' description of his half-sister Elspeth: "About five feet, five feet one. She was short, actually shorter than Mother. Stocky, as I say. Very, very open—she had a keen sense of humor and you never knew what she was going to say.'' He added that she had a dark complexion, and was usually ''sloppy.'' In all of his years of acquaintance with Elspeth—from 1913, when he was born, to 1945—he noticed no change in her appearance, and certainly not any indication she had been ''substituted'' by another person.

Reynolds was more evasive about Elspeth's relations with the Hugheses. Asked by Dinkins' representative to describe Elspeth's relationship with Rupert, whether the two were close, Reynolds responded, ''Well, he sent her an allowance of $300 after they were married.'' That was his only comment. Queried as to how Elspeth referred to Rupert Hughes—as ''Father,'' ''Rupert,'' ''Father Rupert''—Reynolds answered, ''She might have called him—no, I don't think she used his name. She might have spoken of him as Daddy, I don't really remember that.'' According to Reynolds, there was no ''conversational interest'' among his family and Elspeth regarding her connection to Howard R. Hughes, Jr., despite the fact that she was his first cousin and he was a world-famous millionaire. ''She never said anything,'' Reynolds noted. ''I guess they probably never knew each other, never in contact or anything.''

William Reynolds, Jr., also confirmed what Dinkins' research had already suggested: that his parents retired to Jacksonville in 1923, not too long after Elspeth's wedding. It was then they purchased a home a few blocks from Alston Cockrell, Jr.'s, parents. ''Mother knew Stevie Cockrell'' (Patterson Dial's sister), Reynolds admitted, ''but I don't know—it wasn't too long after then that Patty (Patterson Dial) committed suicide. . . . Sister told us. I don't know what she did, take drugs or cut her wrists or what.'' Patterson Dial's death was in March 1945; Elspeth died two months later. Reynolds offered an explanation for the mysterious illness Elspeth was suffering the year before her death, as indicated in her strange letters to and from Rupert Hughes during that period. ''When she was at Mother's funeral (in 1944), she was going to see the doctor,'' Reynolds explained. ''He had been treating her for nervous indigestion. Then I got a letter from Bobby (Barbara Cameron) about a month later maybe, and said they had operated on Elspeth and just saw that she had stomach cancer, that it was too far gone. They just sewed her up again.'' Asked if Elspeth had emotional problems before those diagnosed in 1944 and 1945, Reynolds said, ''Well, I wouldn't know. Now, she had brown spots, a lot of them, all over her body, of the nerve terminals. My mother claimed that came from nervousness and emotional upset.''

Reynolds also verified that his mother, Agnes Hughes Reynolds, spent the last three or four years of her life in Eastern State mental hospital. ''That was probably the saddest thing I can recall in my life, was seeing her. You know, when somebody that was really brilliant and then just fell apart." Reynolds offered an intriguing theory as to his mother's cause of death in 1944. "The doctor thought that . . . .she was having an anemia of the brain, the brain wasn't getting all the blood it should have—now he thought it might have come from maybe something she had picked up in her first marriage. I don't know, I'm not medical, and I don't know all the ins and outs of venereal disease." Reynolds believed Agnes' death may have been caused by a latent venereal disease contracted during her marriage to Rupert Hughes. "He thought it was caused by that," he repeated. "It was just latent in her system, for all the years. I don't know. I wouldn't mean to give that as a firm medical opinion. See, I heard it second hand, mostly from my mother-in-law who was a nurse. She had talked to the doctor up there at Eastern State."

This was not the only oddity William Reynolds, Jr., discussed concerning Rupert Hughes. He also repeated an observation about him once made by his mother: "She told me once that he had a habit. He always took and carried toilet paper with him. In his pocket, you know." Asked why, Reynolds said, "Well, I don't know. It just—if he had to wipe off or clean off or anything in a hurry." Aside from that, he said, "she never spoke of him any to speak of."

Finally, Reynolds repeated the following anecdote about his half-sister, Elspeth: "Well, Daddy (William H. Reynolds, Sr.) was a veteran of the Spanish-American War, and Mother, to be entitled to a widow's pension, which was $30 a month, she had—'course the lawyers handling the Estate handled all this—she had to show forth, first, that Daddy had died, and that she was legally married to him. And that if she had ever been married before she had to show that she was legally divorced. And she had to show that she was legally married to that husband. Why, I don't know—that's just red tape. Sister (Elspeth) made that off-hand remark: 'Gee, I hope I'm legitimate!' "

After the Reynolds interview, Dinkins' associate halfway closed the case. After all, Robert Hughes had been severely discredited in a number of significant respects: William H. Reynolds, Jr., Elspeth's half-brother, remembered seeing her or pictures of her, from 1913 until the time of her death in 1945, and could attest to the fact that it was the same person continuously. That alone seemed to dismiss the theory that Rupert Hughes' "real" daughter Leila drowned in 1920 or 1921, and was then substituted by Elspeth Dial, Elizabeth Patterson Dial's daughter. Furthermore, Alston Cockrell, Jr., substantiated the important facts relative to Patterson Dial's background, and it had been demonstrated that her surname was Dial, not Patterson. There was also a notation in a 1902 Madison newspaper as to the birth of a baby girl Dial—not in the 1890s, as Robert Hughes suggested. Neither *All for a Girl* nor any of the other newspaper or magazine articles Robert Hughes contended supported his family's theory could be located. There were still disturbing inconsistencies about Elspeth, to be sure, but neither Dinkins' associate nor his genealogist Mary Fay could put their fingers on the problem.

Several more pieces of evidence in support of the Barbara Cameron version of the Rupert Hughes family history came in, too: Dinkins' colleague contacted the St. Mary's School in Peekskill, New York (suggested by William Reynolds, Jr.), and discovered school records for an "Elspeth Hughes" for the spring term—February–June 1914, and the full academic years 1914–1915, and 1915–1916. She withdrew without graduating in June 1916. With this school record, Dinkins plugged in the gap between Elspeth's known attendance at the Madeira (1911–1914) and National Cathedral Schools (1916–1917). Elspeth's whereabouts before 1911 were still a complete mystery, however. The St. Mary's Episcopal School records also revealed that Elspeth had been baptized, and that she was confirmed one month after her arrival at the school: March 24, 1914. Her parish was stated to be Presbyterian. Her birthdate was stated to be May 23, 1897; her age sixteen at the time of enrollment in 1914. Her father was listed as Mr. Rupert Hughes of Bedford Hills, New York.

At the same time, the School Board in Jacksonville located a high school record for a "Betty P. Dial" for the freshman year 1917–18. Again, this seemed to clarify that Elizabeth Patterson Dial was born a Dial, not a Patterson. Why she was using the name Betty, however, is anyone's guess.

A Mysterious Drowning

Just when things looked bleakest for Robert Hughes, a strange thing happened. A distant Hughes cousin named Roberta Joyce Hughes Reed, not connected with either George Parnham's midwestern clients or with Robert Hughes' branch of the family, took on special significance in the heirship proceedings. She, like scores of other remote Hughes relations throughout the country, was affiliated with an "heir-finder" named W. A. Jones. Jones collected a fee from each of his "clients" to represent them in the distant hope that the Howard R. Hughes, Jr., inheritance would reach second, third, fourth, or even fifth cousins— many of whom he signed on as clients. Jones, however, was not an attorney. He called himself the president of the official "Heir-Finders Club," and passed out business cards to prove it. Some of Jones' group were from the same area of the Midwest as Parnham's clients; others were scattered throughout the country, all in varying degrees of kinship, sharing the common bond of being remote relatives of Howard R. Hughes, Jr., with little or no hope of inheriting his estate.

Roberta Reed, in her mid-thirties at the time of the heirship investigation, first became interested in her genealogy in approximately 1965, when the first of her children was born. She is Mormon by faith, and part of the Mormon training is an awareness of one's genealogy. She thus began to trace her "roots" with her children's births, though she was always aware of her distant kinship to Howard R. Hughes, Jr. After Howard's death, her interest "obviously increased," and she began hiring researchers "back East" on a sporadic, casual basis to "go through newspaper clippings, get vital statistics." Like George Parnham's clients, Mrs. Reed heard through her grandmother that "Rupert Hughes had the mumps when he was a youngster and could not father children." Her purpose, therefore, in intensifying her genealogical research after Howard, Jr.'s, death was to look into "the accusations that I had heard of Elspeth being Rupert's daughter, which she is not."

Most of the researchers she hired were graduate students at various universities in New York. She asked these students to review back issues of newspapers for clippings pertaining to Rupert Hughes, and the researchers would in turn telephone Mrs. Reed with their results and to ascertain which articles she wished to have copied. It was during one of these telephone calls that Roberta Reed met with startling news. "I had some people doing research for me back East," she explained in her deposition, "and I was asking them to get all the stuff on the Hugheses that they could. One of the college kids that I had working for me had found a newspaper article, and it had said something to the effect that Elspeth, the child of Rupert, had drowned at his house, the Arabian nights home, or whatever they call it." Mrs. Reed explained that when she was first told this, she instructed her researcher not to bother to copy the article—thinking that this must not be the same Rupert Hughes, since she had never heard of a drowning in the Hughes family. Later, however, she thought better of this decision, and tried to contact the college student who had found the drowning article. "When I recontacted him back again," she recited, "he couldn't find the copy. Then I tried to get him back. I could not get him back. He was a part-time student . . . and so I cannot trace the kid."

This news was riveting to Dinkins. Not only was Mrs. Reed not related to Robert C. Hughes, she had never heard of either him or his theory about the Hughes family. (In fact, when she was first informed of the newspaper account of a drowning, she attached no significance to it.) Her discovery of a newspaper article describing the drowning of Rupert Hughes' daughter in a swimming pool at his home was a completely independent verification of Robert Hughes' drowning story.

Naturally, this caused Dinkins and his two assistants to reevaluate the other aspects of Robert Hughes' version of Rupert Hughes' personal life. Dinkins also began a comprehensive search for the drowning article itself, trying to trace the college student Mrs. Reed engaged to do the original research. Unfortunately, Mrs. Reed hired several different students at a number of universities after Hughes' death, and it was impossible to pinpoint either the school or the student with any degree of accuracy. (Another point of interest in Mrs. Reed's deposition was her comment that she "had heard from someone that Rupert had lived with Marion Mould for four years. That's—he wasn't married to her." This marked the second reference to a relationship between Rupert Hughes and Adelaide Manola's mother.)

Just about this time, Dinkins also came to learn about a gentleman from Missouri who remembered reading a poem by Rupert Hughes in which Hughes mentioned the drowning death of his daughter. Like Roberta Reed, the Missourian had no apparent connection to Robert Hughes. Regrettably, he could not recall the name or the date of the poem.

With two independent corroborating sources to suggest that a daughter of Rupert Hughes' had drowned, Dinkins began to pursue with increased interest the only unexplored element of Robert Hughes' theory: Leila B. Hughes, the person Robert claimed was Rupert Hughes' "real" daughter. Robert Hughes and his attorneys had provided a clipping from a 1913 newspaper with a picture of Leila, as she appeared in a musical production called *My Little Friend* in New York City. It was this actress, Hughes contended, who died in Rupert Hughes' swimming pool, later impersonated by Elspeth Dial. At the same time, as the search for more material on Leila Hughes intensified, Dinkins' associate collected every source authority imaginable on Adelaide, Elizabeth Patterson Dial, Marion Manola, and Agnes. Dinkins hired a researcher in Syracuse, New York, to go through back copies of the Syracuse newspapers (Agnes Hedge Hughes Reynolds' hometown) for information on Agnes Hedge, or detailed accounts of her divorce from Rupert Hughes—hoping to find some further clue regarding Rupert and Agnes' marriage, the birth (or death or alias) of their daughter, or something else. Although Robert Hughes was convinced that Rupert Hughes' daughter had drowned, and there were now two other sources to suggest the same thing, it was possible he was mistaken as to the year of her drowning, the place it occurred, or some other relevant detail. Since Hughes relied solely on his memory, the margin of error was great. Consequently, Dinkins had reason to question every period in Rupert Hughes' life.

At just about this stage in their investigation, to add to the growing confusion, Dinkins and his investigators were presented with a new wrinkle on Elspeth. The second and third cousins of Howard R. Hughes, Jr., who grew up in the Keokuk area (later represented by George Parnham) were making noises to the effect that cousin Rupert Hughes was actually sterile. Although no details of their allegations had yet been advanced, and no official claims made, this possibility was added to the swelling list of suspicions about Rupert Hughes and his enigmatic daughter or daughters, Elspeth and Leila. With all the competing rumors and theories about Rupert Hughes in mind, Dinkins' associate began a sweeping investigation into the private lives of everyone connected with Rupert Hughes, not knowing what she would find or what exactly to look for.

After the news of Roberta Reed's accidental discovery, these investigative efforts were concentrated on Leila Hughes, the actress whom Robert Hughes claimed was Rupert's real daughter (by Agnes). With nothing more to go on than Robert Hughes' 1913 clipping picturing Leila B. Hughes in her starring role in *My Little Friend*, Dinkins' associate set out to trace the actress. Using arcane dramatic reference books and the services of the New York Public Library for the Performing Arts, the ad litem's clerk was able to amass a collection of clippings reflecting Leila B. Hughes' stage career. Many of these articles discussed her personal life and background as well. Leila's career, which began in 1912 with the leading role in a musical production called *The Chocolate Soldier*, ended in 1915. In addition to her performance in *The Chocolate Soldier* in 1912, Leila appeared in leading roles in *Two Little Brides* (1912–1913); *My Little Friend* (1913); *Maid of Athens* and *Red Canary* (1914); and *A Modern Eve* (1915).

The clippings on Leila Hughes from the Billy Rose Theatre Collection (a part of the New York Performing Arts Library) make no mention of Rupert Hughes. They do, however, provide information about her background. Curiously, this information is strikingly inconsistent. In most of the newspaper articles about Leila, she is reported to be the daughter of "L. C. Hughes," a "prominent St. Louis resident." These articles state that her father objected to Leila's singing career, and sent her to the Royal Academy of Music in London around 1911, hoping she would forget the stage and return to St. Louis. While in Europe, Leila performed in light operas in Paris and England.

The *St. Louis Globe-Democrat* reported in 1915 that Leila Hughes attended the Columbia School, Yeatman High, and the Strassberger School of Music, all in St. Louis. However, in an interview promoting *The Chocolate Soldier* given in Boston in 1913, Leila Hughes told a reporter that she attended St. Margaret's Protestant Episcopal Seminary at Upper Alton, Illinois, when she was not quite seventeen, after which she went to St. Louis and landed a small part in a musical production. Another 1913 interview with Leila relates that she "grew up in Illinois," had a slight weight problem, and lived in a northern New Jersey bungalow the summer of 1912. A third version of her background surfaced in the September 10, 1913, edition of the *Minneapolis Journal*. While publicizing the opening of Leila Hughes' next musical, the *Journal* quoted her as saying she "hailed from southern Virginia, where her grandfather owned a big plantation." This same interview reported that her father died when she was very young, and that Leila began to appear in "musicales," later went to Paris to study, and was offered the prima donna role in a light opera.

Why did Leila offer three different versions of her past? Was she, as most of the articles related, the daughter of L. C. Hughes, a "distinguished citizen of St. Louis"? Did she grow up in Illinois? Or was she raised on her grandfather's plantation in Virginia after the death of her father? The most consistent biographical fact about Leila B. Hughes in all of the clippings was her age. In all of her publicity she is described as "young," and much is made of the fact that she was offered leading roles when still a child. ("One of the youngest ever on stage," etc.) In 1912, she was said to be nineteen ("I was born on Thanksgiving Day," she told the reporter); in 1913, she was described as "barely out of her teens" in one article, "considerably under twenty" in another, and that she "turned nineteen three years ago" in a third. From the references to her age or birthdate in the complete collection of Leila Hughes' clippings, it was apparent that she was born in either 1891, 1893, or 1895.

Dinkins' associate began to cast about for birth or school records on Leila Hughes (in Illinois, Virginia, and St. Louis), as well as for any information on the "L. C. Hughes" of St. Louis said to be her father in several of the clippings. There was no explanation in her theatre file as to why her career ended in 1915. In an interview in 1913, however, she was reported to be in love with a man named Alfred E. Aarons, "whom she wished to marry." Aarons was thirty years older than Leila, with a "matrimonial record." Leila's parents, a "prominent St. Louis family," urged her not to marry Aarons. Whether she did marry Alred Aarons was not clear from the clippings, as his name did not appear after the 1913 reference.

The response to Dinkins' colleague's queries about Leila Hughes was at first overwhelmingly negative: there were no records of her birth in Virginia, Illinois, or Missouri, and none of the schools she professed to attend (the Columbia School, Strassberger School of Music, Yeatman High, and the Upper Alton, Illinois, Episcopal School) were still in existence in 1979. When the door to Leila Hughes' past was finally opened, the help came from, appropriately enough, St. Louis, Missouri—the state that provided Dinkins with Howard R. Hughes, Sr.'s, marriage licence to Francis Geddes, and Greta's marriage certificate to Alexander S. More.

From St. Louis came two records of special interest to the ad litem. The first was a reply from the School Records Division, first noting that there was no Columbia Grammar School in their files, and second enclosing a high school record for a Leila Hughes. Leila, according to the document, entered Yeatman High in September 1905 at the age of sixteen years, nine months. Her place of birth was not shown, but her father was reported to be Lisle C. Hughes, Greer Avenue, St. Louis. Obviously, Lisle C. Hughes was the "L. C." Hughes mentioned in the Theatre Collection of clippings on Leila's career. This school record was consistent with the biographical information on Leila most often repeated in her publicity clippings: that she was from St. Louis, the daughter of L. C. Hughes. What was not consistent was her age. According to information in the Yeatman High School record she would have been born in either December 1888 or January 1889. How could one reconcile that information with the biographical data in her publicity clippings, which clearly stated or implied that Leila was born between 1891 to 1895, and on Thanksgiving Day?

At approximately the same time as the school record arrived, Dinkins received clarification on the identity of L. C. Hughes. His associate earlier made inquiries in St. Louis concerning Mr. Hughes' death, reasoning that his probate proceedings, if available, might mention a daughter Leila, which in fact they did. The Probate Division of the St. Louis Circuit Court had an estate on file for one Lisle C. Hughes. Hughes died in St. Louis on July 24, 1916. His will read as follows:

WILL

I, Lisle C. Hughes, of the City of St. Louis, State of Missouri . . . declare this to be my last will and testament . . .:

FIRST; I direct that all my lawful debts, and the expenses of my last illness, and the expenses of my funeral, be first paid;

SECOND; To my daughter Leila Blake Hughes, I give and bequeath the sum of one dollar absolutely;

THIRD; To my son Elmer Lisle Hughes, I give and bequeath the sum of one dollar absolutely;

FOURTH; I give, bequeath, and devise, absolutely, all the rest, residue, and remainder of my property . . . to my wife Martha M. Hughes. . . .

(Dated February 7, 1912;
Signed Lisle C. Hughes)

In the application for probate of Hughes' will, his daughter is again stated to be Leila Blake Hughes of New York. (Also mentioned are his son Elmer Lisle Hughes of St. Louis, and wife Martha M. Hughes of St. Louis.) With the discovery of Lisle C. Hughes' estate proceedings, naming Leila B. Hughes as his daughter, and the supporting Yeatman High School record, Dinkins' colleague put aside the search into Leila Hughes' background. It seemed abundantly clear from the records at hand that Robert C. Hughes was mistaken in his belief that Leila was actually the "real" daughter of Rupert and Agnes Hughes. There were still certain questions about her, such as the odd references in the newspaper clippings describing her upbringing on a Virginia plantation by a grandfather after the death of her father, and/or her childhood spent in Illinois—along with the dual versions of her age—but these inconsistencies did not seem important enough to justify a deeper search into her past. Instead, Dinkins' associate concentrated on the more pressing problems of Elspeth, Agnes, Adelaide, and Marion Manola—women involved with Rupert Hughes whose backgrounds were still in question.

The Kensico Cemetery Mystery

The year was 1979, and Dinkins' investigation of Howard R. Hughes' heirs had been rocking along for almost three years. The trial to determine officially the Hughes relatives and divide the estate was now within sight, tentatively scheduled for 1980. (It was later postponed until 1981.) The paternal heirs presumed to prevail at trial were Barbara Cameron and her sisters; and Rush and Avis (Bissell) Hughes. The allegations concerning Elspeth, however, continued. Robert C. Hughes and his attorneys still endeavored to locate the newspaper and magazine clippings Hughes so earnestly believed would prove what his uncle John related to him about Rupert Hughes, and what he professed to have seen in the clippings locked in the family trunk. Roberta Reed persisted in her quest to locate the drowning article reported to her by a college student hired to do Hughes research for her in 1978. And a group of second and third cousins of Howard R. Hughes, Jr. (descendants of Felix Hughes', father, Joshua W. Hughes), in the tri-state area surrounding Keokuk had by this time marshalled forces to launch their position that Rupert Hughes was rendered sterile by a case of the mumps or measles while a student at St. Charles School in St. Charles, Missouri, and that Elspeth was in fact the daughter of Agnes Hedge Hughes by an adulterous liaison during her marriage to Rupert Hughes.

While the ad litem's probe into Rupert Hughes' personal life gained momentum, his associate's simultaneous investigation into the lives of the other Hughes family members continued to ebb and flow. Greta's mysterious past was unfolding in a particularly confusing pattern; the majority of her marriage and divorce records had still not been discovered, and Dinkins' associate had intensified efforts to collect the necessary certificates and decrees in anticipation of the expected 1980 heirship trial, at which time Dinkins would be called upon to document the events in the lives of all the Hugheses, Greta included. It was at this moment that Dinkins' colleague happened to study her death certificate in the distant hope it would provide a clue to her past. As reported earlier, it merely perpetuated the mystery.

The death certificate reported that Greta Witherspoon died in New York on February 21, 1916. She was stated to be forty-five years old, although her month, day and year of birth were not filled in. (Dinkins' associate later confirmed that Greta was born in 1866, which would mean that she was actually fifty years old, not forty-five, in 1916.) Because the year of Greta's death was in conflict and because the cause of Greta's death was a continuing mystery, Dinkins' associate examined the controversial death certificate with a surgeon's eye for detail.

This chance perusal, it developed, led Dinkins' associate into the most stirring mystery of the heirship case.

It was then that she discovered that, although Greta's date of death was reflected on the certificate as February of 1916, her date of burial was handwritten by the undertaker as April 23, 1911. This was either a minor clerical error or a major revelation. Obviously, both dates could not be correct. On the other hand, Dinkins' associate speculated, perhaps the date of *death* was incorrect on the certificate. Greta might well have been buried in 1911, if she died in 1911, and the 1916 date of death was a mistake. Obviously, the only way to remove all doubt was to check the undertaker's records. There were now three different dates given for Greta's year of death: 1911, 1913 or 1914, and 1916. Which, if any, was correct?

As a reminder of the number of years since the characters in this unusual legal drama had been alive, Dinkins' associate learned that the undertaker who handled Greta's funeral was no longer in business. She then tried to find the cemetery where Greta was buried. Cemetery records, Dinkins' clerk reasoned, should clarify the confusion surrounding Greta's death, and her tombstone might dispel whatever doubts might remain after that.

Greta's death certificate showed that she was buried in Kensico Cemetery, which Dinkins' associate eventually learned was located in Valhalla, New York. After a search of several days, however, the employees at Kensico Cemetery could find no record of interment for Greta under any of her various surnames, including the stage name she allegedly adopted during her singing career, "Jeanne Greta." By this time, the Kensico employee was perplexed by the apparent fact that Greta did not appear in their records, when her death certificate plainly stated that she was buried in Kensico Cemetery. She talked to the director of the cemetery, who mentioned that Kensico records were also set up according to plot owners, and suggested that Greta's records might be filed under the name of whoever purchased the cemetery plot in which she was buried.

With that in mind, Dinkins' associate asked the cemetery employee to look under the names of Greta's parents, Felix and Jean Hughes (who were both alive in 1916, when she died); Herbert Witherspoon (her last husband); and Fred Howell (her second husband). If someone other than Greta purchased her cemetery plot, the most logical choices would be her parents or one of her ex-husbands. Then, on a caprice, Dinkins' assistant also requested that the Kensico employee check the cemetery records for several other names: Rupert, Elspeth and Leila Hughes.

Several days later, the Kensico record keeper called back to report the results of her search. Although she could still not locate any records relative to Greta Hughes Witherspoon, she had discovered a huge cemetery plot owned by *Rupert* Hughes. The plot was purchased in 1924, and was large enough, the Kensico director observed, to accommodate twelve bodies. Not only was Greta Hughes not buried in this plot, the Kensico worker related, no one else was, either! To add to the irony of the situation, the directors of the cemetery had been trying to locate Rupert Hughes for a number of years to question him about his property at Kensico. They assumed that the plot was intended for Rupert's use, and they were seeking further clarification on its care and upkeep, since it had remained unused and ignored for over fifty years. When the Kensico employee telephoned Dinkins' associate, it was in part to ask how to contact Rupert Hughes about this cemetery plot. The Kensico representative was shocked to discover from Dinkins' colleague that Rupert Hughes had died in 1956, that he was cremated, and that his ashes were reposited at Forest Lawn Cemetery in Los Angeles, next to the ashes of his last wife, Patterson Dial. The cemetery director stated that it was "highly unusual" that a lot owner would die without

323

Kensico's being notified. Only a lot owner's heirs (in this case, Rupert's) may be buried in his or her lot. More disturbing at the moment to Dinkins' colleague was her recollection of Alston Cockrell, Jr.'s, statement that Rupert Hughes thought funerals were barbaric and wanted nothing to do with the burial process. Why in the world, then, did he own a massive cemetery plot in Valhalla, New York, apparently never used and never acknowledged?

By this time, the director of Kensico Cemetery, Chet Day, had taken an interest in Dinkins' associate's inquiries, and undertook an investigation of his own to explore Rupert Hughes' purchase and to find Greta Witherspoon's body. While examining the history of Rupert Hughes' lot, he discovered that "someone else looked into this" several years earlier, according to notes made at the time. He also reported that, in addition to the large, empty circular lot already credited to Rupert, he had found another cemetery lot once owned by Rupert Hughes. According to the record of interments, there were two individuals interred in this lot: Greta Hughes Witherspoon and Marion Gates.

Who was Marion Gates, and what was she doing in Rupert Hughes' cemetery plot? Finally it clicked: Marion Gates was the same person as Marion Manola, Adelaide Manola's mother! Early in the investigation, Dinkins' colleague had found an obituary for Marion Manola in the October 1914 *New York Dramatic Mirror*. After outlining Manola's career as a light opera singer, the obituary recited that she was married three times: to Henry Mould of Cleveland (Adelaide Mould's father), John Mason (another stage performer), and George G. Gates. Hence when Marion Manola died in 1914, she was Mrs. George Gates: Marion Gates. But why were Greta H. Witherspoon and Marion Gates buried side by side in a lot owned by Rupert Hughes in Valhalla, New York? Why, in fact, did Rupert Hughes own the lot at all?

To investigate these questions, the ad litem sent his associate to Valhalla to look through the cemetery records herself. Kensico, she discovered, is an expansive (461 acre) and beautiful cemetery located several miles north of White Plains, New York, in an exclusive community not far from Rupert Hughes' Bedford Hills farm. There, assisted by Chet Day, she traced Rupert Hughes' purchases at Kensico. By the end of the afternoon, both Day and the ad litem's clerk were completely baffled.

Kensico Cemetery has a dual record-keeping system. There are separate volumes recording who is buried in the cemetery and who owns the lots. To determine who is buried in the cemetery, one consults huge books called the *Index to Interments*. The index is arranged in alphabetical order. One simply looks under the name of the person whose burial information is sought and in this way finds the relevent cemetery records.

There are separate cards reflecting lot owners, kept in alphabetical order. On the back of each lot owner's card is a drawing of his particular lot in the cemetery, with each grave numbered. Each time an individual is buried in that cemetery lot, his or her name is recorded on the back of the lot owner's card, next to the number of the grave, as depicted or the corresponding drawing.

Dinkins' associate first looked up various individuals in the *Index to Interments*, in order to determine which of the Hughes cast of characters might be buried in the cemetery. She located Marion Manola Gates, Greta H. Witherspoon, and Adelaide Manola (the second Mrs. Rupert Hughes). Next, Dinkins' assistant and Chet Day retraced Rupert Hughes' acquisitions from the information on his two lot owner's cards (since he had purchased two separate lots in the cemetery.) Using this dual system, the two discovered that Rupert Hughes first purchased 100 feet of property in the Pocantico section of the cemetery in October 1914, on the occasion of his mother-in-law Marion Manola Gates' death. (At the time, Rupert Hughes was married to Adelaide and living in Bedford Hills.) According to the *Index of Interments,* Marion Gates died at the age of forty-eight in New Rochelle, New York. She was cremated and her ashes were placed on the Rupert Hughes lot. There was no undertaker; her records show "Mr. Hughes in charge."

Several months later, in January 1915, Rupert Hughes bought an additional 100 feet next to his original purchase. In February 1916, Greta H. Witherspoon died (according to her death certificate). Her name is in the "Record of Interments" on the back of Rupert Hughes' lot owner's card, showing that her body was placed in the cemetery mausoleum on February 23 and removed to Rupert Hughes' lot on May 27, 1916. That same day Rupert Hughes purchased another 236.61 feet in the Pocantico plot.

On December 14, 1923, Adelaide Manola Hughes committed suicide in China. Her name is included in the *Index to Interments* at Kensico, indicating that her remains were placed in a mausoleum in February 1924. Oddly, her name does not appear in the "Record of Interments" on the back of Rupert Hughes' lot owner's card, which would suggest that she was not interred in his Pocantico lot next to Marion Manola Gates and Greta Witherspoon.

Rupert Hughes' next acquisition at Kensico occurred in April 1924, when he arranged to buy a second lot, in the Katonah section of the cemetery, some distance from his first lot. (The records reveal that a different salesman sold Hughes this second lot—not the same man who sold him the three separate pieces of land in his Pocantico lot.) Hughes'

Katonah lot is circular in shape, measuring 1000 feet in circumference. According to Day, it can accommodate at least twelve persons. Rupert Hughes paid $3250 for this new cemetery plot in 1924, a sizable sum of money. However, at the time of the purchase, Hughes deeded his original smaller lot in the Pocantico section back to Kensico cemetery, to be applied as a credit toward his new purchase. The deed to the larger Katonah lot was issued to Rupert Hughes in 1925. The reverse side of his lot owner's card for this plot of land is completely blank; there are no names reflected in the Record of Interments.

With this in mind, Chet Day and Dinkins' associate drove out to examine both the Katonah and Pocantico lots, owned at different times by Rupert Hughes. Their first stop was the smaller lot in the Pocantico section. To their amazement, they found three large monuments. The first was in the shape of a giant urn with the inscription "Mother." This was the grave marker of Marion Manola Gates. Reflected on it was her year of death: 1914. Across from this was an identical urn bearing the name Adelaide Manola Hughes, and the date of death, 1923. In between these monuments was a life-sized statue of a woman in repose, marked simply as Greta Witherspoon. There was no date of death on Greta's monument.

Chet Day was as astonished as Dinkins' associate. The Pocantico lot belonged to Kensico Cemetery, not to Rupert Hughes. Why, then, were there three monuments to individuals associated with Rupert on this property?

Putting this question aside for the moment, Day and his confused companion drove on to the large circular lot that Rupert Hughes owned in the Katonah section of the cemetery. As they made their way, they passed the usual assortment of headstones, monuments, and markers typical of any cemetery. As they approached the Rupert Hughes lot, they were struck by one thing: his vast 1000 feet of land was the only empty spot in a totally occupied section of the cemetery! An examination of the site confirmed what the "Record of Interments" on Hughes' lot owner's card suggested: there were no headstones, markers, or monuments on the lot. Intrigued, Day inspected the ground in the circular lot. It was his opinion that the condition of the ground was "peculiar." While he would not go so far as to suggest that this indicated there was someone buried in the Hughes lot, he did not deny that this was a realistic possibility. (There was even an unaccounted for cornerstone on the site.) Day did recommend a procedure called "sounding"—the use of a stake to penetrate the surface of the ground—to determine if indeed there was something or someone buried in Rupert Hughes' lot. Asked by Dinkins' associate if it would have been possible for Rupert Hughes, or someone else, to bury an individual in the lot without the knowledge of the Kensico authorities, Day replied, "We hope not. [Pause] It's against the law."

By 1924, Hughes was living permanently in Los Angeles, California, thousands of miles from Kensico. He had told Alston Cockrell, Jr., that he thought funerals were barbaric, and he was an outspoken advocate of cremation. What possible reason could he have had for buying a cemetery lot large enough for twelve persons? Rupert's parents had a family plot in Keokuk; Howard, Sr., would be buried in Houston; and Rupert's brother Felix with his current wife. There was no logical explanation for this purchase. This thought was made odder by the fact that Rupert Hughes' own ashes were ultimately placed in Forest Lawn Cemetery in Los Angeles, next to Patterson Dial's. He never sold the Kensico lot, never contacted the cemetery directors for any reason, and seemingly never informed anyone of its existence. (It did not show up, for instance, in the list of assets in his estate in 1956, yet it was then and is now a valuable piece of property.)

Finally, was there a reason that three of the mystery figures in his life—Greta, Adelaide and Marion Manola—were removed to this cemetery and placed together in the same lot? And why did Rupert Hughes assume responsibility for Marion Manola's cremation? She was married at the time to George G. Gates. Wouldn't her husband have handled her burial arrangements? And why was there no undertaker listed in her records?

Then there was Greta. Her monument has no date of death inscribed, calling to mind the recurring contradictions about the year and cause of her death. Dinkins' associate was further reminded of Avis' chilling testimony about Greta's death in 1913 or 1914 (not 1916, as her death certificate stated), and the fact that Rupert fell into a thirty-six hour state of shock at the news. Peculiarly, Avis was asked during her second deposition (after the Kensico plot was discovered), if she knew where Greta was buried. She replied that she did not, yet she mentioned later in the questioning that she had visited her mother, Adelaide's, grave several times. How could she visit Adelaide's grave at Kensico and fail to see the life-sized monument to Greta Witherspoon not two feet away? In an even more bizarre twist, Robert Hughes' attorney showed Avis two pictures of Greta taken from *The Keokuk Connection* during the same deposition and asked her if she could identify the woman in the photographs. She could not.

Plots and Counterplots

The discovery of the two Rupert Hughes plots, however compelling, was not the only mystery at the Kensico Cemetery. While examining the cemetery records in the manager's office (before discovering the monuments in Rupert Hughes' old lot and the emptiness of his new one), Dinkins' associate checked the *Index to Interments* for a number of names. The *Index* was combed for a reference to either "Elspeth" or "Leila" Hughes, with the idea in mind that Rupert Hughes' allegedly drowned daughter might be buried in his forgotten cemetery lot. There were none. There was, however, a "Leslie" Hughes reflected in the *Index to Interments*. Following a hunch, Dinkins' clerk asked for the complete records on Leslie Hughes. Leslie, she discovered, died in July 1916 and was buried in a lot owned by Martha Hughes. Seeing this, Dinkins' clerk felt the shock of recognition: the probate proceedings for Lisle C. Hughes (Leila B. Hughes' father) had arrived in Dinkins' office shortly before her departure for Kensico. She remembered that Lisle died in 1916 and that his wife's name was Martha. Could it possibly be the same person? The odds were overwhelmingly against it. Furthermore, the 1912–1915 newspaper clippings in Leila Hughes' Theatre Collection file referring to her father, L. C. Hughes, reported that he was a prominent resident of St. Louis who was opposed to his daughter's career and urged her to return to Missouri at every opportunity. It made no sense that the same man whose probate proceedings were on file in St. Louis would be buried in Kensico Cemetery in Valhalla, New York.

Chet Day pulled the lot owner's card for Martha Hughes. On the back of the card was the "Record of Interments," indicating who was buried in her cemetery lot. It was filled in as follows:

	Record of Interments	Date of Burial
1.	Martha Hughes	5-20-61
	Lisle	
1.	~~Leslie~~ Hughes	7-26-16
4.	Myra Tappan	7-7-48
4.	Elmer E. Tappan	6-22-23
5.	Leila Aaron	9-4-39
6.	Alfred Aaron	11-18-36

Dinkins' associate gasped as she read the back of the card. There was no doubt in her mind that this was the same Hughes whose estate proceedings were on file in St. Louis and who was said to be the father of Leila B. Hughes in much of her publicity. Lisle Hughes' name had been misspelled as "Leslie" in the *Index of Interments*, and this mistake was carried over to the lot owner's card, until someone later crossed it out and wrote in "Lisle." What was even more astonishing was the irrefutable fact that Leila B. Hughes was buried alongside him. ("Leila

Aaron's'' records were cross-referenced and revealed that her full name was "Leila Blake Aarons," filled in by Martha Hughes.) The full impact of this discovery was overwhelming. Not only did Rupert Hughes have a secret cemetery lot (or two) at the Kensico Cemetery in Valhalla, New York, but Leila B. Hughes, the actress whom Robert Hughes claimed was his real daughter, was buried in the very same cemetery! Could this possibly be a coincidence?

To add to the intrigue, Day consulted his notes and discovered that "an attorney from Houston" telephoned him shortly after Howard R. Hughes, Jr.'s, death, "making inquiries" about Rupert Hughes' purchases at the cemetery. Unfortunately, his notes made no reference to the attorney's name or the nature of his inquiry. Who was it who always seemed to be one step ahead of Dinkins' investigation? And what were they looking for—or trying to hide?

After discovering the Kensico cemetery lot where Leila Hughes Aaron was buried, Dinkins' associate was ultimately able to trace her life from birth to death. The others in the lot beside Leila were Lisle and Martha Hughes (Leila's parents), Alfred Aaron, Myra Tappan, and Elmer E. Tappan. Dinkins' colleague remembered the name Alfred Aaron from one of the newspaper clippings in Leila's theatre collection. "Alfred E. Aarons" was identified in a 1913 New York newspaper as Leila Hughes' (thirty years) older boyfriend with a "matrimonial record," the man she "wished to marry." It made sense that Leila and her husband would be buried in Leila's parents (Lisle and Martha's) cemetery lot. But who were Myra and Elmer E. Tappan? Dinkins' clerk recalled that in Lisle C. Hughes' 1916 estate proceedings in St. Louis, his heirs were his wife Martha, daughter Leila, and son Elmer Hughes. Still, Elmer Tappan couldn't be the same person as Elmer Hughes. Who was Elmer Tappan?

Ignoring the mysterious Tappans at first, Dinkins' associate was able to find evidence that Leila B. Hughes married Alfred E. Aarons, a successful theatrical manager and producer, about 1915. Aarons was a native of Philadelphia (born 1865), who moved to New York in 1890. He was married three times, including his marriage to Leila, though all of his obituaries and biographies list only two marriages. His first wife (who is never cited in accounts of Aarons' life) was named Ella M. Rich, a Philadelphian. Ella and Aarons were married in 1886 (in Philadelphia) and had a son named Alexander, born in 1890. Alexander Aarons followed in his father Alfred's footsteps, and became a noted stage and screen producer. His first show was *Lady Be Good* with Fred and Adele Astaire, and he is credited with giving Ethel Merman her first big part. Alexander Aarons was married at least twice. He died in Beverly Hills in 1943 at the age of fifty-two, then employed by RKO Studios—owned at the time by Howard R. Hughes, Jr.

Alfred E. and Ella Rich Aarons, Alexander's mother, were messily divorced in New York City in 1899, on charges that Ella Aarons committed adultery with a Dr. Walter L. Clark. (In a strange coincidence, the physician whose name appears on the controversial 1897 birth certificate of Elspeth Hughes was a Dr. Walter L. *Carr*.) Shortly thereafter, in 1899 or 1900, Aarons married Josephine Hall, who reportedly died in the 1920s. During this period—the early 1900s to 1920—Aarons was producing plays in a number of theatres in New York City. Oddly enough, Rupert Hughes' plays were appearing on the Broadway stage at the same time, and it is likely they knew (or knew of) each other.

Leila B. Hughes and Aarons were married around 1915; he fifty years old, she twenty-seven. Leila apparently retired from the stage, and she and Alfred Aarons had two children: Lisle Blake Aarons (born 1916) and Ruth Hughes Aarons (born 1918). Alfred Aarons died in 1936, his wife Leila Hughes Aarons in 1939. Both were reported to be buried in Kensico Cemetery.

In addition to chronicling Leila's later years, Dinkins' associate was eventually able to secure documentation on her childhood. A birth certificate for "Leila Hughes" was found in Troy, New York, dated November 27, 1888 (Thanksgiving Day—just as she told a reporter in her publicity clippings). Her parents were Lisle C. and Martha Reynolds Hughes. Lisle Hughes was an insurance agent (just as Agnes' father, Charles Hedge, was) for the Metropolitan Life Insurance Company. He worked in upper New York State, close to Canada, for four years from 1890 to 1894, when he moved to Missouri: first to St. Joseph (through 1899), later to St. Louis (1899–1916). Elmer Hughes, Leila's brother, was born in February 1895. He is mentioned in his father Lisle Hughes' estate proceedings in St. Louis in 1916, after which he could not be traced.

Even with all this documentation on Leila to refute Robert Hughes' assertion that it was she who was Rupert Hughes' real daughter, accidentally drowned in his swimming pool in the 1920s, there were still a few questions about her that puzzled Dinkins' associate. There was, for instance, the matter of her birthdate. The forty or so publicity clippings in Leila Hughes' complete Theatre Collection file (highlighting her 1912–1915 singing career) all state or imply she was born in 1891, 1893, or 1895, and make much of the fact that she was one of the youngest performers ever to appear on the New York stage. (On September 25, 1912, for example, Leila was interviewed by the *Musical Courier*. She told the reporter that she was nineteen years old, born on Thanksgiving. That would mean she was born in 1893. According to her birth certificate, she was born in 1888, five years earlier.) She is described as a "teen" in 1912 and 1913, when she would have been twenty-four and twenty-five. In these same publicity interviews, she presented three different versions of her background: that she was the daughter of L. C. Hughes of St. Louis; that she was raised in Illinois and attended Upper Alton, Illinois Episcopal Seminary; and that her father died when she was young and she was raised by a grandfather on a plantation in Virginia.

Obviously, newspaper reports are not always accurate. What is peculiar, however, is the consistency with which Leila's age and background is erroneously or variously reported in her publicity interviews, particularly when there was no apparent reason on her part to deceive either the press or the public. At twenty-four, Leila was not at an age when she would need to conceal her birthdate, and there was seemingly nothing embarrassing about the Lisle Hughes family that would cause her to alter or suppress her autobiography.

The most powerful evidence in support of Robert Hughes' theory, however, is unquestionably Leila's burial at Kensico Cemetery. Despite the fact that Dinkins' associate found an 1888 birth certificate, a 1939 death certificate, and other supporting data in conflict with Robert Hughes' claim that Leila B. Hughes was the real daughter of Rupert Hughes, drowned in the 1920s, the fact that the same Leila B. Hughes is buried in the very cemetery in New York where Rupert Hughes owned a mysterious plot was downright disturbing. Was it only a startling coincidence? The odds were overwhelmingly against it.

Furthermore, what possible motivation would Leila's parents, Lisle and Martha Hughes, have had in 1916 to select a cemetery plot in Westchester County, New York? Lisle Hughes had been a prominent resident of St. Louis for twenty years prior to his death in 1916, and was an outspoken critic of his daughter's career in New York City. His only period of residence in the State of New York was a four-year interval between 1890 and 1894 selling insurance in the northern region of the state, close to Canada—nowhere near Kensico.

Still, Dinkins' associate could find nothing in Leila Hughes' background to support the details of Robert Hughes' claim. The biggest mystery that remained about her past was the apparent disappearance of her brother Elmer Hughes and the identity of Elmer and Myra Tappan—the two individuals buried in the Lisle Hughes plot along with Leila and Alfred Aarons and Leila's parents. Dinkins' associate could never piece together who this pair was. A death certificate was eventually secured for Elmer E. Tappan, who died in New York City on May 27, 1923. He was reported to be sixty-two years old, employed as a ''floor walker'' at the Hotel Norogonsett in Manhattan. There was no date of birth shown for Tappan, and his place of birth was described only as ''United States.'' What really captured the attention of Dinkins' associate when she studied Tappan's death certificate, however, was the appearance of the handwriting on the record. To her practiced eye, it was a stunning facsimile of Rupert Hughes'!

Ultimately, the exploration of Leila B. Hughes Aarons' past came to a close. Dinkins' associate traced her two children by Alfred Aarons— Lisle Blake and Ruth Hughes Aarons—to their deaths, and this pair was the end of the line. (Neither married and each died childless.) Lisle Aarons, she discovered, took over as president of Aarons Theatrical Management, established by his father Alfred years earlier. He died in New York City in 1966. His sister, Ruth Hughes Aarons, once his partner, continued as a successful theatrical personal manager after her brother's death. She eventually moved from New York City to California, where her clients and friends included Imogene Coca, Shirley Jones, and Celeste Holm. Ruth Hughes Aarons, last of the Leila B. Hughes descendants, died under controversial circumstances in Beverly Hills on June 6, 1980. She left her estimated one-million-dollar estate to her doctor, and stated in her will that she had no heirs.

Actress Shirley Jones, a close friend of Miss Aarons', confirmed that Ruth had no other relatives to speak of. "She talked often about how there was nobody left," Miss Jones explained. Jones was aware of the fact that Ruth's mother was Leila Hughes, "a singer," but she never heard Ruth mention the name Rupert Hughes in any context, nor was she ever led to believe that her friend was related to either Rupert or Howard Hughes. "We talked about Howard Hughes a lot," Jones stated, ". . . about his life and so forth. And she never mentioned they were related." Unfortunately, Shirley Jones had never heard of Elmer and Myra Tappan, nor did she know what became of Elmer Hughes (Leila's brother; Ruth Hughes Aarons' uncle), though Ruth did speak of an aunt and uncle in Kansas City.

The conversation with Shirley Jones closed the door to any further investigation into Leila Hughes' possible connection to Rupert Hughes.

Patterson Dial: A Strange Footnote

Dinkins' colleague later stumbled onto a strange corollary to the Rupert/Leila Hughes imbroglio, involving Patterson Dial. A few odds and ends about her past continued to filter into the ad litem's office from time to time in the last stages of the investigation. Mrs. Fay, for instance, located a reference book published by the American Film Institute, noting that actress Patterson Dial's first film in Hollywood was made in 1921, entitled *Get-Rich-Quick Wallingford*. She made several more films in 1921 and 1922; three films in 1923; and five films in 1924. This fact was not entirely consistent with the background that Alston

Cockrell, Jr., provided. Cockrell told Dinkins' colleague that Patterson lived in New York from 1919 to 1923, followed by a brief period of residence in Jacksonville with his parents (Alston and Stephena Cockrell), when she received the fateful "telegram" from Hollywood enclosing a movie contract. It was his belief that his aunt did not move to Los Angeles until around 1923. The Film Institute's reference book, however, indicated that Patterson was actually working in Hollywood by 1921, which increased the chances that she might have met Rupert Hughes while he was still married to Adelaide (Adelaide died in December of 1923), possibly contributing to their marital difficulties. All of this made Robert Hughes' increasingly discredited version of Rupert Hughes' life more plausible.

Dinkins' colleague also located a series of reviews and programs in the Billy Rose Collection relating to the 1919 New York stage production of *Aphrodite*. Cockrell recalled that his aunt began her career as a dancer in that show, after moving away from Jacksonville. Programs from the musical confirm that a "Patterson Dial" was cast in the minor role of Theano in the 1918–20 production of *Aphrodite*, described in a review printed in the December 2, 1919, edition of the *New York American* newspaper as "vulgarly indecent." (Critic Alan Dale's headline read: "Almost Nude Blacks and Semi-Naked Women Disgust Throng in Play Founded on Art, but Which Caters to Low Passions.") These clippings verified that Patterson Dial was already pursuing her career in New York City in 1918, when she was sixteen years old (assuming she was born in 1902, as her records suggested).

It seemed from these clippings that Alston Cockrell, Jr., had the time sequence of Patterson Dial's careers in New York and Hollywood somewhat askew. It also seemed slightly out of the ordinary that Patterson Dial was appearing in a "lewd" production in New York City at the tender age of sixteen. Such suspicions were brought to the forefront when Dinkins' associate spoke again to Mrs. Betty Rimell Westbrook, Elspeth's former maid of honor. Mrs. Westbrook attended an engagement party in her honor, given by her mother's cousin Rupert Hughes and his wife Patterson Dial, at the Los Feliz mansion in 1925. Betty Rimell was then twenty-one years old (born in 1904); Patterson Dial should have been twenty-three (born in 1902). "She was older," Mrs. Westbrook related. "Maybe in her thirties." Informed that Patterson should have been twenty-three on this occasion, Betty Westbrook replied, "Oh, she couldn't have been. No!" Mrs. Westbrook's observation was consistent with Frances M. Smith's (whose mother was also Rupert Hughes' first cousin; Mrs. Smith attended the Cathedral School with Elspeth one year), who also believed Patterson Dial to be in her thirties in 1925.

The evidence pointed more and more to the contrary. There was the notation in the Madison, Florida, newspaper announcing the birth of the Dials' daughter unnamed, in May 1902 (the same birthdate Patterson Dial used); the family photo album with pictures of seven-year-old Patterson standing next to her seventeen-year-old sister Stephena, clearly showing the age difference; and a 1900 census that Mrs. Fay secured, showing William and Sara Dial and their daughter Stephena in Madison, Florida (no daughter Elizabeth Patterson). All of these demonstrated without a doubt that Patterson Dial was born in May 1902. The only document Dinkins lacked was her birth certificate. (Avis and Rush also supported the 1902 birthdate.) Avis testified that Patterson was "about a year" younger than herself. Since Avis was born in December 1900, and Patterson Dial professed to be born in May 1902, this would be consistent. Rush Hughes said much the same thing, and added that he had never met Miss Dial prior to her engagement to Rupert Hughes.

Since there was still some doubt about the circumstances under which Patterson Dial met Rupert (the timing of Adelaide's China trip and subsequent suicide), Dinkins' colleague took the time to review Dial's biographical and film file on record at the Motion Picture Academy in Beverly Hills. Though there was no personal data in Patterson's file, there was a small collection of reviews for the several films in which she appeared from 1921 to 1924. One in particular caught Dinkins' associate's eye.

The name of the film was *Reno*, made on location in 1923 (Adelaide committed suicide in December of 1923), featuring "Pattison Dial" in a small role. The picture, according to the review, was written and directed by one Rupert Hughes. Also in the cast was Rush Hughes. This discovery interested Dinkins' associate for two reasons: it demonstrated clearly that Rupert Hughes and Patterson Dial were acquainted before the death of Adelaide; and it revealed that Rush Hughes appeared in a 1923 film with Patterson, long before she became engaged to Rupert. Yet he testified in his deposition that he did not know Dial when she married Hughes in 1924.

As if these two revelations were not enough, the review also featured a plot synopsis. It was, to say the very least, unexpected:

RENO

Goldwyn-Cosmopolitan picture written and directed by Rupert Hughes with J. J. Mescall the photographer.

Mrs. Emily Dysart Tappan	Helene Chadwick
Guy Tappan.	Lew Cody
Walter Heath	George Walsh

Mrs. Dora Carson Tappan	Carmel Myers
Mrs. Kate Norton Tappan	Hedda Hopper
Miss Alida Tappan	Dale Fuller
Yvette	Kathleen Key
Jerry Dysart	Rush Hughes
Marjory Towne	Marjorie Bonner
Henry Nish	William Orlamond
Judge Norton	Howard Truesdale
Paul Tappan	Robert de Vilblas
Ivy Tappan	Virginia Loomis
Arthur Clayton	Richard Wayne
Justice of Peace	Hughie Mack
Hal Carson	Boyce Combe
McRae, the detective	Victor Potel
Lemile Hake	Percy Hemus
Mattie Hake	Maxine Elliott Hicks
Tod Hake	Billy Eugene
Mrs. Towne	Adele Watson
Hod Stoat	Jack Curtis
Mrs. Hod Stoat	Pattison Dial

Not without many a comedy insertion the story attempts to follow the love affairs of Guy Tappan at one time confronted by a trio of Mrs. Tappans who are, or are not, his lawful wives according to the states wherein they may reside. Another annexation to the story is pinned to the two Tappan children. Over them is a continuous struggle due to the father's wealthy aunt who will not reimburse the financially embarrassed parent unless he procures the custody of his offsprings (Paul and Ivy).

Then there is the second wife and mother of the children, her hectic maneuvers, chasing about the country, and mental anguish given to the cause of finding and holding on to her boy and girl, while the former lover is also at her elbow to assist, also willing to accept she and the children.

The tale covers much territory before the sequence of events concludes but will mostly interest in the passages confined to the Yellowstone park area wherein is displayed some beautiful exteriors and the "kick" of the action through a fight between the versatile Tappan and his second wife's champion. It results in the former's falling into the mouth of a geyser which begins to erupt, tossing and suspending his body in midair to culminate in his death.

. . . Lew Cody is the amorous gentleman, thrice married . . . while George Walsh (appears) as the faithful suitor . . . Beyond that duo comes to light a corking donation in Rush Hughes, who assigned as the brother of the second wife and in the midst of an affair of her own, assuredly equals any other member of the male end on strength of work.

335

Was the plot of Rupert Hughes' film *Reno* a case of art imitating life? The parallels were certainly striking, featuring as it did, a "thrice married" gentleman in a screwy romantic entanglement, with ex-wives and assorted relations of ex-wives all intertwined in amorous encounters, loosely connected to a scheme to win custody of two children by the husband's second wife named Paul and Ivy (Rush and Avis?), upon which an inheritance from a wealthy aunt hinges, and ending in the accidental death of one of the characters. Could one somehow hope to understand Rupert Hughes' tangled marital situation from the story line of this confusing film? Was the plot of *Reno* suggested by a financial incentive behind one of the custody battles in Rupert's own life? It was certainly true that Rupert's father, Judge Felix Hughes, supported Rupert and Agnes during the ten years of their marriage, and possibly for a time thereafter. Was his financial support somehow conditioned upon Rupert's having a child, or some variation on this theme?

The film, with its complicated story of multiple marriages, putative divorces, and continuing custody battles, indicated, if nothing else, that its author, Rupert Hughes, was capable of devising intricate matrimonial scenarios. It reminded Dinkins' associate of a comment made by Louis Kaminar, the attorney who drafted Rupert Hughes' 1954 will. Kaminar recalled that the only "legal" advice he offered Hughes in the six years of their relationship, were those occasions when Rupert would telephone him wanting to know "what the law was" in order to get one or more of his characters out of whatever legal entanglement he had created in his latest piece of fiction.

Knowing this, Dinkins' associate considered that Rupert would certainly relish the complicated bit of business his own life had become for those whose task it was to follow the tortuous path of his personal life through three (or more) marriages, one case of insanity, two suicides, one disputed child, two possibly "equitably" adopted stepchildren, one legal ward, and several individuals nearly adopted—all of which were riddled with inconsistencies and incongruities. Was the confusion in Rupert Hughes' life, as more and more it seemed, a creature of his own design? If so, what was the purpose?

Not the least of the questions about *Reno* was, of course, the use of the name "Tappan" for the protagonist and his many wives. Was there any significance to this choice? If indeed Rupert Hughes had some connection to Leila Hughes, in whose Kensico cemetery lot the unidentified Tappans were interred, was his use of the surname "Tappan" a subtle wink?

During the same period, Dinkins' colleague located a copy of a 1939 issue of *Liberty* Magazine. It featured a short story by author Patterson Dial. The title of the story was "The Secret Child." Although the plot

336

seemed free from any similarity to Patterson's own life, the subject matter and title of her story was eery indeed, given Robert Hughes' allegations that Patterson was the mother of Elspeth Dial, substituted for Rupert's drowned daughter. In fact, Dial implied to her nephew Alston that there was a special, somewhat mysterious significance to the story. Little did Patterson Dial know when she wrote this piece of fiction in 1939, that "The Secret Child" would foreshadow an investigation into her own past for a mystery daughter, culminating in a careful study of her magazine article for possible clues.

Adelaide and Marion: The Mysterious Manolas

The discovery of the Rupert Hughes plot at Kensico Cemetery reawakened a dormant interest in Adelaide Manola, Rupert's second wife, and her mother, actress Marion Manola. Adelaide's activities had already been the subject of some scrutiny, in that she was the mother of Rush and Avis, who claimed to be the "equitably" adopted (step)children of Rupert Hughes, effected during Adelaide's marriage to Hughes, Rush and Avis' claim to the Howard Hughes estate therefore turned upon Rupert's treatment of and attitude toward them after his marriage to their mother in 1908, since they had no formal adoption papers to prove their case. As a consequence, the marriage of Rupert and Adelaide was one of the many separate inquiries that made up the heirship investigation. As the attorney ad litem, Dinkins was responsible for exploring whether Rupert Hughes' behavior was ever inconsistent with Rush and Avis' position that Rupert wished to adopt them in 1911 (at the time of Rush's arrival in Bedford Hills), that he was blocked in these efforts by George Bissell (the pair's natural father), and that he thereafter considered the two to be his adopted children, as distinct from his stepchildren.

This continuing interest in Adelaide, Rush, and Avis was augmented somewhat by the report from Keokuk, not taken seriously, that Rupert Hughes was perhaps once married to Adelaide's mother, Marion Manola (erroneously described as Adelaide's daughter in the piece by author Ray Garrison). Chancing upon the vast and apparently unused Kensico cemetery lot purchased furtively by Rupert Hughes, and stumbling onto the monuments to both Adelaide and Marion (together with the ever-mysterious Greta) interred in a lot paid for by Rupert at the time of Marion Manola's death—and which he no longer owned—raised the red flag for Dinkins' associate to investigate Rupert's connection to both of these women in greater depth. (There was, in addition, Alston Cockrell, Jr.'s, belief that it was Adelaide, not Agnes, who was the mother of Elspeth.)

337

It was becoming clearer that Rupert Hughes harbored more than one secret about his personal life, and it was impossible to tell where one wife left off and the other began. It was even possible that Rupert's several wives, daughters, mothers-in-law, and stepchildren were somehow intertwined in a complicated plot of Rupert's design. (The script he devised for the film *Reno* proved that he had the imagination to do so, and his scathing magazine pieces on marriage as a "bunco game," combined with his comprehensive knowledge of divorce laws in each of forty-eight states, suggested a man obsessed with the subject of mixed-up matrimony.)

Prior to the accidental discovery of the Kensico cemetery plots, Dinkins' associate had collected a variety of materials on Adelaide, and some on Marion Manola. Rush and Avis informed the ad litem that their mother was born in Cleveland (said Rush) or Pittsburgh (said Avis) on May 7, 1884 (said Rush), or 1882 (said Avis), to Henry Mould and his wife Marion Stevens Mould. Rush "thought her family emanated from Flint, Michigan," and stated that Adelaide was an only child. Avis maintained that Henry (also called "Harry") Mould (Marion's husband; Adelaide's father) was from Cleveland. Rush also testified that his grandmother, Marion Mould, was a "musical comedy star" who adopted the stage name of Marion Manola. He knew nothing further about her background. Avis related that Marion Manola "studied in Rome" and was an operetta star. Her daughter Adelaide Mould was "educated in Paris": Avis testified that Adelaide lived at the Sacred Heart Convent in Paris from the ages of six through twelve.

Adelaide Mould married Rush and Avis' father, George Bissell (a resident of Brooklyn, New York), on January 12, 1900. Rush reported that his father was an electrical engineer "who traveled the world on assignment." The newly married Bissells moved to Kobe, Japan, where their daughter Avis was born eleven months later on December 19, 1900. Adelaide became pregnant for the second time in September 1901. According to Avis, Adelaide became ill with dysentery and was advised to return to Bissell's parents' house in Brooklyn, bringing Avis with her. Rush Marion Bissell was born in New York City on May 14, 1902.

In 1903, Avis testified, her parents were divorced. Rush remained with his father (and was sent to live with the Bissell grandparents in Brooklyn), while Adelaide Mould Bissell got custody of Avis, then three years old. Details of the next several years are vague. Avis testified that she started school in Detroit at age five, while living with Adelaide's grandmother and parents (Marion Manola and husband). It was somewhere during this period (1906–1908) that Adelaide (now using the stage name Adelaide Manola) met Rupert Hughes, by Avis' fuzzy recollection. The two were introduced by Avis' godmother, actress

Blanche Bates, at Miss Bates' country estate. Since her mother was "traveling and performing on the stage," Avis rarely saw her. In her first deposition in the Hughes case, taken in September 1976, Avis testified that Rupert and Adelaide married in 1907 or 1908, while Avis was staying at Blanche Bates' home. After the marriage, Avis joined Rupert and Adelaide, and can't recall using the name Bissell again.

Adelaide's life from this point has already been established: she, Rupert, and Avis spent the winter season in an apartment in Manhattan and summered in a series of rented (later their own) country estates in Bedford Hills, near White Plains, New York. Rush Bissell joined the trio in 1911, taken out of the House of Providence in Syracuse, New York, and from this point forward he and Avis considered themselves Rupert Hughes' adopted children. Adelaide retired from the stage, did some writing, and raised canaries. Rupert Hughes pursued his career as a playwright and author of short stories, novels, and novellas. Elspeth spent summers with Rupert and family roughly between 1908 or 1909 to 1919. Rush and Avis were tutored privately in Bedford Hills until 1912, when Rupert began sending them to boarding schools.

From 1916 to 1918, Adelaide and Rupert lived alternately in New York and Washington, during Rupert's tenure with the Army Intelligence Division. Rupert was wooed by Sam Goldwyn in the teens and had begun writing scenarios for the movies by 1916, occasionally assisted by Adelaide. Before 1918, Rupert and Adelaide were living part of the year in California, and this arrangement was made permanent by 1920 or 1921. The early 1920s are something of a blur: Adelaide took two trips to China, the Hughes marriage began to disintegrate, Rupert Hughes met Patterson Dial, the house on Los Feliz with the unusual swimming pool was or was not purchased (stories differ on when Rupert Hughes moved into the mansion), and finally there was Adelaide's macabre suicide in December 1923.

Such was Rush and Avis' portrayal of Adelaide and Marion Manola's background, and their own. To confirm this, Dinkins' associate found the Bissell marriage certificate, which showed that George E. Bissell, Jr., age twenty-four, married Adelaide S. Mould, age nineteen (born in 1881; not 1884 or 1882, as Rush and Avis stated) on January 12, 1900, in New York City, just as Rush recalled. The witness was Marion Elixia Mason, Adelaide's mother. After a tortuous search, the ad litem also secured Adelaide and Rupert Hughes' marriage license. The two were married on June 22, 1908, in Jersey City, New Jersey. On this application, Adelaide said that her date of birth was 1882. She cited Cleveland as her place of birth on both certificates. Dinkins' associate also requested copies of several newspaper accounts of Adelaide's death in 1923. The

339

obituaries all repeated basically the same information about Adelaide Manola Hughes: that she was born in 1884, and was a widow (not divorced from George Bissell) at the time of her marriage to Rupert Hughes in 1908.

About Marion Manola, Dinkins' associate knew less. Ruby Hughes has written that Adelaide's mother was married twice: to Henry S. Mould, whom she divorced in 1891; and to a stage actor named John Mason, whom she divorced in 1900. However, an obituary found in the 1914 *Dramatic Mirror* reported that Manola was married three times: to Mould, Mason, and "George G. Gates." After Dinkins' associate happened upon the Kensico site, the Gates marriage was verified.

Upon leaving Kensico Cemetery in Valhalla, Dinkins' clerk drove to Bedford Hills, Rupert Hughes' place of residence from 1908 to 1918. There, she found back issues of a newspaper called the *North Westchester Times*, published during the years Rupert and Adelaide lived in Westchester County. Like the Keokuk *Gate City,* the *Times* printed the social comings and goings of the residents of Westchester County, including Mount Kisco and Bedford Hills, two of the communities in which Rupert Hughes owned or rented country estates. Rupert Hughes and Adelaide are mentioned frequently, as are Rush and Avis (referred to in the paper as Rush and Avis Bissell, not Hughes, until approximately the year 1916). Interestingly, Dinkins' colleague studied the volumes for the years 1911 to 1917 and did not find one reference to Elspeth or her summer visits to the Hughes farm.

The paper printed a eulogy to Marion Manola in the October 9, 1914 edition:

> Marion Manola, a famous light opera star of 20 years ago and wife of George G. Gates, an accountant, died in the New Rochelle Hospital Thursday night after an operation. She was 48 years of age and was born in Oswego, N.Y., the daughter of John Stevens, an inventor. She studied for grand opera under Madame Marchesi in Paris and made her debut in London in the title role of the light opera "Maid Marian."
>
> Later Miss Manola became well known to American theatregoers through her leading roles in . . . many musical productions. Her chief dramatic successes were won in "Friend Fritz" and "If I Were You" in which she appeared with John Mason, who at that time was her husband.
>
> Mrs. Gates was the mother of Mrs. Rupert Hughes, wife of the novelist and playwright.

The *North Westchester Times* confirmed again Marion Manola's marriage to George G. Gates, with the further information that he was an accountant. This news caused Dinkins' colleague to question anew why it was Rupert Hughes who handled Marion Manola's funeral arrangements, and not her husband, George Gates. (It was on the occasion of Marion Manola's death in 1914 that Hughes made his first purchase of property at Kensico Cemetery.) The *Times* obituary also added an interesting piece of trivia about Manola: it stated that she was once a student of Madame Marchesi in Paris, the same voice teacher who had instructed Greta Hughes—perhaps even at the same time. (Curiously, there is no similar obituary in the *Westchester Times* to Greta Witherspoon in February 1916, the date on her death certificate. As Greta was buried in nearby Kensico, and her brother was a famous local resident, it seemed the newspaper would eulogize her as they had Rupert's mother-in-law. The volumes pertaining to the years 1912 to 1914 were incomplete; it was therefore impossible to determine whether an obituary for Greta appeared during the years Avis testified that she died: 1913 or 1914.)

Based on the information in her obituaries and on her death certificate, Marion Manola was born in 1867, which meant that she was only five years older than Rupert Hughes—actually closer to his age than her daughter Adelaide was. If Adelaide had been born in 1884, as the *Los Angeles Times* reported, she would have been twelve years younger than Hughes. Learning this, Garrison's statement in *Goodbye My Keokuk Lady*—that Rupert Hughes was once married to Marion Manola—seemed at least plausible. However, none of the obituaries on Manola made reference to a marriage to Hughes, and Dinkins' associate had no idea when such an event could have even occurred.

As a precaution, however, the ad litem's investigator began to collect the marriage and divorce records on Marion Manola. There was little or no information about when the events in her life took place, other than Ruby Hughes' suggestion that Manola divorced her first husband Henry Mould in 1891 and her second husband John Mason in 1900. Since she died as Mrs. Gates fourteen years later, it was reasonably safe to assume there was no one in between Mason and Gates. Furthermore, Rupert Hughes married Adelaide Bissell in 1908, and was not divorced from Agnes until 1904. With such busy marital calendars, there did not seem to be a conceivable point of intersection for Hughes and Marion Manola.

The next enlightening piece of information on the Manolas was provided, indirectly, by Rupert Hughes. The ad litem learned about a book of poems written by Adelaide in the early 1920s and published posthumously by Rupert Hughes. At the beginning of the small volume, Hughes included a memorial to his late wife. In it, he discusses both Adelaide and her mother Marion. It is reprinted here in part:

341

MEMORIAL

As a young woman, Adelaide went through alternations of wealth and want. For a time she was dependent upon her own resources for the support of herself and her two children by her first marriage; but she endured the alternating hardships and successes of stage life with equanimity.

When we were married we had not much money. Later she had a good deal, for a writer's wife. Then she indulged herself as best she could in as much splendor as she could afford. She was called by many the best-dressed woman in America.

Her first ambitions were for the stage. Her mother was "Marion Manola," the delightful, the classic figure in light opera, a pupil of Marchesi and for a few years a reigning queen in her field. Adelaide, whose maiden name was Mould, was born in Cleveland, Ohio, May 7, 1884, and loved to use her mother's stage name, "Manola," which had been chosen for her by Madame Marchesi.

After an early marriage, Marion Stevens Mould went with her husband to Paris, both of them to study for opera. They took the infant Adelaide with them and her early years were spent abroad. On a later visit to England, Marion left Adelaide, then five, in a convent to be cared for until her return. . . .

As she grew into girlhood she developed such a likeness to her beautiful mother that she now and then took her mother's place on the stage and no one was the wiser.

Hughes goes on to mention how he met Adelaide while writing a never-finished play for actress Blanche Bates, Adelaide's closest friend. "Marriage followed soon," he noted.

In his memorial to Adelaide, Hughes paints a curious portrait of a tortured soul: " . . . always a sufferer from frenzies of melancholy and from onsets of acute pain; . . . a personality of extraordinary vividness, a mingling of extreme bravery and timorous self-distrust, an exceedingly keen wit, and a very profound power for agony; . . . I have known her to weep for whole days and nights in despair so black that I lived incessantly in the dread that she should take her own life, as at last she did one lonely midnight on a French ship in the harbor of Haiphong in French Indo-China . . . she had hanged herself by a trunk strap swung over her electric fixture—a ghastly and desperate conclusion, like Sappho's leap from the Leukadian cliff."

Unfortunately, Adelaide's and Marion's exotic backgrounds were mysterious and difficult to trace. Avis testified that Adelaide was educated in the Sacred Heart Convent in Paris, while Rupert Hughes wrote that she was placed in a convent in England. Neither could be confirmed. Their ages were somewhat perplexing, as well: if Marion Manola were born in 1867 (as her death certificate and Bedford obituary stated), she would have been seventeen when Adelaide was born in 1884. Adelaide, by those dates, would have been sixteen at the time of Avis' birth in 1900 and fifteen when she married Bissell.

Finally, Dinkins' associate was haunted by Rupert's declaration that Adelaide so closely resembled her mother Marion that she often took her mother's place on the stage "and no one was the wiser." This slightly eery disclosure brought to mind a review of Adelaide's performance in Rupert Hughes' 1908 play, *All for a Girl,* furnished earlier in the investigation by Robert Hughes. The critic described Adelaide as "the beautiful daughter of a once more beautiful mother," as if to imply that Marion Manola were either no longer alive, or that something tragic had befallen her, though the review was written six years before Marion Manola's reported death in 1914. The quote that followed was more curious still: "Oh, this insatiable maw of the stage, which swallows up beauty and youth and genius and leaves us only memories." What was the reason for this strange allusion to Marion Manola in 1908? (She would have been, after all, only forty-one years old.)

A Scandal in Syracuse

For the moment, the ad litem put the Manolas aside and turned his thoughts to Agnes Hedge, Rupert Hughes' first wife. The investigation of the Hughes family was into its fourth year; the trial to determine Howard, Jr.'s, heirs was scheduled for the next year, and neither Dinkins nor anyone else associated with the heirship case had been able to locate the final decree of divorce between Rupert and Agnes. The only document to that effect was the 1903 decree of separation. It was clear from deposition testimony that the alternate custody arrangement was not practiced, and everyone concerned was anxious to find the final judgment to see what provisions it contained for the daughter whose identity was so much at issue. The ad litem was further interested in the possibility that there might be transcripts or additional pleadings from the divorce (or separation) trial, to see what sort of allegations and cross-allegations were made concerning Agnes' (or Rupert's) infidelity, as it related to Elspeth's legitimacy.

In that regard, Dinkins' associate engaged a graduate student from Syracuse University to study back issues of the Syracuse newspapers for some mention of the date or place of Rupert and Agnes Hughes' divorce. Agnes' son William Reynolds, Jr., had apprised Dinkins' associate that his mother was born in Buffalo, New York, and moved to Syracuse at the age of eight (in 1882), when her father, Charles L. Hedge, an insurance agent, received a promotion. By Reynolds' description, the Hedges were rather prominent in the city of Syracuse, and Dinkins' associate correctly guessed that the society column of the Syracuse newspaper might provide a running account of Agnes Hedge's activities, both before and after her marriage to Rupert Hughes. The student researcher was thus instructed to peruse the society columns during the years of the Hughes marriage for some mention of Elspeth; and to review the substantive sections of the paper during the 1903 separation proceedings, for either an account of the trial testimony or some indication as to where Rupert and Agnes were ultimately divorced.

Dinkins' Syracuse researcher proved able to trace Agnes' social calendar with amazing regularity and precision, from her years at the Keble School in Syracuse to the first years of her marriage to Rupert Hughes. In addition, there was front page coverage of each day's lurid testimony at the Hughes separation proceedings in 1903—the same trial that inspired headlines in the *New York Times.*

It appeared from the Syracuse research that Agnes graduated from the Keble School (the finishing school recalled by Reynolds, run by two maiden ladies) on June 17, 1892, at age seventeen. Keble, according to Dinkins' Syracuse researcher, was a school "for bright and up and coming girls of the middle to upper class . . . a cut below the upper crust." The summer following graduation, Agnes and her former classmates took a tour of Europe, and on her return, Agnes enrolled in Evelyn College. Agnes Hedge's name appeared frequently in the newspaper society column during these years, when she socialized often with a regular circle of friends, most of whom were in the same middle- to upper-middle-class social strata as herself. One of her more notable beaus was Robert J. Grant, later named as a co-respondent by Rupert Hughes in their separation proceeding.

On December 12, 1893, Agnes married Rupert Hughes in New York City, where they made their home. Although there was no formal announcement in the Syracuse paper of their wedding, Agnes is described as "Mrs. Rupert Hughes" in the January 7, 1894 "In Society" column of the *Syracuse Evening-Herald*, printed two weeks after the wedding. She and Rupert were shown to visit the Hedges several times during the first few months of their marriage. These are the only notations of Rupert Hughes' presence in Syracuse. For the remainder of 1894, and all of 1895 and 1896, Agnes returned alone to visit her parents approximately four or five times a year.

Elspeth Hughes, according to her birth certificate, was born in New York City on May 23, 1897. The May 30, 1897 *Syracuse Evening-Herald* printed this significant item in the society column: "Mrs. Rupert Hughes and her daughter are to spend the summer months with Mrs. Hughes' mother, Mrs. Charles Hedge, of West Onondaga Street.''

Here was further proof that a child was born to Agnes H. Hughes in May 1897, the month Elspeth is alleged to have been born to Rupert and Agnes. Unfortunately, the daughter is not mentioned by name. A similar item appeared in the social news section of the Syracuse paper two months later. Again, the daughter's first name is not stated: ''Mrs. Rupert Hughes and her daughter of New York are the guests for the summer of Mrs. Hughes' mother, Mrs. Charles L. Hedge of West Onondaga Street.'' On August 29, 1897, the same gossip columnist noted that ''Mrs. Rupert Hughes returned to her home in New York.''

The Syracuse social columns confirmed that Agnes Hughes gave birth to a daughter in May 1897 and that she and the child spent the following summer with Agnes' mother, Julia Hedge, in Syracuse. Unfortunately, this was the last mention of Agnes, Rupert, or their daughter in the Syracuse newspapers until the time of their highly publicized separation proceedings in 1903.

The newspaper accounts of the Hughes' separation trial extended from October to November 1903, when they were a daily feature in the Syracuse newspapers, complete with sketches or photographs of the principal witnesses as they appeared in court.

The Syracuse newspaper descriptions of the separation proceedings provide a running account of the Hughes marriage and reiterate that a daughter was born to the couple in 1897. In two of these articles she is referred to by name as ''Elspeth.'' The October 20, 1903, *Syracuse Journal,* however, reported that efforts were being made ''to bring about . . . some satisfactory arrangement by which (Agnes) might have her baby boy in a separate home.''

Rupert and Agnes' child's nursemaid appeared as one of the witnesses and was identified as Jeanne Crepin, a young French woman. (In conflict with that, William Reynolds, Jr., stated during the heirship investigation that his half-sister Elspeth's nanny was a British woman called ''Miss Page,'' who returned to care for him when he was a young child. Miss Page is nowhere mentioned in the separation proceedings.) Another point of interest was the stated fact that Rupert and Agnes went from London to Shanghai, China, sometime after or during Rupert's period of employment with the Encyclopedia Britannica in England from 1900 to 1901. Coincidentally, it was during this same period, 1900 to 1902, that George Bissell and Adelaide Manola Bissell were living in Kobe, Japan, not a great distance from Shanghai. When asked to list his places of residence in later years, Rupert Hughes never once mentioned China, though he scrupulously recounted all other locales, including London.

The most shocking disclosures in the trial, however, stemmed from the prolific charges of adultery brought by Rupert against Agnes. Hughes named eight co-respondents:

1. Captain Henry R. Lemly
2. Max Karger, "a distinguished musician"
3. Lieut. William H. Reynolds (whom Agnes married a year later)
4. James C. Beebe of Keokuk, Iowa
5. Crowell Campbell
6. Arthur Conover
7. J. Marmaduke Robinson
8. Robert J. Grant of Syracuse (Agnes' former beau before she married Rupert)

Although Agnes' lawyer staunchly denied that the men were anything more than "friends" of his client, much of the testimony suggested otherwise.

Certain other significant points taken from the newspaper accounts of the proceedings follow:

•Oct. 14, 1903: "Mrs. Hughes testified that once Hughes called her a Bowery washerwoman and had told her she was living an adventurous and adulterous life. . . . It was at the time Hughes called her a Bowery washerwoman and referred to her alleged adulterous life that he told her he would no longer live with her, she testified. He wanted her to get a divorce, and said if she did not he would make the name of Hughes so odious that she would be glad to get rid of it, and gave her to understand that he had no further use for her."

"It was on August 20th, 1901, that her husband called her a Bowery washerwoman. She fixed the date in her complaint by consulting her diary, which she had since destroyed. . . . Pressed to tell why she destroyed the diary, Mrs. Hughes broke down and wept. Her mother did likewise. When her composure returned, witness said that the diary contained personal references of a close nature and records of the early life of her child. . . ."

•Agnes Hughes testified on October 14, 1903, that she and Rupert did not become any way prosperous until they went to Europe: "Of the $6,000 a year that it took Mr. Hughes and I to live, a great deal of it came from my mother's pocketbook."

•Agnes' attorney, Lyman Spaulding, charged that "Mr. and Mrs. Witherspoon, the brother-in-law and sister of Hughes, were responsible for the whole trouble through their dislike of his client." (October 15)

•On October 15, Rupert's attorney introduced a letter he claimed was written by Agnes Hughes to Crowell Campbell, one of the named co-respondents. It stated in part:

> "I am here all by myself, sweetheart, and I am thinking of you so hard that I find it impossible to keep from writing you to tell you that I love you, oh so much. . . ."

•William Herbert Reynolds testified on October 10 that he met Agnes Hughes on the Battleship Texas in 1896, and called on her (and Rupert Hughes) thereafter.

A key witness in the separation proceedings was a woman named Tashleene Jarvis, described as the widow of a former member of the "big law firm" of Reed, Simpson, Thatcher, and Barnum. Mrs. Jarvis was at one time friendly with both Rupert and Agnes Hughes, but sided with Agnes at the time of the trial. Mrs. Jarvis and Agnes Hughes met in Montclair, New Jersey, in 1895, where Mrs. Jarvis ran a boarding house. "It is at Mrs. Jarvis' boarding house at Clifton," the October 19, 1903 *Evening Herald* reported, "that much of the kissing to which Mr. Hughes takes exception is alleged to take place." According to Agnes Hughes' testimony, Rupert Hughes was "very friendly" with Mrs. Jarvis, and often borrowed money from her. Both Agnes and Rupert Hughes stayed at Jarvis' summer house in Trenton at no cost in 1896, and saw her regularly thereafter.

Called to the stand as a witness for Agnes, Mrs. Jarvis denied Rupert Hughes' allegations of improper behavior at her boarding house: "Mrs. Jarvis testified that she and Mrs. Hughes slept together while Mr. Reynolds was at her house, and that Mr. Reynolds occupied a room opposite the room occupied by Mr. Hughes," reported the *Post—Standard*. The newspaper went on to cite the "friction" that later developed between Tashleene Jarvis and Rupert Hughes. She explained that this was because "Hughes refused to corroborate certain evidence in her divorce from a Colonel Earley, and that she did not care to consider him a friend thereafter." Later in the trial, Agnes' lawyer asked her: "Did you ever see Mr. Hughes kiss Mrs. Jarvis?" On hearing this, according to the *Evening-Herald,* "Rupert Hughes sat bolt upright." Agnes then added, "I have seen Mr. Hughes kiss nearly every woman who ever came into our house."

As detailed and sensational as the Syracuse newspaper accounts of the Hughes separation proceedings were, Dinkins' local researcher could not find any mention of the couple's divorce. The serial installments of each day's testimony ended at the point of the November 1903 *New York Times* piece, with an announcement that Rupert and Agnes reached an out-of-court separation agreement with provisions for alternate custody of their daughter. This merely restated the terms of the separation decree already in Dinkins' possession, and left unanswered the question many in the heirship case were asking: where did Rupert and Agnes Hughes ultimately obtain a divorce? Dinkins' associate had checked in every place imaginable: Westchester County, Syracuse, even Washington, D. C. (since Agnes and Reynolds moved to D. C. after the November 1904 marriage) — all to no avail. The decree of divorce could not be found. The 1903 separation proceedings were filed and tried in New York County (Manhattan), where Rupert and Agnes Hughes then resided, and continued until November of that year. Twelve months later Agnes Hughes married William H. Reynolds, also in Manhattan. Dinkins was truly puzzled as to why the Hugheses did not secure their divorce in the same court as their separation action. He was further bothered by the fact that the separation file itself had only one document (the separation agreement). Considering the full-blown, several-week trial that generated massive press coverage, there should have been numerous pleadings filed by both Rupert's and Agnes' lawyers, not to mention a possible transcript of the proceedings. Where were the missing documents?

Though the research in the Syracuse papers yielded nothing about the location of the Hughes' divorce, it did provide a comprehensive account of the separation proceedings and shed considerable light on Rupert's and Agnes' personalities, as well as painting a vivid portrait of their marriage. It also lent a certain credence to the allegations of George Parnham's clients: that Rupert Hughes was sterile, and Elspeth was actually the daughter of Agnes and a paramour. Though Agnes and her attorney denied Rupert's accusations of adulteries with the eight men named as co-respondents, the circumstantial evidence and testimony introduced during the trial created at the very least a strong likelihood that this occurred: the love letter that Agnes allegedly wrote to Mr. Crowell Campbell; her entertainment of male guests in a scandalous "pink silk wrapper"; the stolen kisses observed by the French nanny; and most incriminating of all, the fact that she married one of her alleged lovers (William Reynolds) within months after the trial. All of this evidence and testimony suggested something else: that Rupert and Agnes were running with a rather fast crowd. The key to much of the confusion seemed to be Mrs. Tashleene Jarvis, the friend of both

348

Agnes and Rupert who ran a boarding house (''of questionable repute,'' according to Rupert) where much of the scandalous behavior was alleged to take place. Was she the neighbor whom Agnes later told her son, William Reynolds, Jr., that Rupert Hughes was ''carrying on with''? And what exactly caused the serious falling out between Tashleene and Hughes?

Then there was Elspeth. By the Syracuse accounts of the trial, Rupert and Agnes had a daughter by this name in 1903, and Agnes Hughes ''and daughter'' had visited the home of Mrs. Julia Hedge in 1897. Curious, however, was the gap between this visit in 1897 and the trial in 1903. Why were Agnes and her daughter not mentioned in any subsequent Syracuse social columns? Why, too, was the child's nanny identified during the 1903 proceedings as Jeanne Crepin, a French nursemaid, when Agnes Hughes Reynolds told her son, William, Jr., that Elspeth was attended by a ''Miss Page,'' the same British nanny who cared for William, Jr., as a child in 1913? And why did Rupert Hughes never acknowledge his period of residence in Shanghai, China, in 1900 and 1901?

A Secret Divorce

While supervising the eleventh-hour research through Syracuse newspapers for references to Agnes, Elspeth, Rupert, or the Hughes' separation or divorce proceedings, Dinkins' associate dispatched a new set of routine queries for information on documents inspired by certain of William Reynolds, Jr.'s, recollections and observations about his parents. From two such seemingly innocuous requests came stunning revelations concerning Rupert, Agnes, and Elspeth.

First, Dinkins' colleague was able to find a set of guardianship proceedings relative to Agnes Hedge Hughes Reynolds. Mrs. Reynolds died in Eastern State hospital for the insane in 1944. She had been declared incompetent, however, six years earlier, in 1939, and was hospitalized in a sanitarium in Cleveland. Elspeth Lapp, identified in the proceedings as her daughter, was appointed Agnes' guardian. (She resigned this position three years later, in 1941, and a successor guardian was named.) Included in the original guardianship file was a schedule of services prepared by Elspeth Lapp's attorney, reflecting the legal work he provided in connection with Agnes Reynolds' guardianship. Reviewing the file, Dinkins' colleague was struck by three entries in the attorney's calendar:

Nov. 17, 1939:	Mrs. Tashleene (Teddy) M. Robertson lives at 'The Hedges' — Route 2 — Excelsior, Minn., c/o Carroll Brown . . .
	Had thorough conference with Mrs. Robertson, who related the mental condition and the actions of Mrs. Reynolds, before, at the time of, and after she signed the Trust Agreement and Will at Jacksonville, Fla.
	. . . stayed a long time with Mrs. Robertson and took copious notes so as to prepare a full typewritten statement.
Nov. 24, 1939:	Took extensive "deposition" of Mrs. Tashleene Robertson, as to condition of Mrs. Reynolds.
Jan. 5, 1940:	Carefully went over Florida Inheritance Code of 1933, to try to determine what *interest* (Elspeth) Lapp would have in Mrs. Reynolds' estate, if there were *no* will and *no* trust agreement.

Could the "Tashleene (Teddy) Robertson" whose deposition was taken in connection with Agnes H. Reynolds' guardianship in 1939 possibly be the "Mrs. Tashleene Jarvis" who testified on behalf of Agnes in her separation action against Rupert Hughes in 1903, and who figured so prominently in the lives of both Rupert and Agnes during their marriage? Or was Tashleene Robertson actually Tashleene Jarvis' daughter? Common sense would suggest that they were either the same person or intimately related. How many "Tashleenes" could there possibly be who were well acquainted with Agnes Hedge Hughes Reynolds?

The other point of interest in the guardianhip proceedings was the fact that Elspeth Lapp's attorney made note of his "careful" study of the Florida Inheritance Code to determine what "interest" his client, Elspeth Hughes Lapp, would have in Agnes Reynolds' estate if Mrs. Reynolds' 1938 will were declared invalid due to her possible incompetence at the time it was executed. Why, one might well ask, would it be necessary for Elspeth's attorney to check the Florida law of inheritance so closely—unless there was some question in his mind that Elspeth was Agnes' daughter?

At the same time Dinkins' colleague ordered Mrs. Reynolds' guardianship papers, she also requested copies of the application for a widow's pension made by Agnes after Navy Captain William Reynolds' death. Their son, William, Jr., once mentioned that to prove herself entitled to the pension, Agnes had to show that she was legally married to Reynolds, and legally divorced from her husband previous to him. (This prompted Elspeth's "offhand" remark: "Gee, I hope I'm legitimate!") Dinkins' associate hoped, therefore, that the pension file might in some way suggest when and where Agnes finally divorced Rupert Hughes.

Typical of the bureaucratic system, Reynolds, Sr.'s, Veterans Administration file was almost the size of *War and Peace*. It was, however, well worth the time and trouble to read, for several interesting reasons. It indicated, for instance, that Reynolds—like Rupert, Agnes, George, and Adelaide Manola Bissell—was in the Far East (Shanghai) in late 1900, stationed on the *U.S.S. Brooklyn*. The file also contained copies of the Letters of Guardianship concerning Agnes Reynolds. These were necessary for the government to release Agnes' pension check to her legal guardian during her period of incompetency: first Elspeth H. Lapp, and later Charlotte S. Boush (a relative of William Reynolds, Jr.). In that regard, Agnes' next-of-kin were required to demonstrate their relationship to her. Consequently, there is a copy of William Reynolds, Jr.'s, birth certificate in the Veterans Administration file. For no stated reason, however, there is no birth certificate on record for Elspeth. Even more interesting, there is a form dated December 16, 1939, in the pension file, addressed to the chief attorney for claims. The form in question directs that Agnes Reynolds' pension check be suspended, to be sent to her legal guardian (at that time, Elspeth H. Lapp). Shown on the form to be the next of kin or "next friend" of the incompetent (in this case, Agnes), is Elspeth H. Lapp. In the blank to indicate her relationship to Agnes Reynolds, the word "daughter" has been typed in, and beneath it, also typed, is "(alleged)."

Were the allusions in these two files that Elspeth's relationship to Agnes was somehow in question simply red herrings, or was there some significance to them? Why did it seem that Elspeth's identity was always at issue?

As interesting as these disclosures in Reynold's pension file were, the real pearl in the oyster was yet to come. Just as her son William, Jr., had implied, Agnes was put through miles of red tape before she qualified for her widow's pension. Enclosed in the file were a blizzard of letters between Agnes' Jacksonville attorney and the director of claims for the V.A. office, marking the progress of her application for a widow's pension. The chief stumbling block, as this correspondence suggested, was the continuing effort to secure a copy of Agnes' final divorce from Rupert Hughes. As her attorney wrote in 1938: "Some time ago I made application for Mrs. Reynolds for the ordinary and customary widow's pension to be paid to the widows of deceased navy officers. It took some time to get a certified copy of the decree of divorce in Brooklyn, N. Y. but when that was furnished in January, I assumed that everything necessary was completed to enable the Department to award this pension."

Not only did William Reynolds' V.A. records contain this reference to the long-missing final divorce decree, there was a copy of the elusive document in the file! The final judgment of divorce between Rupert and Agnes Hedge Hughes was dated July 12, 1904 (eight months after the separation decree and four months before Agnes' marriage to William H. Reynolds). It was filed in the Supreme Court of Queens County, New York, one of the five boroughs in New York City. Why, Dinkins' associate wondered, did the Hugheses change venue from the borough of Manhattan (where their separation action was pending) to the neighboring borough of Queens for their divorce? The judgment itself was only two pages long. It indicated that Agnes Hughes filed for the divorce in January 1904 (shortly after the November 1903 separation agreement), and she was awarded an interlocutory decree of divorce from Rupert Hughes in April (effective July 12) by default (i.e., Hughes did not file an answer to Agnes' complaint). The final judgment was interesting for three reasons:

(1)   Rupert Hughes did not answer Agnes' petition, nor did he appear to contest or countercharge, despite the months of mud-slinging in the separation action of several months before. Why would he fight Agnes so bitterly in the separation trial and lose by default in the divorce, allowing *her* to get the divorce from *him*?

(2)   Why the change of venue from New York County to Queens County?

(3)   Most significantly, why was there no provision in the final judgment of divorce for custody of Elspeth? The separation agreement filed in Manhattan in November 1903 providing for alternate custody was not incorporated in the divorce decree, therefore it did not apply. How could there be a final judgment of divorce without custody provisions for the couple's child?

352

More Questions About Elspeth:
A Case of Mistaken?

After the almost accidental discovery of Rupert and Agnes' final judgment of divorce with its conspicuously absent custody provisions, Dinkins' associate paused to reevaluate the allegations about Elspeth. With less than six months to go before the heirship trial, Robert Hughes had been largely discredited in certain important respects: Patterson Dial was safely assumed to have been born in 1902, which made it impossible for her to be Elspeth's mother (though she appeared older to several people, possibly the result of long hours and emotional strain); her maiden name appeared to be "Dial," not "Patterson"; Leila Hughes' life had been traced from birth to motherhood to death; no birth certificate could be located for an Elspeth Dial, or death certificate for a drowned Leila Hughes; Elspeth Hughes looked much the same from 1920 to 1945, according to William Reynolds, Jr.; and Robert Hughes could find none of the magazine or newspaper articles he insisted he saw in his uncle's trunk, and which he so fervently believed would confirm his version of Rupert Hughes' life.

Still, Robert Hughes never faltered in his statements about Rupert and the others, and he and his attorneys persisted in their search for the missing clippings and refused to be intimidated by the subtle scoffs and jeers of the lawyers representing the more established potential heirs. In defense of his unsuccessful search for *All for a Girl* and the other articles or interviews Hughes swore would prove his case, he testified at the time of his 1979 deposition: "If I had the names of the books and magazines I would have the material before you here. The span of time has taken a little bit of toll and my mind will not put those back at my fingertips." If Robert Hughes' story were 100 percent inaccurate, how could one explain his dogged efforts to prove it? By all appearances, Robert Hughes was publicizing his version of Rupert's life before the death of Howard R. Hughes, Jr. He insisted the allegations about Elspeth and Rupert Hughes had been in his family for years. Why else would he spend hours reviewing magazines and newspapers, if he knew that what he was saying was a complete fabrication? Furthermore, Hughes had engaged a conservative and highly respected law firm to represent him in his claims, and his attorneys shared his convictions.

All things considered, it was hard to believe that a hallucination, fabrication, or fantasy (as Rush and Avis' Houston attorney described Hughes' tale) could be as detailed and specific as Robert Hughes' story was. Then, too, there was the Harvard Alumni Report (filled in by Howard R. Hughes, Sr.), which showed that "Felix Moner Hughes" was

Howard, Sr.'s, father, and the two independent sources who encountered references to the drowning of Rupert Hughes' daughter, not to mention the eery discovery of both Leila Hughes and a secret Rupert Hughes lot at Kensico Cemetery. As genealogist Mary Fay remarked long after the heirship trial, there had to be a "grain of truth" in what Hughes related.

Robert Hughes' heirship counterparts were the group of Hughes cousins from the Midwest, represented by George Parnham, who stated that it was "common family knowledge" that Rupert Hughes was sterile, caused by a childhood disease. Like Robert Hughes, they had no documentary proof of their claim, although at least fifteen relations signed sworn affidavits attesting that Hughes was infertile. This set of would-be heirs claimed that Elspeth's father was one of Agnes Hughes' lovers during her marriage to Rupert.

Despite the fact that many of the points Robert Hughes advanced concerning Rupert, his wives, and Elspeth were shattered, and that the Parnham group had no medical evidence to support their claim that Hughes was sterile, both Dinkins' associate and his genealogist Mary Fay were convinced there was something about Elspeth that just didn't hang together.

In preparation for the approaching heirship trial, Dinkins' associate tried to put together a chronological profile of Elspeth's life. In doing so, she made some disturbing discoveries.

Assembling all the material extant on Elspeth, Dinkins' clerk studied the pattern of her life. From these papers, interviews, documents, etc., certain truths emerged. It was clear, for instance, that a girl baby was born in May 1897: not only was there a birth certificate with the name "Elspeth Hughes" (which Robert Hughes claims was forged), but the Syracuse society column made note of Agnes Hedge Hughes' visit to her parents' house "with daughter" (no first name mentioned) between May and August 1897. Then, oddly, there is no further mention of the Hedges' granddaughter in the Syracuse social column until 1903, when the Syracuse papers provided daily coverage of the sensational trial in New York City concerning Rupert and Agnes' legal separation. In 1903, the daughter is referred to as "Elspeth" in both the newspaper accounts of the trial, and in the November 1903 separation agreement between Rupert and Agnes, with provisions for alternate custody of Elspeth. In two of the many newspaper articles covering the trial in 1903, the child is described as a six-year-old; in another, as a "baby boy." Simple misreporting? Or was there some confusion?

Where was Elspeth between the summer of 1897 (when she visited Syracuse with Agnes) and the trial in 1903? Rupert and Agnes were in Europe between 1900 and 1901, which would explain why the Hedges'

354

granddaughter was not mentioned in the Syracuse columns for that year and a half. That does not explain, however, why she was not shown to visit her grandparents in Syracuse from the fall of 1897 to early 1900. Agnes and Rupert were then living in New York City, and Agnes had always been a frequent visitor to her parents' home in Syracuse during her marriage. Just as faithfully, the Syracuse social column made note of these visits. Agnes' name does appear in the "In Syracuse Society" section on a few occasions after 1897, but her daughter is never mentioned. As close as Agnes was to her parents, and as often as Agnes' name made the social column, this omission seemed slightly peculiar.

Elspeth's whereabouts after the separation and custody trial are even more mysterious. First, there is a genuine question about who in fact retained custody: Agnes or Rupert? Second, based on all the information then available to Dinkins' associate, there was not a single clue as to Elspeth's residence from 1904 (the divorce) until approximately 1908. In 1908 or 1909, Elspeth resurfaced. Avis remembered the first of Elspeth's summer visits to Rupert's home in Bedford Hills about that time, and understood that she lived with her mother in Washington the remainder of the year. Yet William Reynolds, Jr., Agnes' son by Lieutenant Reynolds, had said that it was Rupert, not his mother, who received custody of Elspeth. He knew nothing about her whereabouts until her enrollment at St. Mary's School in Peekskill, New York, in February 1914. Where was Elspeth between 1904 and 1908, when she began her summer visits to Rupert's farm? She was not with Rupert, nor was she with Agnes those five years.

Beginning in 1908, Elspeth's *summers* were accounted for by Avis (and later Rush, beginning with his first summer at Bedford Hills in 1911). Where was she the remainder of the year? Elspeth's first known school records begin in 1911, with her enrollment at the Madeira School outside Washington, and from that point forward her residence and association with Agnes and William Reynolds, Sr., is established via William Reynolds, Jr. Young Reynolds has pictures of Elspeth with his family from 1913 through 1945, the year of her death. (Perhaps significantly, his mother had no earlier pictures of Elspeth, to his knowledge.) From 1911 to 1914, Elspeth attended Madeira, and in 1914 she transferred to St. Mary's in Peekskill. Elspeth left St. Mary's in June 1916 and enrolled the following fall at the National Cathedral School in Washington, which she attended for one year. This left the period between 1908 and 1911 still unaccounted for, except for summers, which were then spent at Rupert's farm (according to Avis).

From 1917 (after Cathedral School) to 1922, Elspeth apparently lived in Washington with the Reynoldses, and William, Jr., remembered that she was employed for a time as a stenographer. She made her debut in the winter of 1921–22 and was married to Ed Lapp in March of 1922. After her marriage to Lapp, Elspeth's life ceased to be mysterious. She gave birth to three daughters (Agnes, Elspeth, and Barbara) between 1923 and 1925, as Ed Lapp tried out various occupations in Washington, and later Jacksonville (where Agnes and William Reynolds then lived). In the mid-1920s, the Lapps moved from Jacksonville to Cleveland, where they remained permanently. There Elspeth died in 1945.

With this sketchy outline of Elspeth's life, Dinkins' associate worked to fill in the holes, mostly of Elspeth's childhood and adolescence. A full-scale effort was launched to locate a baptismal record, which would confirm both Elspeth's name (Elspeth or Leila), and her exact year and date of birth. This was a dismal failure. The ad litem's investigators made inquiries at the church in Keokuk where Howard, Jr., was christened (attended by the Felix Hugheses), the church where Rupert and Agnes were married in New York, and other likely churches in New York City (both Presbyterian, Agnes' faith, and Episcopalian, then Rupert's). One of Dinkins' employees managed to find out which church the Hedges attended in Syracuse (Park Central Presbytary) and learned that Agnes retained her membership until 1901 (after the 1897 birth). However, there was no record to indicate that Agnes brought her daughter back to Park Central in Syracuse to be baptized. The Hedge family was originally from Buffalo (before Charles Hedge's move to Syracuse when Agnes was eight) and attended Westminster Presbyterian Church in that city. Though they retained a number of ties to Buffalo, there was no record of baptism for Elspeth at the Westminster Church.

The apparent absence of Elspeth's baptismal record was particularly puzzling in light of William Reynolds, Jr.'s, statement that his mother Agnes "was an ardent Presbyterian and was always strict about her children going to Sunday School." Reynolds himself was baptized, and was certain "Sister" would have been, too. Reynolds also related that, after moving to Washington around 1905 (Agnes and William Reynolds, Sr., were married in November 1904), his parents joined the Church of the Pilgrims Presbyterian Church, which was "just around the corner" from their house at 2230 Q St. N.W. "There may be a record of Sister's Sunday School attendance at the Church of the Pilgrims from 1905 to 1911," he suggested. "That would tell you if Sister was living with Mother at the time."

A call to the church confirmed what Dinkins' other records already suggested: that Elspeth did not live with Agnes until 1911, when she was enrolled at the Madeira School. The church coordinator and the church historian/associate pastor reviewed the parish records and discovered that the date of admission for "Elspeth Hedge Hughes" was October 6, 1912. According to the Pilgrims coordinator, she was "received by profession,'' which is the process of confirmation in the Presbyterian Church. Elspeth's address was shown as 2230 Q St., the home of William and Agnes Reynolds. The only other notation concerning Elspeth appeared on April 2, 1917, when she was dropped from membership ''to become a member of the Episcopalian Church.'' There was no record of Elspeth's baptism in the church records, nor was her date of birth shown.

In addition to revealing that Elspeth did not attend the Church of the Pilgrims until as late as 1912 (not 1905, when Agnes and Reynolds moved to Washington), the church records also pointed out another significant paradox concerning her life. The church coordinator related that Elspeth Hughes was confirmed Presbyterian at the Church of the Pilgrims in Washington on October 6, 1912, received by profession. The oddity in this was the fact that Elspeth's records at St. Mary's in Peekskill clearly stated that she was confirmed at the school on March 24, 1914 (one month after her arrival)—also in the Presbyterian faith. (Her St. Mary's records also show that she was baptized.) Why would Elspeth be confirmed twice in the same faith, within two year's time? Why, further, would she drop her membership at the Church of the Pilgrims in 1917 ''to become Episcopalian,'' only to marry as a Presbyterian in 1922—again at the Church of the Pilgrims?

There almost seemed, as others would later observe, to be two Elspeths. Whether this was somehow tied to Robert Hughes' tale of a drowning and later substitution was impossible to tell, but there were clearly many things in Elspeth's background that didn't fit together. After the detection of Elspeth's double confirmations, the ''missing years'' in her childhood, and the ambiguous or nonexistent custody arrangements for her after Rupert and Agnes' divorce, the ad litem's associate began to question her identity seriously. Not only were these few facts disturbing, but there was also the inconsistent 1976 testimony of Avis McIntyre (and Rush, who was by this time deceased) concerning Elspeth's age. Avis, who was born on December 19, 1900, had testified shortly after Howard R. Hughes, Jr.'s, death that Elspeth was ''about a year'' older than she. By this calculation Elspeth would have been born early in 1900, not in May of 1897, as her birth certificate stated. It seemed peculiar that Avis would be mistaken about this, since she was eight years old when she first met Elspeth, and saw her every summer until she was about sixteen. This abnormality was underscored by the seemingly incongruous report of Elspeth's formal debut in Washington in 1921–22, at the age of twenty-five, and the corresponding articles about her wedding in the Washington society section, all emphasizing the ''youthfulness'' of the bride. If Elspeth were born in early 1900, rather than May 1897, she would have been twenty-one at the time of her debut, which would have made much more sense. Elspeth's dual confirmations were also considered in this new light. She was confirmed for the first time in October of 1912—at what would be fifteen-and-a-half years old. If she had been born instead in 1900, she would have been twelve-and-a-half—the standard age for confirmants. The second confirmation, in 1914, made even less sense in connection with an 1897 birthdate: Elspeth would have been seventeen-and-a-half years old on this occasion, much older than the norm.

In light of these new concerns, and by virtue of Robert Hughes' continuing claim that Elspeth Hughes Lapp was not the daughter born to Rupert and Agnes Hughes in 1897, Avis' deposition was taken for a second time. Since she was the only person still living who had been acquainted with most of the individuals whose lives were in question, Avis was in the best position to respond to the queries about Elspeth. (By this time, of course, Avis and Rush were included in the settlement agreement with Elspeth's daughters and the maternal heirs to divide Hughes' estate privately.)

During this second deposition, Robert Hughes himself was in attendance, seated next to his attorney, Ollie Blan. Avis, put to the test of answering more questions about Rupert, Elspeth and the others, was her usual prickly self. "Just don't let us take up time if we don't have to," she snapped at Dinkins. "Time is running," she later admonished him. "George (George Dean, Avis' personal attorney) said that it would take an hour, and it's nearly an hour now, and we're only half through!" On more than one occasion, Mrs. McIntyre expressed irritation at answering questions about her background—as if she were not aware that millions of dollars were at stake, and that her claim to the Hughes inheritance as an equitably adopted daughter of Rupert Hughes was in serious dispute.

Despite such resistance and impatience, Avis eventually offered new insight on some old problems.

For example, she furnished what was now the third version of the origin of Elspeth's name. (The first was Robert Hughes' theory that "Elspeth" was an acronym for "Elizabeth Patterson Dial"; the second came from William Reynolds, Jr., who maintained that his mother Agnes was reading James Barrie's *Sentimental Tommy* while pregnant with "Sister," and chose the name after a minor character in the book, named "Elspeth.") Mrs. McIntyre stated that "Elspeth" was Welsh for Elizabeth:

Interviewer: While we're on that Welsh for Elizabeth, do you want to tell me a little bit about that name? It seems like a very unusual name to me, particularly the spelling.

Avis: Well, Rupert liked the name cause—I don't know if (Robert) Hughes knows this, but Hugheses are mostly Welsh—and Rupert liked the name derivation of Elizabeth. At least that's what I was told, of course.

Interviewer: You were told that by . . . Rupert?

Avis: Yes.

Interviewer: So, he was Welsh extraction?

Avis: Well, much on his father's side, yes—Hughes side.

Interviewer: And so the name "Elspeth" he was reverting to the Welsh?

Avis: To the Welsh, yes.

Interviewer: And did he indicate that he had selected that name for Elspeth?

Avis: Well, I think he did. Yes, I am sure he did. He explained it to me.

It was during this second deposition of Avis McIntyre in 1979, taken three years after the first, that the dialogue concerning Elspeth's age, repeated earlier in this text, occurred. She was questioned first by an attorney from Paul Freese's firm (representing Barbara Cameron et al.), who asked how old she thought Elspeth was the summer they met. "She was a year older that I," Avis stated. This same attorney came back to the question a second time, toward the end of his examination. Again, Avis responded: "Elspeth was a year older than I, yes." This was then repeated for emphasis. Later, Ted Dinkins cross-examined Avis. It was at this point that she was asked to repeat her statement that Elspeth was a year older than herself, which she did; then she was asked if she was "sure there was that one year disparity in age," which she said she was. Finally Dinkins asked, "Could Elspeth, say, have been three years older than you?" to which Avis responded adamantly: "No. She was a year older than I." All told, Avis McIntyre repeated this observation six times in the course of her second deposition. She was given the opportunity to amend her statement, but she refused to do so.

Avis also attempted to clarify Patterson Dial's age. The two met in 1924, when Avis was twenty-four. "I think she was about twenty-two," Mrs. McIntyre observed. "I knew she was 'cause Rupert said that she was so young." Avis' impression of Patterson's age was consistent with the 1902 birthdate she used on all official documents, and suggested again that Patterson at times appeared older than she was, during her mid-twenties to thirties.

Dinkins remembered Elspeth's treatment for nervous indigestion in the year before her death and William Reynolds, Jr.'s, comment that his half-sister had "brown spots of the nerve terminals all over her body," which Agnes claimed came from nervousness and emotional upset. He asked Avis if Elspeth appeared to be a nervous individual, or had any kind of nervous problems. Again, the facts did not match up. "I don't remember that she had any nervous problems," Avis replied. Nor did Avis recall that Elspeth either spoke or studied any foreign languages.

Before concluding the deposition, Robert Hughes' attorney questioned Avis about the private settlement agreement:

Interviewer: Are you aware that a formal written agreement has been drawn up in which the three girls, the daughters of Elspeth, concede you and your brother Rush to be heirs and agree upon a percentage distribution of the estate of Howard Hughes, Jr.?

Avis: Well, I would think so. George would be able to answer that better if he were here.

Interviewer: And do you understand that that agreement was based upon the fact that they would concede you and Rush to be heirs of the estate?

Avis: Absolutely, yes.

Here, Avis steadfastly denied that she, Rush, or their attorneys had ever implied that there was some doubt about Elspeth's relationship to Rupert:

Interviewer: Was that agreement to concede that you and Rush were heirs of the estate based upon your agreement to testify that Elspeth was the daughter of Rupert Hughes?

Avis: Well, I don't think that ever came into it because I don't think there is any question about it.

Interviewer: Has that been your position then at any time that you are discussing it with—

Avis: There has been no question about Elspeth being a daughter of Rupert Hughes, no.

Dinkins, having recently discovered Rupert Hughes' two cemetery lots at Kensico in Valhalla, New York, took the opportunity to question Avis further about Greta Witherspoon's death. It was Avis who testified several years earlier that Greta died in 1913 or 1914, rather than 1916, the date on her death certificate. In addition, Greta's monument was found located next to the grave markers of Adelaide and Marion Manola, Avis' mother and grandmother.

Interviewer: What about, can you pinpoint the date that she died, the date of her death?

Avis: Well, I know that it was that first—it might have been the second year. It might have been 1914, and I was at school in Virginia, and I got a letter from Mother saying how Greta had died, and that Rupert hadn't slept for thirty-six hours. I mean, he went into shock because they were very devoted brother and sister. And that's all I remember of that.

Interviewer: In other words, you think that her death would have been in 1913 or 1914?

Avis: I think so. I was in school in Virginia.

Interviewer: Okay.

Avis: I think it was the first or second year.

361

Interviewer: Would that be when you were in Foxcroft?

Avis: Yes. . . .

Interviewer: Do you know where the funeral services for Greta were held?

Avis: No.

Interviewer: You don't know where she would be buried, do you?

Avis: No.

Interviewer: No?

Avis: No, I don't.

So ended the second deposition of Avis McIntyre. No new or enlightening information about Elspeth's past or background was offered, the mystery about Greta's death (and the Kensico burial situation) was further perpetuated, and the question of Elspeth's age became a critical point of identification. Avis was dead certain—emphatic, even—that Elspeth was a year older than she, when by their birth certificates Elspeth would have been nearly four years older. Unlike the possible confusion concerning Patterson Dial, this could be no mistake in appearance. Avis was eight or so years old when she met Elspeth, and she saw her every summer until she was sixteen. Combined with Rush's deposition testimony that Elspeth was "a bit older" than Avis (he wasn't even sure at first who was the older or younger, and thought they were nearly the same age), it now appeared that there was a genuine conflict concerning Elspeth's year of birth.

Faced with this confusion, Dinkins' associate studied Elspeth's school records more closely for some possible explanation. Instead, the paradox deepened. Elspeth's first known school was Miss Madeira's, a private and expensive boarding school, then outside Washington, D.C. Madeira's records did not reflect any school or schools that Elspeth previously attended. What they did reveal was that she enrolled at Miss Madeira's in the fall of 1911 as an eighth grader (age fourteen). Elspeth withdrew from the school two and one half years later without graduating, on February 4, 1914, after the spring semester had begun. (During her enrollment at Miss Madeira's, Elspeth was confirmed as a

Presbyterian at the Church of the Pilgrims in Washington: October of 1912.)

It was William Reynolds, Jr., who provided the information leading to Elspeth's next school. He had never heard she attended Miss Madeira's, but knew that she was a student at St. Mary's and National Cathedral Schools. (Avis, in contrast, knew only of Madeira's.) Sister Mary Jean, the archivist for St. Mary's School (now St. Mary's Convent) in Peekskill, New York, examined and analyzed Elspeth's records. She determined that Elspeth entered St. Mary's Episcopal School in February 1914 (the month she withdrew from Madeira's) at age sixteen, in the middle of the ninth grade. (Oddly, Elspeth enrolled at Miss Madeira's two and one half years earlier as an *eighth* grader.) The next month, she was confirmed at the school as a Presbyterian. As at Miss Madeira's, there was no record in St. Mary's files of her previous schooling. Stranger yet, Sister Mary Jean discovered that Elspeth repeated the ninth grade (at which she entered) twice—in other words, for the duration of her years at St. Mary's. She withdrew (again without graduating) in the spring of 1916. Thus when she withdrew from St. Mary's in 1916, Elspeth was nineteen years old and in the *ninth* grade!

Asked to comment on this, Sister Mary Jean wrote, "Staying in one grade for three years and being nineteen in early high school does seem unusual." She added, "It is unusual that the record does not list her previous school: most of them do." The school archivist was also perplexed by Elspeth's confirmation at the school as a Presbyterian in March 1914, after being earlier confirmed at the Church of the Pilgrims in 1912. "It *does* seem odd that she was confirmed only six weeks after entering St. Mary's, as there was considerable stress on instruction and her Presbyterian training would not have been considered at all equivalent."

Through Sister Mary Jean, Dinkins' associate was able to find a former classmate of Elspeth's at St. Mary's: Marjorie Scott Kenyon. A letter was written to Mrs. Kenyon, asking her if she had been acquainted with a fellow student named Elspeth Hughes. Mrs. Kenyon remembered Elspeth, and discussed her with another friend who attended the school with her, before responding to Dinkins' inquiry. Marjorie Scott Kenyon was born in July 1900 and graduated from St. Mary's in 1916 at age sixteen. Judging from the information on Elspeth's birth certificate, Elspeth would have been three years older than Mrs. Kenyon. Yet this is not how Mrs. Kenyon related it. She wrote that Elspeth was not in her class, "nor in a friend's who was in the class *below* me." She described Elspeth as "a rather odd girl, rather a loner, erratic in study hall, restless and not at ease." Mrs. Kenyon and her friend both remembered that

Elspeth "mingled with the *younger* girls," and later added, "We *older* girls never saw much of her."

Here was yet another person who seemed to believe Elspeth was born in 1900 or later. Obviously, something was amiss. All in all, it was a strange set of circumstances. To add to the confusion, Elspeth went on to enroll at the National Cathedral School in the fall of 1916 as a nineteen-year-old. She attended Cathedral for one year, until the spring of 1917, when she withdrew—still without graduating. This meant that Elspeth was beginning her attendance at National Cathedral at an age when most students are in their sophomore or junior year in college.

She appears to have been from two to five years behind the norm, all of which would comport with the recollections of Avis, Rush, and Elspeth's St. Mary's classmate (Mrs. Kenyon) that Elspeth was born sometime around 1900. A 1900 birthdate would also be more compatible with her "youthful" wedding and debut in 1921–22 (when she would have been twenty-one instead of twenty-five), and her confirmation at age twelve, rather than age fifteen, in 1912. Still unexplained were Elspeth's two confirmations as a Presbyterian, her withdrawal from membership at the Church of the Pilgrims to become Episcopalian in 1917, and her subsequent marriage in 1922—at the same Pilgrim Presbyterian Church from which she had withdrawn.

William Reynolds, Jr., could not solve the mystery of Elspeth's past. He was fully informed about Elspeth's studies at St. Mary's School and remembered that his grandmother (Julia Hedge) "knew and often spoke highly of Sister Mary Anthony, the principal then." He was also familiar with Elspeth's attendance at National Cathedral in Washington, and did not seem to doubt her enrollment at Miss Madeira's (although he had no personal knowledge of it). These schools covered Elspeth's education from 1911 to 1917. "That still leaves a gap covering Sister's elementary schooling," he admitted. "I have no information on that and can't recall any talk of it." His only suggestion was that Elspeth "may have been with her father in New York some of that time." Yet it was clear Elspeth was not with Rupert, certainly not from 1908 to 1911 (when she summered, only, in Bedford Hills), and by all indications not between 1904 (the time of Rupert and Agnes' divorce) and 1908 (the beginning of the summer visitations).

Reynolds had certain other interesting observations to make in this late stage of the investigation. He related, for example, that his mother (Agnes) told him that she met his father (William H. Reynolds, Sr.) aboard the Battleship Texas in 1902 or 1903. By this statement it was made perfectly clear that Agnes Reynolds presented her son with a carefully edited version of her past: the Syracuse newspaper accounts of the Hughes separation trial reported on several occasions that Agnes met

Reynolds aboard the Texas in 1897—six years before she informed her son the acquaintance was made. William, Jr., was able to verify that his father was in Shanghai (and Japan) at certain times between 1899 and 1902, but denied that Reynolds, Sr., was ever in London while Rupert and Agnes were there in 1900 and 1901. Yet this fact, too, was made known through Reynolds, Sr.'s, testimony at the separation proceedings.

In response to another query, William, Jr., tried to identify Jeanne Crepin (the French nanny who attended Elspeth, according to the newspaper accounts of the Hughes trial). "I'm not familiar with a Jeanne Crepin, as such," he wrote. "I recall Mother speaking to my sister and my grandmother of a Jeanne on some occasions, but did not know what it was about. Possibly I was considered too young for such business." Reynolds persisted in his understanding that his sister Elspeth's nanny was a Britisher named Miss Page, the same woman who cared for him as a child. Why did Elspeth Hughes Lapp refer to her nanny as Miss Page, while the divorce accounts clearly show that the Hugheses' daughter had a French nursemaid named Jeanne Crepin?

Reynolds' statements illustrated two things: that whatever he repeated about Elspeth's early years was from other sources, since he was not born until 1913, and therefore was not a witness to these events; and that whatever he was told by his mother Agnes was very selectively edited.

More confused than ever about Elspeth's background, Dinkins' associate talked at greater length with Betty Rimell Westbrook, the daughter of Rupert's cousin Jenny Rimell (Electa Summerlin's daughter), who served as Elspeth's maid of honor and who knew her just before her wedding in 1922, when Betty was a student at the National Cathedral School. Mrs. Westbrook, a bright and charming seventy-six-year-old, met with Dinkins' associate at her home in Riverside, California, joined by her daughter, Mrs. Martha Pafe, also an alumnus of the Cathedral School. In what was by then an expected outcome, this conversation further confused, rather than clarified, the situation involving Elspeth.

Although Mrs. Westbrook had never been told that Elspeth was anyone other than Rupert's daughter, the circumstances surrounding her acquaintance with Elspeth merely added to her strange mystique. Betty Westbrook reiterated that she first met Elspeth in the fall of 1921, when Betty first enrolled at Cathedral in Washington. Though Rupert Hughes was very close to Betty's mother, Jenny Rimell (and to her grandmother Electa), and visited them rather often in Riverside, Mrs. Westbrook did not learn about Elspeth's existence until she was twelve, in 1916. (At this time her cousin, Frances McLain (Smith) was introduced to Elspeth for the first time, while Frances and Elspeth both attended the National Cathedral during the academic year 1916–17. Frances later told Betty she had met Elspeth.)

Betty Rimell Westbrook was born in July 1904. She knew Elspeth in 1921–22, at the time of her wedding to Ed Lapp. Asked how much older than herself Elspeth was, she replied, "I would say three years." Mrs. Westbrook was then informed that Elspeth's birth certificate showed she was born in 1897, which would make her eight—not three—years older than herself. Asked if that seemed possible, she responded, "I don't think so! I don't see how!" Pausing, she added, "I would say three to four years older, and that would be the most." Both Mrs. Westbrook and her daughter were confused by Elspeth's apparent age at the time she enrolled at Cathedral in 1916. By her birth certificate, she was nineteen years old. Mrs. Pafe, Mrs. Westbrook's daughter and a graduate of National Cathedral, found that highly unusual, and added, "That's when you *graduate*: at seventeen or eighteen."

Mrs. Westbrook also expanded on her earlier recollections about her attendance as maid of honor in Elspeth's wedding. She confirmed that she had known Elspeth only six or seven months before the wedding occurred (Betty Rimell enrolled at Cathedral in September 1921, and Elspeth married Ed Lapp in March 1922:)

Interviewer:	So you really only just met. Did it strike you as slightly odd that she would ask you to be her maid of honor on such short acquaintance?
Westbrook:	Quite . . . I was family, and nobody knew me, and I was just a figurehead as the maid of honor, you see, and very—nobody could say anything about it.
Interviewer:	And Rupert was not there?
Westbrook:	No.
Interviewer:	Did you ever wonder about that?
Pafe:	Not at his daughter's wedding?!
Westbrook:	He was not there.
Interviewer:	Did that seem sort of strange?

Westbrook:	I thought it was strange, but then Elspeth and her father were not very compatible, you see.
	Very strange wedding. Really was.
Interviewer:	What family folk were there that you can remember? Was Frances (McLain) there?
Westbrook:	No! There was no one I knew—no one I knew at all.

As Mrs. Westbrook went on to explain, that was the last time she ever saw Elspeth:

Interviewer:	And once Elspeth returned from her honeymoon . . . then did she and Lapp settle in Washington, so that you saw her as a newlywed?
Westbrook:	I thought they did. I thought they did. He ran a laundry business.
Interviewer:	And did you see them as a couple, then, or—?
Westbrook:	No.
Pafe:	You never saw them?
Westbrook:	No.
Pafe:	Strange! They never came to school to get you out, or take you to dinner or anything? Because the school was very strict, so, you know, you were always looking for ways to get out for dinner. Even when I went there.
Westbrook:	No. No. Huh-uh. No, they never did. I'd served my purpose, you see.
Interviewer:	So you really only saw her for about—well, from September of '21 to March of '22, when she married?

Westbrook: That's about the only time I was around her.

Asked if Elspeth ever said anything about her background, Rupert, or what she had been doing, Mrs. Westbrook replied, "She never said a word about *anything*!" She also repeated her earlier comment that Rupert and Elspeth were not close. "I wonder what caused the difference between father and daughter," Mrs. Pafe asked her mother. "I have no idea," Mrs. Westbrook replied. "You see, Elspeth wouldn't talk."

Mrs. Westbrook's admissions made it unanimous: *every person contacted* who knew Elspeth as a child (or teenager) and was a contemporary was under the distinct impression that she was born circa 1900. This included Rush (who was born in 1902 and who knew her as a child), Avis (who was born in December 1900 and who knew her from the age of eight to around seventeen), Margaret Kenyon (who was born in July 1900, and who was a classmate of Elspeth's at St. Mary's from 1914 to 1916), and Betty Rimell Westbrook (who was born in July 1904, and who acted as Elspeth's maid of honor in 1922). All of these individuals knew Elspeth during her childhood or adolescence, and all were born at or near the same time. Each was of the definite opinion that Elspeth was not born before 1900. William Reynolds, Jr., Elspeth's half-brother, repeated the established line that "Sister" was born in 1897, but it must be remembered that this is what he was told, and he was born in 1913, and therefore did not know Elspeth until she was an adult (and he was still a child) — when age disparities are not so readily apparent.

Combined with the peculiar pattern of Elspeth's schooling, her dual confirmations (and her apparent age at the time), and her formal debut at twenty-five, an intriguing hypothesis began to take shape: could it be that the Elspeth who married Ed Lapp in 1922 and who had three daughters was actually born circa 1900 and not 1897? To lend further support to this theory, Rupert and Agnes were in Europe (and China) during this period, 1900–1901, which might explain how such a birth could go undetected. Could this also explain how and why Agnes told William H. Reynolds, Jr., that Elspeth Hughes Lapp had a British nanny named "Page" as a *baby,* since the Hugheses were in *London* in 1900 while Rupert worked for the Encyclopedia Britannica, and the French nursemaid, Jeanne Crepin, was not employed until 1903, when Elspeth was a small child, not an infant? If this theory were true, then what became of the child who was clearly born in May 1897? Were there, after all, two Elspeths? Or one Leila, and another Elspeth? Or some other variation? As far-fetched as this (and Robert Hughes' theory) seemed on its face, the *circumstances* of Elspeth Hughes Lapp's life did not match the facts on her birth certificate. The two were in direct conflict. Yet what could possibly be the motivation for such an outrageous deception? That was the question that preyed on the minds of the ad litem and his two colleagues.

Why did Elspeth abruptly withdraw from the Madeira School in Washington in the middle of the semester in 1914? Was it the same person who then enrolled at St. Mary's School in Peekskill? Could the Elspeth at Madeira have possibly died in February 1914, only to be impersonated by someone else who enrolled at St. Mary's? The most obvious flaw in this theory was the fact that those who knew Rupert's daughter before February 1914 and who saw her afterward would seemingly have had to be aware of the "substitution." Did the mysterious drowning of Rupert's daughter allegedly reported and clearly rumored, actually take place in 1914? This brought to mind a chilling thought: 1913 or 1914 was the year Avis vividly recalled Greta's death (in defiance of Greta's 1916 death certificate), 1914 was the year Marion Manola died, and 1914 was the year Rupert Hughes made his first purchase at the Kensico Cemetery. Was there some sinister connection?

In search of the truth about Elspeth and her ambiguous background, Dinkins' associate knocked on every door imaginable. Just as the newspapers in Agnes' hometown of Syracuse were scoured for some mention of visits by or references to Rupert, Agnes, or their daughter (which might indicate her name, age, or some other significant detail of her life), so were the Keokuk back issues painstakingly perused for the same. A quartet of trivia in the gossip columns in the Keokuk *Gate City* added yet another subplot to an already crowded scenario. A local genealogist discovered an item in the "Personal" column of the *Gate City* dated April 12, 1896. It reported: "Rupert Hughes sails on the 'New York' for Paris Wednesday and expects to arrive there in time to be present at Mrs. Howell's Paris debut on April 23, when she will sing at Salle Erard with orchestra. The other soloist is M. Garski, said to be the best violinist in France."

Three contemporaneous entries confirmed that Rupert Hughes sailed alone:

> *May 12, 1896*: "Mrs. Rupert Hughes is expected to arrive today for a visit with the family of Hon. F. T. Hughes, during her husband's absence in Paris."
>
> *May 28, 1896*: Mrs. Felix T. Hughes of this city and Mrs. Rupert Hughes of New York, are at Iowa City visiting the former's son, Howard Hughes, who is attending school at the Iowa State University."
>
> *June 28, 1896*: Mrs. Rupert Hughes has returned to New York after a visit with her husband's parents, Hon. and Mrs. F. T. Hughes."

It was clear from these items in the Keokuk social columns that Rupert Hughes sailed for Europe in the spring of 1896, without his wife Agnes, who visited his parents in Keokuk, and then returned to her home in New York. There is no reference in the same column to Hughes' return, yet it mentions Greta's arrival in Keokuk in July "for a visit." It is impossible, therefore, to determine exactly how long Rupert Hughes stayed in Europe, though by inference he did not return with Greta in July. Based on the *Gate City*'s travelogues, it was possible (though by no means certain) that Rupert Hughes was in Europe at the time of Elspeth's (or whoever was born in May 1897) conception! Using a calculation nine months back from May 1897, Agnes' daughter was conceived in the late summer or early fall of 1896. Now, in addition to the developing hypothesis that Elspeth Hughes Lapp (the woman who married Ed Lapp, moved to Cleveland, and died in 1945) was perhaps born in Europe or Shanghai in 1900 or 1901, there was also some additional support for the Keokuk relatives who passionately believed that the daughter born to Agnes Hughes during her marriage to Rupert was not his child (the daughter born in 1897, anyway). Of course the newspaper entries were only circumstantial evidence of Rupert Hughes' separation from Agnes at the time of conception, and they did not plainly state that Hughes was still in Europe by August or September 1896; this was only implied. Still, it raised a spectre of doubt.

The facts and circumstances of Rupert's marriage to Agnes (and the subsequent birth of one or possibly two children) had by this time crystallized to suggest that the critical period of time in the lives of the couple was the interval between 1896 and 1901. The name that appeared as a common denominator between the two during these crucial years (and possibly thereafter) was Mrs. Tashleene Jarvis: the woman who ran the boarding house "of ill repute" in New Jersey, whom Agnes met in 1895. Based on the Syracuse newspaper accounts of the New York separation proceedings, Mrs. Jarvis was an intimate of both Agnes and Rupert who entertained at various times nearly all of the gaggle of co-respondents named in Rupert's divorce action, and seemed to be acquainted with the entire cast. She also had a mysterious falling-out with Rupert, was alleged by Agnes to be romantically involved with him (or at least kissed him), yet testified on Agnes' behalf at the trial. If there were an elaborate deception, drowning, substitution, 1900 secret birth, or some other wild scheme, Mrs. Jarvis was a person likely to know. If, further, she had kept in touch with Agnes Hughes Reynolds up to the time of Agnes' confinement in a sanitarium for the insane in 1939, she would probably be able to complete the chronology of Elspeth's life, filling in the "missing years" between 1904 (the divorce) and 1908 (Elspeth's appearance in Bedford Hills), when neither Rupert nor Agnes had actual custody of their alleged daughter.

Spurred on by the fact that a Tashleene *Robertson* had surfaced as recently as 1939, when her deposition was taken in connection with Agnes Reynolds' commitment proceedings (thirty-six years after the sensational Hughes divorce trial), Dinkins' associate decided to try to trace Tashleene Jarvis via the Minneapolis address listed for Tashleene Robertson in 1939. There was no realistic hope that Mrs. Jarvis herself was still alive in 1980, on the eve of the approaching heirship trial; but it was at least possible that she had a child, children, or grandchildren to whom she related the story of her friendship with the Hugheses— particularly if she remained close to Agnes until 1939, as the guardianship file suggested.

Simultaneous with this search for Tashleene Robertson, Dinkins' associate tried to scrape together some background information on the Tashleene Jarvis who testified at the separation trial in New York in 1903. The ad litem was able to confirm, for example, that a Samuel F. Jarvis, Jr., was employed as an associate at the Reed, Simpson law firm in New York from 1899 to 1901. (Mrs. Jarvis was described in the 1903 newspaper divorce accounts as the widow of a former member of that law firm.) Contemporary New York City directories showed that the last listing for Samuel F. Jarvis, Jr., was in 1900–01. The next two years, 1901–02 and 1902–03, Tashleene Jarvis is shown as the widow of Sam Jarvis, residing at 180 W. 81st Street: the same address used by Rupert Hughes at the turn of the century, and the address Greta Howell used on her marriage application to Herbert Witherspoon in September 1899! Tashleene Jarvis' last New York City directory listing was in 1903.

The search for Tashleene Robertson was at once a success and a failure: Dinkins' associate traced her, only to discover that she died in 1959. The 1939 reference to Ms. Robertson showed her at an address called "The Hedges" in Excelsior, Minnesota, in care of a Carroll Brown. Dinkins' associate eventually learned that Carroll Brown was Tashleene Robertson's son. Brown died in 1946; his death certificate stated that he was born in 1888 to Ralph Brown and Tashleene *Little* Brown. Tashleene (Little Brown) Robertson's burial information showed that she was born in Massachusetts in 1870 (two years before Rupert; four years earlier than Agnes) and died in 1959 at the age of eighty-nine. She was interred in a plot in Minneapolis next to her son Carroll Brown and her last husband, John Robertson. She was also shown to have had a son by Robertson, still living in 1959. It seemed reasonable to assume, from these disclosures, that Tashleene Robertson and Tashleene Jarvis were one and the same. If so, it was clear that Tashleene's social life was as hectic as Rupert's and Agnes', if not more so; based on the available evidence, her husbands would have included

Ralph Brown (the father of her son Carroll Brown), attorney Samuel Jarvis (who apparently died about 1900 or 1901), and John Robertson (by whom she had a son, John). Since there was not enough information to trace Tashleene's son John, Dinkins' associate abandoned the search.

Still bothered by Elspeth's missing years, Dinkins' associate continued to hunt for more information. Surprisingly, Elspeth's daughters knew even less about their mother's past than did the ad litem. Barbara Cameron knew her mother had attended the Madeira and National Cathedral Schools (though, interestingly, she guessed her mother attended Cathedral in 1913, not 1919) but had no further information. The ad litem had nowhere else to turn: Elspeth's half-brother, William Reynolds, Jr., had already admitted there was a "gap" in Elspeth's schooling through the eighth grade that he could not clarify: now her daughter perpetuated this mystery. "I . . . that's all vague to me," Cameron conceded. "I really, I can't chronologically put it together. It's very difficult for me to put it together." She had "no idea" where Elspeth went after the 1904 divorce, nor did she know where Elspeth attended school up to the eighth grade. Mrs. Cameron "just assumed" that her mother's early schooling was in Europe, when Rupert Hughes was with the Encyclopedia Britannica (although Rupert and Agnes Hughes were only in Europe part of the years 1900 and 1901.) As for the custody arrangements, Cameron stated "she was more with her mother." (Yet William Reynolds, Jr., related that custody of Elspeth went to Rupert, and suggested Elspeth was with her father for the missing years.) Again, the question remained: where was Elspeth?

Stranger yet, though Elspeth visited Rupert Hughes' home in Bedford Hills as a child every summer from roughly 1908 to 1917 (according to Avis), Elspeth's daughters had effectively never heard of Adelaide, Avis, or Rush. According to Barbara Cameron, Elspeth rarely talked about her childhood. One name, however, that was familiar to Barbara Cameron was Tashleene Robertson. Asked who she might be, Mrs. Cameron replied, "She was the midwife to Grandmother (Agnes) when Mother (Elspeth Lapp) was born." She confirmed that Tashleene Robertson and Tashleene Jarvis were the same person, and that Tashleene and Agnes were "very dear friends." ("I referred to her as Grandmother," Mrs. Cameron observed.) "Teddy" (as she was called) Robertson's connection to Agnes and Elspeth went even deeper. Mrs. Cameron commented that the only pictures Barbara Cameron and her sisters have of their mother Elspeth as a child (aged approximately three to ten) is a small collection that belonged to Teddy. (Even William Reynolds, Jr.'s, photo albums, which belonged to Agnes, do not show Elspeth before age fourteen.) The photographs were forwarded to Barbara Cameron just before Teddy's death in 1959, by either Teddy herself, or by her son

John Robertson's wife. (Barbara Cameron believed it was Teddy's daughter-in-law.)

Tashleene Little Brown Jarvis Robertson, already an intriguing figure in the heirship investigation, took on increasing interest after the comments made by Barbara Cameron, which confirmed the feeling that Tashleene might indeed be the key to some of the confusion surrounding Elspeth and Rupert and Agnes. Not only was Tashleene a boon companion of both Agnes and Rupert throughout much of their marriage (from 1895 on) and involved in their social activities in an integral way, it now appeared that Tashleene served as a midwife to Agnes when Elspeth was born. On top of that, Tashleene apparently had, for reasons known only to her, Agnes, and Rupert, the only known pictures of Elspeth as a little girl. It was interesting, too, that these pictures were only sent to Elspeth's daughters after Elspeth's death—and perhaps not by Tashleene, but her daughter-in-law. Whatever secrets Elspeth's past held, Tashleene almost certainly knew of—or participated in—them.

A Surrogate Mother?

Unravelling Tashleene Robertson's past to see how it related to Rupert, Agnes, and Elspeth proved to be an adventure of the highest order. Dinkins' associate discovered that Teddy had been married four (not three) times, with a secret marriage unknown even to her youngest son;and that she had a first husband whom she divorced but told almost everyone (including his son and grandson) was dead. There was also a possibly unaccounted-for child.

Through information that Barbara Cameron provided, Dinkins' associate was able to find John Robertson, Tashleene's son by her last marriage. (Carroll Brown, her son by her first husband, Ralph Brown, died in 1946). Robertson was born in 1905 in New York City. He related that his mother was from Stockbridge, Massachusetts, first married to a man named Brown. By Brown she had one child , a son Carroll, born in 1888. The Browns divorced, and his mother married Sam Jarvis. Robertson knew nothing about Jarvis ("just that she married him"). He stated that his parents married in New York in October 1904 (the month before Agnes Hughes and William H. Reynolds, Sr., married). His father's full name was John Marmaduke Robertson (the "J. Marmaduke Robinson" who was named by Rupert Hughes as one of the eight co-respondents in his divorce action against Agnes).

Robertson confirmed that his mother and Agnes "were very close" ("She was Aunt Agnes to me"), although he wasn't given many of the details of their early friendship. Robertson was at boarding school much of the time and did not meet Elspeth and Agnes until 1919, when

Elspeth spent an occasional summer or fall at his mother's house. He rejected the suggestion that his mother Tashleene acted as midwife to Agnes when Elspeth was born. "I don't think Mother did—she didn't have a nursing background," he said. "She—I think Mother helped raise Elspeth." "They (Tashleene and Agnes) were close friends—and I don't know whether Mother was living with Agnes or Agnes with her, or just what the details were."

Just as interesting was Robertson's statement that his mother accompanied Rupert and Agnes on their trip to Europe in 1900 and 1901. As he understood it, the three traveled together (Tashleene's husband, Mr. Jarvis, was not included) extensively when Rupert was working abroad for the Encyclopedia Britannica. "I think they were in London and Paris, and where else on the continent, I have no idea." He was given no further details of the trip and did not know whether it included a period of residence in Shanghai. "Mother was, I guess, was sort of part of the family," he offered in explanation. "I don't know."

For all that, Robertson had no further information about Elspeth's school history. Tashleene's son, too, contributed to the mystery about Elspeth's age:

Interviewer:	When did you meet Elspeth?
Robertson:	When I was about fourteen and she was about eighteen.
Interviewer:	Well, let's see, how—you were born in 1905, and how much older than you did she appear to be?
Robertson:	I think she was only about four years older than I was.
Interviewer:	Okay.
Robertson:	In 1901?
Interviewer:	We have her date of birth as 1897.
Robertson:	1897? Well, then she would have been eight years older. She didn't seem that much older.
Interviewer:	Did it seem—

374

Robertson:	She would have been more than twenty-one.
Interviewer:	Yeah.
Robertson:	She didn't seem that old.

Although Robertson and his wife remembered seeing the pictures of Elspeth as a child, neither recalled sending the photographs to Barbara Cameron, as she believed it happened. Overall, Robertson was not told much about his mother's relationship with Agnes; he just knew they were all "sort of part of the family." He stated that his half-brother, Carroll Brown, who was born in 1888, was closer to Agnes and Elspeth than he, because Carroll was around at the time the friendship was most intense.

John Robertson's observations about Rupert, Agnes, Elspeth, and his mother merely underscored the potential importance of Tashleene's role in Elspeth's life. Whatever plot concerning Elspeth might have been devised by Rupert et al.—if there was one—Tashleene was obviously mixed up in it. The hypothesis that Elspeth Hughes Lapp was perhaps born in 1900 or 1901, supported by all the circumstances and none of the documents, was made even more intriguing with the additional knowledge that Tashleene Jarvis was with Rupert and Agnes during their sojourn in Europe in that same period. Barbara Cameron was told that Tashleene acted as a midwife to Agnes when Elspeth was born. Her son John Robertson claimed his mother helped raise Elspeth. What was the strange connection between Rupert, Agnes, Elspeth, and Tashleene? How were they, as Robertson stated, "sort of part of the family?" Could Elspeth have been with Teddy during those missing years after the divorce? Was a child born to Agnes—or Teddy?—during the 1900–01 residence in Europe, and did that explain the confusion about Elspeth Hughes Lapp's age?

Carroll Brown's son, unfortunately, knew little or nothing about his grandmother "Teddy's" relationship with Agnes, Elspeth, and Rupert Hughes. His father, Carroll, died when he was thirteen; therefore the two had little occasion to discuss that part of Carroll's life. The younger Brown knew little about his grandmother's background, only that she was "high society," from Boston. He was told that her first husband, his grandfather, was a lawyer named Ralph David Parsons Brown. Ralph Brown, the grandson was told, died when his son Carroll was about five. He knew nothing about Teddy's subsequent marriages, save her last one to John Marmaduke Robertson.

After a thorough investigation, Dinkins' associate was able to piece together a chronology of Tashleene's life. She was born Tashline Merry

Little to William and Josephine Baldwin Little in Huntington, Massachusetts in March 1866. Her father, William Little, was a "bedstead-maker" who was poisoned (an overdose of belladonna) in Moline, Illinois, in 1873. Tashline grew up in Stockbridge, Massachusetts (where her son claims she attended a finishing school) and married Ralph Brown on April 12, 1887, in Hartford, Connecticut. Their son, Carroll Brown, was born in 1888. The Browns lived first in Rye, and later in New York, New York. In 1893, they moved to Bordertown, New Jersey. Somewhere along the way Tashline changed her name to Tashleene, for Tashleene Brown sued her husband for divorce in 1895 on the grounds that he deserted her the day after their arrival in Bordertown.

According to Tashleene's petition, Brown, a lawyer, left with a suitcase for Chicago "to look for work" and never returned, called, or wrote. Tashleene hired a detective to trace her estranged husband, who had by then moved to Denver. Brown later became a doctor, remarried, and had three daughters. In a bizarre twist, Ralph Brown's grandson (Carroll Brown's son) had been informed by his father and grandmother Teddy that his grandfather Ralph Brown died when his father Carroll was five. Indeed, Carroll himself thought his father, Ralph Brown, was dead. Tashleene told everyone she was a widow.

Tashleene Brown was granted a divorce from Ralph Brown in February 1896. On April 29, 1896, Tashleene Little married William H. Earley, a plump and mustachioed colonel, in Trenton, New Jersey. (According to the Brown divorce records, Tashleene moved to Trenton after Brown deserted her in 1893, where she "took in boarders." Agnes met her in Montclair, New Jersey, in 1895.) Tashleene was twenty-nine at the time of her second marriage, in 1896. Earley was forty-nine and divorced. The marriage to Earley was another of Tashleene's coverups: her son, John Robertson, had never heard of Earley or the marriage. Dinkins' associate traced it through a reference in the Syracuse newspaper accounts of Rupert and Agnes' 1903 separation proceedings; the paper reported that Tashleene Jarvis became embittered toward Rupert Hughes when he refused to corroborate certain evidence in her divorce from a "Colonel Early." The facts do not support this. The Earleys divorced in 1899, yet Tashleene reportedly went to Europe with the Hugheses around 1900. What was the real cause of the friction?

The Earleys were married from April 1896 to November 1899 and lived continuously in New Jersey. (This would be the period in which Agnes became pregnant with Elspeth, giving birth in 1897, according to the birth certificate.) Would Tashleene have been a midwife to Agnes or raised Elspeth during this period? It seemed unlikely, since the Earleys lived in New Jersey and the Hugheses in New York. In late 1899,

Tashleene sued the colonel for divorce on the grounds of adultery. Her corroborating witness was Samuel F. Jarvis, Jr. (who was to be her next husband).

Seven months later, in June 1900, Tashleene Merry Little Brown Earley (calling herself a widow) married Samuel F. Jarvis, Jr. It was the groom's first marriage, the bride's third. Jarvis was a lawyer with the firm of Reed, Simpson, Thatcher, and Barnum. Tashleene Jarvis, married less than a month, sailed for Europe with Rupert and Agnes Hughes (according to her son John Robertson). The Hugheses were in Europe and Shanghai from May 1900 to November 1901. In yet another bizarre twist, Samuel Jarvis, Tashleene's new husband, died in June 1901, less than a year after they were married. He was thirty-three years old. (The cause of his death was reported variously as "overwork," "sudden death of pneumonia," "worn out over the incorporation of a new locomotive trust," or "cerebral apoplexy.") Based on her son's report, this would mean that Tashleene Jarvis was in Europe with Rupert and Agnes Hughes during the full extent of her marriage to Samuel Jarvis, and that he died while she was abroad. (A niece of Jarvis' said she heard through the family that her uncle "got sick and died." She knew he was once married, but "heard" he was divorced. She described him as religious, and said she would be "shocked" to hear he married someone who had been married previously.)

It was in 1903 that the Hughes separation proceedings were aired, when "Mrs. Tashleene Jarvis" testified as a key witness in the trial. The Hughes' divorce was granted in July 1904; in October 1904 Tashleene Jarvis married John Marmaduke Robertson, one of the co-respondents named by Rupert in his divorce action against Agnes; and in November 1904 Agnes Hughes married William H. Reynolds, Sr., yet another of the co-respondents.

What really happened between Rupert, Agnes, Tashleene, and Elspeth will probably always be a mystery. Certainly the known facts about Teddy's life do nothing to disprove the hypothesis that Elspeth Hughes Lapp was born in Europe in 1900 or 1901. Indeed, this seemed perhaps more plausible than before. Tashleene Jarvis was, after all, with the Hugheses in Europe that year and a half. She could have been, as Barbara Cameron was told, the midwife to Agnes quite easily—if Elspeth were born during their trip overseas. Elspeth's birth in London in 1900 or 1901 would also explain how and why a British nanny (Miss Page) was engaged to care for Elspeth as an infant. A more provocative variation on this theory would be to suggest that the hypothetical baby born in 1900 or 1901 was actually born to Tashleene while she was abroad with the Hugheses. That, in turn, could explain her son's comment that she "helped raise Elspeth" . . . that Rupert and Agnes and Tashleene and Elspeth were all a "sort of part of a family." And it is consistent with descriptions of Tashleene in later years: that she was "flaky," "never had a sensible thought," and "nothing she did or was capable of doing would [be surprising]." It might further explain where Elspeth was during the missing years of her early childhood—perhaps she was with Tashleene. That would certainly clarify how Teddy came to possess the only known pictures of Elspeth taken during her childhood, Elspeth's reluctance to talk about her past, Rupert's ambivalent attitude toward her, and the questions about "where she came from."

Even if Elspeth Hughes Lapp was actually born in 1900 or 1901, there is the question of another child, too—the one born in 1897. The records (a birth certificate and an item in the 1897 Syracuse newspaper) document the birth of a daughter to Agnes in 1897. What became of this child, and when did this occur? There were, after all, *two* confirmations, and the fact that the student at Madeira's and the student at St. Mary's almost seemed to be two different people. Certain other inconsistencies in the recollections of those who knew the adult Elspeth versus those who knew her as a child would come out more distinctly at the heirship trial.

What was not clear in any of this hypothesizing, of course, was the motivation for such deception. Assuming the theory of dual identities to be true (or at least the 1900 or 1901 birthdate for Elspeth Hughes Lapp), why (and how) would Rupert and Agnes Hughes, plus several accessories, concoct such a cunning and complex scheme to camouflage the true identity or background of Elspeth? Was Greta, whose death in 1916 (or 1913–14) was shrouded in mystery, somehow mixed up in this as well? And what of Marion (and Adelaide) Manola, both interred in the secret Kensico lot? Was Leila Hughes a part of the confusion? Did the unused and unknown circular lot Rupert Hughes purchased at Kensico play any part? There was no explanation that made sense.

Rupert and Agnes: Divorced at Last

It was in the dying days of the heirship investigation that the plot took its final twist. Almost from the moment of Dinkins' appointment as attorney ad litem in 1976, he and his associate had been attempting to collect all of the pleadings, transcripts and other documents pertaining to Rupert and Agnes Hughes' divorce. For several years, their only document in this regard was the November 1903 separation agreement.

When finally, in 1980, Dinkins' associate came upon a copy of the Hughes final judgment of divorce among the many papers in William H. Reynolds' Veterans Administration pension file, the ad litem redoubled his efforts to secure the complete records of the Hughes' matrimonial action. Common sense suggested that both the Hughes separation file in Manhattan, and the divorce file in Queens County, contained numerous other documents, in addition to the separation and divorce decrees.

Dinkins' clerk finally met with some success in 1980. One of the functionaries in the New York County Clerk's office had at last produced "a few" additional pleadings in the Manhattan separation action. After four years of struggle, the ad litem's associate's suspicions were confirmed that more divorce records existed. At approximately the same time, the Manhattan clerk's counterpart in Queens County acknowledged by phone the existence of certain other documents (besides the final judgment) in the divorce proceedings. With the confirmation that more papers were available, a sweeping effort was instituted to secure copies of all the documents in the two files—the separation action in Manhattan, and the later divorce action in Queens County.

Through the concerted and coordinated efforts of Dinkins' associate and a member of a New York law firm engaged by Dinkins to assist his colleague in her journey through the labyrinth of the New York court system, by 1981 the elusive matrimonial files were at last examined and copied, to be introduced as evidence at the heirship trial that began in August 1981. (Amazingly, these efforts continued up to and during the trial itself: Dinkins' New York cocounsel and a local attorney engaged by George Parnham, counsel for the Keokuk group who believed Rupert Hughes was sterile, were still endeavoring to assemble the complete proceedings from the New York court system even while Paul Freese was presenting his case on behalf of Elspeth's daughters.)

Using the pleadings in their separation and divorce files as a guide, a rough chronology of Rupert and Agnes' matrimonial discord can be summarized as follows. In November 1901, the Hugheses (with Tashleene Jarvis) returned from Europe. According to various pleadings, Rupert Hughes ordered Agnes out of his house in July 1902. In August, Agnes filed for legal separation and custody of their daughter Elspeth. Rupert Hughes threatened to file a separate action for divorce against her in police court, but did not. Instead, he and Agnes filed affidavits stating his or her presentation of the facts, and engaged their parents and others to do likewise. Their accusations against each other are bitter in the extreme.

In her original complaint, Agnes Hughes claimed that Rupert forcibly and violently ejected her from a hotel in New Jersey where they were summering in July 1902, after accusing her of being immoral and depraved. She further charged Hughes with habitual cruelty for the prior three years of their marriage, and sought custody of their child "Elspeth Hedge Hughes, born May 23, 1897" (then in the custody of Rupert). Her supporting affidavit is more vitriolic. In it, Agnes claimed

379

that she married Hughes against her parents' wishes. She described Hughes as a man of "degenerate tastes and habits . . . utterly and totally depraved . . . (who) boasted openly of his illicit relations with other women." She recited that she and Hughes lived in New York throughout their marriage "with the exception of about a year and nine months, when they were sojourning in Europe, in . . . the year of 1900–1901." She also stated that she and Hughes "employed a French governess for their child." Finally, Agnes declared that Rupert "harassed and hounded" her into bringing an action for divorce, against her "religious training and the best interests of her child." She accused Hughes' mother (Jean) and sister (Greta) of "aiding and abetting" him and charged that they were "people totally unfit to have the custody and control of any child by reason of their morals and degenerate conversations."

There is also an affidavit filed by Julia Hedge, Agnes' mother, seeking custody of the child on behalf of Agnes, due to the "disgusting immorality" of Rupert and his "near relations."

Rupert Hughes offered affidavits from two colleagues at the New York office of the Encyclopedia Britannica, swearing to the fact that he was "in every sense a gentleman." His attorney's affidavit suggested that Rupert Hughes had "conclusive proof" of Agnes' adulteries with at least seven different men in the past four years. He further stated that Agnes was living in concealment at the Staten Island home of "Mrs. Jarvis." In her sworn statement, Jean Hughes denied Agnes' allegations, and charged that "through her profligacy and immorality (she) ruined my son's life." The affidavits of Greta Witherspoon ("I am a respectable married woman") and Felix T. Hughes were much the same.

Rupert Hughes' affidavit is the most illuminating. He denied all of Agnes' allegations but two: he admitted calling her "worse than a harlot," and that he ejected her in July 1902 ("for I discovered (she) had been guilty of the grossest immorality and scandalously untrue and unfaithful to her marriage vows.") He recounted that Agnes had an "unhappy girlhood," that he had met her while he was a graduate student at Yale, and that his father Felix supported them with a weekly allowance for some time. He stated that his marriage to Agnes was happy "until my wife formed the acquaintance of a Mrs. Jarvis." He went on to recount that this "ripened into the most intimate friendship." "It is from this friendship that dates my wife's downfall," he concluded.

Hughes also stated that he "earnestly desired to have a son" and that Agnes "frequently said she would have no more children because of the bother and trouble they caused."

He stated that Agnes was three months pregnant in February 1900 and that she brought on an abortion. The next month, March 1900,

Agnes went to Europe, and stayed six months. (Hughes accused Agnes of self-inducing five abortions altogether.) Of additional interest was Hughes' further statement that Elspeth was once sent to Syracuse as a child, where she caught whooping cough, had no medical treatment "and was on the point of death."

Based on these affidavits, the justice handling the case issued an order in August 1902 (modified slightly in November 1902) that provided for temporary alimony for Agnes and that placed Elspeth in the temporary custody of Rupert Hughes. The judge further appointed a "referee" (a local New York attorney) to hear testimony on the fitness of both parents. After the reference hearing, the appointed referee was instructed to issue an opinion regarding the ultimate custody of Elspeth. Oddly, there are no papers in the file referring to the reference hearing, nor is the referee's report on record.

Nine months later (from October to November 1903), the celebrated separation trial occurred in New York City. It was here that Rupert Hughes outlined the specific instances of adultery he alleged that Agnes had committed during their marriage. According to the pleadings Hughes filed, these affairs began in 1896, as follows:

1. James C. Beebe: Keokuk and Iowa City, April–June 1896. (This is when Rupert Hughes was in Europe, according to the Keokuk papers.)
2. Max Karger: all of 1896 in New York.
3. William H. Reynolds: 1899 and parts of 1902; New York.
4. Henry R. Lemly: March 1898 in Virginia and September 1900 in London.
5. Crowell Campbell: 1902, New York.
6. Robert J. Grant: August 1901, France, and November 1901, Syracuse.
7. Arthur Conover: Summer of 1902, New York and New Jersey.
8. J. Marmaduke Robinson: (Tashleene's fourth husband) 1902.

It was at the conclusion of this trial that Rupert and Agnes reached an out-of-court settlement that culminated in the separation decree of November 1903, granting Rupert Hughes primary (nine-month) custody of Elspeth.

The next development in the dissolution of the Hughes marriage was strange indeed. On January 29, 1904, roughly two months after their separation decree was filed, Agnes Hughes filed for divorce (a separate proceeding from her original cause of action, which was for legal separation only). In her complaint, she charged Rupert Hughes with adultery. In contrast to the separation proceedings in Manhattan, the divorce action was nothing if not discreet. A few short months later, Agnes was granted her divorce from her husband by *default judgment*! A hearing was set (before the judge only; no jury was present) in Patchogue, New York, where Agnes presented her evidence to show that Rupert Hughes committed an isolated act of adultery on January 27, 1904, with an unnamed woman. (Agnes' detective testified that he entered Hughes' apartment and found the anonymous woman in the bedroom "partially clothed.") Although Hughes did not file an answer to Agnes' complaint, his attorney was present at the trumped-up hearing. As a consequence, Agnes Hughes was granted an interlocutory decree of divorce from Rupert Hughes on April 7, 1904. The divorce became final on July 12th.

It seemed exceedingly strange that, after bringing to court eight co-respondents and alleging that his wife committed numerous acts of adultery, naming specific dates and places (often even the time of day), Rupert Hughes would consciously and willingly fail to answer his wife's subsequent petition for divorce, allowing the divorce to be granted in her name on the basis of a default judgment (particularly since Hughes' attorney was present during the staged hearing). It was clear from this collusive divorce action that Rupert Hughes and Agnes had struck a private bargain of some sort. But what was the quid pro quo? What sort of leverage did Agnes have over Rupert that caused him to give the divorce to her without a fight? If one were to concede anything to the other, the facts would suggest that it would be Agnes who would give the divorce to Rupert.

Before the divorce action was filed, Rupert Hughes clearly had the greatest bargaining power. He, after all, was originally given custody of Elspeth by the Supreme Court justice, based on the affidavits filed in Agnes' separation action and pending the official opinion of the referee appointed to hear testimony on the fitness of the parents. The next step in the Hughes' marital battle was the scandal-filled separation trial in New York City, resulting in the November 1903 separation agreement in which Rupert again had the upper hand. Yet it was only two months later that Agnes filed for divorce outside Manhattan in Queens County (possibly to avoid further publicity), and Rupert Hughes did nothing to challenge her action. The single act of "adultery" by Rupert Hughes, observed by Agnes' detective, was clearly staged for the benefit of meeting New York State's strict grounds for divorce. Yet why would Rupert Hughes act in complicity with Agnes to allow her to obtain her divorce against him when it seemed reasonable, even probable, to assume that he would prevail if he challenged her suit for divorce? What was the nature of their complicity? Who paid off whom and why? Did it have anything to do with Elspeth?

This last question pointed out the most striking anomaly of the divorce proceeding: Elspeth's name is nowhere mentioned in the documents included in the *Hughes* v. *Hughes* divorce file in Queens County. There is no provision for—nor even a discussion of—the custody arrangements for a child. This seemed particularly odd after the messy battle of affidavits between Rupert and Agnes to see who got custody in the 1902 separation action.

Thus, after four years of effort to secure copies of the separation and divorce proceedings, the attorneys in the heirship case still had no idea what the custody arrangements for Elspeth were, and they could think of no logical explanation why no provisions were made in Rupert and Agnes' final divorce decree. This unusual omission only contributed to the genuine mystery of Elspeth's whereabouts after the divorce. By the time of the heirship trial, it was still not known where Elspeth was during the years of 1904 to 1908, when she mysteriously reemerged to spend the summers at Rupert Hughes' farm, from which time her age and background were a continuing paradox.

Marion Manola: Rupert Hughes' Darkest Secret?

The lack of custody provisions for Elspeth, Dinkins' associate discovered, was not the only point of interest in the *Hughes* v. *Hughes* divorce file in Queens County. Another significant document was filed several months after the final judgment of divorce in July 1904. In December 1904, Rupert Hughes formally petitioned the court for "Request for Leave to Re-Marry." According to the laws of New York State in 1904, whoever had been adjudged to be the "guilty" party in a divorce action needed the express permission of the court to remarry within one year following the date of the final decree of divorce. Since Agnes had been granted the divorce, Rupert Hughes was the so-called guilty party, which explained his formal petition.

In his pleading, Hughes cited his ex-wife Agnes' November 1904 marriage to William H. Reynolds as justification for his request, and stated: "I am desirous of an opportunity to contract and enter into a marriage and not go without the jurisdiction of this State." A hearing was held on this request on Christmas Eve 1904, when Rupert Hughes appeared before the judge in Patchogue, New York (some distance from Manhattan), to elicit his consent. On December 28, the "Order Granting Leave to Re-Marry" was signed by the judge and entered in the record. Unfortunately, Hughes did not mention the name of his bride-to-be.

This discovery, made only weeks before the heirship trial, threw Dinkins' investigation into a mild panic. Rupert Hughes' request to remarry was granted on December 28, 1904; yet his next known marriage—to Adelaide Manola—did not occur until June 18, 1908. Whom did Rupert Hughes marry between his marriages to Agnes Hedge and Adelaide Manola? And why was this marriage (like Greta's to Alexander More and Howard, Sr.'s, engagement to Frances Geddes) kept secret? This unexpected evidence of a hidden fourth marriage for Rupert Hughes brought to mind the reference to Rupert in Ray Garrison's book, *Goodbye My Keokuk Lady*, discredited by Ruby Hughes and others, in which Garrison reported that "the story has persisted through the years that one of Hughes' several wives was Marion Manola." Was there some truth in Garrison's report after all? Was Marion Manola the woman whom Rupert Hughes married after his divorce from Agnes and before his marriage to Adelaide?

That Hughes married *someone* was almost a certainty. Why else would he go to the extreme effort of having his attorney draft a formal petition, and then travel to Patchogue, New York, on Christmas Eve for the judge to rule on his request? The woman he had in mind was almost certainly not Adelaide: he did not marry her until three and a half years later. As further proof of this, there was Hughes' comment in his memorial to Adelaide in her book of poetry, published posthumously in 1924, in which he said that while he was writing a play for actress Blanche Bates, "I met Adelaide, and our marriage followed soon." No, there had to be another Mrs. Hughes in between Agnes and Adelaide. (Significantly, in his June 1908 marriage license to Adelaide Bissell in Jersey City, Hughes left blank the space opposite "Number of marriage"[sic].)

Dinkins' efforts to find a marriage license for Rupert Hughes between December 1904 and June 1908 were not successful. His associate requested searches in all of the cities Hughes was known to visit in those years (including, most notably, St. Louis), but came up blank each time. To find a marriage certificate for Rupert Hughes under those circumstances was like groping in the dark: Hughes was producing his plays in hamlets and major cities all over the country in those years, and he could have conceivably married his second wife in any of them. He was also a frequent visitor to Europe, and a search for a license in every city in the United States and abroad was simply out of the question. Without more information to go on, a blind search for the license was futile.

While the quest for a Hughes marriage license continued, Dinkins' associate tried to determine whether Marion Manola, the woman Raymond Garrison reported to be Hughes' rumored "secret wife," was actually available for matrimony during the years between Rupert's marriages to Agnes and Adelaide. If she were married to someone else at the time Rupert Hughes received court permission to remarry, then Dinkins could dismiss the possibility that it was Marion Manola who was Hughes' undercover wife. With this fresh incentive, Dinkins' associate searched for any information on Marion Manola's past, particularly the dates of her marriages and divorces.

From the biographical outline supplied by Rush and Avis, Dinkins' associate eventually found a marriage certificate for Marion E. Stevens and Henry S. Mould in Cleveland in 1879. Marion E. Mould was granted a divorce from Henry S. Mould in Boston in April 1891 and retained custody of their daughter Adelaide.

On May 1, 1891 (shortly after her divorce from Mould), Marion Manola married singer John Mason in London. In approximately 1895, they formed the Mason-Manola Company and toured together performing light operas for several years. The Masons were divorced in New York City in May 1900.

This was as much information as Dinkins' associate could put together about Marion Manola. Her next known marriage was to accountant George Gates, to whom she was married at the time of her death in 1914, when they were living in New Rochelle, New York. Dinkins' associate could find no record of Manola's marriage to George Gates. Obviously this was a critical document. Since Marion was Mrs. George Gates in 1914, then if the marriage to Gates occurred *before 1904* (when Rupert Hughes received a judge's permission to remarry), she would have been unavailable to marry Rupert Hughes during his free years. Dinkins' associate needed to discover how long the Gates marriage lasted, whether Marion Manola was married to George Gates between 1904 and 1908—when Rupert Hughes was between marriages. If the Manola-Gates marriage took place after 1908, it was at least possible that it was Marion Manola who married Rupert Hughes after his divorce from Agnes.

Since nothing further was known about Gates, the ad litem tried to collect more information on Marion Manola, in search of clues about the Gates marriage or anything else in her past that seemed relevant. In the process, the team found several interesting articles. On September 26, 1891, the *Illustrated American* devoted an entire page to Marion Manola, part of their ''Gallery of Players.'' The profile went into great detail about her background:

> Miss Manola is very small. She has a most shapely figure, fine dark eyes, and a wealth of auburn hair. . . .
>
> Miss Manola was born in Cleveland, and there she spent her earlier days. When she was sixteen years old, her father, Captain Martins, met with a most tragic death. He was the captain of the steamer ''Mohawk,'' . . . known as the fastest of the boats plying be-

tween Cleveland and Detroit. He had one rival, the "Toronto" . . . One night the two boats raced for the last time. . . . Seven only were saved. Among the drowned was Captain Martins.

Marion Martins had a phenomenal voice as a child. . . . She joined the church choir in her city and there she met and was wooed by Henry S. Mould. . . . Much to the surprise of his friends, Mr. Mould married the young choir singer, who was then barely seventeen. . . . Then clouds came in the shape of business embarrassments, and the Moulds suddenly disappeared from Cleveland and went to Europe. . . .

In Paris Mrs. Mould took lessons from Mme. Marchesi . . . and . . . turned to the light opera stage. . . Fortune treated them well, and Mrs. Mould, having adopted the stage name of "Manola," was offered an engagement in a company.

The article in the *Illustrated American* went on to mention Manola's daughter Adelaide, then eleven, who was reported as being "educated at the Convent of Mt. St. Vincent, near New York" (the third convent associated with Adelaide's education). In closing, the piece announced Manola's upcoming marriage to actor Jack Mason ("generally known as 'Handsome Jack' "). What was strange about the biographical information was that both Avis and Rush had testified that Marion Manola's father was an inventor named John Stevens, and it was Stevens' name that appeared on her death and marriage certificates. Who, then, was Captain Martins, described in great detail as her father?

The *New York Times* printed an even more intriguing item about Marion Manola on October 11, 1894, during her marriage to John Mason:

MARION MANOLA'S CONDITION
The Obstinacy of the Singer Regarded as
a Hopeful Sign of Improvement

Marion Manola is still at her country home in Winthrop, Mass. . . . An expert in insanity, who has examined her condition, says he can cure her if she will come to New York. . . . She has improved greatly mentally since she left the institution at North Conway, where she was taken when her insanity first developed, but her bodily health does not seem to improve, and she is in a pitiable condition. . . . Manola at times is quite rational. Her memory seems to return, and she talks reasonably of old times and her present condition. In the midst of these lucid intervals her mind suddenly leaves her, and her hallucinations come back. She imagines that Sheriffs are pursuing her, and that their object is to take her child from her, and she cries and wrings her hands in despair. These attacks occur regularly three or four times a day. . . .

The New York physician assured her husband, John Mason, that if he could have Manola constantly under his care he could effect a permanent cure, but said if she remained at Winthrop, without proper treatment, her case would soon become hopeless. . . . The husband would not consent to her forcible removal, and so she remains in Massachusetts, hovering between reason and insanity.

To those who know Manola intimately, her obstinacy regarding removal is a good sign.

The cause of Marion Manola's mental illness was never diagnosed, but her career biographies note that she went on to appear in many light operas with John Mason for four or five years after her apparent breakdown. In 1900, after her divorce from Mason, the articles and publicity about Manola ceased, suggesting she retired from the stage or somehow dropped out of sight at that time. As a consequence, there was no newspaper coverage of her subsequent marriage to George Gates (or Rupert Hughes), which occurred sometime between 1900 and her death in October 1914. As a result, the ad litem's associate decided to trace the date of the marriage through possible obituary information on George Gates. By pure luck, a death certificate was located for Gates in New York. It was learned that George Gersham Gates died at the St. Lawrence State Psychiatric Hospital in 1946, having been a patient in that institution for six years. This discovery paved the way for some startling revelations.

An obituary was secured for Gates, who died at age seventy-nine. He was described as an expert accountant who lived in many communities. His first wife was listed as Marion Manola, "who died many years ago." He "later" married a Marion Martin, who died in 1940. (Oddly, Marion Martins was the maiden name shown for Marion Manola in her profile in the *Illustrated American.*) The death notices for Marion Martin Gates (who died in 1940) indicated that she was married twice. Her first husband was Eli LaFrancis of Springfield; her second husband was George Gates of New Rochelle, whom she reportedly married in March 1915.

Disappointingly, these obituaries did not reveal the date of George Gates' marriage to Marion Manola. Dinkins' associate then ordered a copy of Manola's obituary from the newspaper in New Rochelle, her residence at the time of her death in October 1914, when she was married to Gates. The article states that her death occurred at the local hospital after an operation for gall stones. She was identified as Mrs. George Gates, the former Marion Manola, "until her retirement one of the best known light-opera stars." She was reported as one of the first legitimate actresses to go into vaudeville (in 1900), where she played for three years and then retired (in 1903). Her daughter, Adelaide Manola Hughes (''the wife of Rupert Hughes, a playwright, Bedford Hills''), was listed as her only survivor. The New Rochelle obituary then stated that Marion Manola ''made her home'' with Adelaide and Rupert Hughes in Bedford Hills until May 1914, when she came to New Rochelle. In yet another strange twist, the *New Rochelle Pioneer,* in eulogizing its famous resident, stated that Marion Manola Gates was to be buried at the local ''Beechwoods'' Cemetery—not at Kensico. Why this discrepancy? And why, again, did Rupert Hughes handle Manola's cremation, instead of her husband, accountant George G. Gates?

Still hoping to discover when Marion Manola married George Gates, Dinkins' associate ultimately traced and talked to his two daughters by his last wife, Marion Martin Gates. The conversation was most enlightening.

From it, Dinkins' colleague learned that George Gates was actually married three times: to Rozella Forrester, Marion Manola, and Marion Martin. His two daughters by Marion Martin Gates did not know when any of these marriages occurred; however, Dinkins' associate found the marriage certificate for Gates and his first wife Rozella. George Gates and Rozella Forrester were married in August of 1907. With this fact came the knowledge that Rupert Hughes and Marion Manola *could* have been married: Rupert Hughes was free between 1904 (his court request to remarry was granted December 28, 1904) and 1908, and it was now known that Marion Manola did not marry Gates until after 1907.

George Gates' daughters had even more scintillating information to offer. They were told by their parents (George and Marion Martin Gates) that their father's second wife, Marion Manola, was once married to Rupert Hughes! Even more amazing, they were under the impression that Hughes had also once been married to someone named Lucy Gates, though they knew nothing more about this marriage.

The older of the two daughters was born in February 1914 in Bedford Hills; her sister was born in 1919. Neither knew when their parents married, nor did they know when their father was married to Marion Manola.

This information both intrigued and perplexed Dinkins' associate. It provided corroboration for Garrison's report that Rupert Hughes and Marion Manola were once married, and the source of this information was certainly authoritative: Marion Manola's last husband repeated this fact to his daughters. It seemed reasonable to assume that Gates would be knowledgeable about his wife's previous husbands. However, there was something about the dates that didn't hang together. It was clear that George Gates was married to Rozella from 1907 to an undisclosed date. (Gates' daughters said she died during the marriage.) In October 1914, at the time of her death in New Rochelle, Gates was married to Marion Manola. Sometime after Marion Manola's death, Gates married Marion Martin, and the couple had two daughters (the two women whom Dinkins' associate contacted). Yet the older of these daughters was born in February 1914—nine months before Marion Manola's death. Since Marion Manola was supposed to have been married to George Gates in October 1914, and Gates was supposed to have married Marion Martin *after* Manola's demise, how was it that Marion Martin gave birth to the oldest Gates daughter in February 1914, when Gates was still married to Marion Manola?

A second conversation with the Gates daughters did little to clarify this discrepancy. The oldest still maintained she was born in Bedford Hills in February 1914 and that her parents were George Gates and Marion Martin Gates. She and her sister added that their mother, Marion Martin, was a maid to Marion Manola before she married Gates. The two repeated their earlier statement that Rupert Hughes was once married to Marion Manola, and said that their father, George Gates, often told them he despised Rupert Hughes, though he would never say why. They still insisted there was a Lucy Gates who was once married to Rupert Hughes, as well. Neither had ever heard of Rupert Hughes' daughter.

Dinkins' associate could still make no sense of the sequence: it seemed clear that the oldest Gates daughter was born during her father's marriage to Marion Manola, before Manola's death and before his subsequent marriage to Marion Martin. While puzzling over this state of affairs, Dinkins' associate received a shocking letter from the younger Gates daughter (born in 1919):

I am writing in regards to Marion Manola and George Gates, my father. I know everything is very confusing for all concerned, but my sister is not George Gates' daughter. She does not know this, although she has been confused about her birth and where she was born for many years. I would not have known this if I hadn't heard my parents in an argument and my father threatened to tell me about (my sister), however my mother told me herself. She didn't go into any details and I never asked.

However, her birth being in February of 1914 and mine in May 1919. My father must have been married to Marion Manola between these dates at least. I hope this will be of some help to you. Also if you can find out where (my sister) was born and under what name you can tell her?

389

This news was, to say the very least, unsettling. After piecing together the known facts, and locating the oldest "Gates" daughter's birth certificate, Dinkins' associate uncovered a most provocative scenario. Marion Manola (and possibly George Gates) was living with her daughter Adelaide in the Rupert Hughes household in Bedford Hills (Westchester County, New York) for a period of time until May 1914, when she and Gates moved to New Rochelle. Marion Martin was Marion Manola's maid. In February 1914, Marion Martin gave birth to a daughter, while working as a maid to Marion Manola in the Rupert Hughes household. The birth is registered in Westchester County. Beside the blank for "name of father," Marion Martin gave the name of her first husband, Eli LaFrancis. Dinkins' associate later discovered that LaFrancis died in 1910—four years before the birth of Marion Martin's daughter!

According to Marion Martin Gates' younger daughter, neither her mother nor father would discuss the identity of her older sister's father. In fact, Mr. and Mrs. Gates rarely discussed their past at all. She knew only that Gates hated Rupert Hughes and offered no explanation; that Hughes and Marion Manola were once married; and that a "Lucy Gates" somehow figured in the plot.

Though the evidence is entirely circumstantial, the facts surrounding the birth of Marion Martin's older daughter lend themselves to the possible conclusion that Rupert Hughes might have been the father. After all, Marion Martin was living in Hughes' household as a maid to Marion Manola at the time, and it was certain that George Gates was not the father. It was even clearer that the father was not the man stated on the birth certificate. Added to this incriminating mise-en-scène is the additional fact that George Gates despised Rupert Hughes, though he would never say why. Most persuasive, however, is the fact that Marion Martin's older daughter, born in February 1914 in Westchester County, New York, bears an uncanny resemblance to Rupert Hughes, the lord of the Bedford manor. (It was impossible under the circumstances not to recall William H. Reynolds, Jr.'s, earlier statement that his mother Agnes divorced Rupert "because she caught him with the maid.")

Apart from this stunning development, Dinkins' associate could never put together the connection between Marion Manola and Rupert Hughes. No marriage certificate could be located for the period between 1904 to 1908. Whatever marriage occurred—whether it was indeed to Marion Manola, or to someone else—was one of Rupert Hughes' better-kept secrets, and he had many. In concert with the doubts about his alleged natural daughter Elspeth, the questionable adoption claim of Rush and Avis, his strange connection to Greta (and her mysterious death), the several individuals he wished to adopt or became a guardian to, his unused Kensico cemetery lot, the unidentified "Lucy Gates" he was purported to have married, and the still-missing secret fourth marriage (to Marion Manola? or someone else?) between 1904 and 1908, there was added the possibility that Rupert Hughes had an illegitimate daughter in 1914 by Marion Manola's maid, who was then living in his house.

11

The HeirshipTrial:
Looking Back

The discovery of a possible fourth marriage for Rupert Hughes and the suspicious circumstances involving Marion Manola, Marion Martin, and George Gates were the last of the attorney ad litem's investigative efforts. The day of the trial to determine Howard R. Hughes, Jr.'s, paternal heirs finally dawned, in August 1981, and with it came the end of Dinkins' five years of research. The outcome of the trial was almost a foregone conclusion: unless some compelling top-secret evidence were introduced from one of the groups disputing Elspeth's relationship to Rupert Hughes, it was a near certainty that Barbara Cameron and her sisters would be declared heirs-at-law of Howard R. Hughes, Jr. The law of evidence was on their side.

393

By 1981 the ad litem's research had punctured holes in most of the subplots connected with Robert Hughes' master theory that Rupert Hughes' "real" daughter Leila (born in 1897) drowned, and was substituted by Elspeth Dial (born in the early 1900s), the daughter of Elizabeth Patterson Dial. Yet there were elements of Robert Hughes' strange theory that seemed to be supported by the circumstances of Rupert and Elspeth's lives: the odd duality to Elspeth's personality and background, the 1900 or 1901 birthdate consistently attached to Elspeth Hughes Lapp, Elspeth's missing years, the drowning article corroborated by Roberta Reed's student researcher as well as a midwesterner who read of the same in a Rupert Hughes poem, certain inconsistencies in Patterson Dial's life, and the mysterious connection between Leila Hughes and Rupert Hughes' secret plot at the Kensico Cemetery.

The claim of George Parnham's Keokuk-based clients that Rupert Hughes was rendered sterile by a case of measles or mumps in boyhood, and that Elspeth Hughes Lapp was the daughter of Agnes and a paramour, was arguably the most plausible of the theories discrediting Elspeth's identity, yet this group had no proof—no medical evidence— of their allegations. As with Robert Hughes' suspicions, the circumstances lent credence to this theory, as well. If Elspeth's father were actually one of the eight co-respondents named by Rupert in the 1903 separation action (as the midwesterners believed; in fact, several had narrowed this down to one man, Max Karger), it might well explain Rupert's ambivalent attitude toward his supposed daughter, which was in direct contrast to his exaggerated paternal interest in others, witnessed by his eagerness to adopt or become a guardian to a great number of individuals. The sterility theory might also explain why Hughes did not list a daughter on his *Who's Who* or Case Western information forms (though he included her in the latter by 1949), and it would support Alston Cockrell, Jr.'s, allusions to Rupert's "so-called" daughter. Then there was the obvious connection in *Hughes* v. *Hughes*, which demonstrated that Agnes' alleged adulteries did not begin until 1896, the year Agnes became pregnant with Elspeth (according to her birth certificate), after four childless years of marriage to Rupert. In line with that was the entry in the Keokuk personal column that announced Rupert Hughes' departure for Europe in May 1896, but neglected to mention his return—opening the door to speculation that Hughes was abroad at the time Elspeth was conceived. Yet the sterility theory did not explain the apparent confusion over Elspeth's age, and it was in direct conflict with the implications that Rupert Hughes may have been the father of an illegitimate daughter by Marion Manola's maid.

Though everyone connected with Dinkins was in agreement that the accepted Hughes genealogy was flawed, none could devise an alternate theory that tied together all the loose ends, answered all the questions, or explained the motivation for the grand deceptions necessary to suppress or distort the Hughes lineage.

After five years of investigation, the attorney ad litem was left with a mass of unanswered questions about the Hughes family. Yet for all these questions, there was no conclusive (that is, legally sufficient) evidence to disprove the accepted Hughes genealogy: that Elspeth Lapp was the only paternal first cousin of Howard Hughes, Jr., and that her children are his heirs apparent. All the circumstances, common sense, and gut instincts suggested otherwise, but this was not the evidence that the law upheld. In this way, the heirship trial proved to be a disappointing anticlimax to five years of overwhelming suspicions about the Hughes family.

Are the real heirs of Howard Hughes, Jr., still not apparent?

Epilogue

It is strange to note, in reflecting on the distribution of the Hughes estate, that the person whose interests were most at stake was the individual whose wishes were least considered: Howard R. Hughes, Jr., himself. When all was said and done, the Hughes fortune was divided three ways: to his family, in a trial to determine his heirs-at-law; to the United States government, in the form of estate and inheritance taxes; and to lawyers, who benefited handsomely in countless ways by Hughes' apparent neglect to make a will. Yet it takes scant study of Hughes' life to note that he had little time for his family (in fact, he disinherited his father's relatives in the only will he was known to execute); he viewed attorneys with suspicion; and he held the government in the highest contempt.

Perhaps, in the end, the question of who should inherit the Hughes estate is a moral, not a legal, one. In the case of a man like Howard Hughes, with millions of dollars and no close relatives, it seems a travesty that his fortune should pass arbitrarily to far-flung relations, many of whom were complete strangers to him, by a judicial process that resembled nothing so much as a high stakes game of legal roulette. Isn't there a better solution? Should the estate of an intestate person automatically pass by law to a relation, no matter how distant? Shouldn't there be some outer limits on inheritance rights?

One possible alternative might be to hold a hearing, similar to an heirship determination, to explore the intentions of the deceased. Witnesses could include close friends, business colleagues, confidantes, personal attorneys—who would testify concerning the statements made or thoughts expressed by the decedent during his lifetime as to where he wanted his money to go. Had this been accomplished with respect to Hughes, there is little doubt that the bulk of his billion-dollar estate would now be set aside for medical research, not divided willy-nilly among the disputed descendants of an uncle he loathed, the nieces and nephews of an aunt he loved but rarely saw, and the outstretched palms of Uncle Sam.

Obviously, Howard Hughes, Jr., is an extreme example but he illustrates the miscarriage of justice that can occur when one fails to leave a last will and testament—if indeed Hughes did. Surely this is the mystery that will haunt his memory long after the many enigmas of his extraordinary life are forgotten.

Biographical Notes

Because the story of Howard Hughes, Jr.'s family, past and present, comes to encompass what at times seems to be a cast of thousands, there follows an alphabetical listing of certain of the individuals involved in the legal drama to claim his estate, with a short description of the role each plays.

George E. Bissell, Jr. First husband of Adelaide Manola, by whom he had two children, Rush and Avis.

Ollie Blan. Birmingham attorney who represented Robert C. Hughes in his claim of heirship against the Howard R. Hughes, Jr., estate.

Katherine/Kitty (Mrs. Carl) Callaway. Maternal first cousin of Allene Gano Hughes and possibly the relative to whom Howard, Jr., was closest after the death of his parents.

Barbara (Lapp) Cameron. Youngest daughter of Ed and Elspeth Hughes Lapp; alleged granddaughter of Rupert and Agnes Hughes. First cousin-once-removed to Howard Hughes, Jr., and an heir to his estate.

Alston Cockrell, Jr. Nephew of Patterson Dial; only child of Alston and Stephena Dial Cockrell. Close to his aunt Patterson, and lived with her off and on during herr marriage to Rupert Hughes.

Stephena Dial Cockrell. Patterson Dial's older sister; wife of Alston Cockrell, Sr. A minor writer, encouraged by her brother-in-law, Rupert Hughes.

George Dean. Close friend and personal attorney to Avis McIntyre; counsel to Rush Hughes and Avis McIntyre in their claim against the Hughes Estate.

Elspeth (Lapp) DePould. Middle daughter of Ed and Elspeth Hughes Lapp; alleged granddaughter of Rupert and Agnes Hughes. First cousin-once-removed to Howard Hughes, Jr., and an heir to his estate.

Elspeth Dial. According to claimant Robert C. Hughes, she allegedly assumed the identity of Rupert and Agnes' daughter (Leila) after Leila drowned, calling herself Elspeth Hughes and later marrying Ed Lapp.

Patterson Dial. Actress/writer Elizabeth Patterson Dial Hughes. Last wife of Rupert Hughes. Alleged to be the mother of Elspeth Dial.

Sarah Burton Whitner Dial. Mother of Patterson Dial; wife of William Henry Dial of Madison, Florida.

O. Theodore Dinkins, Jr. Partner at Butler and Binion law firm in Houston, appointed attorney ad litem in the Texas Hughes proceedings.

Mary Smith Fay. Houston genealogist hired by Ted Dinkins to assist in his determination of Howard Hughes, Jr.'s, heirs.

Wayne Fisher. Houston trial attorney who served as local counsel to Rush Hughes and Avis McIntyre in their claim against the Hughes estate.

Paul Freese. Los Angeles trial attorney who represented Barbara Cameron and her two sisters (Rupert Hughes' alleged grandchildren) in their legal efforts to be declared Howard Hughes, Jr.'s, paternal heirs.

Allene Gano. Mrs. Howard Hughes, Sr., and mother of Howard Hughes, Jr.

Raymond E. Garrison. Onetime Keokuk newspaperman who wrote several books about Keokuk homes in the late 1950s, including *Goodbye My Keokuk Lady*, which featured a short piece on the Felix Hughes family. Only one to report rumored third and fourth marriages for Greta and Rupert Hughes, respectively.

George Gates. New York accountant who was the last husband of actress Marion Manola.

Lucy Gates. Reportedly once married to Rupert Hughes, presumed to be a daughter of Marion Manola.

Frances Geddes. Frances Geddes Bendelari Hubbell. Joplin beauty who took out a license to marry Howard Hughes, Sr., in 1900, four years before his marriage to Allene Gano.

Pat Gregory. Houston probate judge assigned to oversee the Texas estate proceedings of Howard Hughes, Jr.

Agnes Hedge. Agnes Wheeler Hedge Hughes Reynolds. First wife of Rupert Hughes, alleged to be the mother of his only child, Elspeth. Later married to William H. Reynolds.

Charles and Julia Wheeler Hedge. Parents of Agnes Hedge; paternal grandparents of Elspeth Hughes.

Francis J. Helenthal. Keokuk newspaperman and author of "The Keokuk Connection," a 1976 pamphlet describing Howard Hughes, Jr.'s, midwestern relatives.

Adele Widdifield Howell. Second wife of Fred Howell.

James Frederick Howell. Descendant of a newspaper publishing family in Keokuk and second husband of Greta Hughes.

Lida Gordon Howell. Sister of Fred Howell and a former grande dame of Keokuk society.

Elspeth Hughes. Elspeth Hedge Hughes Lapp. Alleged daughter of Rupert and Agnes Hedge Hughes and only paternal first cousin of Howard Hughes, Jr. Married to Ed Lapp.

Felix Hughes. Youngest child of Felix and Jean Hughes; brother of Howard Hughes, Sr.

Felix Turner Hughes. Former Keokuk lawyer, mayor, and judge. Father of Howard Hughes, Sr. One branch of the Hughes family claims he was born Felix *Moner* Hughes and wrongfully assumed the identity Felix Turner Hughes, after betraying his family during the Civil War.

Greta Hughes. Greta Hughes More Howell Witherspoon. Oldest child of Felix and Jean Hughes of Keokuk and Howard, Jr.'s, only paternal aunt.

Jean Hughes. Jean Amelia Summerlin Hughes. Howard, Jr.'s, paternal grandmother. Wife of Felix T. Hughes and mother of Greta, Howard, Rupert and Felix Hughes.

Leila Hughes. Alleged by claimant Robert C. Hughes to be the "real" daughter of Rupert and Agnes Hughes, drowned in Rupert's swimming pool and later impersonated by Elspeth Dial.

Robert C. Hughes. Agri-business teacher from Wilsonville, Alabama, who claimed heirship to Howard R. Hughes, through the allegedly bogus identity of Howard's grandfather, Felix Turner Hughes. Propounded the Felix Moner Hughes theory, as well as the drowning and impersonation of Rupert and Agnes Hughes' daughter derived through a several-generation surveillance of the Felix Hughes family.

Ruby Hughes. Ruby Helen McCoy Parrott Hughes. Widow of vocal coach Felix Hughes; aunt by marriage of Howard Hughes, Jr. Only member of original Hughes family living at the time of Hughes' death in 1976.

Rupert Hughes. Brother of Howard Hughes, Sr., and paternal uncle of Howard, Jr. Well-known author, playwright, screenwriter, and speaker. Reputedly the father of Howard, Jr.'s, only paternal first cousin.

Rush Hughes. Also known as Rush Bissell. Son of Rupert Hughes' wife Adelaide Manola by her first marriage to electrical engineer George Bissell, Jr. Claimed to be Rupert's "equitably" adopted son.

Edward John Lapp. Elspeth Hughes' husband and the father Barbara Cameron, Agnes Roberts, and Elspeth DePould.

Annette Gano Lummis. Allene Gano Hughes' younger sister; Howard, Jr.'s, maternal aunt. After the death of Allene Hughes in 1922, Annette Lummis helped raise Howard, Jr., for several years while his father was in California. In 1976, she was Hughes' closest known living relative.

William Rice Lummis. Attorney son of Annette Lummis and first cousin of Howard, Jr. Appointed the coadministrator of the Hughes estates in Nevada and Texas, later the chief executive officer of Summa Corporation, Hughes' corporate alter-ego.

Adelaide Manola. Adelaide Russell Mould Bissell Hughes. Adopted the stage name of "Manola" after her mother, singer Marion Manola. Daughter of Henry and Marion Mould of Cleveland; wife of Rupert Hughes. First married to engineer George Bissell, with whom she had two children, Rush and Avis.

Marion Manola. Marion Elixia Stevens Mould Mason Gates. Mother of Rupert Hughes' wife Adelaide Manola, and rumored to have been married to Rupert herself. Light opera singer given the stage name "Manola" by French voice instructor Madame Marchesi.

402

Marion Martin. Once a maid to Marion Manola, she married Manola's husband George Gates after Marion Manola Gates' death. According to certain sources, "Marion Martin" was also the maiden name of Marion Manola.

Avis McIntyre. Also known as Avis Bissell or Avis Hughes. Full name Avis Bissell/Hughes Saunders Golden McIntyre. Daughter of George and Adelaide Manola Bissell. Stepdaughter of Rupert Hughes, never formally adopted. Claimed to be Rupert's "equitaby" adopted daughter.

George Parnham. Houston attorney who represented fifty-odd second and third cousins of Howard Hughes, Jr., from the Midwest who claimed that Rupert Hughes' alleged daughter Elspeth was illegitmiate, based on their belief that Rupert was sterile.

Adella Prentiss. Adella Rouse Prentiss Hughes. First wife of Howard, Jr.'s, uncle Felix Hughes.

William Herbert Reynolds. Second husband of Agnes Hedge and stepfather of Elspeth Hughes.

William H. Reynolds, Jr. Only child of William and Agnes H. Reynolds; half-brother of Elspeth Hughes Lapp.

Ella Rice. Howard Hughes, Jr.'s, first wife. Full name Ella Botts Rice Hughes Winston.

Marshall Ricksen. Born Marshall Ericksen, Rupert Hughes was appointed his legal guardian in 1924. Ricksen lived with Hughes and Patterson Dial at their home in Los Angeles while attending college.

Agnes (Lapp) Roberts. Oldest daughter of Ed and Elspeth Hughes Lapp; alleged granddaughter of Rupert and Agnes Hughes. First cousin-once-removed to Howard Hughes, Jr., and an heir to his estate.

Tashleene Robertson. Full name Tashleene Merry Little Brown Earley Jarvis Robertson. Intimate friend of Rupert and Agnes Hughes said to have served as midwife to Agnes at the time of Elspeth's birth. Possibly "raised" Elspeth.

Stephena Cockrell Scott. Alston Cockrell, Jr.'s daughter; grand-niece of Patterson Dial, and granddaughter of Alston and Stephena Dial Cockrell.

Frances McLain Smith. Her grandmother (Electa Summerlin) and Rupert Hughes' mother (Jean Summerlin) were sisters. Her mother, Rupert's first cousin, lived with the Hughes family in Keokuk while attending college. Frances attended boarding school with Elspeth. Rupert wanted to adopt her.

Ruth A. Stonehouse. Former silent film star who was the second Mrs. Felix Hughes.

Elizabeth Rimell Westbrook. Another granddaughter of Electa Summerlin, Jean Summerlin Hughes' sister. Her mother, Jenny Rimell, and Rupert Hughes were first cousins. Served as maid-of-honor in Elspeth's wedding.

James O. Winston, Jr. Married Ella Rice after her divorce from Howard R. Hughes, Jr. Founded Rowles, Winston.

Herbert Witherspoon. Famous opera singer and third husband of Greta Witherspoon. She reportedly died in despair over the breakup of their marriage.

Chronology

1862/
1863   November 17   Birth of Marion Manola* in Oswego, New York? (To conceal her age, Manola later reported her year of birth anywhere from 1864 to 1868.)

1865   August 1   Marriage of Felix T. Hughes and Jean A. Summerlin, Memphis, Missouri.

1866   June 4   Birth of Greta Hughes, Lancaster, Missouri. (To conceal her age, Hughes later reported her year of birth anywhere from 1868 to 1876.)

1869   September 9   Birth of Howard Robard Hughes, Sr., Lancaster, Missouri.

1872   January 31   Birth of Rupert Hughes, Lancaster, Missouri.

1874   March 20   Birth of Agnes Wheeler Hedge, Buffalo, New York.

1879   August 4   Marriage of Marion Manola (identified as Marion Stevens) and Henry S. Mould, Cleveland.

1880   May 7   Birth of Adelaide Russel Mould, Cleveland? (To conceal her age, Mould later reported her year of birth anywhere from 1882 to 1886.)

1886   Felix Hughes family moved to Keokuk.

     November 11   Henry Mould deserted Marion Manola, Philadelphia.

1887   August 31   Marriage of Greta Hughes and Alexander S. More, St. Louis; Mores move to Santa Barbara.

     December 26   Greta abandoned More.

*Born as either Marion Elixia Stevens or Marion Elixia Martin.

405

1888		Rupert Hughes enrolled at Adelbert College, Cleveland (through 1892).
	February–March	Greta More visited Keokuk, then left for parts unknown.
	October 12	Alexander More filed original complaint of divorce against Greta (later withdrawn).
	November 27	Birth of Leila Hughes, Troy, New York. (Also reported as 1891 to 1895).
	December 31	Divorce granted to Alexander More.
1889	January–May	Greta studied at Chicago Conservatory of Music.
	May 22	Marriage of Greta Hughes and J. Fred Howell, Milwaukee; Howells moved to Denver.
	June 1	Strange death (murder?) of Alexander More, Santa Barbara.
1890		Adelaide Mould said to be enrolled at the Sacred Heart Convent in Paris or London, or the Convent of St. Vincent near New York.
	October 3	Marion Manola sued Henry Mould for divorce, Boston.
1891	April 17	Marion Manola granted divorce from Mould and given custody of Adelaide.
	May 1	Marriage of Marion Manola and John Mason, London.
	September 24	Marriage of William H. Dial and Sara B. Whitner, Madison, Florida.
1892		Howells moved to Keokuk from Denver. Rupert Hughes graduated from Adelbert College.

	June	Agnes Hedge graduated from Keble School, Syracuse.
	July 12	Birth of Stephena Dial, Madison, Florida.
	September	Rupert Hughes began graduate studies at Yale; Agnes Hedge enrolled at Evelyn College near Princeton.
1893	December 12	Marriage of Rupert Hughes and Agnes Hedge, New York City.
1894		Greta abandoned Fred Howell. Rupert Hughes began first job as a cub reporter for the *New York Sun* or *Journal*.
	June 1– October 1	Howard Hughes studied law at the University of Iowa.
1895		Agnes Hughes met Tashleene Brown, Montclair, New Jersey.
1896		Agnes Hughes' alleged adulteries began.
	March 28	Divorce granted to Tashleene from Ralph Brown, New Jersey.
	April 12	Rupert Hughes sailed for Paris aboard the *New York*.
	April 29	Marriage of Tashleene Brown and William H. Earley, Trenton.
	April– June 6	Agnes Hughes visited Keokuk while Rupert in Europe.
	July 28	Greta Howell returned from Paris without Rupert.
	July 30	The Howells separated.

	August/ September	Elspeth Hughes was conceived.
	September 20	Agnes Hughes visited Syracuse.
	October 5	Howard Hughes applied to Iowa State bar and moved to Colorado for two years.
1897	April	Agnes Hughes in Fortress Monroe, Hampton, Virginia, with Tashleene Earley; alleged affair with Captain Lemly.
	May 23	Birth of Elspeth Hedge Hughes, New York City.
	Summer	Agnes Hughes "and her daughter" in Syracuse. (This is the last mention of Agnes' daughter in the Syracuse social column, though Agnes herself appeared again from time to time.)
1899		Howard Hughes drifted to Missouri.
	February 6	Fred Howell granted a divorce from Greta, Iowa.
	September 25	Marriage of Greta Howell and Herbert Witherspoon, New York City.
	November 15	Tashleene Earley granted divorce from William Earley, New York City.
1900		Possible year of birth for Elspeth Hughes Lapp.
	January 12	Marraige of Adelaide Mould and George Bissell, Jr., New York City.
	February	Agnes Hughes pregnancy, treated for blood poisoning and sent to Europe alone after alleged self-abortion.
	May 1	Marion Manola granted divorce from John Mason, New York City.

	May	Rupert Hughes arrived in London to join staff of *Encyclopedia Britannica;* George and Adelaide Bissell moved to Japan.*
	June 7	Marriage of Tashleene Earley and Samuel F. Jarvis, Jr., New York; Tashleene soon joined the Hugheses in Europe for the following year.
	October 16	Marriage license taken out by Howard Hughes and Frances Geddes, Joplin.
	November 22	Marriage of Fred Howell and Adele Widdifield, Manila.
	December 19	Birth of Avis Bissell, Kobe, Japan.
1901	January	Howard Hughes left Joplin for Independence, Missouri, then Beaumont, Texas; Frances Geddes entered convent.
	June	Death of Samuel Jarvis, Tashleene's husband of less than a year.
	November	Rupert and Agnes Hughes returned from abroad; Adelaide Bissell returned to New York from Japan with infant Avis.
	December 21	''Surprise'' marriage of Frances Geddes and Arthur Bendelari, Joplin.
1902	May 14	Birth of Rush Marion Bissell, New York City.
	May 19	Birth of Elizabeth Patterson Dial, Madison, Florida.
	July 19	Rupert Hughes ordered Agnes to leave his house and retained custody of Elspeth.
	August 1	Rupert Hughes first consulted an attorney about a divorce.

*The Hugheses also spent time in Shanghai, as did William Reynolds.

	August 4	Hughes Separation papers filed; Agnes filed separate Custody and Separation Complaint in Manhattan.
	August 27	New York Supreme Court granted Rupert Hughes custody of Elspeth pending Referee's report and final divorce.
1903		Marion Manola retired from opera and joined a vaudeville circuit.
	October 8– November 25	Sensational separation trial between Rupert and Agnes Hughes, New York City.
	November 25	Private agreement reached between the Hugheses resulting in Decree of Judicial Separation. Rupert granted nine-month custody of Elspeth.
	December	Agnes Hughes commenced divorce proceedings in Suffolk County, New York.
1904	January 29	Agnes Hughes filed for divorce in Queens County, New York.
	March 26	Agnes Hughes and Julia Hedge testified at hearing in trumped-up divorce proceeding in Queens County.
	April 7	Agnes Hughes granted Interlocutory Decree of Divorce against Rupert by default.
	May 24	Marriage of Howard Hughes and Allene Gano, Dallas
	July 12	Final Judgment of Divorce granted to Agnes Hughes, Queens County. No provisions for custody of Elspeth.
	October 5	Marriage of Felix Hughes and Adella Prentiss, Cleveland.

	October 12	Marriage of Tashleene Jarvis and John Robertson, New York City.
	November 15	Marriage of Agnes Hughes and William H. Reynolds, New York City.
	December 28	Rupert Hughes requested and received permission to remarry from Queens County divorce judge.
1905	December 25	Birth of Howard Robard Hughes, Jr., Houston.
1908	June 22	Marriage of Rupert Hughes and Adelaide Bissell, Atlantic City.
1909		Elspeth began to spend summers with Rupert Hughes; other months unaccounted for.
1911	September	Elspeth enrolled at Miss Madeira's in Washington as an eighth grader. First known school attended.
	December 20	Rush Bissell withdrawn from Syracuse orphanage and taken to Rupert Hughes' home.
1912	October 6	Elspeth confirmed Presbyterian at Church of the Pilgrims, Washington.
1913	May 18	Birth of William H. Reynolds, Jr., Washington, D.C.
	September	Avis Bissell enrolled at Foxcroft, Virginia.
	November	Date of first known pictures of Elspeth in William Reynolds, Jr.'s, collection.
1914		Thought to be the year of Greta Hughes' death (or 1913) by Avis McIntyre.
	February 4	Elspeth withdrawn from Madeira School.
	February 23	Birth of Evelyn Marian "Gates," daughter of Marion Martin, Bedford Hills.

February	Elspeth enrolled at St. Mary's in Peekskill, New York as ninth grader.
March 24	Elspeth confirmed Presbyterian at St. Mary's.
May	Marion Manola moved out of Rupert Hughes house in Bedford Hills, to New Rochelle, as Mrs. George Gates.
October 6	Death of Marion Manola Gates, New Rochelle (cremated).
October 12	Rupert Hughes' first purchase at Kensico Cemetery.
1915 January 4	Rupert purchased additional 100 feet at Kensico.
May 5	Witherspoon divorce accomplished by Felix Hughes, Iowa.
1916 February 21	Death of Greta Witherspoon, New York (cremated).
May 27	Rupert purchased additional 236 feet at Kensico.
June	Elspeth withdrawn from St. Mary's as ninth grader.
July 24	Purchase of Kensico plot by Leila Hughes family.
October	Elspeth enrolled at National Cathedral in Washington.
1917 April 2	Elspeth dropped from membership at Church of the Pilgrims by becoming Episcopalian.
May	Elspeth withdrew from National Cathedral.
June	Avis graduated from Foxcroft.

	Fall	"Betty P." Dial enrolled at Duval High School, Jacksonville.
1918		Rupert Hughes began movie work.
	November	Patterson Dial began career in New York City.
1919/ 1920		Rupert Hughes began bicoastal living arrangements.
1921		Patterson Dial's first film in Los Angeles.
1922	Winter	Elspeth made formal debut in Washington society.
	January 8	Marriage of Avis "Hughes" and John "Monk" Saunders, New York City (Rupert Hughes gave bride away).
	March 20	Marriage of Elspeth Hughes and Edward Lapp, Washington (Rupert Hughes not present).
	March 29	Death of Allene Gano Hughes, Houston; Sonny sent to California wtih Annette Gano and Kitty McLaurin.
	September–November	Adelaide's first trip to the Orient.
1923		Felix and Adella Prentiss Hughes divorced.
	January–July	*Reno* filmed, featuring Patterson Dial and Rush Hughes, written and directed by Rupert Hughes.
	August	Adelaide left California for second trip to China.
	Summer	Alston Cockrell, Jr.'s, first trip to Los Angeles; Patterson Dial and Rupert Hughes courting.

	September	William and Agnes Reynolds moved to Jacksonville.
	Fall	Howard Hughes, Jr., enrolled at Rice Institute, Houston.
	December 14	Suicide of Adelaide Hughes, Haiphong, China.
1924	January 15	Death of Howard Hughes, Sr., Houston; Sonny moved to Yoakum house with Fred and Annette Lummis.
	January 18	Birth of Agnes Lapp (Roberts), Elspeth Hughes' daughter.
	April 9	Rupert Hughes purchased new 1000' circular plot at Kensico and re-deeded original lot to cemetery.
	April 18	Rupert Hughes appointed legal Guardian of Marshall Ricksen, Los Angeles.
	December 31	Marriage of Rupert Hughes and Elizabeth Patterson Dial, Los Angeles.
1925		Marshall Ricksen lived with Rupert and Pat Hughes through 1927.
	March 27	Birth of Elspeth Lapp (DePould), Elspeth Hughes' daughter.
	June 1	Marriage of Howard Hughes, Jr., and Ella Botts Rice, Houston.
1926	September 4	Birth of Barbara Patterson Lapp (Cameron), Elspeth's daughter.
	October 20	Death of Felix T. Hughes, Los Angeles.
1928	November 4	Death of Jean Summerlin Hughes, Los Angeles.
1929	December 9	Ella Rice Hughes granted divorce, Houston.

1931	March 21	Marriage of Felix Hughes and Ruth Stonehouse, California.
1937	November 29	Death of William H. Reynolds, Jr., Jacksonville.
1939	November 20	Agnes Reynolds declared incompetent, Cleveland.
1941	January 13	Agnes admitted to Eastern State Mental Hospital, Williamsburg, Virginia.
	May 12	Death of Ruth Stonehouse Hughes, Los Angeles.
1943	October 22	Marriage of Felix Hughes and Ruby Parrott, California.
1944	October 10	Death of Agnes Reynolds, Williamsburg, Virginia.
1945	March 23	Death of Patterson Dial Hughes, Los Angeles (cremated).
	May 14	Death of Elspeth Hughes Lapp, Cleveland (cremated; Rupert Hughes not at funeral).
	December '46–December '48	Barbara Lapp Cameron lived with Rupert Hughes, Los Angeles.
1949	November	Alleged shipboard wedding ceremony between Howard Hughes, Jr., and actress Terry Moore.
1950		Rupert Hughes sold Los Feliz home and moved in with Felix and Ruby Hughes.
1954	January 8	Rupert Hughes executed will; alleged to have become senile.
1956	September 9	Death of Rupert Hughes, Los Angeles (cremated).
1957	January 12	Marriage of Howard Hughes, Jr., and Jean Peters, Tonopah, Nevada.

415

1961   September 9   Death of Felix Hughes, Los Angeles.

1971   June 18   Divorce granted to Jean Peters, Hawthorne, Nevada.

1976   April 5   Death of Howard Hughes, Jr., aboard plane en route to Houston.

Sources

The sources below are specifically mentioned in the text and appear in the order in which they are cited in the book. They are not intended to represent the complete body of research material that forms the basis of this work.

Books and Pamphlets

Noah Dietrich, *Howard, the Amazing Mr. Hughes*, Fawcett Book Group, Greenwich, Connecticut, 1972.

Harvard Class Reports, Class of 1897, First-Fifth Reports, Cambridge, The University Press and Crimson Printing Co., the Plimpton Press, 1900-1917.

Francis J. Helenthal, *Howard Hughes: The "Keokuk Connection"*, published by Francis J. Helenthal, Hamilton, Illinois, 1976.

Raymond E. Garrison, *Goodbye My Keokuk Lady*, Lois Hamilton and Raymond E. Garrison, Publishers, Keokuk, Iowa, 1962.

Raymond E. Garrison, *Tales of Early Keokuk Homes*, Lois Hamilton and Raymond E. Garrison, Publishers, Keokuk, Iowa, 1959.

American Film Institute: Feature Films , 1921–30, R. R. Bowker Company, New York and London.

In re Estate of Crozier, 232 N.W.2d 554 (Iowa 1975) (Taken from section on "Lost or Destroyed Wills," *Palmer's Trusts and Succession,* 3rd ed., Wellman, Waggoner, and Browder, Foundation Press, 1977.

"Men of Texas," from *The New Encyclopedia of Texas*, Volume 1, Texas Development Bureau, Dallas, 1929.

Pioneers in Texas Oil, Rare Book Collection, Barker Texas History Center, University of Texas at Austin.

Story of Lee County, Iowa, 1914 (Volume 2).

Portrait and Biographical Album of Lee County, Iowa, 1885.

Thompson and West, *History of Santa Barbara and Ventura Counties and Biographical Sketch of Its Prominent Men and Pioneers*, Howell-North Publishers, 1961.

Magazines

Rupert Hughes, "My Mother," *The American Magazine*, September 1924.

Rupert Hughes, "My Father," *The American Magazine*, August 1924.

Time, September 17, 1956.

Rupert Hughes, "Why I Quit Going to Church," *Cosmopolitan*, October 1924.

Rupert Hughes, "I Am in Favor of Divorce by Mutual Consent," *Cosmopolitan*, August 1924.

Adela Rogers St. Johns, "Is Marriage a Bunco Game?" (an interview with Rupert Hughes), *Photoplay*, July 1921.

Stephen White, "The Howard Hughes Store," *Look Magazine*, February 9, 1954.

The Illustrated American, September 26, 1891.

Newspapers

Philadelphia Inquirer, May 31, 1976.

Houston Chronicle, September 17, 1981, May 25, 1983.

Author's review of Carthage and Joplin, Missouri, newspapers at *Carthage Press*, July 1977.

Dallas Morning News, April 13, 1977.

Mary Swindell, "I'm Kin to Howard Hughes," *Cleveland Press*, December 31, 1977.

Ruby H. Hughes, "Loving Memories of Felix Hughes," *Shoppers Free Press*, 1977–78.

Adella Prentiss Hughes, "Sentimental Photos, No. 88," *Cleveland News* (from her Vassar Alumnae file).

New York Times, October 11, 1897, February 22, 1916.

Keokuk Daily Constitution-Democrat, February 21, 1916.

The Daily Independent, Santa Barbara, California, June 1, 1889. Catharine Cranmer, "Rupert Hughes," *Missouri Historical Review*, October 1925.

Madison Enterprise-Recorder, May 22, 1902, January 3, 1913.

Florida Times-Union, October 15, 1944.

Los Angeles Times, December 15, 1923.

North Westchester Times, October 9, 1914.

David Sloane's research of Syracuse newspapers, 1890–1905.

New Rochelle newspaper (unnamed), October 10, 1914.

New Rochelle Pioneer, October 10, 1914.

Documents and Records

Report of Richard C. Gano, Jr., Special Administrator Regarding Will Search Activites, No. P 621 359 in the Superior Court of California, Los Angeles County, Estate of Howard R. Hughes, Jr., March 15, 1977.

Settlement Agreement, filed in Cause #139,362, Harris County, Texas, Howard R. Hughes, Jr., Estate.

Supplemental Agreement to Settlement and Ancillary Agreements of July 1976 Between the Then Known Heirs-at-Law of Howard Robard Hughes, Jr., filed in Cause#139,362, Harris County, Texas, Howard Hughes, Jr., Estate.

Brief in Support of Motion in Limine filed by Paul Freese on behalf of Barbara Cameron et al., August 14, 1981, Cause #139,362, Harris County, Texas.

Estate of Howard R. Hughes, Sr., Cause #11791, Harris County, Texas.

Estate of Rupert Hughes, Cause #382,466, Los Angeles County Superior Court.

Last Will and Testament of Felix T. Hughes, Lee County, Iowa, filed November 10, 1926.

Last Will and Testament of Jean A. Hughes, Los Angeles County, filed November 17, 1928.

Estate of Alexander S. More, Superior Court, Santa Barbara, California.

Estate of James Frederick Howell, Cause #563 P 1951, Surrogate's Court, Suffolk County, New York.

Estate of Elizabeth Patterson Dial Hughes, Cause #242093, Los Angeles, California.

Estate of Lisle C. Hughes, St. Louis Circuit Court, Probate Division, July 1916.

Death certificate of Greta H. Witherspoon, #6108, New York City Health Department.

Howell v. *Howell*, Lee County, Iowa, at Fort Madison, 1889.

Book 1, Divorce Records of Fort Madison, Iowa.

Witherspoon v. *Witherspoon*, Cause #4273, District Court, Fort Madison, Iowa.

More v. *More*, Cause#1662, #1668, Superior Court, Santa Barbara County, California.

Hughes v. Hughes, Cause #714-1904-GA-H-1, New York Supreme Court, New York County.

Hughes v. *Hughes*, Cuase #29203-04, New York Supreme Court, Queens County.

Witherspoon marriage registration, #HD 147761-99hc., C24524.

Marriage certificate of Greta Hughes and Frederick J. Howell, Milwaukee, Wisconsin.

Marriage license of Greta Hughes and Alexander S. More, Certificate #24367, St., Louis Recorder of Deeds.

"In Re Agnes H. Reynolds, Incompetent," Cause #278069, in the Probate Court of Cuyahoga County, Cleveland, Ohio: Schedule of Services Rendered by James Metzenbaum, October 28, 1940.

Pension file of William H. Reynolds, U.S.N., (Letter from J. R. Hornberger to Director of Claims, March 18, 1938).

Leila Hughes school record, Yeatman High, St., St. Louis Missouri.

Author's review of Kensico Cemetery Records, Valhalla, New York, October 1979.

Court Proceedings

Based on trial testimony or author's observation of the trail to determine Howard R. Hughes, Jr.'s, domicile, 1977–78, the Heirship Determination, Phases I, II, III, 1981, and the hearing re claim of Rush Hughes and Avis McIntyre, September 16, 1981, all in the Estate of Howard Robard Hughes, Jr., Cuase #139, 352, Probate Court 2, Houston, Harris County, Texas.

Interviews

Baptist Hospital Administrators; Sidney L. Brown; Carl B. Callaway; Barbara Lapp Cameron; Darlene Cameron; Wesley Cameron; Mrs. Patrick Canty; Alston Cockrell, Jr.; Sister Mary Corita; Rosario Curletti; Charlotte Delahey; O. Theodore Dinkins Jr.; Florence Eaves Geddes Ettinger; Mary S. Fay; Doris Foley; Evelyn Gates; Ruth Gates; James Geddes III; Opal Geddes; Judge Pat Gregory; Francis J. Helenthal; Rock Houstoun; Ruby H. Hughes; Shirley Jones; Keokuk, Iowa, residents; Arthur Leeds; Cornelia Geddes Marks; Mrs. Robert McClure; Pat McLernon; Richard Millar; Mrs. Raleigh Minor; Father David Patrick; William H. Reynolds, Jr.; Mrs. Marshall Ricksen; John T. Robertson; Stephena Cockrell Scott; David Sloane; Ellen Smith; Frances McLain Smith; Sabra Staley; Birdwell Sutlive, Jr.; William L. Talbot; Jacqueline Taylor; Laurie Thompson; Mary Van Conway; Elizabeth R. Westbrook; Richard Whitesell, Jr.; James O. Winston, Jr; Frances Geddes Writer; and author's confidential sources.

Correspondence

Faye Beelman to Mary Fay; Evelyn Castle and Ruth Donie to author; Mary Fay O. Theodore Dinkins, Jr.; Mary Fay to author; M. Christine Gallery to author; Ray Garrison to author; Ruby H. Hughes to Francis J. Helenthal; Ruby H. Hughes to E. A. Ebersole; Rupert Hughes to Alston Cockrell, Jr.; Rupert Hughes to Stephena D. Cockrell; Rupert Hughes to Ray Garrison; Collection of Rupert Hughes correspondence, Iowa State University; Sister Mary Jean to author; Margaret Scott Kenyon to author; William H. Reynolds, Jr., to author; M. A. Robison to Mary Fay; David Sloane to author; Vicar Mark Walden to author; Farnces Writer to author.

Depositions

(Estate of Howard R. Hughes, Jr.)

Gregson Bautzer; Barbara Cameron; Dr. Norman Crane; Roy Edward Crawford; Eleanor Boardman d'Arrast; John F. Egger; Dale Eunson; Colleen Moore Hargrave; John Holmes; Elizabeth Jean Peters Hough; Robert C. Hughes; Ruby H. Hughes; Rush Hughes; Cornwell Jackson; Louis Kaminar; Ron Kistler; Annette Gano Lummis; William R. Lummis; Nadine Henley Marshall; Avis Hughes McIntyre; Terry Moore; Glenn Edward Odekirk; Lee Harrell Palmer; Dr. Jack Titus.

Other

Leila B. Hughes file, the Billy Rose Theatre Collection, New York Library of the Performing Arts at Lincoln Center.

Reno, California Theatre Program, December 9, 1923 (Patterson Dial file, Academy of Motion Picture Arts and Sciences, Beverly Hills, California).

Ruth Stonehouse file, Academy of Motion Picture Arts and Sciences, Beverly Hills, California.

"Howell" envelope, Keokuk Public Library, Keokuk, Kowa.

Information on the Geddes family assembled by author from entries in the Joplin City Hall, Joplin, Missouri.

Author's notes taken from Keokuk city directories, Keokuk, Iowa.

Terry Moore Press Conference, as reported on "Good Morning America," ABC, May 25, 1983.

Report of Mary S. Fay, September 1, 1977.

Index